MANCHESTER CITY
THE BIRTH OF THE BLUES 1880 – 1894

St. Mark's Church

ST. MARK'S FOOTBALL CLUB
1880-1881

WEST GORTON (ST. MARK'S) FOOTBALL CLUB
1881-1883

WEST GORTON ASSOCIATION FOOTBALL CLUB
1883-1884

GORTON ASSOCIATION FOOTBALL CLUB
1884-1887

ARDWICK ASSOCIATION FOOTBALL CLUB
1887-1894

MANCHESTER CITY FOOTBALL CLUB
1894

Paul Toovey

MANCHESTER CITY
THE BIRTH OF THE BLUES 1880 – 1894

First published in Great Britain in 2009 by
Paul Toovey
42 Fernwood Marple Bridge
Stockport SK6 5BE

Copyright © Paul Toovey 2009

The right of Paul Toovey to be identified as author of this work has been asserted in accordance with Section 77 of the Copyright, Designs and Patents Act 1988. A catalogue record for this book is available from the British Library.

All rights reserved. No part of this publication may be reproduced or stored in a retrieval system, or transmitted, in any form or by other means, electronic, mechanical, photocopying, recording or otherwise without prior permission in writing of the copyright holder, nor be otherwise circulated in any form or binding or cover other than in which it is published and without a similar condition being imposed on the subsequent publisher.

ISBN 978-0-9561910-0-7

Printed and bound in Great Britain by
RDW DIGITAL,
Specialist Printing and Bookbinders,
HUDDERSFIELD HD2 1YE
www.rdwdigital.co.uk

CONTENTS

i	Foreword	4
ii	Introduction	5
iii	Acknowlegements	6
1	St. Mark's Church West Gorton	7
2	St. Mark's Cricket Club	11
3	St. Mark's Football Club 1880-81	16
4	West Gorton (St. Mark's) Football Club 1881-82	24
5	West Gorton (St. Mark's) Football Club 1882-83	30
6	Belle Vue Rangers 1882-83	35
7	West Gorton Football Club 1883-84	38
8	Gorton Association Football Club 1884-85	43
9	Gorton Association Football Club 1885-86	50
10	Gorton Association Football Club 1886-87	54
11	Ardwick Association Football Club 1887-88	62
12	Ardwick Association Football Club 1888-89	72
13	Ardwick Association Football Club 1889-9	84
14	Ardwick Association Football Club 1890-91	101
15	Ardwick Association Football Club 1891-92	131
16	Ardwick Association Football Club 1892-93	155
17	Ardwick Association Football Club 1893-94	182
18	Manchester City Football Club 1894-The Birth of the Blues	210

FOREWORD by GARY JAMES

The roots of all football clubs are important. It is essential supporters and others in love with the game understand how their own particular club came into being and what obstacles the pioneers faced.

Since Manchester City won the FA Cup for the first time in 1904, the Blues have been recognised as one of the game's giants. However, less than 25 years before that initial national success the side embarked on its very first season. Playing on rough ground in a densely populated industrial landscape the club made its first tentative steps.

Much has been written about the birth of the Club and how St. Mark's Church in West Gorton gave life to the side, but year after year, generation after generation, a number of myths have developed or been enlarged upon. Some have written as fact rumours while others have been happy to use the work of earlier journalists and historians instead of performing their own detailed research. This is an approach I abhor and so I was delighted when I was contacted around two years ago by Paul Toovey.

Paul immediately impressed me. He told me he had been reading some of my own work and that he had new information. I often get calls like this, but what made Paul's different is that he did actually have new information. He had done what all historians should do and sought his own information from original sources. I am proud of my work and the efforts taken to record City's history, but I know that there are many, many stories still be told. No individual can hope to fully record every aspect of City life.

I guess the first piece of information Paul had uncovered that impressed was the name of the first person to score for the Club. During the 1980s I had uncovered a brief match report of St. Mark's first known game, but Paul had gone one step further and found a much more detailed report. Within that report were details of the first goal and other significant match information. This information has never previously been published and it truly is a major breakthrough in our knowledge of City's roots. It should also make the family of James Collinge very proud.

Following my first conversation with Paul he provided more information. Inevitably, I helped along the way, but Paul didn't really need any support as he continued to review long forgotten newspapers and investigate leads.

The result of Paul's work has now at long last been published. Paul's story takes the Club from the mid 1870s through to its transformation into Manchester City in 1894 and it is a very interesting tale. Match reports, player profiles, news stories and the like help paint a picture of how the Club developed but, more importantly, it highlights facts not the perceived fiction that many believe is true.

I fully recommend this book. It is a worthy addition to the shelves of City fans and football historians.

Gary James
March 2009

INTRODUCTION

It was in the 1960's that I read a book on the history of the Football League from 1888 to 1938 and I decided that one day I would research the early history of City. I have supported City all my life and follow in the footsteps of my grandfather who supported City from earliest times. When I retired in 2007 the opportunity to carry out the research and to write this book arose.

The early history of St. Mark's Church is well documented. However, I was surprised to find that several early reports existed of matches played by St. Mark's Cricket Club which was founded in 1875. Cricket was very popular with many sides playing in the area. By 1879, St. Mark's had a junior team and there were five match reports with the names of nine junior cricketers who were to play for St. Mark's Football Club in the first match against Macclesfield Baptists on 13th November 1880. The book contains a detailed report of the first match which was prepared by a player or official of the Baptist side as well as details of eight other matches played during the first season whereas a total of only seven matches had been previously recorded.

The Church Football Club played for three seasons as St. Mark's (West Gorton) and later as West Gorton (St. Mark's) before merging with Belle Vue Rangers to form West Gorton in the 1883-84 Season.

In October 1884, the former St. Mark's players left West Gorton and formed Gorton Association Football Club. The club grew and prospered due largely to the considerable efforts of Walter Chew and Lawrence Furniss, and in 1887, a tenancy was secured of land which was to become the Hyde Road Ground, Ardwick. As the club had moved from Gorton to Ardwick the name was changed to Ardwick Association Football Club.

In 1890, Lawrence Furniss and John Allison, who were on the Ardwick Committee, went to Scotland and signed five players. They also signed eight experienced players from Lancashire clubs, including David Weir, who was an England International. Ardwick then had a very capable team and could compete against teams from the Football League (founded in 1888) and the Football Alliance (founded in 1889). At the end of the 1890-91 Season, Ardwick came close to gaining a place in the Football League.

In 1891 Ardwick joined the Football Alliance and in 1892 the Second Division of the Football League.

In April 1894, Ardwick became defunct.

Manchester City were formed as a limited company on 16th April 1894, and on 21st May 1894, City were elected to the Second Division of the Football League.

The book contains a detailed history of the football club from 1880 to 1894 including details of many of the matches, players and officials as well as an account of the successes and problems which were experienced.

ACKNOWLEDGEMENTS

I should like to thank the British Library, National Archives and the librarians in the Manchester Central Library, Manchester Metropolitan University Library and the Local Studies Libraries at Tameside, Stockport, Macclesfield and Bolton who provided great assistance when researching the newspapers and periodicals of the period. In particular, I found the Athletic News, the Athletic News Annuals, The Umpire, the Sunday Chronicle, the Manchester Evening News, Gorton Reporter, Macclesfield Courier, Cheshire County News and the Manchester City News to be most informative.

I spent several days at the National Football Museum at Preston where I was able to inspect many rare books and records. I received considerable assistance from Peter Holme, a Research Officer at the Museum, for which I am most grateful.

Most of the very early City records were destroyed many years ago. Important early books on Manchester City and the Lancashire clubs were:

"History of Manchester City Football Club"
Fred Johnson 1930

"History of the Lancashire Football Association"
C.E.Sutcliffe and F.Hargreaves 1928

Frank Hannah, the distinguished President and Chairman of the Manchester F.A., very kindly sent to me a copy of the Souvenir Centenary Brochure entituled

"The History of the Manchester County Football Association"
which he compiled in 1984.

Chris Williams of Sportingold Limited provided the Official Cards for two of the early away matches of Ardwick as well as giving great support.

I received tremendous assistance from Gary James who also provided several photographs.

I should like to thank the printers of this book.

Finally, I should like to thank Linda Moore, who was my secretary for thirty five years, who helped prepare this book and my wife, family and friends for their support.

Paul Toovey

March 2009

CHAPTER 1

ST. MARK'S CHURCH WEST GORTON

The origin of Manchester City Football Club is directly traceable to St Mark's Football Club, West Gorton which was formed in 1880, although its roots go back much further to 1875, when members of St. Mark's Church established St. Mark's Cricket Club. It was when the junior members of St. Mark's Cricket Club decided to play association football during the winter months that St. Mark's Football Club came into being with the first football match being played on 13th November 1880. The history of St. Mark's Football Club begins with St. Mark's Church and the St. Mark's Cricket Club.

St Mark's Church West Gorton

In the early 1860's the West Gorton area was growing rapidly due to the heavy industrialisation which was taking place in Gorton and the surrounding areas. Whilst many people were employed in the new industries there was still unemployment and many problems with crime, overcrowding, poor sanitation and pollution. The major cause of death in the area was bronchitis. The Gorton Local Board of Health was founded in 1863 to provide local services and to address many of these problems.

West Gorton was outside the boundaries of Manchester, but was within the Diocese of Manchester. The Diocese decided that in view of the population growth there was a need for a new Church in West Gorton. Mr Beyer of Beyer and Peacock, an engineering company in Gorton, had met the expense of building St. James Church, Gorton and he met most of the expense of building St. Mark's Church. On 30th November 1865 **St. Mark's Church**, Clowes Street, West Gorton was consecrated. The Church was assigned a District from the parishes of St. James, Gorton; St. Barnabas, Openshaw; St. Thomas, Ardwick and St. Johns, Longsight.

ST.MARK'S CHURCH

The Reverend Arthur Connell

The first Rector of St Mark's Church was Arthur Connell who had been curate of High Harrogate, Yorkshire for seven years. Arthur Connell received a letter from the Rector of Bradford-cum-Beswick informing him that there was a vacancy at West Gorton and that the district afforded a "fair field for ministerial usefulness". Influenced by the contents of the letter, he came to preach at St. James, Gorton on a Sunday morning and St. Marks in the evening. "Believing the call to be from God", he resigned his position in Harrogate and came to West Gorton with his wife, Anna and his two daughters Anna (born in 1851) and Georgina (born in 1853).

The Rev. Arthur Connell, with the assistance of his wife (and later his two daughters) and the Churchwardens (a Curate was not appointed for many years), quickly established the Church. The congregation was initially very small, but grew rapidly. Within a short time, the church was crowded at the Sunday evening services with a large, attentive and devoted congregation.

In 1865, the St. Mark's Day and Sunday Schools were not of the standard Arthur Connell wished them to be. The Day school had no certificated teacher and few scholars. The Sunday school had but "a sparse attendance of both teachers and scholars". Mr Beyer generously supported the schools and certificated teachers were engaged. Arthur Connell placed the Day school under government inspection which enabled the school to obtain grants. The grants allowed the school to secure the best teaching power possible, both as regards quantity and quality. The number of scholars greatly increased and the school was soon receiving the maximum grant. By 1878, four extensions had been built to the school, with Mr Beyer meeting most of the cost. The scholars received a good education.

In addition to Church services and the Day and Sunday Schools, the Church established a Penny Savings Bank, a Mutual Improvement Society, a Choral Society and a Drum and Fife Band. The Church also arranged entertainment evenings and concerts as well as many other events

The Parish grew and prospered. There were some 7000 to 8000 people in the Parish and his inability to visit every household caused Arthur Connell much anxiety and distress. In 1878, Arthur Connell asked the Bishop of Manchester for the services of a Curate but as West Gorton was not in Manchester (it became part of Manchester in 1890) it was beyond the limits for which grants were made.

Tribute to Arthur Connell

On 11th April 1878, a gold watch was presented to the Rev. Arthur Connell and a china tea service was presented to his wife, Anna, by the Churchwardens, the scholars of the Day and Sunday Schools, the Church Committee and the parishioners.

More than one hundred and eighty members of the Church attended the presentation. A very moving address was given expressing their high appreciation of the earnest, devoted and faithful manner in which the Rev. Arthur Connell had performed the various duties connected with the church and schools. The address was followed by loud and prolonged cheering.

Georgina Connell- St Mark's Mothers Meetings

In 1877, Arthur Connell's younger daughter, Georgina originated St Mark's Mothers' Meetings. The first meeting was attended by only seven mothers and was held in the vestry of the Church. Georgina worked hard and the membership increased, outgrowing the available accommodation. In 1878, the Rector and Church Wardens raised funds and a parish room, capable of accommodating 100 persons, was erected at a cost of £400. The Mothers' Meetings were then transferred to the parish room. Georgina addressed the meetings which were held each Monday and the meetings were extremely popular. On 4th April 1883, the members of St. Mark's Mothers Meetings made a presentation to Georgina and expressed their respect and gratitude.

Anna Connell- St Mark's Working Men's Meetings

In the 1870's, the West Gorton Working Men's Institute, had been established. However, by January 1877, it was reported that it was likely to collapse for want of support amongst the working men of West Gorton. William Henry Beastow was President of the Institute and he held a meeting of the members in the Institute's premises in Robert Street, West Gorton. Only about forty paying members had joined the Institute out of the many thousands of local inhabitants. Lectures on various subjects of interest had been held in an endeavour to bring in new members but to no avail. William Henry Beastow had done everything possible to continue the Institute and was even prepared to settle the Institute's debts. However, after an adjournment, the meeting was reconvened and the members decided to close the Institute. All the Institutes assets and furniture were sold to meet the debts.

William Henry Beastow was prominent in local public affairs and was keen to arrange for the local working men to have a place to go to "where they could obtain enjoyment of a rational character."

In 1879 Arthur Connell's elder daughter, Anna, originated the St Marks Working Men's Meetings with the assistance of William Henry Beastow and Thomas Goodbehere, who were both Churchwardens. Anna Connell visited most of the homes in the parish and only three men first responded to her invitation to attend a Working Men's Meeting. However, Anna Connell persevered and with the assistance of William Henry Beastow and Thomas Goodbehere, Anna Connell enrolled a membership upwards of one hundred working men by 1882. William Henry Beastow and Thomas Goodbehere attended the weekly meetings, held on a Tuesday evening, which were addressed by Anna, and the average weekly attendance was between 60 and 70. Anna succeeded where the Institute had failed

Tribute to Anna Connell

On 12th March 1883, a special tribute and presentation was made to Anna Connell.
"ST MARK'S, WEST GORTON an interesting social gathering took place at St Mark's School on Monday 12th March 1883, the occasion being a presentation to Anna Connell by the members of the Working Men's Meeting. About 100 of the members sat down to a comfortable tea and after tea singing and prayer, the Rector, who presided said that he would reserve what he had to say to a later period of the evening, the object of the meeting was peculiar and uncommon. It was most

gratifying to him to see such a large gathering of respectable, intelligent-looking working men, who appeared to be all of one heart and mind, and deeply interested in the object that had called them together. Three members of the committee then each in suitable and touching words referred to the reverent estimation in which Anna Connell was held by all the members, and the spiritual good which many of them experienced under her earnest and fervent addresses. Several of the working men present then rose and gave corresponding testimony to the benefit they had arrived from their weekly meetings. The presentation consisted of a large and valuable Bible beautifully bound in Morocco, which was inscribed

"Presented to Anna Connell by the Members of the Working Men's Meeting as a token of respect and esteem and in appreciation of her services as conductor of the above meetings St Mark's West Gorton 12 March 1883"

Miss Connell in rising to speak was received with loud and long continued applause. She said that she could not find words to express the gratitude she felt for the valuable presentation they made and the kind and encouraging words spoken by so many of the members present. Her heart was too full to give expression to her thoughts and therefore she would ask her father to be the exponent of her feelings"

The Archdeacon of Manchester described Arthur Connell as the father of the parish, and as having, by his ministry and earnest labours, wrought a very great change for the better in the district. He spoke of Mrs Anna Connell as the mother of the parish and their two daughters, Anna and Georgina, as the curates of the parish.

Anna continued her work for the Church and the community until July 1897 when her father was forced to resign as Rector of St Mark's Church due to ill health. Anna's mother had died two years previously. Arthur Connell was suffering from chronic bronchitis and Anna moved with her father to Southport to look after him. It was hoped that the sea air would improve his health. Arthur Connell died in February 1899.

On 3rd September 1889 Georgina Connell married the Rev. John William Dixon, the Curate of St. Brides Church, Old Trafford and who was previously associated with St. Mark's Church and Schools. In 1899, after her father's death, Anna went to live with Georgina and her husband in Walsall. John William Dixon later became rector of Darlaston Church.

Anna died, after suffering a heart attack, on 21st October 1924 and Georgina died on 9th September 1933.

Anna Connell is credited by many as being the founder of the St. Mark's Football Club, mainly on the basis that she had founded a Working Men's Club and that the Church cricket and football clubs had emanated from the Working Men's Club. However, this is not correct. Anna founded St. Mark's Working Men's Meetings (which was not a Club) and it was not until 1882 that the Meetings became well established, which was some time after the Church cricket and football teams had been formed. There were many tributes paid to Anna but they were all in respect of the Working Men's Meetings and no mention is made of any association with the Church cricket and football clubs

St. Mark's Church was demolished in 1974 after the properties in the surrounding area had been cleared.

CHAPTER 2

ST. MARKS CRICKET CLUB

William Henry Beastow

William Henry Beastow was born in 1835 and lived most of his life in West Gorton. He was employed as an engineer by the Union Iron Works, which was the largest employer in West Gorton. At the 21st Anniversary Dinner of the Union Iron Works held at Belle Vue Gardens on 11th September 1880 which was attended by the Managers and Foremen representing about 700 employees at the Works, William Henry Beastow responded to the main speech of the evening made by S.H. Brooks who owned the Company. He worked at the Union Iron Works for thirty years, retiring in 1899 when he was sixty four years of age.

He took a keen interest in municipal affairs serving as a member of the Gorton Local Board of Health for many years, retiring in 1888. He was overseer of the poor for the West Gorton district for twenty five years. He was elected to Manchester City Council in 1897 as a Conservative representative for the St. Mark's, West Gorton ward. He retained his seat until he retired in 1907, when he moved to live with his daughter and son-in-law in Chorlton-cum-Hardy. He was appointed a Justice of the Peace in 1902. He died on 16th November 1912 aged seventy seven years.

In 1880, William Henry Beastow lived at 178 Clowes Street West Gorton with his wife and family, close to St Marks Church and to the Union Iron Works. He was the Parishioners Churchwarden at St Mark's Church and was Chairman of St. Mark's Cricket Club. He had worked closely with Anna Connell in establishing the St. Mark's Working Men's Meetings, and whilst Anna Connell would have been supportive, it was William Henry Beastow and the junior cricketers of the St Mark's Cricket team who formed St Mark Football Club.

St. Marks Cricket Club

St. Mark's Cricket Club was formed in 1875. The earliest reported matches took place on 12th June 1875 against The Crown, Newton Heath and on 28th August 1875 against Cheadle Bulkeley. The following details were published:-

12th JUNE 1875		At West Gorton	
St. Mark's, West Gorton		**Crown, Newton Heath**	
T. Williams b W. Taylor	5	W. Whitelegge b Cragg	4
C. Jackson b J Dixon	6	W. Taylor c Warhurst b Barton	2
A. Seaton b J Dixon	3	R. Barrett c Underwood b Barton	9
W. Meredith c Whitelegge b J.Dixon	3	I. Blackwell b Barton	3
H. Barton b J. Dixon	9	J. Dixon b Barton	4
H. Cragg b I Blackwell	0	C.G.Tinker lbw	5
J.Cragg b I Blackwell	6	J. Martin run out	11
R. Warhurst b J Dixon	2	B. Wilson c Cragg b Hardy	0
W. Cuthwaite c Whitelegge b Blackwell	0	T. Whitehead c Seaton b Cragg	25
C. Hardy b Blackwell	0	J. Hall b Cragg	0
L. Underwood not out	0	W Davies not out	2
Extras	17	Extras	11
Crown won by 25 runs	51		76

28th AUGUST 1875			At West Gorton	
St. Mark's, West Gorton			**Cheadle Bulkeley**	
J. Cragg c Hiney b Lowe	1		Jones b Barton	6
L. Underwood run out	3		Sargent b Barton	1
J. Twiss c Tommis b Barnshaw	17		Pearson b H.Cragg	9
J. Haslam c and b Barnshaw	3		Lowe c Twiss b H. Cragg	9
H. Barton c Tommis b Barnshaw	7		Barnshaw b H. Cragg	7
J. Ringrose b Barnshaw	17		Barrington b H. Cragg	4
T. Williams b A. Lowe	9		Hiney b Barton	22
Jackson c Barrington b Barnshaw	2		Tommis not out	0
A. Seaton c and b Lowe	9		Wright b Barton	0
W. Meredith b Lowe	1		Hemmings run out	0
H. Cragg not out	1		Barton c Twiss b Barton	0
Extras	4		Extras	4
St. Mark's won by 12 runs	74			62

In 1876, the Cricket club continued with one team. Although many matches went unreported, the local newspapers did give the results of several games.

The reported matches in 1876:

ST. MARK'S				
6th May 1876	Pendleton Excelsior	41	lost to	ST.MARK'S	62
13th May 1876	ST.MARK'S	98	beat	Whaley Bridge Mechanics Institute	28
20th May 1876	Hurst	45	beat	ST.MARK'S	43
27th May 1876	Stockport Perseverance	53	lost to	ST.MARK'S	67
8th Jul. 1876	Whaley Bridge Mechanics Institute	18	drew with	ST.MARK'S	18
5th Aug 1876	St James, Gorton	29	lost to	ST.MARK'S	53
12th Aug 1876	Hurst	59	beat	ST.MARK'S	56

The Cricket Club grew and was well supported.

By 1877, St. Mark's had increased its membership and ran two teams.

The reported matches in 1877:

FIRST XI					
5th May 1877	Openshaw Methodists	57	drew with	ST.MARK'S	57
12th May 1877	ST.MARK'S	46	beat	Openshaw Methodists	16
16th Jun 1877	ST.MARK'S	97	beat	Hyde Road Methodists	70
SECOND XI					
5th May 1877	ST.MARK'S	61	beat	Openshaw Methodists	21
9th Jun 1877	Openshaw Excelsior	17 & 21	lost to	ST.MARK'S	99
16th Jun 1877	Openshaw Perseverance	54 & 11	lost to	ST.MARK'S	48 & 86
23rd Jun 1877	Ardwick Juniors	52	beat	ST.MARK'S	19
30th Jun 1877	ST.MARK'S	44	beat	Helsby Juniors, Moss Side	21 & 21
7th Jul 1877	St James, Gorton	39	lost to	ST.MARK'S	56
4th Aug 1877	St Barnabas, Openshaw	16 & 42	lost to	ST.MARK'S	44 & 38
11th Aug 1877	ST.MARK'S	47	beat	St.James, Gorton	21
1st Sep 1877	ST.MARK'S	16	beat	St Barnabas, Openshaw	15
21st Sep 1877	Helsby Juniors, Moss Side	47 & 21	lost to	ST.MARK'S	44 & 38

In 1878, St. Mark's also had a junior team.

The reported matches in 1878:-

FIRST XI					
20th Jul 1878	St James, Gorton	73	lost to	ST.MARK'S	87
JUNIOR XI					
27th Apr 1878	ST. MARK'S JUNIORS	30	lost to	Droylsden 2nd XI	76
11th May 1878	Stanley, Beswick	45 & 44	lost to	ST. MARK'S JUNIORS	47 & 75
1st Jun 1878	ST. MARK'S JUNIORS	29 & 96	beat	Stanley, Beswick	27 & 65
15th Jun 1878	Openshaw Methodists	2 for 1wkt	drew with	ST. MARK'S JUNIORS	42
22nd Jun 1878	ST. MARK'S JUNIORS	29	beat	Gorton United	21
13th Jul 1878	ST. MARK'S JUNIORS	99	beat	Openshaw Methodists	55
27th Jul 1878	ST. MARK'S JUNIORS	75	beat	Droylsden 2nd XI	35
7th Sep 1878	ST. MARK'S JUNIORS	28	lost to	Ardwick Juniors	59

The St. Marks junior cricket team had played very well in the 1878 Season against other clubs second elevens or junior teams, winning five, drawing one and losing two of the matches which were reported. Unfortunately, there are no details of the players in that seasons junior team.

By 1879, William Henry Beastow and James Moores presided over the meetings of the Cricket Club. James Moores was a sidesman at the Church and also a member of the Gorton Local Board of Health.

Frederick Hopkinson, who was one of the junior cricketers, was secretary.

In 1879, five of the cricket matches of St. Mark's juniors were reported in detail in the local newspapers and contained the names of the players.

It was when the St. Mark's junior cricketers turned to football in the winter of 1880 that the St. Mark's Football Club was formed.

The cricketers who were later to play for the Church football club are shown in capitals in the St. Mark's batting line-up in these matches:

10th MAY 1879

At West Gorton

Gorton Baptist 2nd XI		v	St. Mark's Juniors	
W.H. Draper c R.Hopkinson b Keates	2		A.W.KEATES c Bradburn b Charles	0
J H Quarmby c Keats b Hunt	7		R. Hunt b Charles	4
S. Grimshaw c R. Hopkinson b Hunt	4		C.BEASTOW b Sudworth	3
H. Howarth b Keates	1		J.BEASTOW c Howarth b Charles	1
W. Roberts b Keates	0		W.CHEW c Bradburn b Sudworth	8
J. Sudworth b Keates	8		F.HOPKINSON run out	5
G. Bradburn c Chew b Keates	7		J.COLLINGE run out	7
J. Charles c F. Hopkinson b Hunt	8		R.HOPKINSON b Howarth	0
A.Birch c Hunt b Keates	14		H.HEGGS c Roberts b Howarth	9
J. Border b F.Hopkinson	6		W.Burton c and b Birch	0
W. Brandrith not out	16		A.McDONALD not out	0
Extras	1		Extras	6
	74			43

Gorton Baptist 2nd XI won by 31 runs

14th JUNE 1879

At Whalley Range

St. Mark's Juniors		Helsby	
R.HOPKINSON lbw b H. Capstick	10	J. Kershaw run out	4
F.HOPKINSON not out	22	J. Daly b F. Hopkinson	3
A.W.KEATES b H. Capstick	2	G. Adshead c Kitchen b F. Hopkinson	0
C.BEASTOW c Jenkins b H.Capstick	3	R. Stapleton run out	0
R. Hunt c Rose b H. Capstick	0	H. Capstick b Hunt	0
W.CHEW c Daly b T. Capstick	4	T. Capstick b Hunt	0
J. Foster b H. Capstick	1	S. Jenkins c Larder b Hunt	4
J.BEASTOW hit wkt b T. Capstick	3	G. Cooper b Hunt	7
J.COLLINGE b H. Capstick	3	D. Rose c R. Hopkinson b Hunt	0
T. Larder b H. Capstick	2	H. Rushton c Hunt b F. Hopkinson	4
E. KITCHEN b H. Capstick	0	W. Crossley not out	7
Extras	7	Extras	1
	57		30

St. Mark's Juniors won by 27 runs

5th JULY 1879

At Gorton

Gorton Baptist 2nd XI		v St. Mark's Juniors	
T.Buckley c Larder b F. Hopkinson	2	F.HOPKINSON b Sudworth	13
J H Quarmby st Chew b Hunt	0	R.HOPKINSON b Sudworth	19
J. Buckley run out	1	C.BEASTOW c and b Sudworth	4
J. Sudworth b Hunt	2	J. Foster lbw Bradburn	0
S. Grimshaw b F. Hopkinson	0	G. Harrison run out	9
G. Bradburn c Larder b Hunt	8	R. Hunt b Sudworth	20
W.H. Draper c Hunt b F. Hopkinson	1	E.KITCHEN b Sudworth	0
J. Hackley c Beastow b Hunt	3	A.W.KEATES b Sudworth	0
Harrop not out	3	J.BEASTOW b Buckley	6
Jenkinson lbw F. Hopkinson	1	T. Larder b Sudworth	4
G. Beaumont c Kitchen b Foster	0	W.CHEW not out	4
Extras	4	Extras	15
	25		94

St. Mark's Juniors won by 69 runs

2nd AUGUST 1879

At Whalley Range

Helsby		v St. Mark's Juniors	
T. Capstick c Harrison b F.Hopkinson	16	R.HOPKINSON b T. Capstick	8
H. Capstick c Harrison b F.Hopkinson	3	W.CHEW hit wkt b Daly	0
G.Cooper b Foster	4	F.HOPKINSON b Daly	2
H.Rushton c Larder b Harrison	5	G. Harrison b T. Capstick	3
S.Jenkins c Harrison b F. Hopkinson	0	E.KITCHEN b T. Capstick	0
J.Daly c Harrison b Foster	5	J. Foster c Ormrod b Daly	0
D.Rose c Hopkinson b Harrison	5	C.BEASTOW run out	0
G.Ormrod b Foster	0	J.BEASTOW b Daly	0
R. Stapleton c C. Beastow b Foster	0	T. Larder b T. Capstick	1
W. Crossley c Foster b Harrison	5	J.COLLINGE run out	1
T. Humphreys not out	1	W.CHEW not out	0
Extras	1	Extras	7
	45		22

Helsby won by 23 runs

9th AUGUST 1879

At Beswick

Stanley (Ardwick)		St. Mark's Juniors	
J. Appleton b Foster	0	J. Foster b McDonald	0
J. Crawford b Foster	0	**F. HOPKINSON** b McDonald	0
W. Farrar c and b F. Hopkinson	23	W. Burton b McDonald	4
E. McDonald b Harrison	11	**C. BEASTOW** b McDonald	0
E. Burton c C. Beastow b Collinge	17	**R. HOPKINSON** b Buxton	0
W.R. Livesey c Collinge	5	G. Harrison b McDonald	2
R. Shorrocks b F. Hopkinson	0	**A.W. KEATES** b Sudworth	1
W. Hammersley b F. Hopkinson	13	**J. BEASTOW** b McDonald	0
E. Potts b Collinge	3	**H. HEGGS** b Buxton	0
E. Bailey b Collinge	4	**J. COLLINGE** not out	2
W. Peckett not out	2	W. Hardy c and b McDonald	0
Extras	15	Extras	9
	93		18

Stanley won by 75 runs

The following nine of the junior cricketers, who featured in one or more of these matches, were later to play in the first match of St. Mark's Football Club against Macclesfield Baptists on 13th November 1880:

Charles Beastow, John Beastow, Walter Chew, James Collinge, Henry Heggs, Frederick Hopkinson, Richard Hopkinson, Edward Kitchen and Alexander McDonald.

Albert W. Keates, who was another member of the junior cricket team, did not play in the first football match but did play for the football club later in the 1880-1881 Season against Hurst.

William Sumner and William Downing were not members of the junior cricket team. However, they both played for St. Mark's Cricket Club and they also played in the first football match against Macclesfield Baptists.

W. Hardy, a junior cricketer, acted as umpire, for the football club

St. Mark's Cricket Club prospered. Several events and concerts were held for the Cricket Club at the beginning of each cricket season and also during the year to raise funds.

By 1882, Frederick Hopkinson, Richard Hopkinson, John Beastow, William Downing, William Sumner and Walter Chew were playing in the St. Mark's Cricket Club first team.

In 1883, it was reported that the club was in a good position and was well supported. The club had nearly 40 members and was running two teams.

In the 1883 Season, the club's first team played 13 matches of which 6 were won, 4 were lost and 3 were drawn.

The second team played 18 matches of which 12 were won, 2 were lost and 4 were drawn.

CHAPTER 3

ST. MARKS FOOTBALL CLUB
1880-1881

In 1880, William Henry Beastow, who had a son, John Hunter Beastow, and a step-son, Charles Edward Beastow, both aged 18 years who played for the St Mark's Junior Cricket team, proposed that an association football club should be formed for the young St. Mark's cricketers. This proposal was supported by the cricketers. The football club was founded by William Henry Beastow and the members of the junior cricket team. The football club was at first probably regarded as a section of the cricket club with William Henry Beastow and James Moores presiding over the club and with Fredrick Hopkinson, acting as secretary. There are no separate reports of concerts and events being held for the football club. However, at an event held on 15th April 1882, at the opening of the cricket season, both William Henry Beastow and James Moores, in a few appropriate remarks, spoke of the advantages to be derived by engaging in such healthy games as cricket, football and kindred sports.

In 1880, the dominant winter game in the Manchester area was rugby and there were only a few football clubs playing in accordance with "association rules". The football season ran from October to March. Games were reported in the local newspaper by the Secretary of the Club sending in a report before the deadline set by the local newspaper. St. Mark's would send in reports of Church events on a regular basis and it is perhaps not surprising that in St. Mark's first season there are nine reported matches. Whist other unreported matches will have taken place in this season and later seasons, it is likely that the majority of the games were reported.

Nine of the cricketers in the St. Mark's junior side played in the first football match and W. Hardy was an umpire. Two other cricketers playing in the St Mark's Cricket Club first team also played in the first football match- William Sumner, who was to be the captain of the football team, and Walter Downing.

The first opponents were the Baptist team from Macclesfield and whilst it is not known when that side was founded there are records showing that they were playing football in 1879 and by 1880 they also had a second team.

St. Marks Football Club arranged to play their home matches on waste land, which was also used for cricket, near to Clowes Street, West Gorton.

St Mark's Football Club's first match was reported as follows:

13th November 1880
        St. Mark's (West Gorton)   1   v   Baptist Church (Macclesfield)   2

St. Mark's team: C. Beastow; W. Sumner (captain) and F. Hopkinson; W. Chew, H.Heggs and W.Downing; R.Hopkinson, J.Beastow, J.Collinge, J.Pilkington, E. Kitchen and A. McDonald
St. Mark's goalscorer: Collinge   W. Hardy, Umpire

    A very pleasant and exciting game was played between the above Clubs on Saturday 13th November 1880 at Longsight near Belle Vue. The Longsight captain won the toss and elected to play against the wind. The ball was set in motion at 3:15 by the Baptist captain. The Longsight forwards soon settled to work and in a very few minutes were rewarded for their exertions by scoring the first goal, which was made by COLLINGE. The ball being again started, the Baptist men played more carefully, and, after a few unsuccessful shots at goal, W. Potts got possession of the ball and running it up, shot the ball in the centre of the goal, where Hornby, who was in waiting, very cleverly passed it under the tape, thus making matters equal. Both sides now strode hard to gain supremacy, the ball travelling rapidly from one end of the field to the other, Hornby and Taylor making themselves conspicuous by the neat way in which they passed their opponents. The Longsight men kept working hard, H. HEGGS and J. PILKINGTON especially. Wallworth, now getting possession, passed to Hornby, who made a shot which was well stopped by SUMNER. The Baptist forwards now rushed the ball up, one of the Longsight team kicking it behind, resulted in a corner kick for the Baptists which was entrusted to W. Potts who shot the ball right in the centre again, where Bickerstaff, breasted it in, thus making the second goal for the Baptists. Shortly afterwards the Longsight men got a corner kick but failed to score from it. A few minutes afterwards half-time was called.

When ends were changed the Longsight men exerted themselves still more to make matters equal, but with very little success. PILKINGTON made a good shot, which, however did not score. A very close and exciting scrimmage took place in Baptist quarters lasting over five minutes, which ended by Bennett sending the ball right away. H. HEGGS, however, soon brought it back again by an excellent rush up the side passing four of the Baptist men in succession; just as he was going to deliver the ball he was charged and the ball was taken from him and returned to the Longsight end, where Hornby made another shot which just flew over the tape. Time getting short the Longsight men worked strenuously, and getting near to the Baptist goal KITCHEN made a shot which fell wide by about a yard. Scrimmages now became the order of the day, during one of which time was called, leaving the Baptist winners by two goals to one. SUMNER, HEGGS, R. HOPKINSON and KITCHEN deserve special mention for St. Mark's; as do Hornby, Taylor, Shipley and H. Potts for Baptists.

Until 1891, the game was controlled by two umpires, each nominated by the clubs. The umpires would usually each control one half of the pitch. If there was an incident and a player appealed, the umpire would raise his flag if he agreed. If the other umpire also raised his flag then the appeal was resolved. If the umpires disagreed, then the referee, who would stand on the touchline, would arbitrate. The referee also acted as timekeeper. In early friendly matches it was not unusual for the score in a game to be given but for it to be mentioned that one (or more) of the goals was disputed. In 1891 the referee took full control of the game with two linesmen.

The first players

Unusually, the match was played with twelve players each side. The following three players in the side were to be prominent in running the affairs of St. Mark's Football Club and the successor clubs during the 1880's:

FREDERICK HOPKINSON (born 1863, aged 17). Frederick Hopkinson lived at 71, Clowes Street, West Gorton with his father and elder brother, Richard. He was a Clerk by occupation and was Secretary of St. Mark's Cricket and Football clubs. He remained Secretary of St. Mark's Football Club until 1883. When Gorton was formed in October 1884; he went back on the football committee and read Gorton's first annual report in 1885. He played as a full-back for St. Mark's, West Gorton (St. Mark's) and Gorton making 20 recorded appearances. He took an active part in the activities of St. Mark's Church

WALTER CHEW (born 1865, aged 15). Walter Chew lived at 12, Elizabeth Street, West Gorton with his parents, younger sister and elder brother, William Henry Chew. He was a Warehouse Clerk. He played a leading role in the club's affairs, serving as Secretary of both Gorton and Ardwick and he led the negotiations for the Gound at Hyde Road Ardwick. He played in midfield and as a forward for St. Mark's, West Gorton (St. Mark's), West Gorton and Gorton making 34 recorded appearances. He also played for Ardwick. He was captain of West Gorton (St. Mark's) for part of the 1882-1883 Season. He also played for and captained Belle

Vue Rangers who merged with West Gorton (St. Mark's) in 1883. He later served for sixty years on the Committee of the Manchester and District Football Association (forty six years as Treasurer). He was the most important person in the early history of the club.

Walter's brother, **William Henry Chew** (born 1862 aged 18) played for West Gorton (St. Mark's) and acted as an Umpire for the club. He also served on the Gorton and Ardwick Committees (part of the time as Treasurer).

EDWARD KITCHEN (born 1862, aged 18). Edward Kitchen was born in Bramhall in 1862. He lived with his parents and five younger brothers and sisters at 4 Tank Row, West Gorton. He was a Clerk and he also played an important part in the Club's affairs being Secretary when Gorton was formed in 1884. He played as a goalkeeper and in midfield (also occasionally as a forward) for St. Mark's, West Gorton (St. Mark's) and Gorton making 33 recorded appearances.

St. Mark's Football Club would have had a Committee to run the club's affairs and it is likely that Frederick Hopkinson, Walter Chew and Edward Kitchen would have served on the Committee.

William Henry Beastow and James Moores were active in public affairs and involved in many organisations. They would not have been involved in the administration of the football club although they did attend cricket concerts to raise funds and became involved again when Gorton Football Club was formed in 1884. James Moores died in 1891 and William Henry Beastow in 1912. Their obituaries did not mention their connection with St. Mark's and Gorton football clubs.

The other players in the first match:

WILLIAM SUMNER (born 1861, aged 19). William Sumner was a lodger at 122, Clowes Street, West Gorton and was an engineering student. He played as a full-back and was also Captain of St. Mark's and West Gorton (St. Mark's) during the three seasons he played for the club. He was the club's best player and was mentioned in many match reports for his good play. It is likely that he had played association football before moving to West Gorton as an engineering student. He may well have introduced the St. Mark's junior cricketers to association football and been responsible for the practise referred to in the report of the Arcadians match on 27th November 1880. He later played for Manchester Association, and in 1883, he played for Manchester against Stoke in a Football Association Cup-tie.

WILLIAM DOWNING (born 1861, aged 19). William Downing was born in Bramhall in 1861. He lived with his parents and younger brother at 47, Elizabeth Street, West Gorton. He was a Clerk. He played as a half-back and forward (although on one occasion he played as goalkeeper) for three seasons for St. Mark's and West Gorton (St. Mark's).

RICHARD HOPKINSON (born 1860, aged 20). Richard Hopkinson was a Clerk and the elder brother of Frederick Hopkinson. He lived with his family at 71, Clowes Street. His father was the organist at St. Mark's Church and he later became the Church organist. He played an active part in church concerts and activities. He played as a forward for St. Mark's, West Gorton (St. Mark's) and for Gorton making 13 recorded appearances.

JOHN HUNTER BEASTOW (born 1862, aged18). John Beastow was the son of William Henry Beastow and lived with his parents, sister and step brother, Charles Frederick Beastow, at 178, Clowes Street, West Gorton. He was an Engine Fitter. He played as a forward for St. Mark's for one season.

CHARLES FREDERICK BEASTOW (born 1862, aged 18). Charles Beastow was the step-son of William Henry Beastow and lived at 178, Clowes Street, West Gorton. He was a Clerk in the Iron Works. He played for St. Mark's and West Gorton (St. Mark's) for three seasons as a goalkeeper and forward.

JOHN PILKINGTON (born 1863, aged 17). John Pilkington lived at 5, Dark Lane, Ardwick with his family. He played as a forward for three seasons for St. Mark's and West Gorton (St. Mark's). There is no record of him playing cricket for St. Mark's.

ALEXANDER McDONALD (born 1864, aged 16). Alexander McDonald lived at 11, Butler Street, Ancoats with his family. He was a Cooper by occupation. He played as a forward for three seasons for St. Mark's and West Gorton (St. Mark's).

JAMES COLLINGE (born 1862, aged 18). James Collinge was born in Heywood and was a lodger at 25, Boundary Street West, West Gorton. He was a warehouseman by occupation. He was a forward and played for two seasons for St. Mark's and West Gorton (St. Mark's). He scored St. Mark's first ever goal and in 1882 he scored five goals in a match against Haughton Dale.

HENRY HEGGS (born 1860, aged 20). Henry Heggs was born in Gloucestershire in 1860. He lived with his parent and brothers and sisters at 6 Hampton Street, Ardwick. He was a Mechanic Fitter. He played as a half-back for one season for St. Mark's.

A further eight matches were reported during the 1880-1881 Season.

27th November 1880
     St. Mark's (West Gorton)   0   v   Manchester Arcadians   0

The Arcadians played their second match on 27th November against St. Mark's, Longsight on the ground of St. Mark's. The game was a most even one, and in proof of this, we may say that no goals were scored by either side during the match. St Mark's played very well together, evidently the result of considerable practise. The Arcadians were somewhat deficient in combined play but showed good individual form.

The match on 27th November 1880 was the Arcadians second match of the season and it was also St. Mark's second match. It was difficult to obtain fixtures as there were so few local clubs playing football in accordance with association rules. The report mentioned that the St. Mark's players had played very well together which had been the result of considerable practise. This is a reference to *combined play* (that is play which involved passing and movement which was more successful than individual dribbling) which indicates that someone in the club (probably William Sumner) was very familiar with the game.

St. Mark's then played the first of two fixtures against Hurst who were by far the best local team and who were the first winners of the Manchester & District Challenge Cup in 1885

18th December 1880
Hurst (Ashton-u-Lyne)   3   v   St. Mark's (West Gorton)   0

This match was played on the ground of the former, at Hurst, in very stormy weather. The visitors won the toss, and elected to play with the wind in their favour. Hurst kicked off, taking the ball close to the St Mark's goal, when Lawton, dashing in, shot the ball between the posts. The visitors kicked off from the centre, and after a little give-and-take play in mid-field, the home forwards again came away, and not to be denied, Lawton scored the second goal. Shortly after this, half-time was called.

Ends having been changed, St Marks, with two goals to the bad and a strong wind against them, kicked off. During the second half, the visitors were hard pressed, and many shots were made at their goal, but the wind carried them wide of their mark. Ultimately the St Mark's forwards getting possession, made a good run, and Lomas, the Hurst custodian, had to run out to save his charge, kicking the ball, which rebounded off a St. Mark's player close to the Hurst goal, but Knott, in the nick of time, came to the rescue of Hurst, and kicked the ball out of play. St Mark's took the corner, but nothing resulted, and from this time onwards, St. Mark's had to act on the defensive. Just before the call of time, Axon scored the third goal for Hurst. St Mark's disputed the goal, claiming the ball had been over the goal-line before it was put across, and was therefore out of play, but neither of the umpires saw this, and the visitors kicked off again from the centre. Time was now called, leaving the home team the victors by three goals, one of which disputed, to nil.

At the beginning of 1881, St. Mark's played return matches against the Arcadians and Macclesfield Baptists, who had changed their name to Baptist Rovers.

8th January 1881
Manchester Arcadians   0   v   St. Mark's (Longsight)   0

This match took place on the Arcadians ground at Moston Lane. The ground was in a very bad state through the frost which prevented any fast play, notwithstanding which, a very enjoyable game was witnessed. The Arcadians at times severely pressed their opponents, but were unable to shoot with any precision through the very slippery state of the ground. After an hour's play the game resulted in a draw, neither side scoring.

22nd January 1881
Baptist Rovers (Macclesfield)   4   v   St. Mark's (Longsight)   0

These Clubs met on the ground of the former at London Road Macclesfield. A pleasant though rather one sided game was played; the Rovers from the first showing a decided superiority. It resulted in favour of the Rovers by four goals to nil.

Albert Keates and Edward Groves made their first appearances for St. Mark's in the next match against Hurst

ALBERT W. KEATES (born 1863, aged 17) was born in Crewe and had been a member of the St. Mark's junior cricket team. He was a clerk living at 84, Clowes Street, West Gorton with his uncle. He played as a full-back.

EDWARD GROVES (born 1863 aged 17) Edward Groves lived at 50 Gorton Street, Ardwick with his mother and sister. He was a Warehouseman. He played as a full-back and half-back for St. Mark's, West Gorton (St. Mark's), West Gorton and Gorton making 36 recorded appearances. He also played for Ardwick.

26th February 1881
St. Mark's (West Gorton)   0   v   Hurst (Ashton-u-Lyne)   7

St Mark's team: Cooper; Sumner © and Keates; Groves and Smith; Kitchen McDonald Pilkington Harroway Heggs and another.

This match was played on the ground of the former at Longsight, it being a return match. The ground was in a very sloppy state, and consequently the falls were very numerous. The toss was won by Sumner, the home captain, who elected to play with the ground in his favour. Lawton kicked off for Hurst with a gentle touch to J. Firth, who immediately placed the home goal in imminent danger. The corner-kick which resulted was taken by W.C. Firth, who landed the ball well in front of the uprights, and Berry being on the spot, scored the first goal.

St. Mark's kicked off, but the Hurst backs were equal to the occasion, and quickly returned the ball into mid-field, and the forwards again made for the home goal, but its keeper defended his charge well, and got the ball away, but only for a short while, as Berry, for a second time, scored with a beautiful header.

No other point was made up to half-time, after which St. Mark's, with two goal to the bad, kicked off, but they could make no headway. The Hurst forwards were working together like machinery, scoring goal after goal in such a rapid manner that, at the call of time, they were declared the winners by seven goals to nil, one of which was credited to a St. Mark's player.

The next match was against Manchester Wanderers Reserve

5th March 1881
Manchester Wanderers Reserve   1   v   St. Mark's (West Gorton)   1

St. Mark's team: C. Beastow; Sumner © and Collins; Heggs J. Beastow and Downing; W. Chew Kitchen Collinge and McDonald.
St. Mark's goalscorer: Downing

This match was played at Brook's Bar on the ground of the former (which was rather heavy). The home team put nine men on the field, and the visitors ten, and after an hour's play, each side had scored a goal. Richardson, for the Wanderers, was the first to score, pushing the ball through during a scrimmage near the goal. A free kick passed from the wing to DOWNING at centre was cleverly converted into a goal for St Mark's. Evans and Sterling did very good service for the Wanderers; whilst the grand returns made by SUMNER, the St Mark's captain, gave his forward players the privilege of passing, which was all that could be desired. The game resulted in a draw of one goal each.

St. Marks finished the season with two matches against Stalybridge Clarence and achieved the Club's first victory in the last game of the season.

12th March 1881
Stalybridge Clarence   5   v   St Mark's (West Gorton)   0

The above clubs met at Tame Valley on Saturday for the first time, to play a friendly game. The weather was very fine, which brought out a good number of spectators. The visitors arrived at about 3:30pm, and were soon ready to play. The St. Mark's captain won the toss, and chose the way to play. The Clarence then put the ball in motion, and the ball was kept in the St. Mark's half for some time. The Clarence succeeded in putting the ball twice between the posts. Half-time being called, ends were changed.

St. Mark's put the ball in motion, taking it near their opponents' goal and made several attempts to put it through the posts, but failed. Before time was called, the Stalybridge team scored three more goals, making it five. Time being called, a very friendly game ended in favour of Clarence by five goals to nil.

19th March 1881
Stalybridge Clarence   1   v   St. Mark's (West Gorton)   3

These clubs met to play their return match at Stalybridge, their first engagement having taken place the previous week, when the Clarence won by five goals to nil. Clarence could only muster eight of their own team, but called in the services of three substitutes (one being Booth, captain of Broadbottom).

The Clarence captain won the toss, and playing with a very strong wind, they pressed St. Mark's very much during the first half, but only succeeded in scoring one goal by Booth.

After change of ends, play was all in favour of St. Mark's who scored twice in rapid succession. Their first goal was scored by R. HOPKINSON, after a neat little dribble along the right wing, and the second direct from a corner kick by the same player. J.COLLINGE afterwards kicked a splendid goal for the visitors, who thus won by three goals to one. All worked hard for St Mark's, particularly SUMNER at the back and R. HOPKINSON forward, whilst KITCHEN was excellent in goal.
St. Mark's goalscorers: R. Hopkinson 2, Collinge.

REPORT OF THE FIRST MATCH ON 13th NOVEMBER 1880

This match report, which appeared in local Cheshire Newspapers, appears to have been prepared by the secretary of the Baptist team who referred to St.Mark's as St. Mark's, Longsight whilst a brief report of the match in the Gorton Reporter correctly referred to the club as St. Mark's (West Gorton).

> BAPTIST v. ST. MARK's, LONGSIGHT.—A very pleasant and exciting game was played between the above clubs on Saturday last, at Longsight, near Belle Vue. The Longsight captain winning the toss, he decided to play against the wind. The ball was set in motion at 3-15 p.m. by the Baptist captain. The Longsight forwards soon settled to work, and in a few minutes were rewarded for their exertions by scoring the first goal, which was made by Collinge. The ball being again started, the Baptists then played more carefully, and after a few unsuccessful shots at goal, W. Potts got possession of the ball, and running it up to side shot the ball in the centre of the goal, where Hornby, who was in waiting, very cleverly passed it under the tape, thus making matters equal. Both sides now strove hard to gain supremacy, the ball travelling rapidly from one end of the field to the other. Hornby and Taylor making themselves the most conspicuous by the neat way in which they passed their opponents. The Longsight men still kept working hard, H. Hegys and R. Pilkington especially. Wallworth now getting possession passed to Hornby, who made a shot which was well stopped by Sumner. The Baptist forwards now rushed the ball up, and one of the Longsight team kicking it behind, resulted in a corner kick for the Baptists, which was entrusted to W Potts, who shot the ball right in the centre again, where Bickerstaff breasted it in, thus making the second goal for the Baptists. Shortly afterwards the Longsight men got a corner kick, but failed to score from it. A few minutes afterwards half-time was called, when ends being changed, the Longsight men exerted themselves still more to make matters equal, but with very little success. Pilkington made a good shot which, however, did not score. A very close and exciting scrimmage now took place in Baptist quarters, lasting over five minutes, which was ended by Bennett sending the ball right away. W. Hegys, however, soon brought it back again by an excellent run up the side, passing four of the Baptist men in succession. Just as he was going to deliver the ball he was charged,and the ball taken from him and returned to the Longsight end, where Hornby made another shot which just flew over the tape, time getting short. The Longsight men worked strenuously, and getting near to the Baptist goal Kitchen made a shot which fell wide by about a yard. Scrimmages now became the order of day, during one of which time was called, leaving the Baptists winners by two goals. Messrs Sumner, Hegys, R. Hopkinson, and Kitchen, deserve special mention for the home team ; as do Hornby, Taylor, Shipley, and W. Potts for the visitors. The teams were—St. Mark's; goal, C Beaston; backs, W. Sumner (captain) J Collinge; right wing, J Beaston, R. Hopkinson; centre, E Kitchen, A Macdonald. Baptist: goal, F Shipley; backs, W Robinson, W Bennett; half backs, W Pott (captain), J Radforth; centre, C Rothwell, J Bickerstaff; umpires: E Hardy and A B Houghton.

22

SUMMARY
ST. MARK'S FOOTBALL CLUB 1880-81

DATE		OPPONENT	RES	1	2	3	4	5	6
1880				7	8	9	10	11	
13.Nov	H	Baptist	L 1-2	C. Beastow	W. Sumner©	F.Hopkinson	W. Chew	H. Heggs	W. Downing
12 players		Macclesfield		R .Hopkinson	J. Beastow	J.Collinge1	J. Pilkington	E. Kitchen	A. McDonald
27.Nov	H	Manchester	D 0-0						
		Arcadians							
18.Dec	A	Hurst	L 0-3						
08.Jan	A	Manchester	D 0-0						
		Arcadians							
22.Jan	A	Baptist Rovers	L 0-4						
		(Macclesfield)							
26.Feb	H	Hurst	L 0-7	Cooper	Sumner ©	Keates	E. Groves	Smith	Kitchen
				McDonald	Pilkington	Harroway	Heggs	A.N.Other	
05.Mar	A	Manchester	D 1-1	C. Beastow	Sumner ©	Collins	Heggs	J. Beastow	Downing 1
		Wanderers Res		W.Chew	Kitchen	Collinge	McDonald		10 players
12.Mar	A	Stalybridge	L 0-5						
		Clarence							
19.Mar	A	Stalybridge	W 3-1	Kitchen	Sumner ©				
		Clarence		R. Hopkinson 2		Collinge 1			

Captain: ©

RECORDED MATCHES 1880-81

	P	W	D	L	F	A
Home	3	0	1	2	1	9
Away	6	1	2	3	4	14
Total	9	1	3	5	5	23

RECORDED APPEARANCES 1880-81

PLAYER	APPS.	GLS
1. BEASTOW,C	2	
2. SUMNER,W (© (captain)	4	
3. HOPKINSON,F	1	
4. CHEW,W	2	
5. HEGGS,H	3	
6. DOWNING,W	2	1
7. HOPKINSON,R	2	2
8. BEASTOW,J	2	
9. COLLIINGE,J	3	2
10. PILKINGTON,J	2	
11. KITCHEN,E	4	
12. McDONALD, A	3	
13. COOPER.	1	
14. KEATES,A	1	
15. GROVES,E	1	
16. SMITH	1	
17. HARROWAY	1	
18. COLLINS,W	1	

CHAPTER 4

WEST GORTON (ST. MARKS) FOOTBALL CLUB

1881-1882

Frederick Hopkinson continued as Secretary and William Sumner as Captain.

The club played its home matches this season at Kirkmanshulme Cricket Ground, Redgate Lane, Longsight.

St. Mark's started the season with seven of the players who had played in the Club's first match. Both matches in October against Bentfield and Hurst Clarence were lost.

15th October 188
        Bentfield (Greenfield)   1 v St. Mark's (West Gorton)   0

St. Mark's team: E. Kitchen; W. Sumner© and F. Hopkinson; J. Bottomley W. Downing and H. Hanson; W. Chew J. Clegg J. Pilkington R. Hopkinson and W.H. Chew

This match was played on the ground of the former at Greenfield, and resulted in a victory for Bentfield by one goal to St Mark's nil.

29th October 1881
        St. Mark's (West Gorton)   0 v Hurst Clarence (Ashton-u-Lyne)   3

St Mark's team: E. Kitchen; W. Sumner © and E. Groves; W. Collins and A. McDonald; W. Chew J. Pilkington W. Downing R. Millard R. Hopkinson and J. Clegg

The above teams met for the first time this season to play a game of football (Association rules) on the ground of St. Mark's. The weather was very fine, which brought a good number of spectators to witness the game, which proved to be a friendly one. The St. Mark's team chose the way to play, which was a little downhill, but not much. The Clarence team put the ball in motion, which was kept in play for some time. The Hurst team then got a corner-kick, which proved successful for them, as they scored from it. St. Mark's then put the leather about, both teams showing some good play, but nothing more being done until half-time was called.

After half-time, St Mark's put the ball in motion. Clarence then had the best of it, scoring two more goals. Time being called, one of the most pleasant games ended in favour of Clarence by three goals to nil.

At the end of October 1881, the club became known as West Gorton (St. Mark's).

Most of the players who played in the first season were still playing for St. Mark's and it is unlikely that St. Mark's Church had withdrawn its patronage.

The St. Mark's vicarage was at 17 North Road, Longsight and correspondence relating to the football club would have been sent to the Longsight address. In some of the early reports in the newspapers, particularly those prepared by members of the away team, St. Mark's football club was often referred to as St. Mark's (Longsight). In 1881-1882, home matches were played at Kirkmanshulme Cricket Club which was also in Longsight .

The change of name of the football club to West Gorton (St. Mark's) emphasised the connection with West Gorton.

In November 1881, West Gorton (St. Mark's) played the first "derby" against Newton Heath (LYR) (later Manchester United) at Newton Heath.

12th November 1881
Newton Heath (LYR) 3 v West Gorton (St. Mark's) 0

West Gorton team: Kitchen; Sumner © and F. Hopkinson; Groves and Collins; C. Beastow Pilkington McDonald W. Chew Millard and Perver

This match, under Association rules, was played at Newton Heath, and, after a pleasant game, resulted in a victory for the home team by three goals to nil.

Two goals were scored for Newton Heath in the first half, one by J. Jones, the other being put through the West Gorton goal by one of their own backs whilst attempting to stop a shot from E. Thomas.

E. Thomas scored a goal for Newton Heath in the second half, who won by three goals to nil.

In the next match **EDWARD BOWER** made his first appearance. Edward Bower was born in 1864 at Great Warford, Cheshire and was 17. He lived with his family at 251, Hyde Road, West Gorton. His main position was full-back but he also played in goal. He played for West Gorton (St. Mark's), West Gorton and Gorton making 22 recorded appearances. He later played for Ardwick. He was described as a lengthy full back who could kick with either foot.

Edward Bower played in the side with Walter Chew, Edward Kitchen, Frederick Hopkinson, Richard Hopkinson, Edward Groves and William Sumner. Collectively, they were West Gorton (St. Mark's) best players. There was an improvement in the club's performances and West Gorton won the next two matches, before losing to Broadbottom when they only had nine players.

19th November 1881
Manchester Arcadians 0 v West Gorton (St. Mark's) 1

West Gorton team: E. Kitchen; W.Sumner © and F. Hopkinson; W.Collins and E.Groves; R.Hopkinson W.Chew A.McDonald J.Pilkington E.Bower W.Downing.
West Gorton goalscorer: Pilkington

Played under Association rules on the ground of the Arcadians at Harpurhey, and resulted in a win for the visitors by one goal to nil. The Arcadians won the toss, and elected to play with the wind, but failed to take advantage of it, as, after twenty minutes play, the ball was worked well up to the home goal, where a free-kick ensued on the right-wing, which was centred by CHEW, and during a tight scrimmage PILKINGTON made a splendid shot, which the goalkeeper was unable to stop.

After change of ends, St Mark's had the game all in their favour, the ball being kept constantly at the Arcadians end. Another goal was scored by St Mark's, the ball striking the cross-bar, and falling in a slanting position, which the goalkeeper then knocked back into play. The West Gorton appeal for a goal was, however, disallowed by the Arcadians' umpire. The forward play of West Gorton was the best shown by them this season, whilst the back play was, as usual, very fine.

3rd December 1881
West Gorton (St. Mark's) 3 v Bentfield (Greenfield) 2

West Gorton team: E. Kitchen; W.Sumner © and F. Hopkinson; Taylor Groves and McKenna; R. Hopkinson Collinge Roberts Clegg and C. Beastow.
West Gorton goalscorer: R. Hopkinson 3

The clubs met to play their return match at Longsight today, both sides being fairly represented. St. Mark's elected to play uphill with a slight breeze, the result being that two goals were registered by them in the first half, both obtained by R. HOPKINSON.

After change of ends, Bentfield with a stronger breeze, made several attacks on the St. Mark's goal, and very soon managed to equalise matters, both goals being scored by J. Bradbury. St. Mark's during this time had fallen off considerably, but now played up with renewed effort. When near the Bentfield goal, St. Mark's claimed a free-kick, from which R. HOPKINSON was again successful in kicking the third goal, amidst cheers. Nothing further was scored, and the game ended in a victory for the St. Mark's team by three goals to two.

31st December 1881
Broadbottom 3 v West Gorton (St. Mark's) 0

West Gorton team: J. Clegg; E. Kitchen; Groves and another; Pilkington McDonald W. Chew Millard and Anderson
Umpire: Mr Osborne

These teams (West Gorton had nine players) met for the first time this season at Broadbottom today, when a very interesting game was witnessed. The home captain lost the toss, so the St Mark's captain elected to play slightly down the hill. Dixon, for Broadbottom kicked off, and the ball was soon in the West Gorton quarters, Ashworth putting the ball between the posts for the first goal. St Mark's kicked off from the centre, and after some good passing by the Broadbottom forwards, Wolstenholme put the ball under the bar for the second goal. Up to half-time, no further score was made by either team.

Ends being changed, the West Gorton men pulled themselves together, and they played well in defence, only allowing one more goal, when one of their own backs headed through his own goal from a throw in by Batty.

A very pleasant game thus ended in victory for Broadbottom by three goals to nil.

In January 1882, West Gorton played their better players and drew with Manchester Arcadians and then recorded their best win by eight goals to one against Haughton Dale, when James Collinge scored 5 goals.

7th January 1882
West Gorton (St Mark's) 1 v Manchester Arcadians 1

West Gorton team: Kitchen; Sumner © and F. Hopkinson; Groves and McDonald; Collinge Pilkington, R. Hopkinson Downing C. Beastow, and W. Chew.
West Gorton goalscorer: R. Hopkinson
Umpire: Mr Osborne

These clubs played their return match on the ground of St. Mark's at Longsight, and after the agreed hour's play, the result was a draw, each side scoring one goal. Despite the heavy state of the ground, some good play was witnessed, both sides mustering pretty strong teams. The Arcadians won the toss, and elected to play down the slope, but even with this advantage, failed to score during the first half.

On change of ends, the play became somewhat faster, and after six or seven minutes, the Arcadians scored the first goal. The ball was again set in motion by the home team, and was immediately put through the visitors' uprights by R. HOPKINSON, amidst cheers. No further score was made, although the ball was kept mainly in the Arcadian's territory, and the West Gorton team should have scored several times.

14th January 1882
West Gorton (St. Mark's) 8 v Haughton Dale 1

West Gorton team: Bower; Sumner © and Taylor; Groves and Collins; Collinge, C. Beastow, R. Hopkinson, W. Chew, Anderson and another.
West Gorton goalscorers: Collinge 5, C. Beastow 2 and Anderson

Played at Longsight, on the ground of West Gorton (St. Mark's), and after one hour's play, the result was an easy victory for West Gorton by eight goals to one, the goals being scored by J. COLLINGE with five goals, C. BEASTOW with two goals and ANDERSON with one goal.

The Haughton Dale captain won the toss, and decided to play downhill, and scored a goal, whilst St. Mark's through their good forward play, succeeded in scoring four goals before half-time was called.

On resuming play, Haughton Dale worked hard to retrieve their loss, and broke away several times, but only to be driven back by SUMNER at the rear who exhibited some grand form, and at the call of time, St. Mark's had registered four more goals. St. Mark's won by eight goals to one and recorded their best victory.

At the end of January, West Gorton suffered a heavy defeat against Hurst but the players were not recorded.

28th January 1882

Hurst 6 v West Gorton (St. Mark's) 0

The above Association clubs met at Hurst today. At the call of time, the score was Hurst 6 goals West Gorton (St. Mark's) 0.

St. Mark's turned out strong teams in the last three games of the season. In their next two matches against Broadbottom and Newton Heath, St. Mark's gained revenge for the defeats earlier in the season. However in the last match against Haughton Dale, St. Mark's were surprisingly beaten.

25th February 1882

West Gorton (St. Mark's) 3 v Broadbottom 0

West Gorton team: Kitchen; Sumner © and F. Hopkinson; Groves and Taylor; McDonald Holt Downing R. Hopkinson Clegg and Anderson.
West Gorton goalscorers: Groves, Downing and Clegg.

These clubs played their return match at Longsight today. The St. Mark's captain won the toss, and elected to play uphill with the wind. A visit was at once made to the Broadbottom goal, but several minutes elapsed before DOWNING shot the leather between. This was, however, disallowed, through one of the home players making a wrong appeal. A claim for "hands" was afterwards made, and GROVES kicked right into the goal. The Broadbottom goalkeeper soon afterwards, in knocking the ball out, ran into one of the players and injured himself, and was obliged to go home. Shot after shot was made at the Broadbottom goal, but without avail, until DOWNING at length again put the ball through. At half-time St. Mark's led by two goals to nil.

In the second half, it was expected that St. Mark's would go on the defensive. However, this was not the case; the St. Mark's goalkeeper only handled the ball once and on the other hand, CLEGG scored another goal. SUMNER, for St. Mark's, played splendidly at the back, his sure and timely kicks repulsing all the visitors attempts to score. The game thus ended in favour of West Gorton by three goals to nil.

4th March 1882

West Gorton (St. Mark's) 2 v Newton Heath (L & Y R) 1

West Gorton team: Kitchen; Sumner © and F. Hopkinson; Groves and Downing; Collinge, Pilkington, R. Hopkinson, W. Chew, C. Beastow and Clegg.
West Gorton goalscorers: C. Beastow and Collinge   Umpire: Mr. Osborne

These clubs met to play their match (under Association rules) at Longsight today, when a well contested game ended in a win for West Gorton by two goals to one. SUMNER, the home captain, had the choice of goals, and elected to play downhill, with the wind. St. Mark's were strongly represented, but Newton Heath brought only ten men with them, and were obliged to play a man short. Nothing of note occurred for seven or eight minutes, and then R. HOPKINSON, by a nice piece of head-work, enabled BEASTOW to score the first goal. Newton Heath were next awarded a couple of corner-kicks. The first was well sent in, but St Mark's cleared away all danger; the second fell rather short, and COLLINGE getting possession, ran the ball the full length of the field, and sent it flying through the Railwaymen's uprights, amidst loud cheers. This was a splendid piece of work, and the visitors, nettled by this reverse, played up well. At half-time St. Mark's led by two goals to nil.

After change of ends, some even play was witnessed. Newton Heath, however, did manage to score in this half. Following a throw in and some good passing, the ball was put past KITCHEN the home goalkeeper. West Gorton won by two goal to one.

11th March 1882

Haughton Dale 1 v West Gorton (St. Mark's) 0

West Gorton team: Kitchen; W. Sumner © and F. Hopkinson; Groves and Taylor; R. Hopkinson
W. Chew Collinge Pilkington Clegg and C. Beastow.   Umpire: Mr. Osborne

This match was played at Haughton Dale today, in beautiful weather, when an exciting and enjoyable match was witnessed by the spectators. Haughton Dale winning the toss, St. Mark's kicked off from the centre, up the incline and against a slight breeze, and before long the ball was in the vicinity of the West Gorton goal. Several shots were made by the Haughton forwards without any definite result before SUMNER and HOPKINSON could get the sphere away. After this, the game was of a very even nature, until half-time arrived without a goal having been scored.

Upon the ball being re-started from the centre, St. Mark's came with a rush down the field, and immediate danger threatened the home uprights. Rowbotham made a neat save, and punted the ball well up-field, but the ball was returned by SUMNER, the West Gorton captain and after a prolonged struggle the ball was put out of play. Some give-and-take play now occurred, until a bad kick by one of the St. Mark's backs gave Moores a chance of scoring, which he lost no time in utilising, amidst great excitement. On re-starting the ball, a misunderstanding between the West Gorton forwards gave the Dale men another chance, but after a long dribble the ball went over the line and into touch. Immediately after this, "Time" was called, leaving Haughton Dale the victors by one goal to nil.

All the St. Mark's players who had played in the first match against Macclesfield Baptists played at some stage during the season with the exception of Henry Heggs and John Beastow. West Gorton had played some of the best teams in the locality, including Hurst and Newton Heath (LYR). The club had made good progress.

SUMMARY
ST. MARK'S FOOTBALL CLUB 1881-82

DATE		OPPONENT	RES	1	2	3	4	5	6
1881				7	8	9	10	11	
15.Oct	A	Bentfield	L 0-1	Kitchen	Sumner©	F.Hopkinson	J.Bottomley	Downing	H.Hanson
		(Greenfield)		W.Chew	J.Clegg	Pilkington	R.Hopkinson	W.H.Chew	
29.Oct	H	Hurst	L 0-3	Kitchen	Sumner©	Groves	W.Collins	McDonald	W.Chew
		Clarence		Pilkington	Downing	R.Millard	R.Hopkinson	J.Clegg	

WEST GORTON (ST. MARK'S) FOOTBALL CLUB 1881-82

12.Nov	A	Newton Heath	L 0-3	Kitchen	Sumner©	F.Hopkinson	Groves	Collins	C.Beastow
		LYR		Pilkington	McDonald	W.Chew	Millard	Perver	
19.Nov	A	Manchester	W 1-0	Kitchen	Sumner©	F.Hopkinson	Collins	Groves	R.Hopkinson
		Arcadians		W.Chew	McDonald	Pilkington 1	E.Bower	Downing	
03.Dec	H	Bentfield	W 3-2	Kitchen	Sumner©	F.Hopkinson	Taylor	Groves	McKenna
		(Greenfield)		R.Hopkinson3	Collinge	Roberts	Clegg	C.Beastow	
31.Dec	A	Broadbottom	L 0-3	Clegg	Kitchen	Groves	A.N.Other	Pilkington	McDonald
				W.Chew	Millard	Anderson			9 Players
07.Jan	H	Manchester	D 1-1	Kitchen	Sumner©	F.Hopkinson	Groves	McDonald	Collinge
1882		Arcadians		Pilkington	R.Hopkinson1	Downing	C.Beastow	W.Chew	
14.Jan	H	Haughton Dale	W 8-1	E.Bower	Sumner©	Taylor	Groves	Collins	Collinge 5
				C.Beastow 2	R.Hopkinson	W.Chew	Anderson 1	A.N.Other	
28.Jan	A	Hurst	L 0-6						
25.Feb	H	Broadbottom	W 3-0	Kitchen	Sumner©	F.Hopkinson	Groves 1	Taylor	McDonald
				Holt	Downing 1	R.Hopkinson	Clegg 1	Anderson	
04.Mar	H	Newton Heath	W 2-1	Kitchen	Sumner©	Groves	Downing	Collinge 1	
		LYR		Pilkington	R.Hopkinson	W.Chew	C.Beastow 1	Clegg	
11.Mar	A	Haughton Dale	L 0-1	Kitchen	Sumner©	F.Hopkinson	Groves	Taylor	R.Hopkinson
				W.Chew	Collinge	Pilkington	Clegg	C.Beastow	

Captain: ©

RECORDED MATCHES 1881-82						
	P	W	D	L	F	A
Home	6	4	1	1	17	8
Away	6	1	0	5	1	14
Total	12	5	1	6	18	22

RECORDED APPEARANCES 1881-82			
	PLAYER	APPS	GLS
1	BEASTOW,C	6	3
2	SUMNER,W (c)	10	
3	HOPKINSON,F	8	
4	CHEW,W	9	
6	DOWNING,W	6	1
7	HOPKINSON,R	9	4
9	COLLINGE,J	5	6
10	PILKINGTON,J	8	1
11	KITCHEN,E	10	
12	McDONALD, A	6	
15	GROVES,E	10	1
18	COLLINS,W	4	
19	BOTTOMLEY,J	1	
20	HANSON,H	1	
21	CLEGG,J	7	1
22	CHEW,W.H.	1	
23	MILLARD,R	3	
24	PERVER	1	
25	BOWER,E	2	
26	TAYLOR	4	
27	McKENNA	1	
28	ROBERTS	1	
29	ANDERSON	3	1
30	HOLT	1	

CHAPTER 5

WEST GORTON (ST. MARKS) FOOTBALL CLUB
1882-1883

Frederick Hopkinson continued as Secretary and William Sumner as Captain.

The club played its matches this season at Queens Road, West Gorton.

The club had made progress the previous season and from the reports the main strength of the team was the good play of the defence, with William Sumner and Frederick Hopkinson being very capable. The leading goalscorers had been James Collinge and Richard Hopkinson. Unfortunately, James Collinge ceased playing for the club at the end of the 1881-1882 Season.

The club played the usual opponents such as Hurst, Bentfield and Haughton Dale but the results were poor. A further problem was that in the ten recorded matches the team was under strength in six of those matches. The following matches were reported during the season:-

14th October 1882
>Haughton Dale   0   v   West Gorton (St. Mark's)   0

West Gorton team: Bower; F.Hopkinson and Groves; Kitchen and McDonald; W.Chew W.H.Chew Pilkington Clegg C.Beastow and Anderson.

These clubs met today to play their first match of the season at Haughton Green. West Gorton had the option of playing downhill for the first half, but even with this advantage they were often pressed, and had it not been that their backs played so well, Haughton Dale would certainly have scored.

On change of ends, it was expected that the home team would press the West Gorton team more than ever. Each goal was threatened several times, but the players on both sides played with great determination, and at the call of time, neither side had scored.

28th October 1882
>West Gorton (St. Mark's)   0   v   Bentfield (Greenfield)   2

The match was played at West Gorton, who fielded but ten men, whilst Bentfield could muster only nine. Bentfield winning the toss chose to play against the wind. Some capital passing was witnessed, and just before half-time, Bentfield, getting well on the ball, scored a goal, J. Bradbury shooting the ball between the posts.

After a few minutes' rest, W. Bottomley kicked a splendid goal for the visitors, from half-back. Next to score was A. Bottomley, who shot the ball through for Bentfield's third goal. Not liking this, the Gorton team appealed for off-side, the umpires decided that the last goal be disputed. Time being called, Bentfield were left victors by two goals and one disputed to West Gorton's nil.

4th November 1882
>Hurst Clarence   2   v   West Gorton (St. Mark's)   2

West Gorton team: Kitchen; W. Sumner © and Taylor; Groves; W. Chew Nichol Anderson and C.R. Sumner (eight players). West Gorton goalscorer C.R. Sumner 2

West Gorton brought only eight men to Hurst for this match. On account of the high winds, play was limited to one hour, consisting of two halves, thirty minutes each way.

The West Gorton captain, winning the toss, elected to play with the wind at his back. During the first half, C.SUMNER scored two goals for West Gorton, who led by two goals to nil at half-time.

On resuming, the Clarence commenced to play with great vigour. A shot was sent in which KITCHEN fisted out, but Lees met the ball, and with a good shot sent it between the uprights. There were several corner-kicks in favour of the home side, but nothing came of them until about seven minutes before the call of time, when the ball was played close along the goal-line, and some of the West Gorton players thinking it was out of play, they offered no resistance, whereupon the Clarence kicked a goal, thereby equalising matters.

18th November 1882

Hurst 6 v West Gorton (St. Mark's) 0

This match was played at Hurst. West Gorton, with only ten men, won the toss and took advantage of the wind. Hurst kicked off and at the call of time the score was Hurst 6 goals West Gorton nil.

25th November 1882

West Gorton (St. Mark's) 0 v Manchester Association 1

West Gorton team: Downing; W. Sumner © and Taylor; Kitchen and Groves; Johnson R.Hopkinson Anderson W.Chew Pilkington and C.R. Sumner   Umpire: Mr. Bower

The ground at Gorton was very heavy, owing to the recent incessant rain. Nothing of importance occurred during the first half, except that Manchester claimed a goal from a throw-in, which was received and played by a Manchester player whilst he was off-side. The umpire disallowed the goal.

The second half was noticeable for the dash of the Manchester forwards. On one occasion, DOWNING, the West Gorton goalkeeper, returned the ball into play just at the feet of Rouse, who scored the only goal obtained. The visitors afterwards again put the ball through, but the point was disputed, through the ball being kicked into the centre five or six yards away from the corner flag, instead of taking the corner-kick from the corner flag. The West Gorton forwards lacked considerably in this half, whilst their back play was very good throughout.

2nd December 1882

Marple 1 v West Gorton (St. Mark's) 1

West Gorton team: Kitchen; W. Sumner © and F. Hopkinson; Groves and Bower; Johnson C. Beastow McDonald W. Chew and N. Carrick (ten players).

West Gorton turned up at Marple short-handed, only having ten men. The ground was very hard and slippery. SUMNER, the visitors' captain, had a nasty fall early on in the game and he had to go in goal. This weakened the back division of his side.

The game ended in a draw, each side scoring one goal.

William Sumner was badly injured in the game and did not play for West Gorton again. In the next season he joined Manchester Association.

Walter Chew became captain.

6th January 1883

Greenheys 1 v West Gorton (St. Mark's) 1

This match was played on the ground of Manchester Association Club. West Gorton arrived late with only nine men, but they obtained a substitute when a member of the Blackpool Club who was on the ground agreed to play for them. It was decided to play 20 minutes each way with 10 each side. The game was well contested throughout, and resulted in a draw 1 goal each.

3rd February 1883

Broadbottom 2 v West Gorton (St. Mark's) 0

West Gorton team: Ashworth; F.Hopkinson and Groves; Kitchen and Clark; Nichol, Fletcher, W. Chew © McDonald and Sykes (ten players).

Broadbottom playing at home were victorious by two goals to nil.

17th February 1883

Bentfield 7 v West Gorton (St. Mark's) 0

West Gorton team: Whitelegg; Kitchen and Groves; Millard Anderson and McDonald; Clark, Clegg Nichol W. Chew© and W.H. Chew

Played at Bentfield today for the benefit of J.E. Moss of Hurst F C, who some time since had the misfortune to break his leg whilst playing at Bentfield. West Gorton winning the toss chose to play with the wind. Bentfield kicked off, and took the ball up to the West Gorton full-backs, who just managed to return it down the field, where a nice bit of play by both sides was witnessed. West Gorton at this point getting well on the ball made a capital shot at goal, but only to be returned by the goalkeeper. This was the only chance during the game that the visitors had to score. Bentfield, though playing against the wind, scored two goals before half-time.

On resuming, the Bentfield forwards, playing well together, kept continually shooting at their opponents' goal, which ended in five more goals being scored. A pleasant game resulted in a victory for Bentfield by seven goals and another disputed, to West Gorton's nil.

24th February 1883

West Gorton (St. Mark's) 1 v Middleton 0

West Gorton team: Patterson; Kitchen and Groves; Millard and Anderson; Nichol W. Chew © Clegg and Clark (nine players)

The match was played at Gorton. Neither side was fully represented. A pleasant game resulted in favour of West Gorton by two goals (one of which disputed) to nil.

It had been a disappointing season and it was the end of the first phase of the club's history.

The club in the first three years of its existence was closely connected to St. Mark's Church and to the St. Mark's Cricket Club.

Many matches will have gone unreported during this period and the detail in the reported matches is often sparse. However, in the recorded matches during the first three seasons from 1880 to 1883, the players who made the most appearances and the leading goalscorers were:

APPEARANCES 1880-83	
Edward Kitchen	21
Walter Chew	18
Edward Groves	18
William Sumner	17
Alexander McDonald	13
Frederick Hopkinson	12
Richard Hopkinson	12
John Pilkington	11
Charles Beastow	10
GOALSCORERS 1880-83	
James Collinge	8
Richard Hopkinson	6
Charles Beastow	3

The only players from St. Mark's first match against Macclesfield Baptists who continued to play for the club after the 1882-1883 Season were Walter Chew, Edward Kitchen, Frederick Hopkinson and Richard Hopkinson. Two other St. Mark's players, Edward Groves and Edward Bower, who had not played in St. Mark's first match, also continued to play for the club.

Walter Chew, Frederick Hopkinson and Edward Kitchen were again to take an active part in the running of the club, when Gorton was formed in the 1884-85 Season.

However, in the meantime, West Gorton (St. Mark's) were to merge with Belle Vue Rangers to form West Gorton for the 1883-1884 Season

\multicolumn{10}{c}{SUMMARY}
\multicolumn{10}{c}{WEST GORTON (ST. MARK'S) FOOTBALL CLUB 1882-83}
DATE		OPPONENT	RES	1	2	3	4	5	6
1882				7	8	9	10	11	
14.Oct	A	Haughton	D 0-0	Bower	F.Hopkinson	Groves	Kitchen	McDonald	W.Chew
		Dale		W.H.Chew	Pilkington	Clegg	C.Beastow	Anderson	
28.Oct	H	Bentfield	L 0-2						
		(Greenfield)							
4.Nov	A	Hurst	D 2-2	Kitchen	Sumner©	Taylor	Groves	W.Chew	Nichol
		Clarence		Anderson	C.R.Sumner 2				8 Players
18.Nov	H	Hurst	L 0-6						
									10 Players
25.Nov	H	Manchester	L 0-1	Downing	Sumner©	Taylor	Kitchen	Groves	Johnson
		Association		R.Hopkinson	Anderson	W.Chew	Pilkington	C.R.Sumner	
02.Dec	A	Marple	D 1-1	Kitchen	Sumner©	F.Hopkinson	Groves	Bower	Johnson
				C.Beastow	McDonald	W.Chew	Carrick	10 Players	1 goal *
06.Jan	A	Greenheys	D 1-1						
1883									9 Players
03.Feb	A	Broadbottom	L 0-2	Ashworth	F.Hopkinson	Groves	Kitchen	Clark	Nichol
				Fletcher	W.Chew ©	McDonald	Sykes		10 Players
17.Feb	A	Bentfield	L 0-7	Whitelegg	Kitchen	Groves	Millard	Anderson	McDonald
		(Greenfield)		Clark	Clegg	Nichol	W.Chew ©	W.H.Chew	
24.Feb	H	Middleton	W 1-0	Patterson	Kitchen	Groves	Millard	Anderson	Nichol
				W.Chew ©	Clegg	Clark		9 Players	1 goal *

Captain: ©   Scorer(s) not known: *

\multicolumn{7}{c}{RECORDED MATCHES 1882-83}
	P	W	D	L	F	A
Home	4	1	0	3	1	9
Away	6	0	4	2	4	13
Total	10	1	4	5	5	22

PLAYERS APPEARANCES					
ST. MARKS F. C. 1880-1881					
WEST GORTON (ST MARKS) F.C. 1881-1883					
	1880-1881	1881-1882	1882-1883	TOTAL	GOALS
1. BEASTOW,C	2	6	2	10	3
2. SUMNER,W ©	4	10	3	17	
3. HOPKINSON,F	1	8	3	12	
4. CHEW,W ©	2	9	7	18	
5. HEGGS,H	3			3	
6. DOWNING,W	2	6	1	9	2
7. HOPKINSON,R	2	9	1	12	6
8. BEASTOW,J	2			2	
9. COLLINGE,J	3	5		8	8
10. PILKINGTON,J	2	8	2	12	1
11. KITCHEN,E	4	10	7	21	
12. McDONALD, A	3	6	4	13	
13. COOPER	1			1	
14. KEATES,A	1			1	
15. GROVES,E	1	10	7	18	1
16. SMITH	1			1	
17. HARROWAY	1			1	
18. COLLINS,W	1	4		5	
19. BOTTOMLEY,J.		1		1	
20. HANSON,H		1		1	
21. CLEGG,J		7	3	10	1
22. CHEW,W.H.		1	2	3	
23. MILLARD,R		3	2	5	
24. PERVER		1		1	
25. BOWER,E		2	2	4	
26. TAYLOR		4	2	6	
27. McKENNA		1		1	
28. ROBERTS		1		1	
29. ANDERSON		3	5	8	1
30. HOLT		1		1	
31. NICHOL			4	4	
32. SUMNER, C.R.			2 (2 goals)	2	2
33. JOHNSON			2	2	
34. CARRICK,N			1	1	
35. ASHWORTH			1	1	
36. CLARK			3	3	
37. SYKES			1	1	
38. FLETCHER			1	1	
39. WHITELEGG			1	1	
40. PATTERSON			1	1	

William Sumner was captain in all 17 of his recorded appearances and Walter Chew was captain in 3 recorded appearances.

CHAPTER 6

BELLE VUE RANGERS
1882-1883

Belle Vue Rangers Football Club 1882

There were close links between West Gorton (St. Mark's) and Belle Vue Rangers from the time Rangers was formed. Ranger's first reported fixtures were in January 1882, when they played two matches against Hurst Park Road. Belle Vue Rangers lost the first match against the Hurst first team but drew the second game against the Hurst reserve team. The captain of the team was Walter Chew and Edward Kitchen, Edward Groves and Edward Bower of West Gorton (St. Mark's) played some matches for Rangers.

14th January 1882

        Hurst Park Road   4   v   Belle Vue Rangers   1

Rangers team: J. Payton; Hitchen and E. Bower; D. Donohue and Patterson; Patterson P. Donohue W. Russell J. Hickson and W. Chew ©.
    These two Clubs met for the first time this season on the ground of the former and there was an easy victory for the Park Road by 4 goals to nil, Manifield scoring three goals and Clough one goal.

28th January 1882

        Hurst Park Road Reserves   1   v   Belle Vue Rangers   1

Rangers team: J. Payton; E. Bower and Avery; Wathey and McCabe; right wing J. Hickson and D. Donohue; centres Baker and W. Chew ©; left wing P. Donohue and W. Russell
Rangers' goalscorer: Russell.
    The return match between these Clubs was played on the ground of the latter at West Gorton, when a very even game ended in a draw. W. RUSSELL kicked a goal for the Rangers in the first half from a scrimmage in front of goal. Park Road equalised matters about ten minutes before call of time. For the Rangers WATHEY and BOWER, backs, and BAKER and P. DONOHUE, forwards, were the best players, PAYTON keeping goal well as usual.

Belle Vue Rangers Football Club 1882-1883

In the 1882-1883 Season, Belle Vue Rangers played nine reported matches, five being against club reserve teams.

21st October 1882

        Belle Vue Rangers   6   v   Hurst Park Road Reserves   0

Rangers' team: R. Howarth; E. Bower and H. Wathey; D. Donohue and J. Hickson;
W. Chew © J. Poole J. Fletcher T. Coffey P. Donohue and T. Allen.
Rangers' goalscorers: P. Donohue 2 D. Donohue 1 W. Chew 1 T.Coffey 1 and 1 other goal.
    These teams met at Gorton. CHEW won the toss for the Rangers and elected to play slightly downhill. The Rangers had all the best of the game, which ended in favour of the Rangers by 6 goals to nil. The goals were scored by P. DONOHUE two goals; W. CHEW, D. DONOHUE and T. COFFEY one each (the scorer of one of the goals is not recorded).

4th November 1882

        Belle Vue Rangers   5   v   Endon Reserves   4
    These teams met at Bollington and after a very unpleasant game the Rangers won by 5 goals to 4 and one disputed. They would have won easier but they played against the wind for an hour and

a quarter instead of 45 minutes. Both of the umpires' watches were found to be stopped when time should have been called.

18th November 1882
Belle Vue Rangers   2   v   Macclesfield Wanderers   4

Played at West Gorton and resulting in a victory for Macclesfield Wanderers by 4 goals to 2.

6th January 1883
Hurst Park Road Reserves   3   v   Belle Vue Rangers   1

Rangers played a plucky game at Hurst but suffered a defeat by three goals to one.

20th January 1883
Belle Vue Rangers   3   v   Hurst Clarence Reserves   1

Rangers team: E. Hunt; E. Groves and E. Bower; H. Wathey D. Donohue T. Allen; J. Poole W. Chew © Fletcher T. Coffey and P. Donohue.
The match was played on the ground of the Rangers at West Gorton. After pressing their opponents all through the game the Rangers won by three goals to one goal. E. BOWER and E. GROVES played a splendid back game and H. WATHEY shone conspicuously at half back. The services of the Rangers goalkeeper were never called upon during the game.

27th January 1883
Belle Vue Rangers   1   v   Macclesfield Wanderers   1

Rangers team: Payton; E. Bower and E. Groves; H. Wathey and J. Bowers; E. Kitchen T. Coffey W. Chew © T. Allen J. Fletcher and another.
Played at Macclesfield and ending in a draw each side scoring one goal. The Wanderers played a rough game even charging their opponents when the ball was six yards over the goal line.

10th March 1883
Hurst Clarence Reserves   3   v   Belle Vue Rangers   2

Played on the ground of Hurst Park Road and after a pleasant game of thirty minutes each way victory rested with the Clarence who won by three goals to two.

17th March 1883
Belle Vue Rangers   2   v   Denton   0

Rangers team: J. Payton; E. Groves and E. Bower; H. Wathey and D. Donohue; J. Poole © T. Allen, S. Vale, J. Hickson, P. Donohue and J. Fletcher.
This match was played at West Gorton, and after a rather one sided game, the Rangers won by two goals to nil. The score would have been greatly augmented but for the Denton goalkeeper.

31st March 1883
Stalybridge Athletic   1   v   Belle Vue Rangers   0

Played on the ground of Stalybridge Athletic and after a well contested game resulted in victory for Stalybridge Athletic by one goal to nil.
All played well for the home team. Bickerton played in his usual style and succeeded in putting the ball between the posts just before the call of time.

In the eleven recorded matches of Belle Vue Rangers, the club won four, drew two and lost five of the games. The team was recorded in six of the match reports and Walter Chew captained the Rangers in five of those matches. Many of the matches had been against reserve teams, but Belle Vue Rangers had played well against established teams, such as Macclesfield Wanderers and Denton.

Belle Vue Rangers Rangers and West Gorton (St. Mark's) had a close relationship and discussions were to take place between the two clubs during the summer of 1883 with a view to a merger. Walter Chew is likely to have played a prominent part in those discussions.

SUMMARY								
BELLE VUE RANGERS FOOTBALL CLUB 1881-1882								
DATE		OPPONENT	RES	1	2	3	4	5	6
1882				7	8	9	10	11	
14.Jan	A	Hurst Park	L 0-4	J.Payton	Hitchen	E.Bower	D.Donohue	Patterson	Patterson
10 Players		Road		P.Donohue	W. Russell	J.Hickson	W.Chew ©		
28.Jan	H	Hurst Park	D 1-1	J. Payton	E. Bower	Avery	H.Wathey	McCabe	J. Hickson
		Road		D.Donohue	Baker	W.Chew ©	P.Donohue	W.Russell 1	
BELLE VUE RANGERS FOOTBALL CLUB 1882-1883								
21.Oct	H	Hurst Park	W 6-0	R.Howarth	E. Bower	H. Wathey	D.Donohue1	J. Hickson	W.Chew © 1
		Road Res.		J.Poole	J.Fletcher	T.Coffey 1	P.Donohue2	T.Allen	1 goal *
04.Nov	A	Endon Res	W 5-4						
18.Nov	H	Macclesfield	L 2-5						
		Wanderers							
06.Jan	A	Hurst Park	L 1-3						
1883		Road Res							
20.Jan	H	Hurst Clarence	W 3-1	E.Hunt	E.Groves	E. Bower	H. Wathey	D.Donohue	T. Allen
		Res		J. Poole	W.Chew ©	J. Fletcher	T. Coffey	P.Donohue	3 goals *
27.Jan	A	Macclesfield	D 1-1	J. Payton	E. Bower	E. Groves	H. Wathey	J.Bowers	E.Kitchen
		Wanderers		T. Coffey	W.Chew ©	T. Allen	J. Fletcher	A.N.Other	1 goal *
10.Mar	A	Hurst Clarence	L 2-3						
		Res							
17.Mar	H	Denton	W 2-0	J. Payton	E. Groves	E. Bower	H. Wathey	D.Donohue	J. Poole
				T. Allen	S.Vale	J Hickson	P.Donohue	J. Fletcher	2 goals *
31.Mar	A	Stalybridge	L 0-1						

Captain: ©   Scorer(s) not known: *

RECORDED MATCHES 1881-1883						
	P	W	D	L	F	A
Home	5	3	1	1	14	7
Away	6	1	1	4	9	16
Total	11	4	2	5	23	23

RECORDED APPEARANCES OF ST. MARK'S PLAYERS		
PLAYER	APPS.	GOALS
1. CHEW,W ©	5	1
2. BOWER,E	6	
3. GROVES,E	3	
4. KITCHEN,E	1	

CHAPTER 7

WEST GORTON FOOTBALL CLUB
1883-1884

On 8th October 1883, the football correspondent (Dribbler) in the Manchester Courier wrote:-

"I am informed that Sumner who played for West Gorton last season, and which club has broken up, will play for Manchester Association next Saturday against Macclesfield, and his services will add greatly to the strength of the club."

On 15th October 1883, the Courier carried the following notice:-

WEST GORTON ASSOCIATION F.C.-The Hon. Secretary of this club writes:

"I noticed in your last issue a paragraph to the effect that the West Gorton Association F.C. was no more. Permit me to contradict that report as being untrue. Besides, such a statement tends to mislead clubs with whom we have engagements."

On 22nd October 1883, Dribbler wrote in the Courier:-

"It appears I was right after all about the West Gorton Club having been abolished. The Belle Vue Rangers, the Secretary of which wrote on the subject that the statement was misleading, have taken on the name of the deceased West Gorton, hence the misunderstanding."

However, what had happened was that West Gorton (St. Mark's) and Belle Vue Rangers had amalgamated, with the amalgamated club retaining the name of West Gorton and continuing to play at West Gorton (St. Mark's) ground at Queens Road.

There were already close ties between the two clubs going back as far as January 1882 and continuing throughout the 1882-1883 Season, with Walter Chew, Edward Groves, Edward Bower and Edward Kitchen playing some matches for the Rangers. West Gorton (St. Mark's) were more established than Belle Vue Rangers and had a much better fixture list.

In the 1882-1883 Season, West Gorton (St. Mark's) had only won one match, and had difficulty during the season in raising a full team. Belle Vue Rangers did not experience such problems. Walter Chew and Edward Kitchen probably considered that a merger with Belle Vue Rangers would have advantages for both clubs.

From the report in the Courier it would seem that the secretary of West Gorton was the former secretary of Belle Vue Rangers. The captain of West Gorton was J. Poole, who succeeded Walter Chew as captain of Belle Vue Rangers.

From a playing point of view, the new season was a great success, and thirteen matches are known to have been played by the first team of West Gorton. Many of West Gorton (St. Mark's) regular fixtures were maintained including matches against Bentfield, Broadbottom, Furness Vale, Greenheys, Haughton Dale, Manchester Arcadians and Marple.

West Gorton ran two teams and some of the former West Gorton (St. Mark's) players probably played for the second team. Only Walter Chew, Edward Bower and Edward Groves of the St. Mark's players are known to have played for the West Gorton first team but the full West Gorton team is only recorded in two of the match reports in the 1883-1884 Season. The club colours were reported to be scarlet and black.

West Gorton played the following fixtures:

6th October 1883

West Gorton 4 v Hurdsfield 3

The match was played on the ground of West Gorton. The ball was started at 3.20pm, and at half-time the score was equal, three goals each.

On the resumption of play, West Gorton added another goal. As time was drawing to a close, the Hurdsfield men tried their best to score, but in this they were prevented. West Gorton thus winning a good game by 4 goals to 3. The Hurdsfield team are a fine lot of fellows, hailing from Macclesfield, but as seen above West Gorton held their own against them

13th October 1883

West Gorton 1 v Furness Vale 0

1000
West Gorton team: J. Payton; E. Groves and E. Bower; H. Wathey, R. Howarth and J. Cathels; J. Poole © T. Allen, W. Angus, W. Chew and P. Donohue.
West Gorton goalscorer: P. Donohue.

The match was played at West Gorton. The Furness Vale team was very strong and heavy, whilst West Gorton had two of their best players missing, for whom substitutes had to be found. The West Gorton captain won the toss, and elected to play with the wind. The game was hotly contested all through, the backs of both teams defending in splendid style. About two minutes from half-time, the ball was run down to the Furness Vale goal by ALLEN and ANGUS, and passed to P.DONOHUE, who shot the leather between the posts.

This was the only goal scored, and West Gorton won a grand game by one goal to nil. Special mention should be made of HOWARTH, who played magnificently for West Gorton at half-back.

26th October 1883

West Gorton 2 v Manchester Arcadians 0

West Gorton team: J. Payton; E. Bower and E. Groves; H.Wathey R. Howarth and D. Donohue; J.Poole © W. Angus T. Allen, T. Coffey and P. Donohue

This Association match was played today at West Gorton. In spite of the rain, the match was witnessed by about 100 spectators. The ground was very wet and heavy, and West Gorton had matters very much their own way and finally won by two goals to nil.

3rd November 1883

West Gorton 4 v Broadbottom 0

Played at West Gorton and resulted in a win for West Gorton by 4 goals to nil.

17th November 1883

Pendleton Olympic 1 v West Gorton 7

The game was very pleasantly contested at Pendleton and at the call of time West Gorton had won by 7 goals to 1.

24th November 1883

Marple 1 v West Gorton 5

West Gorton won at Marple by 5 goals to 1.

24th November 1883   West Gorton (2nd) 6 v Marple (2nd) 0   at West Gorton

1st December 1883

       Bentfield 2 v West Gorton 1

The match was played at Bentfield. Bentfield came off victorious by 2 goals to 1

8th December 1883

      Furness Vale Rovers 0 v West Gorton 0

The game, which was played at Furness Vale came to a conclusion fifteen minutes before time, on account of an off-side goal scored by the home team, who left the field because West Gorton disputed the goal. The game thus ended in a draw.

 8th December 1883   West Gorton (2nd) 3 v Clifton (2nd) 0   at West Gorton

22nd December 1883

       Haughton Dale 1 v West Gorton 4

This fixture was contested at Haughton. In the first half West Gorton scored two goals to one by Haughton Dale put through by a West Gorton player.

In the second half West Gorton increased their score to four goals, at the same time preventing Haughton from scoring again, thus winning by four goals to one.

 22nd December 1883 West Gorton (2nd) 1 v Haughton Dale (2nd) 0 at West Gorton

12th January 1884

       West Gorton 2 v Levenshulme 2

The West Gorton ground was not fit to play on being five to six inches deep in mud, but owing to the great interest in the game, the match proceeded. After a tight struggle, the game ended in a draw with each team scoring twice.

2nd February 1884

       West Gorton 2 v Bentfield 1

Played on the Clemington Park ground, West Gorton, before about 600 spectators, and resulted in a win for the home team, who scored three goals (one of which disputed) to one. It is the first time the Bentfield first team has been defeated for two years.

 2nd February 1884   Bentfield (2nd) 2 v West Gorton (2nd) 0   at Greenfield

9th February 1884

       Broadbottom 0 v West Gorton 5

Played at Broadbottom, and after a very pleasant and rather one-sided game, resulted in a win for West Gorton by five goals to nil.

16th February 1884

       Greenheys 1 v West Gorton 5

Played on the ground of the former, at Greenheys, and resulted in an easy win for West Gorton by five goals to one.

 16th February 1884   West Gorton (2nd) 3 v Greenheys (2nd) 0   at West Gorton.

 23rd February 1884   Hurst Clarence 1 v West Gorton (2nd) 1   at Hurst.

22nd March 1884

West Gorton 7 v Gorton Villa 0

After a pleasant and one-sided game at Clemington Park, West Gorton won by seven goals to nil. For West Gorton, POOLE, PRICE and DONOHUE forward, and BOWER, WATHEY, GROVES and HOWARTH behind, played a grand game.

5th April 1884

Levenshulme 1 v West Gorton 1

The game was played at Levenshulme before a large number of spectators and was very exciting throughout. In the first half Levenshulme had by far the best of the game scoring one goal and having several close shaves of scoring more.

In the second half West Gorton played much better, and managed to equalise matters, the game ending in a draw, one goal each.

West Gorton's first team had been very successful winning twelve (including the match played on 4th October 1884), drawing three and losing two of the sixteen recorded matches. The second team had four wins, one draw and one loss in their six recorded matches.

However, the old West Gorton (St. Mark's) players were unhappy with the amalgamation as the former Belle Vue Rangers players and officials had taken over the club and only a few of the West Gorton (St. Mark's) players were playing in the first team.

At the end of the season, Walter Chew and Edward Kitchen decided that they would re-form the club as Gorton Association Football Club but they needed a ground.

After Gorton A.F.C. was formed, the former Belle Vue Rangers players continued as West Gorton playing at Queen's Road. The club subsequently changed its name to "West Gorton Athletic" and played against Gorton in the Manchester and District Challenge Cup in 1887. The club later became "West Gorton Hibernian". Some of the former Belle Vue Rangers players were to play for Gorton, including Payton, Wathey and D.Donohue.

RECORDED APPEARANCES 1883-84	
FORMER ST.MARK'S PLAYERS WHO LATER PLAYED FOR GORTON	
PLAYER	APPEARANCES
1. CHEW,W	2
2. BOWER,E	4
3. GROVES,E	4
WEST GORTON PLAYERS WHO LATER PLAYED FOR GORTON	
PLAYER	APPEARANCES
4. PAYTON,J	3
5. WATHEY,H	4
6. DONOHUE,D	2
7. BOOTH,J	1

SUMMARY
WEST GORTON FOOTBALL CLUB 1883-84

DATE		OPPONENT	RES	1	2	3	4	5	6
1883				7	8	9	10	11	
6-Oct	H	Hurdsfield	W 4-3						
13-Oct	H	Furness Vale	W 1-0	J.Payton	E.Groves	E.Bower	H.Wathey	R.Howarth	J.Cathels
			1000	J.Poole ©	T.Allen	W.Angus	W.Chew	P.Donohue1	
20-Oct	H	Manchester	W 2-0	J. Payton	E. Bower	E. Groves	H. Wathey	R. Howarth	D.Donohue
		Arcadians	100	J.Poole ©	W. Angus	T. Allen	T.Coffey	P.Donohue	2 goals *
3-Nov	H	Broadbottom	W 4-0						
17-Nov	A	Pendleton	W 7-1						
		Olympic							
24-Nov	A	Marple	W 5-1						
1-Dec	A	Bentfield	L 1-2						
8-Dec	A	Furness Vale	D 0-0						
		Rovers							
22-Dec	A	Haughton Dale	W 4-1						
1884									
12-Jan	H	Levenshulme	D 2-2						
2-Feb	H	Bentfield	W 2-1						
			600						
9-Feb	A	Broadbottom	W 5-0						
16-Feb	A	Greenheys	W 5-1						
15-Mar	A	Haughton Dale	L 0-1						
22-Mar	H	Gorton Villa	W 7-0		E. Bower	E. Groves	H. Wathey	R. Howarth	
				J.Poole ©		Price		P.Donohue	7 goals *
5-Apr	A	Levenshulme	D 1-1						
WEST GORTON ASSOCIATION FOOTBALL CLUB OCTOBER 1884									
04-Oct	H	Crewe	W 2-0	J. Payton	E.Groves	E.Bower	R.Howarth	H.Wathey	D Donohue
1884		Britannia		J.Poole ©	W.Chew	T. Allen	T. Coffey	J.Booth	2 goals *

Captain: ©   Scorer(s) not known: *

RECORDED MATCHES 1883-84

	P	W	D	L	F	A
Home	8	7	1	0	24	6
Away	9	5	2	2	28	8
Total	17	12	3	2	52	14

*Includes West Gorton v Crewe Britannia on 4th October 1884

CHAPTER 8

GORTON ASSOCIATION FOOTBALL CLUB
1884-1885

West Gorton F. C.

The 1884-1885 Season commenced before Gorton A.F.C. was formed with Walter Chew, Edward Bower and Edward Groves still playing in the first team of West Gorton. On 4th October 1884, West Gorton played Crewe Britannia at West Gorton. The brief match report gave details of the team and was as follows:

4th October 1884   West Gorton   2   v   Crewe Britannia   0

West Gorton team: J. Payton; E. Groves and E. Bower; R. Howarth H. Wathey and D. Donohue; J. Poole © W. Chew T. Allen T. Coffey and J. Booth.
This match was played at West Gorton and resulted in a win for West Gorton by two goals to nil.

Gorton A. F. C.

Later in October 1884, Gorton Association Football Club was formed by the members of the former West Gorton (St. Mark's) Football Club.

A tenancy had been obtained of a ground at Pink Bank Lane, Longsight.

A notice announcing the formation of Gorton A.F.C. appeared in the *Gorton Reporter* on 25th October 1884:

25th October 1884 "The members of the Old West Gorton Association Football Club have pulled together, and, with the assistance of a few other players, have formed a new club under the name of "Gorton Association". A suitable ground has been secured near Belle Vue Station. Mr E. Kitchen, Railway Cottages, Longsight has been appointed secretary. He is arranging matches for both first and second teams."

A notice appeared in *The Umpire* on 2nd November 1884 announcing the formation of Gorton A.F.C. and the securing of a new ground near Belle Vue Station. The notice also announced that the Hon. Secretary Mr E. Kitchen would be glad to arrange fixtures with first and second teams within a reasonable distance.

The Officers of the Club were:

        Chairman: James Moores
        Vice-Chairman: William Henry Beastow
        Secretary: Edward Kitchen

It is likely that Walter Chew and Frederick Hopkinson were on the committee. Frederick Hopkinson read the annual report at the end of the first season.

The connection with St. Mark's Church was still strong for James Moores was a Sidesman and William Henry Beastow was a Churchwarden. Walter Chew, Edward

Kitchen, Frederick Hopkinson, Richard Hopkinson and Lawrence Furniss (a new member) were also active members of the Church.

The Club's tenancy of the new ground at Pink Bank Lane, Longsight was at a yearly rent of three pounds with a yearly rent of fifteen shillings for a dressing room.

The Club joined the Manchester and District Football Association which was formed in 1884.

The players were still amateurs and paid a membership subscription. The club was well supported from the outset and there were sufficient members to run two teams.

William Henry Beastow presented the club with a set of black jerseys with a white cross.

It is believed that William Henry Beastow is standing on the right of the photograph and that James Moores is seated next to him. The players are not identified but the following players were in the Gorton First team at the beginning of the 1884-1885 Season:

E.Bower
K. McKenzie©   F.Hopkinson
E.Groves   L. Furniss   E. Kitchen
W.Chew   R.Hopkinson   T. Kirk   J.Booth   Owen

Several new players joined Gorton and two were to be very prominent:

LAWRENCE FURNISS was born in Cromford, Derbyshire in 1858 and he initially worked as a railway clerk. By 1884, he had moved to 127, Clowes Street, West Gorton. He became a parishioner at St. Mark's Church and was later a sidesman. He played at half-back and as a forward for Gorton from 1884 to 1886, when he suffered a serious knee injury. He was captain of Gorton in 1885-1886. His injury caused him to retire from playing and his last recorded appearance was on 20th March 1886 in a match against Ashton. In 1886-1887 he served on the club's management committee with Walter Chew, William Henry Chew and William Mayson and jointly they were instrumental in securing a tenancy of the Hyde Road Ground and forming Ardwick. He later became Secretary of Ardwick and a Director and President of Manchester City Football Club.

KENNETH McKENZIE was born in Scotland in 1863 and was 21 when he started to play for Gorton. He played as a full-back and was captain of Gorton in the 1884-1885 Season. He is credited with having found the land which was to become the Hyde Road ground in 1887. He later played for Ardwick and was captain at the beginning of the 1887-1888 Season and in the 1889-1890 Season.

Gorton played the following fixtures:

8th November 1884   Gorton (2nd) 4 v Eccles (2nd) 2

15th November 1884

Gorton 4 v Gorton Villa 0

The match was played at Pink Bank Lane, Longsight and resulted in a win for Gorton by four goals to nil.

22nd November 1884

Gorton 0 v Heywood St. James 0

Gorton team: J. Payton; E. Bower and F. Hopkinson; Prenty Avery and E. Kitchen; Turner © Owen W. Chew J. Booth and J.Mellor.   Umpire: W.H.Chew

There were a fair number of spectators at Pink Bank Lane. Smith won the toss and after OWEN had kicked off for Gorton the ball was quickly returned and carried into Gorton territory. BOWER with a good kick relieved his goal, and some smart level play followed. Gorton got in close proximity to the Heywood goal, but one of their forwards spoiled the chance by a foul. St. James closely pressed their opponents and for the rest of the game had the advantage. TURNER, OWEN, AVERY, BOWER and HOPKINSON were prominent for Gorton.

6th December 1884

Manchester Clifford 0 v Gorton 4

Gorton team: Kitchen; McKenzie © and F.Hopkinson; Bower, Jenkins and Groves; Furniss, W. Chew, Kirk, Booth and Owen.   Umpire: W.H. Chew

The game at Old Trafford was played in a very friendly manner. Clifford passed well, but were weak in front of goal, whilst Gorton took advantage of some good shots at goal and won by four goals to nil.

13th December 1884

Heywood St. James 0 v Gorton 0

Gorton team: Bower; McKenzie © and F. Hopkinson; Groves D. Standring and J.E. Aspinall; Kitchen W. Chew Bowden Furniss and Ackroyd

Played at Heywood and resulted in a draw, neither side scoring. Gorton did not arrive on the ground until after 4.00 p.m., and as darkness set in soon after, the match was proceeded with under great difficulties. In the first half, Heywood pressed their opponents closely and several shots were made at goal but were well stopped by McKENZIE and BOWER.

In the second half, the play was in almost total darkness and no goals were scored.

3rd January 1885

Tottington 3 v Gorton 0

Gorton team: Bower; Kitchen and F. Hopkinson; Booth Groves and Earnshaw; Baker Furniss Fletcher W. Chew and Brooks.

    Gorton won the toss at Tottington and Hamer kicked off for the home side. The play in the first half was of a very even description. In the second half, Tottington pressed their opponents and Butterworth scored three goals. Tottington won by three goals to nil.

10th January 1885

Gorton 5 v Manchester Clifford 0

    The Gorton Association Football Club, newly formed this season, have taken all before them. They beat a strong team of the Manchester Clifford on Saturday by five goals to nil. They have really only lost one match this season, and that was with only half of their team at Tottington Park. This is good form, and the success of the club has caused whispers that it would not be very surprising to hear of them bringing the Manchester and District Challenge Cup to Gorton.

17th January 1885

Gorton 1 v Newton Heath (LYR) 3

Gorton team: Bower; McKenzie © and F. Hopkinson; Kitchen and Groves; Booth D. Melville Kirk Bain Furniss and Mearns.

    Gorton won the toss at Pink Bank Lane and had the assistance of the wind. Newton Heath many times during the first half visited the Gorton quarters, but the Gorton backs played well and saved their side repeatedly, although at times the Newton Heath forwards gave them some trouble. A minute before half-time, from a corner kick, Newton Heath scored.

    With the wind in their favour in the second half, Newton Heath had the best of the game, but Gorton breaking away scored from a scrimmage in front of goal, five minutes after re-starting. Newton Heath played up well, and scored twice in a short time. It had become quite dark, and it was agreed to abandon the game ten minutes before time. Newton Heath thus won a good game by three goals to one.

24th January 1885

Gorton 3 v Manchester Clifford 0

    These teams met for the third time this season at Gorton, the ground being very much against good play. Gorton scored twice in the first half, and once in the second, and had it not been for the goalkeeping of Sankey, the score would have been very much larger.

    Gorton were drawn to play Dalton Hall in the First Round of the Manchester & District Cup, which would have been the most important fixture played by the club since its formation. Six former St. Mark's players were chosen to play for Gorton: Walter Chew, Edward Kitchen, Frederick Hopkinson, Richard Hopkinson, Edward Bower and Edward Groves. The St. Mark's influence was still very strong on the playing side as well as on the administration side of the club

31st January 1885   Manchester & District Challenge Cup   First Round

Dalton Hall (Owens College) 1 v Gorton 0

Gorton team: E. Bower; K. McKenzie © and F. Hopkinson; E. Groves L. Furniss and E. Kitchen; W. Chew R. Hopkinson D. Melville T. Kirk and J. Bain.

    There was a large attendance of spectators at Dog Kennel Lane Manchester to watch these clubs in the first round of the Manchester Cup. Gorton played a very strong team, whilst the Collegians were weakened by some of their players being ineligible. The weather was cold with a strong wind, and considering the amount of rain the ground was in very good condition. McKENZIE won the toss and deputed the College to defend against a very strong wind. The College kicked off, and the ball was well returned by KIRK. His efforts were neutralised by an equally smart return by Tankye, and dribble by Pauls, Gorton conceding a corner five minutes from the start. R.HOPKINSON and FURNISS then made for the College goal, but all danger was averted by Pauls and Sadler. After an appeal for hand ball, Pauls almost scored but the ball just missed its mark. Gorton then got the ball away and a missed kick by a College back gave R.HOPKINSON a chance which he failed to take. Following a handball against the College only the grand defence of the College backs prevented McKENZIE from scoring. Thistlethwaite for the College had a shot at goal which passed just over the bar. F.HOPKINSON, GROVES and FURNISS broke away with a grand passing run and there was a fierce onslaught on the College goal, a brace of corners being repelled by the College backs.

On change of ends, and with the wind in their favour, it was thought that the College would soon score. Gorton had to act strictly on the defensive and shot after shot was grandly saved by the fine play of BOWER, GROVES, KITCHEN and McKENZIE. After the College had numerous unproductive corners, the College had another corner to their credit from which Pauls notched the first and only goal of the game. This reverse dampened the spirits of Gorton, but they did not relax their efforts, the College goalkeeper saving a high shot from GROVES by almost a miracle. A well contested game ended in favour of the College by one goal to nil. GROVES for Gorton was their best player, whilst KITCHEN, BOWER, BAIN and FURNISS put in some good work.

14th February 1885

Gorton Villa 1 v Gorton 1

This match was played on the ground of Gorton Villa before a large number of spectators. McKENZIE won the toss for Gorton and A. Birch set the ball in motion for Gorton Villa. Within a few minutes from the start, Gorton scored from a mistake by one of the Villa's backs, who centred the ball in front of his own posts. This reverse roused the Villa, and Miller running the ball right along the field screwed in one for Villa. Nothing more of importance resulted in the first half.

After change of ends, Villa's forwards worked the ball well up, Gorton's goalkeeper left his posts to meet the ball and missed his kick, Darnley for Villa landed the ball between the posts, but one of Gorton's backs, who, it is alleged, had in the meantime got between the posts, stopped it from going through. Villa claimed a goal but this not suiting McKENZIE, he took his men off the field.

21st February 1885

Newton Heath (LYR) 6 v Gorton 0

This match was played at Newton Heath before a fair number of spectators. Gorton won the toss and Newton Heath kicked off against the wind. It was soon apparent that Newton Heath were in fine form, their combined play being the great feature even at the beginning of the game. Newton Heath scored the first goal with a shot by Blear after ten minutes. Following this came some exceedingly good play and Gorton strove hard to put themselves on equal terms. A somewhat easy chance presented itself, but Gorton failed to utilize the opening. Newton Heath then fired in some magnificent shots, but the Gorton goalkeeper distinguished himself by frustrating all attempts to score in a remarkable fashion. At half-time Newton Heath were leading by one goal to nil.

After half-time, Newton Heath played well. Howles, Black and Davies were especially busy, and by combined passing, two goals were quickly registered to Newton Heath. Newton Heath continued to have the better of the game and the Gorton goalkeeper was very busy repelling the Newton Heath attacks. Black and Mitchell were not to be denied and by really excellent passing three more goals were scored, one when McKENZIE put the ball through his own goal. For Gorton, all played well but Newton Heath's tactics were more combined and their passing at times was very fine.

20th April 1885   GORTON ASSOCIATION FOOTBALL CLUB -The first annual dinner in connection with the above club was held on Monday evening, 20th April 1885 at the Justice Birch Hotel on Hyde Road where there was a good attendance.

Mr and Mrs Pitt served an excellent dinner and it was thoroughly enjoyed. Afterwards, Mr James Moores presided and Mr W.H. Beastow was Vice Chairman. The loyal toasts were honoured, interspersed with songs "Heart of Oak" by Mr Chew and "The Old Brigade" by Mr F.Hopkinson. The toast "The Manchester and District Association" was heartily received and acknowledged by Mr Colbert.

Mr F. Hopkinson read the annual report, which stated that the club only formed in October last, had made considerable progress. It had a membership of about twenty five active members, with a promise of a good increase next season. The first team last season had played sixteen matches, seven of which were won, seven were lost, and two drawn; the number of goals scored was 31 against 21 scored by their opponents. The second team played seventeen matches, winning eight, losing seven, drawing two; the number of goals scored was 25, against 21 by their opponents.

In conclusion the report said that there was a balance on the right side, and all that is required for the success of the club is a good ground.

Other toasts followed and songs were given by Messrs. F. Hopkinson, Furniss, Barber and others, the evening being very agreeably spent. Mr R. Hopkinson ably officiated as pianist.

Gorton's first Balance Sheet

BALANCE SHEET

Balance Sheet for the year ended 30th April 1885			
INCOME	£	s	d
R. Peacock, Esq.	5	0	0
Members Subscriptions	3	2	4
Hon. Members Subscriptions	1	5	0
Gate Money	1	1	10
	£10	9	2
EXPENDITURE			
Rent of ground	3	0	0
Rent of dressing room		15	0
Football requisites	1	16	3
Stationery, printing, postages	1	17	3
Umpire expenses		14	0
Subscription to M. & D. Association		10	6
Comp. tickets for Dinner		7	6
Balance in hand	1	8	8
	£10	9	2

The profit of £1.8s.8d was carried forward.

SUMMARY
WEST GORTON A.F.C. 1884

DATE		OPPONENT	RES	1	2	3	4	5	6
1884				7	8	9	10	11	
04-Oct	H	Crewe Britannia	W 2-0	Payton Poole©	E.Groves W.Chew	E.Bower Allen	Howarth Coffey	Wathey J.Booth	Donohue 2 goals *

GORTON A.F.C. 1884-85

DATE		OPPONENT	RES	1	2	3	4	5	6
15-Nov 1884	H	Gorton Villa	W 4-1						
22-Nov	H	Heywood St.James	D 0-0	Payton Turner ©	Bower Owen	F.Hopkinson W.Chew	Prenty Booth	Avery J.Mellor	Kitchen
06-Dec	A	Manchester Clifford	W 4-0	Kitchen L.Furniss	McKenzie © W.Chew	F.Hopkinson T.Kirk	Bower Booth	Jenkins Owen	Groves 4 goals *
13-Dec	A	Heywood St.James	D 0-0	Bower Kitchen	McKenzie © W.Chew	F.Hopkinson Bowden	Groves Furniss	D.Standring Ackroyd	J.E.Aspinall
03-Jan 1885	A	Tottington	L 0-3	Bower Baker	Kitchen Furniss	F.Hopkinson Fletcher	Booth W.Chew	Groves Brooks	Earnshaw
10-Jan	H	Manchester Clifford	W 3-0						
17-Jan	H	Newton Heath LYR	L 1-2	Bower D.Melville	McKenzie © Kirk	F.Hopkinson J.Bain	Kitchen Furniss	Groves Mearns	Booth 1 goal *
24-Jan	H	Manchester Clifford	W 3-0						
31-Jan MC1	A	Dalton Hall	L 0-1	Bower W.Chew	McKenzie © R.Hopkinson	F.Hopkinson Melville	Groves Kirk	Furniss Bain	Kitchen
14-Feb	A	Gorton Villa	D 1-1		McKenzie ©				
21-Feb	A	Newton Heath LYR	L 0-6		McKenzie ©				

Captain: ©   Scorer(s) not known: *

RECORDED MATCHES 1884-85

	P	W	D	L	F	A
Home	5	3	1	1	11	3
Away	6	1	2	3	5	11
Total	11	4	2	5	16	14
Actual record	16	7	2	7	31	21

RECORDED APPEARANCES 1884-85

Player	Apps.	Player	Apps.
1. CHEW,W	5	15. PAYTON,J	1
2. KITCHEN,E	6	16. AVERY	1
3. HOPKINSON,F	6	17. TURNER	1
4. GROVES,E	5	18. MELLOR, J.	1
5. BOWER,E	6	19. JENKINS	1
6. HOPKINSON,R	1	20. STANDRING, D.	1
7. FURNISS,L	5	21. ASPINALL, J.E.	1
8. McKENZIE, K.	6	22. BOWDEN	1
9. BOOTH, J	.4	23. ACKROYD	1
10. KIRK, T.	3	24. EARNSHAW	1
11. BAIN, J.	2	25. BAKER	1
12. OWEN	2	26. FLETCHER	1
13. MELVILLE, D.	2	27. BROOKS	1
14. PRENTY	1	28. MEARNS	1

CHAPTER 9

GORTON ASSOCIATION FOOTBALL CLUB
1885-1886

Walter Chew took over as Secretary from Edward Kitchen.

Lawrence Furniss was captain of the team.

In the Annual Report for the previous season it was mentioned that all that was required for the success of the Club was a good ground. The accounts for the year ending 30th April 1886 show that the Club received compensation for loss of ground and this presumably related to the Pink Bank Lane Ground which the Club appear to have been required to vacate.

The Club looked for another ground and secured a tenancy of a ground adjoining the Bull's Head Hotel, Reddish Lane, Gorton at a yearly rent of £4 17s 6d, which included changing facilities.

Thirteen matches were reported during the season.

3rd October 1885

Gorton 1 v Earlstown 1

Gorton A.F.C. commenced the season this afternoon, when a match against Earlstown was played on the new home ground, Bull's Head, Reddish Lane, Gorton. Earlstown won the toss, and played with the wind and the sun at their backs during the first half, and scored the first goal after about twenty minutes play. FURNISS equalised shortly afterwards with a splendid shot from half-back, the score at half-time being one goal each.

The game was well-fought, but nothing further was scored in the second half, and at the call of time, neither side held the advantage. The result was a draw each side scoring one goal.

Gorton goalscorer: L. Furniss

10th October 1885

Gorton 2 v Shuttleworth 2

This match resulted in a draw of 2 goals each, after a fast and exciting game at Gorton.

17th October 1885

Gorton 1 v Eccles 3

Gorton team: Gardner; F.Hopkinson and Kitchen; Groves Furniss © and Anderson; Melville Bower Baker W. Chew and Bowker
Gorton goalscorer: W.Chew

A hurriedly arranged fixture was played at Reddish. Immediately after the kick off Eccles, by judicious passing, harassed the Gorton goal and T. Mitchell registered the first goal for Eccles. On restarting Eccles still continued to have decidedly the best of it until a combined rush by the Gorton team allowed them to pay their first visit to the Eccles quarters and CHEW succeeded in equalising matters. Harper, however, was not long in scoring a second goal for Eccles, and eventually W. Mitchell further increased the Eccles total, which gave them the advantage at half-time by three goals to one.

During the second period of the game Eccles severely menaced the Gorton defence, the ability of the Gorton team being taxed to the utmost to prevent Eccles from scoring. Ultimately at the end Eccles were victorious by three goals to one.

17th October 1885   Eccles (2nd) 3 v Gorton (2nd) 0

24th October 1885   Benefit Match

Gorton Villa 4 v Gorton 1

The match was played before a large number of spectators and raised £6 for the benefit of Mr J. Shepherd, a well-known Gorton Villa player, who accidentally broke his leg whilst practising on this ground a month ago. The game was a fast one. A few minutes after the start, Gorton scored a goal, but afterwards the Villa had the best of it, and ultimately won by four goals to one.

14th November 1885

Gorton 3 v Manchester Clifford 0

21st November 1885

Uppermill 1 v Gorton 1

A rough and noisy match played at Greenfield resulted in a draw each side scoring one goal.

28th November 1885

Gorton 1 v Gorton Villa 0

The Villa apparently fancied they had a soft thing on at Gorton. Their anticipations were dispelled, however, as the home club won by 1 goal to nil, the Gorton custodian never handling the ball once. There was a pretty fair attendance of spectators, notwithstanding the unpropitious weather. The way in which Association games "draw" the Manchester public is wonderful, considering that it is not much more than three years since the dribbling code of football was introduced into this district.

19th December 1885   Manchester and District Challenge Cup   First Round

Pendleton Olympic 2 v Gorton 1

16th January 1886

Gorton 3 v Haughton Dale 0

13th February 1886

Gorton 1 v Levenshulme 0

Gorton team: Kitchen; F. Hopkinson and Bower; Clark and Drinkwater; Furniss © Payton Groves W. Chew and Wathey (ten players). Gorton goalscorer: Groves

The Gorton club, having been let down in their ordinary fixture for today, brought off a hastily arranged game with Levenshulme at the Bull's Head Ground. The home team were minus the services of McKENZIE, MELVILLE and RADFORD, and Levenshulme were likewise weakened by the absence of good players due to injury, both teams numbering only ten players. Two former West Gorton/Belle Vue Rangers players PAYTON and WATHEY played for Gorton.

Levenshulme won the toss, and elected to play downhill with the wind. The visitors pressed Gorton for a time, but the good play of BOWER at the back and of KITCHEN in goal prevented them from scoring. Play was transferred to the other end, where the Gorton forwards missed an easy chance in front of goal. Half-time arrived without either side having scored.

After change of ends, Gorton, aided by the wind and the incline, soon began to press Levenshulme, and gained several corners, which were very well sent in by CLARK. From one of these corners, GROVES scored the only goal of the afternoon, the game ending in a win for Gorton by one goal to nil.

20th February 1886

Gorton (2nd) 6 v Miles Platting (1st) 2

The game at Gorton was very fast and even until half-time when Gorton led by 2 goals to 1. After crossing over Gorton played a good combined game keeping the visitors backs fully employed up to the call of time when the score was Gorton 6 goals Miles Platting 2.

27th February 1886

Manchester 5 v Gorton 1

Gorton team: E. Kitchen; J. Ward and E.Bower; E.Groves and T. Drinkwater; W.Chew L.Furniss © J.H. Watmough A. Cliffe and D.Melville (ten players)
Gorton goalscorer: Watmough

The first match between the clubs this season took place on the ground of Manchester. Gorton won the toss and Farrington of Manchester kicked off. CHEW and FURNISS dribbled to the Manchester end but nothing resulted. After about twenty minutes, some pretty passing by the Manchester players enabled Farrington to score the first goal. At half-time Manchester were leading by one goal to nil.

With the advantage of the wind Manchester completely penned their opponents for some time. At length Bagnell scored a second for Manchester with an overhead kick. This roused the Gorton players, who rushed the ball to the Manchester end, and after the Manchester goalkeeper twice fisted out, WATMOUGH succeeded in scoring for Gorton. Gorton again had to go on the defensive, but after some good back play, Farrington scored a third goal for Manchester. Bagnell then struck the crossbar and the ball rebounded to Thistlethwaite who scored a fourth goal. The remaining portion of the game was evenly contested, although just before full-time, Manchester added a fifth goal, thus winning by five goals to one.

20th March 1886

Gorton 9 v Ashton 0

Gorton team: W. Twiss; Bower and Ward; Biddulph Mayson and Groves; Furniss © Watmough Smith Davy and W.Chew

The match was played at Gorton and after a one-sided game, Gorton won by 9 goals to nil.

27th March 1886

Gorton 5 v Oldham Olympic 1

Gorton had played thirteen recorded matches, winning six, drawing three and losing four. The club had continued to make good progress. The search to secure a suitable ground was still continuing as the Reddish Lane ground was some distance away from the club's roots in West Gorton.

Gorton's second Balance Sheet

BALANCE SHEET

Balance Sheet for the year ended 30th April 1886			
INCOME	£	s	d
Balance from 1884-1885	1	8	8
R. Peacock, Esq. MP	2	10	0
S. Brooks, Esq.	1	1	0
Members Subscriptions	4	18	10
Hon. Members Subscriptions	2	8	0
Gate money	2	5	8
Compensation for loss of ground	2	0	0
Receipts smoking concert	2	12	0
	£19	4	2
EXPENDITURE			
Rent of ground	4	17	6
Football requisites	2	3	3
Stationery, printing, advertising etc	3	11	6
Umpires and sundry expenses		16	7
Subscription to M. & D. Association	1	7	7
Expenses, smoking concert		10	6
Balance still with late Treasurer	1	3	10
Balance in hand	3	4	9
	£19	4	2

Gorton had made a small profit of £1 8s 8d from the previous season and with a profit of £1 16s 1d for 1885-86 there was a balance to carry forward of £3 4s 9d.

SUMMARY
GORTON A.F.C. 1885-86

DATE		OPPONENT	RES	1	2	3	4	5	6
1885				7	8	9	10	11	
3-Oct	H	Earlstown	D 1-1					L.Furniss © 1	
10-Oct	H	Shuttleworth	D 2-2						
17-Oct	H	Eccles	L 1-3	Gardner	F.Hopkinson	E.Kitchen	E.Groves	L.Furniss ©	Anderson
				D.Melville	E.Bower	Baker	W.Chew 1	Bowker	
24-Oct	A	Gorton Villa	L 1-4						
14-Nov	H	Manchester Clifford	W 3-0						
21-Nov	A	Uppermill	D 1-1						
28-Nov	H	Gorton Villa	W 1-0						
19-Dec	A	Pendleton	L 1-2						
MC 1		Olympic							
16-Jan	H	Haughton	W 3-0						
1886		Dale							
13-Feb	H	Levenshulme	W 1-0	E.Kitchen	F.Hopkinson	E.Bower	Clark	T.Drinkwater	L.Furniss ©
				J.Payton	E.Groves 1	W.Chew	H.Wathey		10 players
27-Feb	A	Manchester	L 1-5	E.Kitchen	J.H.Ward	Bower	E.Groves	T.Drinkwater	W.Chew
				L.Furniss ©	JWatmough1	A.Cliffe	D.Melville		10 players
20-Mar	H	Ashton	W 9-0	W.Twiss	E.Bower	J.H.Ward	Biddulph	W.Mayson	E.Groves
				L.Furniss ©	J.Watmough	Smith	Davy	W.Chew	9 goals *
27-Mar	H	Oldham Olympic	W 5-1						

Captain: ©   Scorer(s) not known: *

RECORDED MATCHES 1885-86

	P	W	D	L	F	A
Home	9	6	2	1	26	7
Away	4	0	1	3	4	12
Total	13	6	3	4	30	19

RECORDED APPEARANCES 1885-86

PLAYER	APPS.	GOALS	PLAYER	APPS.	GOALS
1. CHEW,W.	4	1	32. GARDNER	1	
2. KITCHEN,E	3		33. ANDERSON	1	
3. HOPKINSON,F	2		34. BOWKER	1	
4. GROVES,E	4	1	35. CLARK	1	
5. BOWER,E	4		36. WATHEY,H	1	
7. FURNISS, L	5	1	37. WARD,J.H.	2	
13. MELVILLE, D.	2		38. CLIFFE,A.	1	
15. PAYTON,J	1		39. TWISS,W.	1	
25. BAKER	1		40. BIDDULPH	1	
29. DRINKWATER, T.	2		41. SMITH	1	
30. WATMOUGH,J.H.	2	1	42. DAVY	1	
31. MAYSON,W.	1				

CHAPTER 10

GORTON ASSOCIATION FOOTBALL CLUB
1886-1887

In 1886, Walter Chew was Secretary and his brother William Henry Chew was Treasurer. Walter Chew, William Henry Chew, Lawrence Furniss and William Mayson were on the Club's Management Committee.

On 9th May 1886, Walter Chew inserted a notice in *The Umpire* that the club had available dates for first and second team matches in the coming season.

The Club retained the tenancy of the ground adjoining the Bull's Head Hotel, Reddish Lane, Gorton.

The reported matches during the season were as follows:

9th October 1886

Marple 4 v Gorton 1

6th November 1886

Gorton 7 v Shuttleworth 1

The teams played at Gorton. The home team played a fine game, their passing being much admired. The Gorton forwards and half-backs were always on the ball, the goalkeeper only having to play the ball once. At the call of time, Gorton had scored seven goals, to one for Shuttleworth, the latter scoring their only goal whilst the home full-backs and goalkeeper were attending to an injured player.
Gorton goalscorers: Hodgetts 3 Payton 2 and Chew 2

13th November 1886

Manchester Clifford 0 v Gorton 2

The above teams met today at Old Trafford, and the encounter resulted in a win for Gorton by two goals to nil. The home team pressed the Gorton defence hard in the first half, but owing to the splendid play of the Gorton backs, they were unable to score.
Shortly after half-time, CHEW broke away and after a fine dribble, CHEW scored with a splendid shot. Most of the play now took place in Manchester Clifford's quarters, and WARD scored the second goal for Gorton from a very fast shot.
Gorton goalscorers: Chew and Ward

20th November 1886

Gorton 0 v Stretford 1

4th December 1886

Gorton 1 v Royton 0

The match was played on the Gorton ground. Gorton, after an even game, defeated Royton by 1 goal to nil, although they played with three substitutes. Gorton played with good combination.

11th December 1886

Gorton 2 v Oldham 1

Played at Oldham. The game was confined to fifteen minutes each way and came to an abrupt end owing to Oldham disputing the second goal after it had been allowed by the referee.

On 8th January 1887, Gorton's fixture with Greenheys was cancelled due to bad weather.

15th January 1887
Pendleton Olympic   0   v   Gorton   0

Gorton team: J. Morton; E. Groves and E. Bower; J. Ward W. Mayson and E. Kitchen; W. Chew J. Hodgetts D. Donohue T. Drinkwater and D. McKenzie

    Played at Pendleton before a very few spectators. The ground, owing to severe frost, was very hard and slippery, but considering the conditions, a very good and even game was played. DONOHUE kicked off for Gorton with a very strong wind blowing across the ground. Play was kept in the Gorton half and Pendleton had several corners. Good play from BOWER and HODGETTS enabled Gorton to take the ball to the other end. HODGETTS passed to DRINKWATER but he shot over the bar. After this Pendleton played the better and pressed Gorton but could not score. Ultimately a pleasant game ended without either side having scored.

    In the first round of the Manchester Cup, Gorton were drawn at home against West Gorton Athletic. When the St. Mark's players pulled out of West Gorton to form Gorton, the former Belle Vue Rangers players in the merged club, continued as West Gorton but later changed the name of the club to West Gorton Athletic. The Gorton team was much too strong for the Athletic and had a comfortable win.

22nd January 1887   Manchester & District Challenge Cup   First Round
Gorton   5   v   West Gorton Athletic   1

Gorton: J. Morton; E.Groves and E.Bower; J. Ward, E.Kitchen and W.Mayson; W. Chew J. Hodgetts D. Donohue T. Drinkwater and D. McKenzie
Gorton goalscorers: Hodgetts 2 and D. McKenzie 3

    This tie was played at Reddish Lane, Gorton, on the Gorton A.F.C. ground before 1000 spectators. From the kick-off, Gorton at once attacked, and after a few minutes play, HODGETTS scored for Gorton from a neat pass by McKENZIE. Shortly afterwards, HODGETTS scored again. The Athletic then put on a spurt, and for some time kept up an attack on the Gorton goal, but no score was made. At length, BOWER relieved the pressure, and the ball was straightway taken down the field, and McKENZIE put it through. Even play followed, and at the halfway period, Gorton were leading by three goals to nil.
    On ends being changed, the Athletic were first to attack, but a corner-kick was their only reward, until their forwards, with a combined rush, ran the ball through amidst loud cheering. This proved to be their only score, and shortly afterwards CHEW put in a nice dribble down the right, and passed across to McKENZIE, who scored. The game had been very fast, but about this period it flagged somewhat. McKENZIE again scored for Gorton, and Jervis of the Athletic sent in a fine shot, but it was fisted out by MORTON. The Athletic had hard lines on several occasions, and but for the excellent goalkeeping of MORTON and the fine back play of BOWER and GROVES, would most likely have made the score more equal, whereas the ultimate outcome was a win for Gorton by five goals to one.

29th January 1887
Gorton   0   v   Manchester Clifford   0

    This match was played at Gorton. The second half was more evenly contested than the first. Clifford just missed scoring with the ball striking the upright and going behind. All the Clifford backs played well, as did BOWER and MORTON, the goalkeeper for Gorton. The game ended without either side scoring

5th February 1887
Halliwell Reserve   5   v   Gorton   2

    This match was played on the Halliwell ground at Bolton and Halliwell won by 5 goals to 2.

19th February 1887   Manchester & District Challenge Cup   Second Round
Newton Heath   11   v   Gorton   1

3,000
Gorton team: J. Morton; E.Groves and E.Bower; J. Ward W.Mayson and J. Bridge; J. Hodgetts E.Kitchen W.Chew D.Donohue and T. Drinkwater   Gorton goalscorer: Drinkwater

    Doughty kicked off for the home team, who scored five minutes after the start. The ball was continually in the Gorton half, Gotheredge adding another goal for Newton Heath. A corner kick for the home team proved futile. Watmough then scored a goal and H. Davies followed up with another. Gorton then rushed the ball up the field, but it was immediately returned, and Davies again scored for the Heathens. Some neat passing on behalf of Newton Heath took place, Davies eventually adding another goal for the home team. The score at half-time was Newton Heath 6 goals Gorton nil.

On re-starting, Newton Heath again scored, H. Bates this time putting the ball through. The Gorton goal was continually being assailed, and their goalkeeper was having a warm time of it. Newton Heath next claimed a corner, but nothing came of it. The Gorton men were again at Newton Heath's goal, but they were repulsed, and the ball was quickly returned, with the result that the Heathens obtained another goal, one of the Gorton men doing the needful by turning the ball over his own goal-line. Three more goals were quickly added for Newton Heath, but in the last minute Gorton scored, DRINKWATER putting the ball through. Final score: Newton Heath, 11 goals; Gorton, 1 goal.

26th February 1887

Gorton 2 v Rainow 4

A very fast game at Gorton resulted in a win for Rainow by 4 goals to 2.

26th March 1887 Ashton Charity Cup First Round

Gorton 1 v Gorton Villa 3

Following a protest made by Walter Chew the tie was awarded to Gorton on Appeal.

9th April 1887

Gorton 3 v Dukinfield 2

The match was played at Gorton. At the beginning play was very even, until the Gorton right, with the wind in their favour, broke away and HODGETTS scored. HODGETTS, playing grandly, scored again. Gorton then notched another goal, thus making the game 3 goals to nil. Dukinfield, after this reverse, gave the home backs plenty to do, which they did in grand style, until a pass from the left resulted in the first goal for the visitors from Ogden. Half-time arrived with Gorton leading by three goals to one.

Soon after re-starting Owen, at full-back for Dukinfield, stopped a splendid rush by the Gorton forwards. Soon afterwards, Harrison ran down the field and scored with a fast shot. That made the game three goals to two in Gorton's favour. After the kick-off the Dukinfield defence was again called upon, Owen clearing his lines in fine style. Nothing further was scored up to the call of time. Gorton goal scorer: Hodgetts 2, scorer of third goal not known.

Denton and Gorton met on 21st May on the Hurst ground at Ashton-under-Lyne to decide their semi-final tie in the Ashton and District Charity Cup competition. Both teams had been preparing for the event, and the encounter attracted keen interest. Hurst took on West Gorton Athletic on the Denton Ground in the other semi-final tie.

21st May 1887 Ashton& District Charity Cup Semi Final
Denton 7 v Gorton 0

Venue: Hurst, Ashton-under-Lyne. Owing to the unsettled weather, the "gate" was not as large as was expected, but there was plenty of excitement nevertheless. The Denton team came out first, and were followed by the Gorton eleven, who were a much lighter lot. Gorton won the toss, and naturally chose the wind and the incline. At four o'clock, Kerfoot started the ball for Denton. A corner soon fell to Denton, which Ingham placed nicely, but the Gorton defence conceded a second corner, which their backs got away to safety. Play was even for the next twenty minutes, at the end of which, Kerfoot, taking advantage of poor kicks by three of the Gorton backs, ran the first goal through for Denton. This roused the Gorton men, whose left wing sent in a stinging shot, but the Denton 'keeper was equal to the occasion. A free kick to Gorton was sent narrowly the wrong side of the post. Denton carried the ball up-field, forcing a corner from MORTON in the Gorton goal. Although well placed, the corner kick did not bear fruit. From a throw-in close up in the Denton half the ball was nearly headed through by two Gorton men, the Denton goalkeeper just managing to fist out in time to prevent the equaliser. Another raid was then made on the Gorton goal and Denton scored a second goal. The Gorton men claimed that the ball had been brought back from out of play, but the referee set aside the claim. Two minutes later Denton increased their score, and when the whistle blew for half-time the match stood at three goals to nil in Denton's favour.

When ends were changed, it was expected that Denton, with the wind and incline in their favour, would pile on a lot of goals, but this proved not to be the case, for although Denton pressed and had the best of play, the Gorton defence was so good that twenty minutes were consumed before a fourth goal was added. Gorton then paid another visit to the Denton end of the field, but Booth caught the ball from a hot shot and threw it out, and the Denton men pouncing on the ball and running it down the field smartly, were able to notch their fifth goal. A few minutes later, Denton again put the ball between the uprights but Gorton claimed that it had again been brought from out of play; and as their appeal to the referee was once more decided against them, they refused to continue the game. Kerfoot thereupon ran the ball through the Gorton goal from the re-start for a seventh time, without opposition, and as the Gorton players had now retired from the field, the referee - Mr Price of Newton Heath - blew his whistle, and play ceased. The Gorton men had played up pluckily against their weightier opponents, and passed the ball fairly well, but the game was not a very scientific one.

Gorton had played fifteen recorded matches during the season and had won seven, drawn two and lost six. The club had also got through to the second round of the Manchester Senior Cup.

Gorton had played for three seasons and their results had improved but they were still only capable of competing with local teams. Better players such as Lawrence Furniss, Kenneth McKenzie and J. Hodgetts had been attracted to the club but the players remained amateurs paying membership subscriptions.

The players who had made the most recorded appearances for Gorton were:

RECORDED APPEARANCES 1884-87	
Walter Chew	14
Edward Bower	14
Edward Kitchen	12
Edward Groves	12
Lawrence Furniss	10
Frederick Hopkinson	8

The St. Mark's players continued to play a very important part in running the club and playing for the first team. In the appearance table five of the six players who had made the most recorded appearances were St. Mark's players.

The leading goalscorers were:

GOALSCORERS	
J. Hodgetts	7
W. Chew	4
D. McKenzie	3

In June 1887, Kenneth McKenzie, who was employed at Bennett's Timber Yard, Hyde Road, West Gorton suggested to the Gorton Committee that some derelict land adjoining the railway arches near Hyde Road would make a good playing pitch for the club.

The Committee agreed.

On 18th January 1887, the secretary, Walter Chew, sent a letter to the agent of the Great Central Railway in the following terms:

Gorton Association F. C.
Sir,
The Committee of the above club are anxious to make arrangements with you to rent the ground situate between Galloway's Works and Bennett's Yard, Ardwick, which I hear belongs to your company. If you decide to let the ground for the above purposes, kindly let me know the lowest terms at your earliest, and I shall have pleasure in placing the same before my committee.
Yours, etc

Negotiations were successful.

As the club was now moving to Ardwick, although still only a short distance from St. Mark's Church and the waste land where the first matches were played, the name of the club was changed from Gorton Association Football Club to Ardwick Association Football Club.

On 17th August 1887, Lawrence Furniss, William H. Chew, William Mayson and Walter Chew as the Managing Committee of Ardwick A.F.C. entered into a Tenancy Agreement with Manchester, Sheffield and Lincolnshire Railway Company acting by their agent who let the land to the Club from 1st September, 1887 to 1st May, 1888 at a rent of £10.

The ground was to become Hyde Road, Ardwick and the home of Ardwick A.F.C. and later Manchester City A.F.C. from 1887 until 1923 when Maine Road was constructed.

SUMMARY
GORTON A.F.C. 1886-87

		OPPONENT	RES	1	2	3	4	5	6
1886				7	8	9	10	11	
9-Oct	A	Marple	L 1-4						
6-Nov	H	Shuttleworth	W 7-1						J.Payton 2
				W.Chew 2	J.Hodgetts 3				
13-Nov	A	Manchester	W 2-0				J.H.Ward 1		
		Clifford		W.Chew 1					
20-Nov	H	Stretford	L 0-1						
4-Dec	H	Royton	W 1-0						
11-Dec	A	Oldham	W 2-1						
15-Jan	A	Pendleton	D 0-0	J.Morton	E.Groves	E.Bower	J.H.Ward	W.Mayson	E.Kitchen
1887		Olympic		W.Chew	J.Hodgetts	D.Donohue	T.Drinkwater	D.McKenzie	
22-Jan	H	West Gorton	W 5-1	J.Morton	E.Groves	E.Bower	J.H.Ward	E.Kitchen	W.Mayson
MC 1		Athletic		W.Chew	J.Hodgetts 2	D.Donohue	T.Drinkwater	D.McKenzie 3	
29-Jan	H	Manchester	D 0-0	J.Morton		E.Bower			
		Clifford							
5-Feb	A	Halliwell Res	L 2-5						
19-Feb	A	Newton	L 1-11	J.Morton	E.Groves	E.Bower	J.H.Ward	W.Mayson	J.Bridge
MC 2		Heath	3000	J.Hodgetts	E.Kitchen	W.Chew	D.Donohue	Drinkwater 1	
26-Feb	H	Rainow	L 2-4						
26-Mar	H	Gorton Villa	WON	Gorton	awarded tie	on appeal			
AC1									
9-Apr	H	Dukinfield	W 3-2						
					J.Hodgetts 2				1 goal *
21-May	A	Denton	L 0-7	J.Morton					
AC SF		S.F.at Hurst							

Scorer(s) not known: *

RECORDED MATCHES 1886-1887

	P	W	D	L	F	A
Home	8	5	1	2	18	9
Away	7	2	1	4	8	28
Total	15	7	2	6	26	37

RECORDED APPEARANCES 1886-1887

PLAYER	APPS.	GOALS	PLAYER	APPS.	GOALS
1. CHEW,W	5	3	37. WARD, J.H.	4	1
2. KITCHEN,E	3		43. HODGETTS, J.	5	7
4. GROVES,E	3		44. MORTON, J.	5	
5. BOWER,E	4		45. DONOHUE, D.	3	
15. PAYTON,J	1	2	46. BRIDGE, J.	1	
29. DRINKWATER, T.	3	1	47. McKENZIE, D.	2	3
31. MAYSON, W.	3				

GORTON A.F.C. RECORDED APPEARANCES 1884-1887					
	1884-1885	1885-1886	1886-1887	1884-1887	1884-1887
	APPS.	APPS.	APPS.	APPS.	GOALS
1. CHEW,W	5	4	5	14	4
2. KITCHEN,E	6	3	3	12	
3. HOPKINSON,F	6	2		8	
4. GROVES,E	5	4	3	12	1
5. BOWER,E	6	4	4	14	
6. HOPKINSON,R	1			1	
7. FURNISS, L	5	5		10	1
8. McKENZIE, K.	6			6	
9. BOOTH, J	4			4	
10. KIRK, T.	3			3	
11. BAIN, J.	2			2	
12. OWEN	2			2	
13. MELVILLE, D.	2	2		4	
14. PRENTY	1			1	
15. PAYTON,J	1	1	1	3	2
16. AVERY	1			1	
17. TURNER	1			1	
18. MELLOR, J.	1			1	
19. JENKINS	1			1	
20. STANDRING, D.	1			1	
21. ASPINALL, J.E.	1			1	
22. BOWDEN	1			1	
23. ACKROYD	1			1	
24. EARNSHAW	1			1	
25. BAKER	1	1		2	
26. FLETCHER	1			1	
27. BROOKS	1			1	
28. MEARNS	1			1	
29. DRINKWATER, T.		2	3	5	1
30. WATMOUGH,J.H.		2		2	1
31. MAYSON,W.		1	3	4	
32. GARDNER		1		1	
33. ANDERSON		1		1	
34. BOWKER		1		1	
35. CLARK		1		1	
36. WATHEY,H		1		1	
37. WARD, J.H.		2	4	6	1
38. CLIFFE,A.		1		1	
39. TWISS,W.		1		1	
40. BIDDULPH		1		1	
41. SMITH		1		1	
42. DAVY		1		1	
43. HODGETTS, J			5	5	7
44. MORTON,J			5	5	
45. DONOHUE,D			3	3	
46. BRIDGE,J			1	1	
47. McKENZIE, D			2	2	3

The First Seven Seasons from 1880-1887

There were three separate phases to the club's early development.

The first phase covered the first three seasons from 1880 to 1883. The club was formed as St. Mark's Football Club and continued as the football club of St. Mark's Church during this period. In the first season and the early part of the second season, the club was called St. Mark's (West Gorton) in reports prepared by the club's secretary, but in some reports written by the opponents' secretary the club was referred to as St. Mark's (Longsight). For most of the second season and during the third season, the club was called West Gorton (St. Mark's) but the club remained the football team of St. Mark's Church.

The second phase lasted for just one season 1883-1884, when West Gorton (St. Mark's) merged with Belle Vue Rangers to form West Gorton. West Gorton ran two teams and only three of the St. Mark's players played in the first team but some will have played for the second team. When the merger did not work out, the former St. Mark's players were still playing for West Gorton in early October 1884 at the beginning of the 1884-1885 Season. However, when Gorton was formed towards the end of October 1884 (the delay was caused because of the difficulty in finding a ground), the St. Mark's players and others immediately joined Gorton.

The third phase was the three seasons as Gorton from 1884 to 1887. From the outset Gorton was well supported and had a good number of members which enabled the club to run two teams. Gorton continued as an amateur club with the players being members of the club. Gorton was well organised and began to attract better players. However, it was only in August 1887, when it was possible to obtain a tenancy of the land which was to become the Hyde Road Ground in Ardwick that the first major step to becoming a leading club was taken and resulted in the change of name from Gorton to Ardwick.

The players who played for the club's first team during the three phases were Walter Chew, Edward Bower and Edward Groves.

Edward Kitchen, Frederick Hopkinson and Richard Hopkinson played for the first team during the first and third phases.

The recorded appearances of the six players are as follows:

RECORDED APPEARANCES 1880-1887				
PLAYER	1880-1883	1883-1884	1884-1887	TOTAL
Walter Chew	18	2	14	34
Edward Groves	18	4	14	36
Edward Bower	4	4	14	22
Edward Kitchen	21		12	33
Frederick Hopkinson	12		8	20
Richard Hopkinson	12		1	13

CHAPTER 11

ARDWICK ASSOCIATION FOOTBALL CLUB
1887-1888

Following the successful negotiations for a tenancy of the new ground Gorton Association Football Club changed its name to Ardwick Association Football Club. Ardwick entered into an agreement for the ground in the following terms:

Agreement made this 17th day of August 1887 between the Manchester, Sheffield and Lincolnshire Railway Company (" the Company") by Edwin Barker of Manchester, their Estate Agent of the one part and the Ardwick Association Football Club (the Tenants") by Lawrence W.Furniss,127 Clowes Street, West Gorton; William H. Chew, 62 Avon Street, Chorlton-on-Medlock; William Mayson, 101 Earl Street, Longsight, and Walter Chew, 12 Elizabeth Street, West Gorton, in the County of Lancaster as Managing Committee ,of the other part.

Whereas the Tenants have applied to the Company for permission to play football upon the land between the London and North Western Railway and Messrs.Galloway's Works at Ardwick and the Company have consented to grant such permission for the season commencing on 1st September, 1887, and terminating on the first day of May 1888.Now therefore it is hereby agreed between the parties as follows:

1. *The rent to be at and after the rate of Ten Pounds for the said period payable by two instalments of Five Pounds on the first day of September and the first day of December, 1887.*

2. *The Tenants hereby indemnify and hold harmless the Company from all accidents, losses, costs and damages caused by or in anywise owing to or resulting from the use of the said land*

3. *The Company notwithstanding anything contained in these presents may at any period on giving the Tenants seven days notice determine this tenancy and enter and repossess the said land or any part thereof which they may require and any such notice may be delivered or sent by post to the last known place of abode of any of the members of the Managing Committee or left upon the said land or any part thereof.*

In Witness whereof the parties hereto have hereunder set their hands the day and year first written above

Signed by Edwin Barker in the presence of John Barker

Signed by Lawrence W. Furniss, William Henry Chew, William Mayson, and Walter Chew in the presence of Donald More McKenzie

It was a very brave and remarkable step taken by the four members of the Managing Committee, for they only had a few pounds at their disposal and they relied in many instances upon their own confidence gained as players of the game.

The move to the new ground, which was later to be called "Hyde Road", laid the foundations of a club which was to grow to an importance far beyond their wildest dreams.

The greatest asset of the club at this time was enthusiasm.

The Agreement for the new ground had only been completed a short time before the new season was to begin and a considerable amount of work had to be carried out.

The energetic Secretary, Walter Chew, enlisted the aid of local tradesmen and the managers and owners of adjacent works to prepare the ground. Chesters Brewery paid for the ground to be turfed.

Walter Chew sent out a notice inviting members of the public to a meeting which was held on 30th August 1887 at the Hyde Road Hotel to discuss the prospects of the Club. Stephen Chesters Thompson, who was a member of the local Chester's Brewery family, was invited to become President. The Hyde Road Hotel, which was a Chesters' public house, became the headquarters of Ardwick and provided facilities for meetings as well as changing facilities for the players.

Hyde Road Hotel
The Officers for the first season of Ardwick were:
President
S. Chesters Thompson JP
Vice Presidents
A. Galloway; E. Tatton; E. Melia; T. Horner; R. Fortune
Match Secretary
W. Chew, 12 Elizabeth Street, Gorton
Financial Secretary
J.H. Lea, 61 Lime Street, Chorlton-on-Medlock
Committee
T .Wood; W.H. Chew; L.W. Furniss; B.G. Clarke; W. Johnson; R. Eccles;
W. Broad; G. France; J.H. Watmough; G. Meredith; H. Robinson and T. Hanks

Four of the members of the committee had previously played for the club: Walter Chew, William Henry Chew, Lawrence Furniss and J.H. Watmough.

Ardwick continued as an amateur club with the players being members and paying membership subscriptions.

Kenneth McKenzie was appointed captain of the first team and J. Hickson captain of the second team. However, within a few weeks, W. Watmough and J. Callagan were appointed first and second team captains. There were three former St. Mark's members playing for Ardwick: Walter Chew (who played in the first match against Macclesfield Baptists), Edward Bower and Edward Groves. Many of the players who played in the previous season for Gorton continued with Ardwick and several new players joined the club. The club had sufficient members to run three teams.

The Players

The following players are known to have played for Ardwick during the 1887-88 Season:

ARDWICK A.F.C. PLAYERS 1887-88	
Goalkeepers:	
J. Morton	(formerly Gorton)
D. Donohue	(formerly West Gorton and Gorton)
Pease	
Full-backs:	
Edward Bower	(formerly St. Mark's, West Gorton and Gorton)
Edward Groves	(formerly St. Mark's, West Gorton and Gorton)
Kenneth McKenzie	(formerly Gorton)
J.H. Ward	(formerly Gorton)
Hartley	
Peck	
Half-backs:	
William Mayson	(formerly Gorton)
W. Watmough	
J. Manning	
J. Nelson	
Matley	
Forwards:	
W. Chew	(formerly St. Mark's, West Gorton and Gorton)
J. Hodgetts	(formerly Gorton)
T. Drinkwater	(formerly Gorton)
Donald McKenzie	(formerly Gorton)
M. Fergus	
J. Parker	
J. Currie	
J. Callagan	
J. Hennefer	
J. Pickup	
Davies	
Wrathall	
Jarvis	

The Managing Committee went to great expense to advertise the first game which was due to be played at Hyde Road against Salford on 10th September 1887. A band was engaged to play during the game. About 500 spectators came to watch the match, but unfortunately Salford failed to turn up.

The first actual game to be played at Hyde Road took place the following Saturday, 17th September 1887.

17th September 1887   Ardwick 2 v Hooley Hill 4
Hyde Road

The teams contested an exciting game in delightful weather before a good number of spectators. The game resulted in a victory for Hooley Hill by 4 goals to 2.

1st October 1887   Marple 4 v Ardwick 1
Marple

22nd October 1887   Earlstown Wanderers 0 v Ardwick 0
Newton Common Earlstown
Ardwick team: D. Donohue; E. Groves and E. Bower; W. Watmough ©, J. Manning and J. Nelson; M. Fergus J. Hodgetts J. Parker J. Currie and D. Mackenzie

The afternoon was fine but the attendance of spectators was very small. The game from start to finish was fairly even, although at one stage one of the Wanderers forwards would have scored but DONOHUE defended his goal well. The result was a draw Earlstown Wanderers 0 Ardwick 0.

5th November 1887   Eccles 2 v Ardwick 3
Eccles

Ardwick were badly handicapped by their goalkeeper not turning up. Eccles kicked off and in less than five minutes their left wing drew first blood. Ardwick now had a look in and led by DRINKWATER, they made several assaults on the Eccles goal, DRINKWATER equalising. The Ardwick forwards played splendidly especially FERGUS, DRINKWATER and HODGETTS, and these three caused Eccles no little trouble. At half-time the score stood at Ardwick three goals Eccles one.

On re-starting Eccles still continued to press, and on several occasions had very hard lines. The above-mentioned trio did splendid work not to mention WATMOUGH and MANNING at half-back and a most stubborn half was witnessed, neither side seemed to have an advantage. This was kept up until almost the close of time, when Eccles scored. Ardwick won a pleasantly contested game by 3 goals to 2.

12th November 1887   Edenfield 2 v Ardwick 4
Edenfield

This match was played before a small number of spectators. Ardwick played with two substitutes. Soon after the kick off HODGETTS ran up and scored a goal. Then the Edenfield centre scored right in front of the Ardwick goalkeeper from a free kick. The goal was objected to but without avail. Ardwick showed very little cohesion in the first half and DRINKWATER (left wing) and HODGETTS (right wing) had all the work to do. HARTLEY at full back for Ardwick stopped several Edenfield sorties. At half-time the score was Edenfield one goal Ardwick one goal.

On the change of ends Ardwick had matters their own way. DRINKWATER on one occasion obtained the ball in the Ardwick goal area and running down to the Edenfield end scored amidst applause. HODGETTS and WRATHALL next had a look in and they both scored. Ardwick still kept the upper hand and finally won by 4 goals to 2.

19th November 1887   Hooley Hill 3 v Ardwick 0
Hooley Hill

26th November 1887   Edenfield 1 v Ardwick 0
Edenfield

3rd December 1887   Ardwick 5 v Lees 1
Hyde Road
Ardwick team: Morton; K. McKenzie and Ward; Manning Marley and Watmough ©; Davies 2 Currie
Substitute 3 Hodgetts and Chew.

Ardwick led off and about a minute from the start DAVIES scored. A long high shot from the right wing of Lees was cleared by Ardwick. The Ardwick centre scored next and then from a scrimmage in the Ardwick goal, Lees scored with an own goal from an Ardwick player. At half-time Ardwick led by two goals to one.

In the second half, Ardwick were always pressing and DAVIES a young reserve player scored twice, one being disallowed on the plea of "off-side". HODGETTS had hard lines in not scoring on two occasions. The Ardwick forwards next broke away and a long shot from DAVIES was helped on by the centre and scored. A good dribble from the Ardwick forwards registered another goal and Ardwick won by 5 goals to 1.

10th December 1887   Ardwick 8 v Lees Street Olympic 0
Hyde Road

17th December 1887   Ardwick 1 v Buxton 1
Hyde Road

The match was played before a fair muster of spectators. Buxton turned up with a good team, but Ardwick were short of K. McKENZIE and DRINKWATER. Ardwick led off with a combined dribble and obtained a corner immediately but it proved fruitless. Give-and-take play followed. Buxton came away with a good dribble but were well stopped by BOWER at full-back who played a splendid game all through. From a good kick the Ardwick forwards took possession and HODGETTS shot. The Buxton goalkeeper fisted out and HODGETTS headed through. This roused Buxton but they had made no impression at half-time when Ardwick led by one goal to nil.

After the change of ends Ardwick by combination and good back play asserted their superiority and were often dangerous. Buxton broke away several times and on one occasion a long high shot from their centre half was only partly fisted out by the Ardwick goalkeeper and from the scrimmage which resulted, Buxton forced the ball through. Shortly before the Buxton goal, one of the Buxton forwards collided with the Ardwick goalkeeper and had his shoulder blade broken. Buxton with ten men played a defensive game and kept Ardwick at bay until HODGETTS scored. He was ruled off side and the game ended in a draw, Ardwick 1 goal Buxton 1.

21st January 1888   Manchester & District Challenge Cup   First Round
Hurst

Lower Hurst 3 v Ardwick 2

Lower Hurst won the toss and decided to play downhill in the first half. Ardwick kicked off and went with a dash securing a corner, which was not improved upon. From the goalkick, the home forwards ran the ball down but the visiting backs relieved. Some give-and-take play now ensued, neither side seeming to have the advantage, the defence of both teams being good. After about ten minutes play Lower Hurst managed to notch their first goal, much to the chagrin of the Ardwick spectators who seemed to be tearing their throats with shouts of "Play up, Ardwick". Resuming, Ardwick seemed to be getting alive to the situation and before half-time managed to secure a goal. The teams crossed over with the score being one goal each.

The second half of the game was played in difficult circumstances due to the wretched state of the ground, owing to the great amount of rain that had fallen but, despite all this, both teams worked energetically, each trying to secure a winning goal. Lower Hurst added two further goals. This seemed to rouse the "Ardwickians" to desperation. They put in all they knew and in a very few minutes they secured another goal which caused great enthusiasm amongst the Ardwick followers who cheered for their team very lustily. Excitement prevailed very much at this stage amongst the spectators, each side shouting for their respective team. Ardwick had slightly the advantage with playing downhill, but the Lower Hurst team got strictly on the defensive and a very fast exciting game was brought to a close in favour of Lower Hurst by 3 goals to 2.

28th January 1888   Ardwick 0 v Astley Bank 2
Hyde Road

4th February 1888   Ardwick 4 v Marple 3
Hyde Road

11th February 1888   Ardwick 5 v Bolton Central 0
Hyde Road

11th February 1888   Openshaw 2 v Ardwick A 0

18th February 1888   Ashton Charity Cup   Second Round
Hyde Road

Ardwick 8 v Hyde 1

Ardwick team: Morton; K.McKenzie and Bower; Watmough © Manning and Mayson; Hodgetts 1 Callagan 2 Parker 2 Drinkwater 1 and D. McKenzie 2

Hyde kicked off against the wind. Ardwick pressed all through the first half. The Ardwick forwards worked with clock-like regularity, the ball passing evenly from wing to wing and they far outshone their opponents. DRINKWATER scored the first goal, followed by a goal from D.

MACKENZIE both from the left wing. No less than thirteen corners fell to Ardwick in the first half and all were admirably placed by WATMOUGH (right) and MAYSON (left). From several of WATMOUGH'S corners MAYSON headed into goal splendidly but failed to score. Soon afterwards PARKER, from a good pass by HODGETTS, scored Ardwick's third goal. At half-time the score was Ardwick three goals Hyde nil.

Playing with the wind and the incline, it was thought that Hyde would hold the upper hand in the second half, but it was not so. Combined dribbles by Ardwick seemed to be the order of the day and through PARKER, HODGETTS and CALLAGAN three more goals were quickly scored. Then Hyde had a look in and from a scrimmage in goal Hyde scored amidst general applause. From the kick off Ardwick dribbled nicely up and again CALLAGAN scored. Then a good run by DRINKWATER and D.MACKENZIE ended in the latter scoring, making the eighth goal for Ardwick. Shortly after time was called and Ardwick won by 8 goals to 1.

The tie was ordered to be replayed at Hyde on account of the sloppy character of the ground at Ardwick.

25th February 1888   Ashton Charity Cup   Second Round Replay
Hyde

Hyde 1 v Ardwick 3

Ardwick team: Bower; K.McKenzie and Ward; Watmough © Manning and Mayson; Hodgetts 1 Callagan 1 Currie Drinkwater and D. McKenzie 1

Hyde chose their Cup Team and Ardwick played their usual First Team. Hyde played with the wind for the first half and had the best of the game. The Ardwick defence was a treat to witness. The Hyde rights Preston and Taylor were often dangerous but BOWER and K. MACKENZIE both played a splendid game. Ten minutes from the start, BOWER saved from Preston and WARD conceded a corner to save another from Barber. The corner was cleared and HODGETTS and CALLAGAN broke loose. They passed prettily together up to the half flag when HODGETTS kicked across to DRINKWATER who centred to CURRIE. CURRIE passed to CALLAGAN who headed to HODGETTS. This enabled HODGETTS to send in a stinger but J. Hall headed well out. Preston then obtained possession passing to Barber and he and Lee ran it down and Lee scored, BOWERS slipping and missing the ball. The score at half-time was Hyde one goal Ardwick nil.

Playing down hill Ardwick completely overpowered their opponents who kicked out deliberately time after time to save their side. Fifteen minutes after half-time CALLAGAN sent in a good high shot from the Ardwick right and scored. From the centre kick Hyde kept the ball in mid-field for a short time but WARD returned it and HODGETTS obtaining possession dribbled down but the Hyde goalkeeper saved at the expense of a corner. This was nicely placed by WATMOUGH and HODGETTS scored. Ardwick completely baffled their opponents and eventually, D. MACKENZIE scored another goal from the left. Ardwick won by 3 goals to 1.

10th March 1888   Ashton Charity Cup   Semi –Final
Hurst

Lower Hurst 3 v Ardwick 1

Owing to the late arrival of Ardwick the ball was not set in motion until 3:40pm. Ardwick kicked off and after some loose play Lower Hurst put the ball through, but it was disallowed on account of off-side. Lower Hurst were not to be denied and shortly afterwards scored their first goal. Ardwick kicked off, CALLAGAN being determined to score caused great laughter through running the ball down the field after the whistle had blown. After some neat play Ardwick scored the equaliser.

At half-time the score was one goal each. After the interval, Lower Hurst started the ball and soon scored their second goal. Ardwick strived hard to avert defeat and their full-backs played very well. However, Lower Hurst scored another goal thus winning a very fast game by 3 goals to 1.

On 10th March 1888, it was reported that during the season the Ardwick A team had only lost three matches, whilst the B team had not so far suffered a reverse.

17th March 1888   Ardwick 6 v Manchester South End 2
Hyde Road

Ardwick were minus BOWER, HODGETTS and SIMISTER but were still too strong for their opponents who only sent in a couple of shots yet through bad management of the Ardwick goalkeeper, PEASE, both scored. HENNEFER centre for the home team played a splendid game. Ardwick won by 6 goals to 2.

On the same day, 17th March 1888, an unusual football match took place, when the Ardwick A team played Jaffe's Employees, which was a team chosen by William Henry Chew, who was a member of the Ardwick Committee. The Jaffe's team was described as being overweight and unfit, with one of their players, Charlie, being described as their greatest offender in this respect. The Jaffe's team used their weight in the first half but made no impression. At half-time Ardwick were leading by one goal to nil.

In the second half the Jaffe's players were described as being "winded" and the Ardwick players ran rings around them scoring six goals but only three were allowed by the referee. Ardwick A won by 4 goals to nil.

31st March 1888   Buxton 7 v Ardwick 0
Silverland, Buxton

Buxton scored three goals in the first half and four goals in the second half.
The Ardwick men played with considerable pluck but their staying powers were not as good as the Derbyshire lads. Buxton were in good form and played a combined game. The crossing by the Ardwick players was somewhat defective. Buxton won by 7 goals to 0.

7th April 1888   Eccles 3 v Ardwick 0
Eccles

21st April 1888   Ardwick 4 v Bolton Borough 3
Hyde Road

The match was played before a large muster of spectators, as Bolton came as a club of good standing. Ardwick with the wind scored soon after the start with a splendid header by JARVIS from a pass by HENNEFER. Soon afterwards Ardwick scored again with a long shot by HENNEFER. From the kick off Bolton got possession and following some good dribbling Bolton scored. After give-and-take play in the centre, HODGETTS passed to CALLAGAN, who passed to HENNEFER, then back to HODGETTS, who running round the backs scored with a scorcher. Bolton obtained possession and following a shot which MORTON caught, the goalkeeper was bundled into the goal despite a gallant effort to save. Just before half-time, HODGETTS scored again making the score Ardwick four goals Bolton two.

In the second half Bolton had the wind in their favour and pressed. Soon after the start MORTON conceded a corner. This was placed under the bar. MORTON conceded another corner which was cleared by WATMOUGH at half-back, who played a champion game. PECK and PICKUP stopped dangerous attacks. Then the Ardwick forwards broke into a good dribble, which ought to have resulted in a goal, but fate ruled otherwise and the final shot from HODGETTS went behind. Shortly before time, Bolton scored through a misunderstanding between the Ardwick backs. The fastest and most pleasant of games played at Ardwick resulted in a win for Ardwick by 4 goals to 3.

28th April 1888   Fairfield 0 v Ardwick 0
Fairfield

Gamben started the ball for the home team against a strong wind. The game at once became very fast. Half-time arrived with a clean score sheet.
HENEFFER re-started and the Fairfield forwards showing some nice passing pressed severely but were weak in front of goal. The Fairfield half backs were almost impassable as they robbed DRINKWATER HENEFFER and HODGETTS repeatedly. Cartledge especially distinguished himself for Fairfield. Fairfield continued to have the best of the game but their forwards were unable to get past MORTON. The game ended in a draw Fairfield 0 Ardwick 0.

5th May 1888   Ardwick 6 v Oughtrington Park 0
Hyde Road

Ardwick had been well supported during the season and the Club's three teams played very well. The first team had played thirty four matches but only twenty three were reported. The club had won eleven; drawn three and lost nine of the reported matches. This was an improvement on the previous year.

Three St. Mark's players Walter Chew, Edward Bower and Edward Groves are shown in the reports as having played in the Ardwick first team. In the following season, only Edward Bower continued to play in the first team.

On the financial side, Gorton had made small profits in 1884-85 and 1885-86 and a small loss in 1886-87 as set out below:-

1884/85:	£1 8s 8d
1885/86:	£1 16s 1d
1886/87:	(2s 3d)

In Ardwick's first season, the club's income had increased to £80 6s. However, expenditure had increased to £93 11s 1d, resulting in a loss of £13 5s 1d. The largest item of expenditure was £24 4s for work on the ground. Overall the result was reasonable in view of the initial cost of developing an open piece of land into a football ground.

Ardwick's first Balance Sheet:

BALANCE SHEET

Balance Sheet for Season 1887-1888			
INCOME	£	s	d
Balance from Gorton A.F.C.	3	2	6
S. Chesters Thompson	4	4	0
Members' Subscriptions	11	19	6
Gate Money	47	9	9
Advertisements		8	0
Receipts-Two Smoking Concerts & Cup-ties	4	12	9
Profit from Draw	8	9	6
Balance	13	5	1
	£93	11	1
EXPENDITURE			
Rent on Ground	10	0	0
Subscriptions to MDFA & ACCC		15	6
Work on Ground	24	4	0
Team's Travelling Expenses	13	6	1
Printing, postages etc.	18	3	0
Postages, Telegrams	2	0	9
Football requisites	11	10	5
Half Gate to Visiting Teams	5	2	10
Protest fee v Lower Hurst	1	0	0
Referee's expenses (cup-ties)	1	1	0
Medical fee		7	6
Expenses Two Smoking Concerts	1	9	0
Police	2	8	8
Sundry expenses	1	2	4
	£93	11	1

The move to the Hyde Road ground was the first really significant step taken by the club. The membership of the club had grown and so had the support. Whilst the first team and also the two reserve teams had played well, efforts were being made to attract better players.

There follows a summary of the season with details, where known, of reported matches, attendances, appearances and goalscorers. Ardwick had played friendly matches and had entered the Manchester and District Senior Cup (MC) and the Ashton Charity Cup (AC)

SUMMARY
ARDWICK A.F.C. 1887-88

DATE		OPPONENT	RES	1	2	3	4	5	6
1887				7	8	9	10	11	
17-Sep	H	Hooley Hill	L 2-4						
01-Oct	A	Marple	L 1-4						
22-Oct	A	Earlstown Wanderers	D 0-0	D.Donohue M.Fergus	E.Groves J.Hodgetts	E.Bower J.Parker	W.Watmough© J.Currie	J.Manning D.McKenzie	J.Nelson
05-Nov	A	Eccles	W 3-2	M.Fergus	J.Hodgetts		W.Watmough© T.Drinkwater1	Manning	2 goals *
12-Nov	A	Edenfield	W 4-2		Hartley J.Hodgetts2	Wrathall 1	T.Drinkwater1		
19-Nov	A	Hooley Hill	L 0-3						
26-Nov	A	Edenfield	L 0-1						
03-Dec	H	Lees	W 5-1	J.Morton Davies 2	K.McKenzie J.Currie	J.Ward Substitute3	J.Manning J.Hodgetts	Matley W.Chew	W.Watmough©
10-Dec	H	Lees Street Olympic	W 8-0						
17-Dec	H	Buxton	D 1-1			E.Bower	J.Hodgetts 1		
1888									
21-Jan MC 1	A	Lower Hurst	L 2-3						
28-Jan	H	Astley Bank	L 0-2						
04-Feb	H	Marple	W 4-3						
11-Feb	H	Bolton Central	W 5-0						
18-Feb AC 2	H	Hyde	W 8-1	J.Morton J.Hodgetts1	K.McKenzie J.Callagan2	E.Bower J.Parker 2	W.Watmough© T.Drinkwater1	J.Manning D.McKenzie2	W.Mayson
25-Feb AC 2®	A	Hyde	W 3-1	E.Bower J.Hodgetts1	K.McKenzie J.Callagan1	JWard J.Currie	W.Watmough© T.Drinkwater	J.Manning D.McKenzie1	W.Mayson
10-Mar AC SF	A	Lower Hurst	L 1-3		J.Callagan				
17-Mar	H	M/c. South End	W 6-2	Pease		J.Hennefer			
31-Mar	A	Buxton	L 0-7						
07-Apr	A	Eccles	L 0-3						
21-Apr	H	Bolton Borough	W 4-3	J.Morton J.Hodgetts2	J.Callagan	Peck Hennefer 1	W.Watmough© J.Pickup	Jarvis 1	
28-Apr	A	Fairfield	D 0-0	J.Morton J.Hodgetts		J.Hennefer	T.Drinkwater		
05-May	H	Oughtrington Park	W 6-0						

Captain: ©   Scorer(s) not known: *

RECORDED MATCHES 1887-1888						
	P	W	D	L	F	A
Home	11	8	1	2	49	17
Away	12	3	2	7	14	29
Total	23	11	3	9	63	46
ACTUAL RESULTS						
First XI	34	14	7	13	91	80
A Team	23	12	8	3	57	49
B Team	14	10	0	4	53	14

The actual results are taken from Fred Johnson's book on "The History of Manchester City"

Twenty three of the thirty four first team matches were reported and the full Ardwick line-up was given in only four matches. The recorded appearances are taken from those four matches.

RECORDED APPEARANCES 1887-88		
PLAYER	APPS.	GOALS
1. MORTON,J	2	
2. DONOHUE,D	1	
3. BOWER,E	3	
4. GROVES,E	1	
5. McKENZIE,K	3	
6. WARD, J.H.	2	
7. MAYSON,W	2	
8. WATMOUGH,W	4	
9. MANNING,J	4	
10. NELSON,J	1	
11. MATLEY	1	
12. CHEW,W	1	
13. HODGETTS,J	4	2
14. DRINKWATER,T	2	1
15. McKENZIE, D	3	3
16. FERGUS, M	1	
17. PARKER, J	2	2
18. CURRIE, J	3	
19. CALLAGAN,J	2	3
20. DAVIES	1	2
21. SUBSTITUTE	1	3

CHAPTER 12

ARDWICK ASSOCIATION FOOTBALL CLUB
1888-1889

The Officers for the second season of Ardwick were:

President
S. Chesters Thompson, JP
Vice Presidents
A. Galloway; E. Tatton; E. Melia; T. Horner; R. Fortune
Match Secretary
W. Chew, 12 Elizabeth Street, Gorton
Financial Secretary
J.H. Lea, 61 Lime Street, Chorlton-on-Medlock
Committee
T. Wood; W.H. Chew; L.W. Furniss; B.G. Clarke; W. Johnson; R. Eccles;
W. Broad; G. France; J.H. Watmough; G. Meredith; H. Robinson and T. Hanks

A new grandstand holding one thousand spectators was built at the expense of Chesters Brewery who were granted sole selling rights for beer at the ground. The club erected the first pay box at a cost of £5 15s.

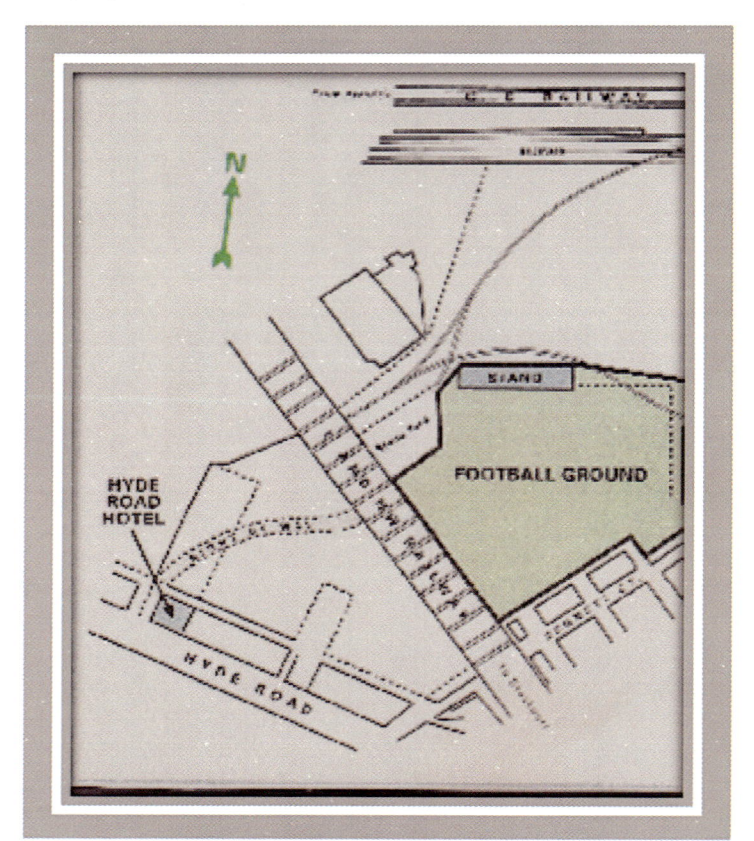

Hyde Road Ground

The football ground and new grandstand are shown on the Drawing. The right of way from the Hyde Road Hotel to the Ground is also shown. Galloway's Works was to the east of the Ground.

W. Watmough continued as Captain.

Ardwick remained an amateur club with the players paying membership subscriptions. Many of the players from Ardwick's first season continued with the club.

The Players

The following players played in the first team during the 1888-1889 Season (with the new players shown in italics).

ARDWICK A.F.C. PLAYERS 1888-89	
Goalkeeper:	
F. Leather	
Full-backs:	
Edward Bower	(the last of the St. Mark's players)
Kenneth McKenzie	(formerly Gorton)
Peck	
Half-backs:	
W. Watmough	
J. Manning	
Siddall	
S. Simster	
Forwards:	
J. Hodgetts	(formerly Gorton)
J. Hennefer	
J. Callagan	
Donald McKenzie	(formerly Gorton)
J. Pickup	
J.Currie	
J.H. Smith	
J. Stanley	
J.O'Brien	
Gallagher	

The following fixtures were arranged by Walter Chew:

1st September 1888   Ardwick 3 v Matlock 3
Hyde Road

This, the opening match of the season, was played at Hyde Road before a good number of spectators. The game was fairly even for some time, but when the teams had settled down, Ardwick had slightly the best of it and managed to score the first goal, a splendid shot from the outside left by STANLEY. Matlock then strove hard to get on level terms but the Ardwick goalkeeper and backs managed to keep them from scoring up to half-time, the game then being one goal to nil in favour of Ardwick.

After change of ends, Ardwick had the best of the game for some time, putting the ball through the opponents' goal four times but two of these were disallowed. The Matlock forwards were let in on several occasions by the home backs, and they managed to draw level by scoring two goals a few minutes before the call of time. The final score was 3 goals each.

John Allison, who was a pioneer in the treatment of sports injuries, attended this match. He paid half-a-crown to enter and declined any change. This generous supporter was soon located and he was later to serve on the Ardwick committee and became a director of Manchester City.

John Allison had set up a sports clinic in Higher Ardwick in the late 1870's and moved to Hyde Road, Ardwick to set up Matlock House Hydro in 1884. He became a specialist in treating muscular and limb injuries at his hydropathic baths.

A Caricature of John Allison

John Allison also opened Turkish Baths at 42 Hyde Road, Ardwick. He advertised the Turkish Baths as being specially recommended to football players "as favouring in high deree the best and most perfect development of the muscles"

ALLISON'S
TURKISH BATHS
42 Hyde Road, Ardwick
First Class 1/6.

8th September 1888   Ardwick 7 v Walkden Park Mill 1
Hyde Road

The visitors kicked off with the wind in their favour. Ardwick soon forced the play and were winning by three goals to one at half-time.

In the second half Ardwick had all the best of the play and added four more goals. Ardwick won by 7 goals to 1.

15th September 1888   Ardwick   10   v   Fairfield   0
Hyde Road

  Ardwick kicked off and immediately took the ball to the Fairfield goal but the goalkeeper defended splendidly and managed to keep his goal in tact for about 20 minutes. However, the Ardwick players kept up the pressure and the score at half-time was Ardwick four goals Fairfield nil.

  On change of ends, Ardwick completely outplayed Fairfield and scored six times, the final score being Ardwick 10 goals Fairfield 0. This score would have been greatly increased but for the Fairfield goalkeeper who defended magnificently all through the game.

22nd September 1888   Oldham Olympic   0   v   Ardwick   4
             Oldham

22nd September 1888   Ardwick A   7   v   Oldham Olympic A   0

29th September 1888   Royton   3   v   Ardwick   5
Royton

  Royton kicked off and had the best of the game for the first few minutes scoring two goals. However, Ardwick soon settled down to good combined play and had much the best of the play up to half-time when the score was Ardwick four goals Royton two.

  In the second half, Ardwick again had the best of the play but could only score one more goal with Royton also scoring one goal. The game resulted in a win for Ardwick by 5 goals to 3.

29th September 1888   Ardwick A   2   v   Royton A   1

6th October 1888   Ardwick   6   v   Marple   4
Hyde Road

  Marple kicked off and, almost immediately, scored. The game became very fast, Ardwick doing their utmost to equalise and this they did after about ten minutes play. Ardwick then had the best of the play and the score at half-time was Ardwick four goals Marple one.

  On resuming, play became very exciting and the ball travelled rapidly from one end to the other. However, Marple could never make up the ground they had lost in the first half and Ardwick won by 6 goals to 4. This makes the fifth successive victory for Ardwick.

13th October 1888   Lancashire Junior Cup   First Round
Hyde Road

         Ardwick   6   v   Manchester Clifford   0

  Ardwick started the game and each side quickly gained a corner. Ardwick pressed for a time and HENNEFER scored. The Clifford were kept on the defensive and CURRIE managed to score a second goal for Ardwick which was followed by a third goal scored by CALLAGAN. Shortly afterwards the ball was headed through by HODGETTS and the score at half-time was Ardwick four goals Manchester Clifford 0.

  From the kick off for the second half Ardwick kept up a continuous attack on the Clifford goal and HENNEFER and a Clifford player each scored for Ardwick. At the close Ardwick had won by 6 goals to nil. (Ardwick later scratched and did not play in the second round of the cup)

20th October 1888 Farnworth Parish Church   2   v   Ardwick   3
Farnworth

  The game was fast and exciting. The score at half-time was Farnworth Parish Church two goals Ardwick nil.

  In the second half, Ardwick had the best of the match and won a good game by 3 goals to 2.

27th October 1888   Ardwick   2   v   Lower Hurst   0
Hyde Road

  There were a good number of spectators in the ground. Lower Hurst objected to playing full time (Lower Hurst only had ten men) and two thirty five minute halves were arranged. Ardwick kicked off and the ball travelled from end to end for the first few minutes. Afterwards Ardwick had all the best of the game but up to half-time could not manage to score.

After change of ends, Ardwick continued to press and scored twice through the efforts of STANLEY. The final score was Ardwick 2 goals Lower Hurst 0

Ardwick had made an excellent start to the season. After drawing the first game of the season, Ardwick had eight successive victories.

It was commented that: *"Ardwick had every prospect of developing into a first rate club."*

3rd November 1888   Davenham   0   v   Ardwick   3
Davenham
Davenham were handicapped with several of their players being engaged in a Cheshire and Derbyshire match. Davenham kicked off and the visitors immediately began to press gaining a corner in the first few minutes of the game, which, however, proved fruitless. Give-and-take play then followed but at length PICKUP scored the first goal for Ardwick. A second goal was headed through by HODGETTS from a capital centre by STANLEY. The former then experienced very hard lines a few minutes later and at half-time Ardwick were leading by two goals to nil.

During the second half, Ardwick had decidedly the best of matters, and eventually, STANLEY scored the third goal for Ardwick, who ultimately won by 3 goals to nil.

10th November 1888   Ardwick   1   v   Oldham Olympic   1
Hyde Road
There were a good number of spectators in the ground. The Olympic brought a strong team being assisted by Barton (Blackburn Rovers), Halliday (Halliwell), O'Donnell (Newton Heath Central) and others. Ardwick played with the wind in the first half and had much the best of the game getting corner after corner but they could not score owing to the splendid defence of the Olympic's backs and goalkeeper. There was no score at half-time.

The Olympics scored from the foot of Barton immediately after change of ends. After this, Ardwick played much better and had the best of the game but could not score until close on time when HODGETTS equalised with a good header, the game ending in a draw of 1 goal each.

10 November 1888   Oldham Olympic A   1   v   Ardwick A   4

17th November 1888   Ardwick   8   v   Manchester   1
Hyde Road
Ardwick Team: Leather; Bower and Peck; Watmough © Manning and Siddall; Stanley 1 O'Brien 4 Hennefer 2 Hodgetts 1 and D McKenzie.

There were a fair number of spectators in the ground. The pitch was in a wretched condition and consequently the time was curtailed to two 35's. The visitors were first to break away but MANNING relieved with a long kick. Manchester again returned and nearly scored. PECK for Ardwick was now seen to advantage with some good kicking enabling O'BRIEN to notch the first goal of the game. Parkington for Manchester put in a good shot which went a little wide. Ardwick now rushed the ball to the other end and O'BRIEN sent in an express shot which Verity fisted out in fine style but HENNEFER got the ball and shot through. Manchester had another look in but failed to score. The ball was again taken forward by Ardwick and STANLEY scored with a grand shot. This brought about half-time with Ardwick leading by three goals to nil.

The change of ends brought no relief for Manchester as Ardwick rushed the ball up but a claim for "hands" in front of goal spoiled the chance of scoring. Some good kicking on the part of O'BRIEN HODGETTS and HENNEFER enabled HENNEFER to add the fourth goal. O'BRIEN of Ardwick put in some brilliant play and quickly notched two goals amidst loud applause. These reverses seemed to rouse Manchester but all to no avail for the ball was again worked up to the Manchester end and O'BRIEN centred for HENNEFER who missed the chance. This, however, did not matter much for directly afterwards HODGETTS sent in a stinger, which Jones in attempting to kick out sent the ball through his own posts. Manchester now made a vigorous raid on the Ardwick goal and after some exciting play scored their first and only goal of the match. The play was now more even and neither side had an advantage until HODGETTS with a good kick sent the ball to the visitors end, and O'BRIEN following up well, scored the eighth goal for Ardwick amidst much enthusiasm. Time was called soon afterwards and a most one-sided game ended in a victory for Ardwick by 8 goals to 1.

24th November 1888   Bacup   7   v   Ardwick   0
Bacup

    Ardwick, who prior to this match held an unbeaten record, were unable to play anything like their usual strength side. Six of their players were unavailable and Ardwick consequently suffered, as was expected under the circumstances, their first defeat of the season. Bacup had the best of matters especially in the second portion but Ardwick bitterly complained of the decisions of the referee. Bacup ultimately won the game by 7 goals to nil.

1st December 1888   Ardwick   4   v   Farnworth Parish Church   3
Hyde Road

    Ardwick played downhill in the first half and had much the best of the game, STANLEY O'BRIEN and HENNEFER each scoring a goal before half-time when the score was Ardwick three goals Farnworth nil.

    In the second half, Farnworth scored two goals in the first few minutes, one of these being a very lucky one as the Ardwick goalkeeper kicked the ball against one of his backs and it rebounded through before he could get back to his position. Play now became very fast and Farnworth scored making the game three goals each. Both sides struggled hard to get the winning goal. STANLEY, at length, scored for the home team by tackling the Farnworth goalkeeper before he could get the ball away. A fast and exciting game resulted in a win for Ardwick by 4 goals to 3.

8th December 1888   Ardwick   4   v   Manchester Clifford   0
Hyde Road   1000

    Ardwick kicked off and for some time play was in their territory from which a corner accrued but through the fine play of BOWER at full back the ball was kicked clear. Ardwick now began to press and had much the best of the game in the first half with HODGETTS and PICKUP both scoring before half-time, when Ardwick led by two goals to nil.

    On resumption Ardwick continued to maintain their superiority with some fine passing by STANLEY and PICKUP on the left wing. Ardwick had all the best of the play and scored two more goals through HODGETTS and STANLEY. A one sided game ended in a victory for Ardwick by 4 goals to nil.

15th December 1888   Ardwick   2   v   Church   1
Hyde Road

    Church won the toss and elected to play downhill. Ardwick kicked off and play at once became fast and exciting. Church were the first to score with a good shot, but after some good passing STANLEY equalised. The score at half-time was one goal each.

    On change of ends both sides played hard to score the winning goal. Ardwick, however, had slightly the better of the play, and at length, O'BRIEN scored a second goal for Ardwick. The final result was Ardwick 2 goals Church 1.

22nd December 1888   Ardwick   3   v   Over Wanderers   2
Hyde Road

    Over kicked off against the wind and the game at once became very even, good play being shown by both sides. The score at half-time was Ardwick two goals Over Wanderers one.

    On change of ends the Wanderers soon made the game even. Ardwick then played up with renewed vigour, and their exertions ultimately were rewarded when STANLEY scored the third goal. The game then continued with much spirit and Ardwick again put the ball through the Over goal, but after a consultation, the goal was disallowed. Ardwick won a fast and exciting game by 3 goals to 2.

29th December 1888   Bolton Borough   0   v   Ardwick   2
Bolton

    In the first half, the game was exceedingly well contested, but notwithstanding the strenuous efforts of both sides to overpower each other, the defence of the back divisions was not to be broken. At half-time no score had been recorded.

    In the second half, Ardwick played excellently and frequently harassed the Bolton defence, with the result that PICKUP and O'BRIEN succeeded in effecting the downfall of the Bolton goal on one occasion each which enabled Ardwick to record another victory to their long list of successes by 2 goals to nil.

5th January 1889   Ardwick   1   v   Darwen Rovers   0
Hyde Road
Ardwick Team: Leather; Peck and Bower; Watmough © Manning and Siddall; O'Brien 1 Hodgetts Hennefer Pickup and Stanley.

     Darwen Rovers had the best of the game during the first half, but there was no score.

     In the second half, Ardwick did most of the pressing and O'BRIEN scored just before the call of time. There was fine play from LEATHER, BOWER and MANNING for Ardwick. The final score was Ardwick 1 goal Darwen Rovers 0.

12th January 1889   Ardwick   9   v   Davenham   2
1500 Hyde Road

     Ardwick kicked off and scored a goal within three minutes. Davenham equalised soon after. Ardwick then took the lead and scored four more goals. At half-time Ardwick led by five goals to one.

     In the second half Ardwick continued to hold the upper hand and added four more goals, finally recording a grand victory by 9 goals to 2.

19th January 1889   Hooley Hill   2   v   Ardwick   2
Hooley Hill

     The match was played before a fair number of spectators. The game was well contested with each side making some good runs. LEATHER saved well for Ardwick. At half-time Ardwick led by two goals to one.

     There was some exciting play in the second half and Hooley Hill equalised. Each side made efforts to score the winning goal but the score at full-time was 2 goals each.

26th January 1889   Ardwick   8   v   Heaton Park   1
Hyde Road

     Heaton Park kicked off but Ardwick immediately began to press and scored their first goal in about five minutes. Heaton Park equalised after a little give-and-take play. After this Ardwick had the best of the game and the score at half-time was Ardwick five goals Heaton Park one.

     Heaton Park played ten men during the greater part of the second half owing to one of their players getting hurt. Ardwick had matters much their own way and finally won by 8 goals to 1.

2nd February 1889   Manchester & District Challenge Cup   Second Round
3000 Hyde Road

                                         Ardwick   7   v   Gorton Villa   0

     Ardwick pressed throughout and in the first half scored on four occasions.

     The second half brought no relief for the visitors and Ardwick scored three more goals. The final score was Ardwick 7 goals Gorton Villa 0.

9th February 1889   Lower Hurst   v   Ardwick
Hurst

     Ardwick won the toss and Lower Hurst kicked off but the match had to be abandoned.

16th February 1889   Ardwick   9   v   Park Lane Wanderers   0
Hyde Road

     Ardwick met Park Lane Wanderers (the holders of the Wigan & District Cup) before a good number of spectators.

     Ardwick kicked off and play at once became very fast, the ball travelling rapidly from goal to goal. Ardwick soon settled down to a splendid passing game and had the best of it at every point. Ardwick scored six goals through HENNEFER (3), SMITH, WATMOUGH and O'BRIEN. At half-time the score was Ardwick six goals Park Lane nil.

     In the second half Ardwick still did all the pressing and STANLEY played splendidly. O'BRIEN, SMITH and WATMOUGH each scored. Ardwick won by 9 goals to nil.

23rd February 1889   Marple   5   v   Ardwick   2
Marple

     The game was played before a fair muster of spectators. HENNEFER started the game for Ardwick and play was at once of a lively character. HODGETTS for Ardwick headed the first goal. On re-starting Marple with some combined dribbling equalised. Shortly afterwards the Ardwick goalkeeper added a second goal to the Marple score. WATMOUGH then equalised with a good shot. At half-time the score was two goals each.

On crossing over Marple began to press and before time was called had scored three more goals, leaving Marple the winners by 5 goals to 2

23rd February 1889   Ardwick A   3   v   Marple A   3

On 26th February 1889, a match was played at Belle Vue Gardens under Wells lights in aid of the Hyde Colliery Explosion Fund between Ardwick & District and Newton Heath (L.Y.R.) and a profit of £140 was made. Newton Heath won by 3 goals to 2.

2nd March 1889   Ardwick   2   v   Witton   5
Hyde Road

The first match between these Clubs took place before a large attendance of spectators. Witton were quickly called upon to defend their position, and STANLEY was not long in scoring with a grand shot, this early success being greeted with loud cheers. Witton, however, responded and Grimshaw went through and equalised. Witton severely harassed the Ardwick defence for some time and the Ardwick goalkeeper was called upon frequently to save. Howarth was then responsible for the second goal for Witton. Both sides alternately attacked, but Grimshaw and Howarth for Witton each added a goal before half-time when Witton were leading by four goals to one.

On changing ends, the Ardwick players gave a much better account of themselves and smart play on the part of HENNEFER and HODGETTS was instrumental in HODGETTS recording Ardwick's second goal. Ardwick maintained their attacking tactics but the Witton's back division played admirably in defence and prevented Ardwick from scoring. Horsfield then scored a fifth goal for Witton. Witton won the match by 5 goals to 2.

9th March 1889   Ardwick   2   v   Royton   1
Hyde Road

Royton played with the wind in their favour and the sun at their backs. Ardwick kicked off but Royton took the ball up field and Dyson scored for Royton. After this, Ardwick had much the best of play but they failed to score before half-time, when Royton led by one goal to nil.

In the second-half Ardwick pressed all through and the Ardwick forwards gave the Royton goalkeeper a lot of work to do. At last J.H. SMITH sent in a good shot which beat the Royton goalkeeper and made the score equal. Ardwick then had much the best of it sending the ball over the bar time after time, and eventually a strong shot from J.O'BRIEN resulted in a second goal for Ardwick. Time was called leaving Ardwick winners by 2 goals to 1.

16th March 1889   Manchester & District Challenge Cup   Third Round
North Road

Newton Heath L&YR   4   v   Ardwick   1

Ardwick Team: F. Leather; K. McKenzie and E. Bower; W. Watmough © J.Manning and S. Simster; J. Callagan J.Hodgetts J. Hennefer 1 J. Pickup and J. Stanley

Newton Heath started and for some time play was pretty even. Ardwick made the first attack and Mitchell cleared. LEATHER then had to stop a fast shot from J. Doughty. Some nice passing by Burke and R. Doughty took place near the Ardwick goal but J. Doughty kicked over. The Ardwick left wing then ran the ball up but Mitchell was again in the way. Some fast play took place at the Ardwick end but the defence was too good. LEATHER made some really fine saves. HENNEFER and STANLEY were next prominent with some splendid play, and a determined rush was made for the Newton Heath goal. A corner fell to Ardwick but they were unable to score. Burke and J. Doughty got away and the latter after a splendid run put in a swift shot which LEATHER was powerless to save. Penley was then called to save from HENNEFER. Following a free kick to Newton Heath the ball was well placed by Mitchell and Gotherage headed it through the Ardwick goal. Gotherage added a third goal a few minutes later. Ardwick then played well and Newton Heath were forced to concede a corner but nothing resulted. The score at half-time was Newton Heath three goals Ardwick nil.

Newton Heath pressed in the second-half but LEATHER was in grand form. At last after a spirited run and some fast play by HENNEFER and STANLEY in the mouth of the Newton Heath goal the ball was rushed through. From the re-start the Newton Heath forwards at once got away and after some exciting play J. Owen scored with a well judged shot. The final score was Newton Heath 4 goals Ardwick 1.

23rd March 1889   Manchester Clifford   0   v   Ardwick   4
Old Trafford
Ardwick Team: F. Leather; K. McKenzie and E. Bower; W. Watmough © J.Manning and S. Simster; J.O'Brien 1 J.Hodgetts 1 J. Hennefer 1 J. Pickup 1 and J. Stanley

    Ardwick played with the wind during the first half and had all the best of the game. STANLEY put in some brilliant centres and O'BRIEN scored the first goal. Ardwick continued to have the best of matters and PICKUP and HENNEFER added a goal each before half-time when Ardwick led by three goals to nil.

    On changing ends Clifford with the elements in their favour gave a better account of themselves, but they proved no match for Ardwick who settled down to a grand passing game. HODGETTS ultimately secured another goal for Ardwick who finally won easily by 4 goals to nil.

30th March 1889   Heaton Park   2   v   Ardwick   3
Heaton Park

    Ardwick played with the wind at their backs in the first-half and had all the best of the game but could not score owing to the erratic shooting of their forwards. The Heaton Park players managed to break away on two occasions and scored two goals before half-time.

    In the second-half Ardwick although playing against the wind still continued to press and scored on three occasions. The final score was Ardwick 3 goals Heaton Park 2.

3rd April 1889   Ardwick   8   v   Sheffield Attercliffe   1
Hyde Road

    The match was played before a good number of spectators. Ardwick had much the best of the game and led by five goals to nil in the first half.

    In the second-half, Ardwick still maintained their advantage and added three more goals whilst Sheffield Attercliffe scored one. The game ended in an easy victory for Ardwick by 8 goals to 1.

13th April 1889   Ardwick   3   v   Church   3
Hyde Road

    The match was played before a good number of spectators. Church played with the wind in their favour during the first-half and had slightly the best of it leading by two goals to nil at half-time.

    After change of ends, Ardwick pressed, and managed to score three times whilst the visitors added one goal to their score. The final result was a draw of 3 goals each.

20th April 1889   Buxton   0   v   Ardwick   2
Silverlands, Buxton

    The match was played before a large number of spectators. Ardwick kicked off against the strong wind and led by one goal to nil in the first-half.

    On changing ends, Ardwick had the best of it and notched another goal. There were few attractive features associated with the match but the better team won. The final score was Ardwick 2 goals Buxton 0.

27th April 1889   Ardwick   4   v   Macclesfield   0
Hyde Road

    The rising Ardwick club received a visit from Macclesfield and they met before a good number of spectators. Macclesfield started and Ardwick at once began to press. A lot of loose play ensued in front of the Macclesfield goal and GALLAGHER scored for Ardwick. Ardwick had most of the play but up to half-time no further score was registered, at which period Ardwick were leading by one goal to nil.

    After crossing over Ardwick again put their opponents on the defensive, but Macclesfield's backs stubbornly resisted their attacks for some time. Finally, HODGETTS got one past the Macclesfield goalkeeper and HENNEFER also scored a goal shortly afterwards. Re-starting Macclesfield put on a rush and forced Ardwick to defend their goal. Several corners were conceded and Macclesfield kept up a vigorous attack but without success. Ardwick eventually broke away and play was even for a time until HODGETTS got clear away and scored a fourth goal for Ardwick. The game ended in a win for Ardwick by 4 goals to nil.

4th May 1889   West Manchester   v   Ardwick   abandoned
Brooks' Bar

    In the first-half West Manchester scored three goals and led by three goals to nil at half-time. In the second-half Ardwick scored a goal whilst West Manchester also scored. The game was brought to a sudden termination and was abandoned owing to two of the players coming to blows with spectators.

Ardwick's results were very good in 1888-89 and much better than in the previous season. Thirty four matches were recorded and Ardwick won twenty six; drew four and lost four. Ardwick had become a very good junior club but they would need to strengthen to compete with the better clubs in Lancashire.

The club's financial position also improved. On the income side, the gate money had increased considerably from £47 to £213. On the expenditure side, the rent on the ground increased from £10 to £15. The Committee had decided on further improvements to the ground as they were confident of increased patronage and support. The expenditure on the ground during the year was £23 16s. The accounts showed a good result, with the loss of £13 5s 1d in 1887-88 being turned into a profit of £33 9s 0d in 1888-89.

Ardwick's Second Balance Sheet:

BALANCE SHEET

Balance Sheet for Season 1888-1889			
INCOME	**£**	**s**	**d**
S. Chesters Thompson	5	5	0
Members' Subscriptions	16	10	2
Gate Money	213	8	11
Share of Cup-ties	16	1	8
Guarantees for Away matches	16	8	5
Hire of Ground		19	0
Profit on ball	1	6	5
	£269	19	7
EXPENDITURE			
By accounts due last year	11	6	3
Rent on ground	15	0	0
Poor Rate		15	0
Subscriptions to MDFA & LJFA	1	16	6
Work on ground	23	16	0
Team's Travelling Expenses	34	9	10
Printing	27	7	8
Posting	9	15	0
Postages & Telegrams	3	13	5
Stationery		8	6
Referee's Expenses	2	8	6
Football requisites	21	8	4
Payments to Visiting Teams	68	17	6
Police	3	2	4
Erection of Paybox	5	15	0
Entertaining own & visiting team	6	0	9
Medical fee		5	0
Entrance fee (Heaton Park Contest)		5	0
Balance in hand	33	9	0
	£269	19	7

The subscriptions of £1 16s 6d were paid to the Manchester and District Football Association and to the Lancashire Football Association.

There follows a summary of the season with details, where known, of reported friendly and cup matches, attendances, appearances and goal scorers. Ardwick entered the Manchester and District Senior Cup (MC) and the Lancashire Junior Cup (LJC).

SUMMARY
ARDWICK A.F.C. 1888-89

DATE		OPPONENT	RES	1	2	3	4	5	6
1888				7	8	9	10	11	
01-Sep	H	Matlock	D 3-3						
								J. Stanley 1	
08-Sep	H	Walkden	W 7-1						
		Park Mill							
15-Sep	H	Fairfield	W 10-0						
22-Sep	A	Oldham	W 4-0						
		Olympic							
29-Sep	A	Royton	W 5-3						
06-Oct	H	Marple	W 6-4						
13-Oct	H	Manchester	W 6-0						
LJC1		Clifford		J.Callagan1	J.Hodgetts1	J.Hennefer2	J.Currie 1		1 own goal
20-Oct	A	Farnworth	W 3-2						
		Par. Church							
27-Oct	H	Lower	W 2-0						
		Hurst						J.Stanley 2	
3-Nov	A	Davenham	W 3-0						
					Hodgetts 1		J.Pickup 1	J.Stanley 1	
10.Nov	H	Oldham	D 1-1						
		Olympic			Hodgetts 1				
17.Nov	H	Manchester	W 8-1	F. Leather	E.Bower	Peck	W.Watmough©	J.Manning	Siddall
				J.Stanley 1	J.O'Brien 4	J.Hennefer2	J.Hodgetts 1	D.McKenzie	
24.Nov	A	Bacup	L 0-7						
01-Dec	H	Farnworth	W 4-3						
		Par. Church			O'Brien 1	Hennefer 1		Stanley 2	
08-Dec	H	Manchester	W 4-0		Bower				
		Clifford			Hodgetts 2		J.Pickup 1	Stanley 1	
15-Dec	H	Church	W 2-1						
					O'Brien 1			Stanley 1	
22-Dec	H	Over	W 3-2						
		Wanderers						Stanley 1	2 goals *
29-Dec	A	Bolton	W 2-0						
		Borough			O'Brien 1		Pickup 1		
05-Jan	H	Darwen	W 1-0	F.Leather	Peck	E.Bower	W.Watmough©	J.Manning	Siddall
1889		Rovers		J.O'Brien 1	J.Hodgetts	J.Hennefer	J.Pickup	J.Stanley	
12-Jan	H	Davenham	W 9-2						
			1500						
19-Jan	A	Hooley Hill	D 2-2	Leather					
26-Jan	H	Heaton	W 8-1						
		Park							
02-Feb	H	Gorton Villa	W 7-0						
MC 2			3000						
09-Feb	A	Lower		Abandoned					
		Hurst							
16-Feb	A	Park Lane	W 9-0				Watmough © 2		
		Wanderers		O'Brien 2		Hennefer 3	J.H.Smith 2	Stanley	

82

Date	H/A	Opponent	Result						
23-Feb	A	Marple	L 2-5				Watmough© 1		
					Hodgetts 1	Hennefer			
02-Mar	H	Witton	L 2-5						
					Hodgetts 1	Hennefer		Stanley 1	
09-Mar	A	Royton	W 2-1						
			5000	O'Brien 1			Smith 1		
16-Mar	A	Newton	L 1-4	F.Leather	K.McKenzie	E.Bower	W.Watmough©	J.Manning	S.Simster
MC 3		Heath		J.Callagan	J.Hodgetts	J.Hennefer1	J.Pickup	J.Stanley	
23-Mar	A	Manchester	W 4-0	F.Leather	K.McKenzie	E.Bower	W.Watmough©	J.Manning	S.Simster
		Clifford		J.O'Brien 1	J.Hodgetts1	J.Hennefer1	J.Pickup 1	J.Stanley	
30-Mar	A	Heaton Park	W 3-2						
06-Apr	A	Sheffield	W 8-1						
		Attercliffe							
13-Apr	H	Church	D 3-3						
			5000						
20-Apr	A	Buxton	W 2-0						
27-Apr	H	Macclesfield	W 4-0						
					Hodgetts 2	Hennefer 1	Gallagher 1		
4-May	A	West		Abandoned					
		Manchester							

Captain: ©   Scorer(s) not known: *

RECORDED MATCHES 1888-89						
	P	W	D	L	F	A
Home	19	15	3	1	89	27
Away	15	11	1	3	50	27
Total	34	26	4	4	139	54
ACTUAL RESULTS						
First XI	43	32	5	6	167	69
Reserves	18	11	2	5	59	22

The actual results are taken from Fred Johnson's book on "The History of Manchester City"

Thirty four of the forty three first team matches were reported but the full Ardwick line-up was given in only four matches. The recorded appearances are taken from those four matches.

RECORDED APPEARANCES 1888-89		
PLAYER	APPS.	GOALS
1. LEATHER,F	4	
2. BOWER,E	4	
3. PECK	2	
4. McKENZIE, K	2	
5. WATMOUGH,W	4	
6. MANNING,J	4	
7. SIDDALL	2	
8. SIMSTER,S	2	
9. HODGETTS,J	4	2
10. HENNEFER,J	4	4
11. CALLAGAN,J	1	
12. McKENZIE, D	1	
13. PICKUP,J	3	1
14. STANLEY,J	4	1
15. O'BRIEN,J	3	6

CHAPTER 13

ARDWICK ASSOCIATION FOOTBALL CLUB
1889-1890

Stephen Chesters Thompson, JP continued as President.

Lawrence Furniss of 128 Kirkmanshulme Lane, Longsight was appointed Secretary of Ardwick in place of Walter Chew who remained on the Ardwick Committee.

John Allison joined the Ardwick Committee.

Lawrence Furniss    John Allison

Kenneth McKenzie returned as Captain replacing W. Watmough.

Until the 1888-1889 Season, the team had been chosen from the members. However, the Ardwick Committee now decided to go further afield for players than their own members. J. Hodgetts had become Ardwick's first professional receiving five shillings per week. The amateurs were also allowed five shillings expenses for each away match.

Several players remained from the previous season, but there were also many new players. F. Leather continued in goal. P. Bennett and J. Heald replaced Edward Bower and Peck at full-back with K. McKenzie moving to half-back. W. Watmough and J. Manning continued at half-back. J. Stanley moved to half-back from the forward line as did J. O'Brien late in the season. Hart, who was a reserve, played in two matches at half-back.

J. Hodgetts, J. Hennefer and J. Callagan continued in the forward line. There were seven new forwards: J.W. Howarth, H. Schofield, W.J. Gregson, A. Booth, R. Walker, W. Tait, from West Manchester but formerly of Newton Heath, and W.

Woodacre from Witton. M. Fergus, who was a reserve, played in one match at outside left and there were several players from other clubs who played for Ardwick in the match against Everton. Towards the end of the season, Walter Rushton and A. McWhirter joined on trial from Bolton Wanderers and Daniel Whittle on trial from Halliwell.

The Players

The following players played in the first team during the 1889-1890 Season (with the new players shown in italics):

ARDWICK A.F.C. PLAYERS 1889-90
Goalkeeper:
F. Leather
Full-backs:
P. Bennett
J. Heald
Half-backs:
W. Watmough
J. Manning
K. McKenzie   (formerly Gorton)
J. Stanley
J.O'Brien
Hart
Forwards:
J. Hodgetts   (formerly Gorton)
J. Hennefer
J. Callagan
M. Fergus
J.W. Howarth
H. Schofield
W.J. Gregson
A. Booth
W. Tait
R. Walker
W. Woodacre

The Club played the following fixtures:

7th September 1889   Ardwick   3   v   Darwen Rovers   5
Hyde Road
   The play was very even in the first-half, both sides scoring two goals each.
   In the second half, Darwen Rovers quickly scored two goals, BENNETT the Ardwick back getting hurt. Darwen scored again and Ardwick then had considerably the best of the play and eventually scored. The final score was Ardwick 3 goals Darwen Rovers 5.

14th September 1889   Hurst   3   v   Ardwick   4
Hurst
   The match was played before a large number of spectators. Garnett started the ball for Hurst. Ardwick ran the ball into the Hurst goal area and from a free kick close in had a chance to score but the ball went outside. Ardwick still pressed and had hard lines in not scoring. Hurst ran the ball to the other end but it went over the line. HODGETTS scored the first goal for Ardwick. Hurst equalised shortly afterwards when BENNETT missed his kick and Parkinson put the ball through the Ardwick goal. Half-time arrived with the score standing at one goal each.
   From the re-start Ardwick rushed up and HODGETTS scored again. Hurst now had a look in and Burns scored their second goal. Hurst continued to press, but the Ardwick backs repelled the attacks. The Hurst goalkeeper had to stop a good shot from HENNEFER. Hurst again pressed and the Ardwick goalkeeper ran out and missed the ball allowing Garnett to give Hurst the lead. Ardwick put on a spurt and O'BRIEN scored twice. The final score was Ardwick 4 goals Hurst 3.

21st September 1889   Ardwick 6 v Bacup 2
Hyde Road

    The match was played before a fair muster of spectators. Bacup kicked off but Ardwick immediately began to press and HOWARTH soon scored a goal. Bacup then played up but the ball was returned and HOWARTH helped through a good shot by WATMOUGH. At half-time the score was Ardwick two goals Bacup one.

    In the second half Ardwick had much the best of the play and scored four more goals, the visitors scoring one. The game ended Ardwick 6 goals Bacup 2.

28th September 1889   Lancashire Junior Cup   First Round
Hyde Road   4,000

Ardwick 4 v Denton 2

    Ardwick kicked off but Denton were the first to attack. The Ardwick left wing got away but his final shot went outside. A good shot by HODGETTS was well stopped by Lowe, the Denton goalkeeper. Ardwick though playing against a strong wind were having quite as much of the play as Denton, and forced Denton to concede a corner but nothing resulted. Denton attacked and from a scrimmage on the line Denton scored the first goal. Ardwick retaliated, but the Denton goalkeeper was not to be beaten. The Denton forwards by a combined run added a second goal. This seemed to rouse Ardwick and from a good run by the left wing, O'BRIEN scored. At half-time the score was Denton two goals Ardwick one.

    Denton re-started but Ardwick at once took the upper hand. SCHOFIELD equalised for Ardwick. STANLEY put in a good shot which deserved to score, but HODGETTS made amends by scoring immediately afterwards. The Denton defence was now severely taxed and HOWARTH beat Lowe with a good shot. Ardwick ran out winners by 4 goals to 2.

5th October 1889   Irwell Springs 3 v Ardwick 0
Bacup

    Ardwick came with nine men and were hard pressed throughout. Irwell scored in six minutes and at half-time were leading by one goal to nil.

    Irwell spent the second half shooting at the Ardwick goal and scored after ten minutes. LEATHER prevented any further score until just before full-time when Bann scored the third goal. Irwell Springs won by 3 goals to nil.

12th October 1889   Manchester Welsh 1 v Ardwick 5
Heaton Chapel

    Manchester Welsh kicked off. Ardwick began to force the game and the Welsh had to clear an awkward shot. Ardwick continued to press but could not get one through. McKENZIE, the Ardwick captain, received a nasty kick over the eye and had to leave the ground for a few minutes. Ardwick forwards then ran down the field and passing nicely, HODGETTS scored. SCHOFIELD added another very soon afterwards. HODGETTS also put in another good shot which Lewis put over the bar. The Welsh forwards visited the Ardwick end, but a goal kick was the only result. The score at half-time was Ardwick two goals Manchester Welsh nil.

    Ardwick re-started and play was rather fast and of a give-and-take character. Ardwick rushed down and BENNETT scored the third goal. GREGSON had hard lines with a good shot going just over the bar. Manchester Welsh now made a spurt and by a bit of determined play managed to get one past LEATHER. Ardwick again pressed and gained a corner from which HODGETTS headed a good goal. O'BRIEN scored the fifth goal. Ardwick won easily by 5 goals to 1.

19th October 1889   Lancashire Junior Cup   Second Round
Hyde Road

Ardwick 6 v Rochdale Clifford 2

    A fast game with each side scoring once in the first-half, but the Ardwick backs were very loose.

    In the second-half Ardwick pressed all through, scoring five goals. The Clifford put the ball through just before the call of time, the Ardwick goalkeeper being down the field. Ardwick won by 6 goals to 2.

26th October 1889   Ardwick 8 v Farnworth Parish Church 1
Hyde Road   1,500

    Ardwick kicked off, and the game was at once very fast and even with each side gaining a fruitless corner. Ardwick played up and had the best of it gaining several corners; but owing to some weak shooting and good play by the Farnworth goalkeeper they could not score. Farnworth worked the ball up and gained a corner but with no result. Ardwick again pressed and GREGSON scored the first goal. SCHOFIELD added a second and HOWARTH added another shortly afterwards. At half-time the score was Ardwick three goals Farnworth nil.

Farnworth re-started and aided by the wind it was thought that they would show up better but Ardwick soon got the upper hand with the forwards playing well. SCHOFIELD scored the fourth goal and added a fifth goal shortly afterwards. Farnworth attacked and after some loose play in front of goal, Entwistle scored for Farnworth. Ardwick again pressed and the visitor's defence had plenty of work to do. HODGETTS scored the sixth goal and then GREGSON and O'BRIEN added one each. Ardwick won easily by 8 goals to 1.

2nd November 1889 Manchester Clifford 1 v Ardwick 6
Greenheys

This match was the opening of the Clifford new ground, which was lately occupied by the Manchester Association Club. Clifford won the toss and Ardwick kicked off against a strong wind, but soon visited the Clifford quarters and gained a corner from which SCHOFIELD scored. Clifford then rushed down, but the ball went over. Ardwick were now pressing and Morton (the former Ardwick goalkeeper) saved a good shot. Clifford relieved the pressure but Ardwick returned and O'BRIEN scored with a fast low shot. At half-time Ardwick led by two goals to nil.

Clifford re-started and Ardwick at once began to press. Morton in goal and Long at back defended well for Clifford. SCHOFIELD then added another goal for Ardwick and keeping up the pressure HOWARTH added a fourth. Clifford tried hard to break away but the backs were too good, STANLEY in particular playing a fine game at half-back. Ardwick then added two more goals scored by O'BRIEN and SCHOFIELD and won a one sided game by 6 goals to nil.

9th November 1889   Lancashire Junior Cup   Third Round
Hyde Road

Ardwick 1 v Heywood Central 1

Heywood Central played with the wind, but Ardwick scored after five minutes play. At half-time the score was Ardwick one goal Central nil.

The second-half was very fast, Central having slightly the best of it but they could only score once. The Ardwick goalkeeper played splendidly. Extra time was played. The result was a draw, Ardwick 1 goal Heywood Central 1.

(Ardwick appear to have scratched for there is no record of a replay and Heywood Central went into the fourth round).

16th November 1889   Marple 0 v Ardwick 5
Marple

A very good and fast game each team pressing in turn. The Ardwick forwards were however better at shooting and quicker in front of goal. Ardwick won by 5 goals to nil.

23rd November 1889   Ardwick 3 v Derby St Luke's 2
Hyde Road 2,500

Ardwick were short of several of their regular players. Derby kicked off but Ardwick intercepted and were the first to attack. Derby retaliated and gained a corner which proved abortive. Shortly afterwards, Smith opened the scoring for Derby from a free kick. For some time the play was of a very even nature. At length the Midlanders gained a corner from which Royle scored their second goal. Stimulated by these reverses Ardwick warmed to their task and Derby were compelled to concede four corners in succession, none of which Ardwick were able to utilise to their advantage. At the interval St Luke's led by two goals to nil.

Ardwick re-started and at once commenced to press. O'BRIEN and HODGETTS were conspicuous for some fine combination play, the last mentioned player heading over the bar. After the Saints had obtained a corner, Ardwick attacked and as the result of a grand forward movement on the part of O'BRIEN HODGETTS and HENNEFER, HENEFFER scored for Ardwick. Ardwick continued to exhibit sterling combination play and attacked vigorously, HENNEFER eventually equalising. Ardwick attacked strongly and whilst repelling a shot, the St Luke's goal keeper injured himself and had to retire. Playing with only ten men for the remainder of the game St Luke's kept their goal in tact until just before the call of time when HENNEFER succeeded in giving his side the lead. Ardwick won by 3 goals to 2.

30th November 1889   Ardwick 3 v Chester St Oswald's 2
Hyde Road 2,000
Ardwick team: Leather; Bennett and Heald; Watmough K. McKenzie © and Stanley; Hodgetts 2 O'Brien A. Booth Howarth 1 and Schofield.

    This was the first encounter of these teams. The Saints kicked off and for a time fast play was witnessed from both sides, but eventually HOWARTH scored for Ardwick, this accomplishment being the outcome of some nice passing by the Ardwick forwards. After Chester had invaded Ardwick's territory Ardwick became the aggressors, a shot from BOOTH going over the bar, whilst shortly afterwards the Chester goalkeeper had to fist out. Ardwick had slightly the best of matters for some time but eventually they were forced to act on the defensive the Saints only being prevented from scoring by excellent play on the part of LEATHER, BENNETT and HEALD. At length O'BRIEN gained possession and then passed to HODGETTS, who scored the second goal for Ardwick and when the teams changed ends Ardwick led by two goals to nil.

    Ardwick re-started and for a time the Saints held a slight advantage, after which Ardwick pressed and some exciting play was witnessed in the Chester goalmouth. Chester got the ball away and their forwards running down the field at great pace were only deprived by HEALD, when appearing dangerous. However, Chester were not to be denied and they came again and Lunt scored their first goal. Ardwick next took up the running and HODGETTS taking advantage of a judicious kick by McKENZIE, scored the third goal for Ardwick. Evans almost immediately afterwards obtained the second for Chester. The game was subsequently of an even character the result being a victory for Ardwick by 3 goals to 2.

7th December 1889   Ardwick 7 v Hooley Hill 1
Hyde Road
Ardwick team: Leather; Bennett and Heald; Watmough Manning and Hart; Hodgetts 1 O'Brien 3 Booth 2 Howarth 1 and Gregson ©.

    Ardwick were not fully represented being short of McKENZIE and SCHOFIELD, their places being filled by reserve men. Hooley Hill kicked-off but Ardwick ran down and O'BRIEN shot the ball through out of reach of the goalkeeper. O'BRIEN added another goal shortly afterwards from a good pass from HOWARTH. Hooley Hill then played up and gained a corner but nothing resulted. From the goalkick, HOWARTH got the ball and, evading all opposition, scored a splendid goal. Hooley Hill then rallied, and from a throw in scored their first and only goal. Shortly afterwards O'BRIEN scored again after a good run. At half-time the score was Ardwick four goals Hooley Hill one.

    Ardwick kicked off in the second half and maintained the pressure. BOOTH scored the fifth goal. Hooley Hill now played up but could not break through the Ardwick defence, HEALD playing a fine game at full back and LEATHER in goal being there when called upon. Ardwick returned to the attack and HODGETTS scored the sixth goal and shortly afterwards from a scrimmage in front of goal BOOTH scored the seventh goal. Ardwick won a one sided game by 7 goals to 1.

14th December 1889   Ardwick v Royton
  This game was abandoned due to fog.

21st December 1889 Newton Heath Central 0 v Ardwick 2
Newton Heath
Ardwick team: Leather; Bennett and Heald; Watmough McKenzie © and Stanley; Hodgetts O'Brien W. Tait 1 Howarth and Schofield 1.

    The ground was in a wretched state and it was agreed to play thirty five minutes each way. The Central had a little the better of the first few minutes play, but the game was afterwards very even and though both teams had chances of scoring, half-time arrived without any score.

    In the second half Ardwick soon began to press and from a nice run by TAIT and O'BRIEN, TAIT scored the first goal. The Ardwick forwards kept up the pressure and several times came near to scoring. Then, the Central forwards ran down the field and attacked but the danger was averted by HEALD and BENNETT. SCHOFIELD added a second goal for Ardwick. Ardwick won by 2 goals to nil.

25th December 1889   Ardwick 2 v Derby Junction 5
Hyde Road 4,000
Ardwick team: Leather; Bennett and McKenzie ©; Watmough Hart and Stanley; Hodgetts, O'Brien 1 Walker Hennefer 1 and Tait.

    The game was played in beautiful spring like weather. Unfortunately, Ardwick were minus HEALD, SCHOFIELD and HOWARTH which placed them at a great disadvantage with their formidable opponents. TAIT started the ball for Ardwick and almost immediately the Junction rushed down to the Ardwick goal and Lester had no difficulty in notching the first goal. Again the Junction bore down on Ardwick and Kennerley scored the second and third goals. This roused Ardwick and some good passing on the part of TAIT, STANLEY and O'BRIEN resulted in a goal for Ardwick. WALKER was next conspicuous with a good transfer to HENNEFER who scored the second goal for Ardwick. Fast play ensued for some considerable time during which both ends were visited. There was no further score and at half-time Derby Junction led by three goals to two.

After change of ends Ardwick began to press but their shooting was too erratic. For a long time Ardwick were on the attack but were unable to score. Ultimately, the Junction broke away and from a free kick in the mouth of the goal Kennerley scored the fourth goal for Derby Junction which was soon followed by a fifth scored by Smith. Play after this was loose and there was no further score with Derby Junction winning by 5 goals to 2.

26th December 1889   Ardwick 2 v Hyde 3
Hyde Road 4,000

There was great local interest in the match. Hyde kicked off and for a time the play was very even. Eventually some capital passing amongst the Ardwick forwards enabled SCHOFIELD to beat Stansfield with a great shot. For some time afterwards Ardwick were seen to their best advantage but their efforts were unavailing. Hyde were now prominent but Ardwick, not to be denied, played with remarkable judgment, their passing being frequently applauded. Ardwick gained several corners but they failed to increase their lead. Hyde next attacked and Wigmore scored a goal. A strong appeal by Ardwick for off-side was not entertained. After Hyde had again pressed BENNETT saved his side from further disaster. Ardwick dominated and SCHOFIELD succeeded in putting his side ahead. The score at the interval was two goals to one in favour of Ardwick.

Ardwick re-started and at once made tracks for the Hyde goal but the ball went behind. For some time afterwards both teams went on the attack alternately and both goalkeepers were called upon to defend. Ardwick subsequently had a distinct advantage and attacked vigorously but they failed to score although they were very near to doing so on several occasions. At length Beresford was instrumental in scoring an equaliser for Hyde. Ardwick next took up the running and on many occasions HODGETTS and TAIT were applauded for fine combinations, but their exertions were un-rewarded. McLuggage finally scored the third goal for Hyde who won by 3 goals to 2.

30th December 1889   Ardwick 7 v Hurst 0
Hyde Road
Ardwick team: Leather; Bennett and Heald; Watmough K. McKenzie and Stanley 2; J. O'Brien 1 Hodgetts 3 W. Tait 1 Howarth and Gregson.

The game was played before a good muster of spectators. Hurst kicked off but Ardwick soon began to press and Lees in goal had to save several good shots. Ardwick forwards were playing grandly and HODGETTS headed a nice goal, the same player adding a second from a good pass by GREGSON. The visitors then tried hard to break away but the home full-backs and half-backs were too good. McKENZIE put in some good work. Ardwick were again busy and TAIT added the third goal and O'BRIEN followed with a fourth goal. At half-time the score was Ardwick four goals Hurst nil.

In the second-half the home team continued the pressure. STANLEY put in a fine shot which was saved by Lees. Hurst were completely beaten by the passing of the Ardwick forwards and HODGETTS again scored. STANLEY added the sixth and seventh goals. Ardwick won a one-sided game by 7 goals to nil.

1st January 1890   Ardwick 4 v Rawtenstall 3
Hyde Road 2,500
Ardwick team: Leather; Bennett and Heald; Watmough K. McKenzie © and Stanley; J. O'Brien 1 Hodgetts W. Tait 3 Howarth and Schofield.

Rawtenstall kicked off and soon began to press with Cowell scoring for them in the first five minutes. Ardwick put in some good play and TAIT equalised. Rawtenstall gained a corner but BENNETT relieved. WATMOUGH was now conspicuous for Ardwick with some good tackling and from a free kick in front of goal O'BRIEN gave Ardwick the lead. Play was now greatly in favour of Ardwick but at half-time the score remained Ardwick two goals Rawtenstall one.

From the re-start Ardwick pressed but SCHOFIELD shot outside. Rawtenstall then took up the ball but LEATHER saved a grand shot. Ardwick attacked and TAIT scored .TAIT then added a fourth goal from a missed kick by one of the backs. Rawtenstall's goalkeeper saved some good shots and their forwards then attacked with Whittaker scoring for them. After a good bit of play by Ardwick,

HODGETTS headed through but was given off-side. Rawtenstall played up and Downes scored a third goal for them. The game ended with a win for Ardwick by 4 goals to 3.

4th January 1890   Ardwick 4 v Marple 0
Hyde Road
Ardwick team: Leather; Bennett and Heald; Watmough K. McKenzie © and Stanley; J. O'Brien 1 Hodgetts 3 Walker Howarth and Schofield.

    The game was played before a fair muster of spectators. The ground was in a very bad condition. Ardwick had much the best from the start. HODGETTS soon scored two goals and O'BRIEN added another before half-time when the score was Ardwick three goals Marple nil.

    In the second half Ardwick continued to have the best of the game and HODGETTS scored again. Ardwick won by 4 goals to nil.

11th January 1890   Manchester and District Challenge Cup   Second Round
Hyde Road 8,000

         Ardwick 5 v Gorton Villa 2

    The two local rivals, Gorton Villa and Ardwick met in the Second Round of the Manchester Cup. There had been great excitement during the week over the impending struggle, with the result that there was a record gate of about 8000 spectators present. Ardwick commenced play with ten men. Villa scored the first goal after ten minutes play but at half-time the score was Ardwick three goals Gorton Villa two.

    From the commencement of the second-half Ardwick had all the play, scoring two more goals. The game finished Ardwick 5 goals Gorton Villa 2.

18th January 1890   Ardwick 4 v Witton 3
Hyde Road 4,000
Ardwick team: Leather; Bennett and Heald; Watmough K. McKenzie © and Stanley; Hodgetts J. O'Brien W. Tait 2 Howarth 1 and Schofield 1

    Ardwick started the match and the game became very fast but Witton pressed and scored. HOWARTH and TAIT then scored for Ardwick but Witton equalised and the score at half-time was two goals each.

    In the second-half Ardwick pressed and TAIT gave Ardwick the lead before Witton again equalised. With only a short time remaining, SCHOFIELD scored the winning goal and Ardwick won by 4 goals to 3.

25th January 1890   Ardwick 6 v Newton Heath Central 1
Hyde Road
Ardwick team: Leather; Bennett and Heald; Watmough K. McKenzie © and Stanley; Hodgetts 1 J. O'Brien W. Tait 1 Howarth and Schofield (4 other goals)

    The teams met for the second time this season, Ardwick having won the first meeting at the Newton Heath Ground by two goals to nil. Newton Heath Central started the ball and made for the Ardwick end, LEATHER having to fist out. Ardwick then pressed and gained a couple of corners but nothing resulted. Ardwick penned their opponents and HODGETTS scored. Ardwick kept up the pressure and scored another goal. The Central's forwards came away with a grand run but the ball was placed behind. Ardwick again brought the ball down the field and gained a fruitless corner. At half-time Ardwick were leading by two goals to nil.

    On change of ends the Central at once made a rush on the Ardwick goal and scored. Ardwick then came away with a neat run and TAIT scored the third goal. Ardwick pressed their opponents and from hands in the goalmouth the ball was again placed between the uprights. Ardwick continued to have the best of the game and when time was called the score was Ardwick 6 goals Newton Heath Central 1.

    On 1st February 1890, Ardwick had a fixture against Newton Heath.

    The match was described *"as a meeting of two local clubs, one just rising to a higher standard in the football world whilst the visitors (Newton Heath) are nearly in the front rank"*.

1st February 1890   Ardwick 0 v Newton Heath 3
Hyde Road 7,000
Ardwick team: Leather; Bennett and Heald; Watmough K. McKenzie © and Stanley; Hodgetts J. O'Brien Tait Howarth and Schofield.

     Both teams were well represented. TAIT formerly of Newton Heath kicked off but Newton Heath first attacked and the ball was put out for a corner but nothing came of it. Ardwick now got the ball past the Newton Heath backs but Hay cleared out of danger. Newton Heath sent in shots and had hard lines in not scoring. Hands in favour of Ardwick looked dangerous but nothing resulted. A corner in favour of Newton Heath was put in very well by Farman and LEATHER saved in fine style. Farman next had hard lines, sending in a quick shot which LEATHER just managed to save. However, shortly afterwards Farman scored. Several corners then fell to Newton Heath and from one of these Craig scored the second. The Ardwick forwards then took the ball down field but nothing resulted. Newton Heath pressed and scored a third goal. HODGETTS next had a chance but the ball was shot wide. A corner fell to Newton Heath but this proved fruitless. Ardwick tried hard to score but could not break through the Newton Heath defence. At half-time the score was Newton Heath three goals Ardwick nil.

     On the re-start, the game was of a very even nature and each side had shots. The Newton Heath players gathered themselves together and some good shots were sent in by their forwards. A corner fell to Newton Heath but this proved fruitless. Newton Heath pressed and had considerable hard lines in not scoring with all the forwards having shots. No further goals were scored in the second half. The final result was Newton Heath 3 goals Ardwick nil.

    On 8th February 1890, J. Stanley and J. Hodgetts played for Manchester and District against Warwickshire. R. Walker and W. Tait took their places in the match against Irwell Springs.

8th February 1890   Ardwick 2 v Irwell Springs 0
Hyde Road
Ardwick team: Leather; Bennett and Heald; Watmough K. McKenzie © 1 and R. Walker; J. O'Brien 1 W. Tait Schofield Howarth and Gregson.

     Irwell started the ball in fine weather before a good number of spectators. Irwell at once began to press and forced a corner but the ball was placed behind. Irwell's right came away with a grand run but owing to bad shooting the ball was put outside. Ardwick attacked and the Irwell goalkeeper had to fist out. Irwell ran the ball up field and gained a corner but it proved fruitless. Ardwick began to press and scored but the goal was disallowed for off-side. At half-time neither side had scored.

     In the second half, TAIT started the ball for Ardwick. The ball was taken into the Irwell end and the Irwell custodian had to save several shots. Ardwick pressed their opponents and from a corner McKENZIE scored the first goal. Ardwick tried hard to add to their score but could not break through the Irwell defence. The Ardwick forwards then came away with a neat run and O'BRIEN scored the second goal. When time was called the score was Ardwick 2 goals Irwell Springs 0.

15th February 1890   Hooley Hill 4 v Ardwick 0
Hooley Hill
Ardwick team: Leather; Bennett and Heald; Watmough K. McKenzie © and Stanley; Tait J. O'Brien Hennefer and Howarth (10 players)

     Ardwick came without four of their team and started with nine men. Hooley Hill at once began to press and Cheetham scored.

     Ardwick were now strengthened but only played ten men until the finish. Hooley Hill had all the best of the play and finally won a poor game by 4 goals to nil.

22nd February 1890   Manchester and District Challenge Cup   Third Round
Hyde Road
                           Ardwick 5 v Hooley Hill 1
Ardwick team: Leather; Bennett and Heald; Watmough 1 K. McKenzie © and Stanley; Hodgetts J. O'Brien 1 Gregson Howarth 2 and Schofield 1.

     Ardwick quickly began to press and SCHOFIELD scored. Directly afterwards, HOWARTH, following some good passing, scored a second goal. WATMOUGH with a dashing run half the length of the field scored the third goal. HOWARTH doing some grand work scored again. At half-time the score was Ardwick four goals Holley Hill nil.

On resumption Hooley Hill pressed and scored a goal. Until the finish Ardwick kept up a complete bombardment on the Hooley Hill goal and O'Brien scored a fifth goal. The final result was Ardwick 5 goals Hooley Hill 1.

1st March 1890   Ardwick   6   v   Manchester   4
Hyde Road
Ardwick team: Leather, Bennett and Heald; Watmough McKenzie © and Stanley; Hodgetts 1 O'Brien 3 Callagan Howarth 1 and Schofield 1.

The Ardwick backs played badly and Ardwick players put the ball through their own goal on two occasions. SCHOFIELD then scored the first goal for Ardwick and HOWARTH and O'BRIEN also scored. At half-time the score was Ardwick three goals Manchester two.

Ardwick pressed at the commencement of the second half but could not score. Manchester quickly got a goal and then O'BRIEN scored two goals for Ardwick. Manchester again scored but Ardwick obtained a sixth goal through HODGETTS. Ardwick won by 6 goals to 4.

8th March 1890   Ardwick   13   v   Welsh Druids   1
Hyde Road
Ardwick team: Leather, Bennett and Heald; Watmough McKenzie © and Stanley 1; Callagan 1 O'Brien 3 Hodgetts 2 Schofield 3 and Howarth 2 (1 own goal)

HODGETTS started the game for Ardwick who at once went into the visitor's quarters and SCHOFIELD placed the ball between the uprights to score Ardwick's first goal. Some passing by the visiting forwards brought the ball to the Ardwick goal, but the defence was too strong. The ball was then transferred to the other end and Ardwick gained a corner but it proved fruitless. There was a neat run by O'BRIEN and HODGETTS scored the second goal. Following this Ardwick continued to press and STANLEY added a third goal. The visitors made a neat run but HEALD cleared with a good kick. Not to be denied the visitors kept up the pressure and gained a corner but it was put behind. At half-time the score was Ardwick three goals Welsh Druids nil.

No time was lost in changing ends. Ardwick pressed and HOWARTH shot over the bar. Shortly afterwards O'BRIEN succeeded in beating the visitors goalkeeper with an express short. The visitors were next conspicuous and LEATHER was called upon to use his hands. The Ardwick forwards then came again with a good run. O'BRIEN and HODGETTS with neat play brought the ball down to the visitor's goals and the visiting full back unfortunately put the ball through his own goal. Ardwick continued to have the best of the game and O'BRIEN and SCHOFIELD both scored two further goals; HODGETTS scored one further goal; HOWARTH scored two goals and CALLAGAN scored a goal with the Druids scoring one goal.

The final score was Ardwick 13 goals Welsh Druids 1.

The next match was against Everton from the Football League. The game was played with the aid of Wells Lights. Despite heavy rain all day, Everton were greeted with a hearty reception by a crowd of 5,000 spectators.

10th March 1890   Ardwick   0   v   Everton   3
Hyde Road 5,000
Ardwick team: Leather; Bennett and Heald; Watmough McKenzie © and Edwards; Bakewell (Derby County) Lea Hodgetts Stanley and Daft (Notts. County).

This was the first visit of Everton to Hyde Road. Mr Chesters Thompson kicked off in favour of the visitors, who at once made a raid on the Ardwick goal, forcing a couple of corners which were cleared. Play was transferred to the Everton end but Hannah relieved with a ponderous kick, placing the ball near the Ardwick goal and Brady scored the first goal for Everton. LEATHER, the Ardwick goalkeeper, had some tough shots to deal with but he was equal to the occasion and saved in a remarkable manner. The Ardwick left wing pulled together and forced a corner off Hannah which was easily dealt with. The Everton right wing attacked and Brady scored again. Both teams were now playing a fast game, each end being visited, but nothing tangible resulted. At half-time the score was Everton two goals Ardwick nil.

The second-half had barely commenced when the Everton forwards came away together and scored the third goal. Corners were now pretty frequent with each side pressing in turn. DAFT (on loan from Notts County) HODGETTS and BAKEWELL (on loan from Derby County) put in some capital forward play for Ardwick whilst the defensive play of Hannah and Doyle for Everton was very conspicuous. Millward and Brady of the Everton forwards were well looked after by HEALD and BENNETT and no further score took place. A good and fast game considering the state of the ground resulted in favour of Everton by 3 goals to nil.

15th March 1890 Bolton Wanderers Reserve 6 v Ardwick 0
Pike's Lane
Ardwick team: Leather, Bennett and Heald; Watmough McKenzie © and Stanley; Hodgetts O'Brien Howarth Schofield and Callagan

Ardwick commenced play and were kept on the defensive for some minutes though Sutcliffe had shots to save. At half-time Bolton led by three goals to nil.

The second-half was much in favour of Bolton who registered three more goals. The final score was Bolton Wanderers 6 goals Ardwick 0.

22nd March 1890   Manchester and District Challenge Cup   Fourth Round
Denton
Denton 1 v Ardwick 1
Ardwick team: Leather, Bennett and Heald; Watmough McKenzie © and Stanley; Hodgetts O'Brien Howarth Schofield and Callagan 1

The match was played before a vast crowd, a good proportion being partisans of Ardwick. At the commencement, each side attacked in turn. Denton then for a considerable time engaged the attention of the Ardwick defence but without being able to score. Ardwick's right wing was seen to advantage, but O'BRIEN was checked when dangerously near to goal. Denton then again dominated but LEATHER, BENNETT and HEALD in particular defended stubbornly. Denton were called upon to defend but there was misfortune for Ardwick when STANLEY sustained a serious injury and had to be assisted off the ground. Not to be daunted by playing in adverse circumstances Ardwick attacked through CALLAGAN and HODGETTS. The game up to the interval was of a fluctuating character, both sides attacking alternately. No goals were scored by half-time.

On resuming, Denton forced the pace and rushed the ball through the Ardwick goal, but the goal was disallowed for an infringement. Denton again attacked vigorously but HEALD relieved grandly and McKENZIE with a powerful kick set up CALLAGAN to score for Ardwick amidst tremendous applause. Stimulated by the reverse Denton attacked for a considerable time but their efforts were unavailing, due to the smart goalkeeping of LEATHER and the grand play of the Ardwick backs. However, eventually their exertions were rewarded with a goal by Plant. Ardwick then took up the running and HODGETTS succeeded in putting the ball through the Denton goal but the goal was disallowed. Ardwick had slightly the best of matters but they failed to score again and the game ended in a draw, Denton 1 goal Ardwick 1.

29th March 1890   Ardwick 2 v Heywood 0
Hyde Road 4,000
Ardwick team: Leather, Bennett and Heald; Watmough McKenzie© and Manning; Callagan Woodacre 1 Hodgetts Howarth 1 and Schofield.

Ardwick were without STANLEY who was still injured. Ardwick included WOODACRE late of Witton. HODGETTS kicked off for Ardwick and after some even play Heywood pressed in a most spirited manner and LEATHER saved a good shot from Ward. A free kick near to the Ardwick goal appeared dangerous but WATMOUGH relieved splendidly. HODGETTS with a fast dribble took the ball to the Heywood end, before Ardwick were again placed on the defensive by some good play by the Heywood forwards. A fine passing movement between HODGETTS and WOODACRE carried operations near to the Heywood goal but Gregory kicked away. HODGETTS then shot just over the cross bar. Subsequently the play and combination of both teams was of a very even and high character but neither side succeeded in scoring. When the interval arrived there was no score.

Ward started the second-half for Heywood but HODGETTS intercepted and passed to SCHOFIELD who after a good run centred to HODGETTS who shot over the bar. The game for a considerable time afterwards was decidedly in favour of Ardwick who kept their opponents strictly on the defensive, but Gregory and Singleton defended in a faultless style and McNab the Heywood goalkeeper on one occasion saved grandly. Ardwick pressed continuously and HOWARTH eventually scored with a grand shot. Shortly afterwards one of the visitor's forwards put the ball through the Ardwick goal but the goal was disallowed. WOODACRE then scored for Ardwick who won a splendidly contested game by 2 goals to nil.

5th April 1890   Ardwick   1   v   Royton   0
Hyde Road

Ardwick team: Leather, Bennett and Heald; O'Brien McKenzie © and Manning; R. Walker Woodacre Hodgetts 1 Howarth and Fergus.

There was a good attendance as both teams were still in the Manchester and District Challenge Cup. WATMOUGH and STANLEY were missing from the Ardwick team. Royton kicked off. Good combination play between HODGETTS and FERGUS took place near to the Royton goal but Dyer fisted out. Play was then of an even nature with the respective backs playing in capital style. At length a fine movement between WOODACRE HODGETTS and FERGUS resulted in play near to the Royton goal with a shot going over the bar. Royton exhibited good speed and combination and attacked vigorously but a good shot was repulsed by LEATHER. The play was subsequently in favour of Ardwick, Dyer on one occasion negotiating a grand shot from O'BRIEN but at half-time neither side had scored.

On resuming Royton made matters difficult for the Ardwick backs but were unable to score. At length Ardwick pressed and after O'BRIEN had shot just over the bar Royton conceded two corners which were fruitless. Royton's forwards then chose an excellent combination but their shooting was ineffectual. After the respective goalkeepers had made good saves, play was taken near to the Royton goalmouth but WOODACRE spoiled Ardwick's chance by handling the ball. Play was contested near the Royton goal, with a shot from HOWARTH going over the cross bar, whilst afterwards McKENZIE shot wide. The play was then of a very open character with HEALD and BENNETT playing well for Ardwick. Eventually HODGETTS scored for Ardwick and Ardwick won by 1 goal to nil.

7th April 1890   Chester St. Oswald's   3   v   Ardwick   1
Chester

St. Oswald's kicked off and immediately scored. Ardwick forced the play for a little while after this but were quickly forced back and before half-time St. Oswald's registered two more goals and were leading by three goals to nil.

In the second-half Ardwick were aided by the strong breeze, but despite the fact that they were continually on the attack they could only break through the St. Oswald's defence once when they scored. Ardwick worked hard to reduce their opponent's lead but had to finally retire beaten by 3 goals to 1.

12th April 1890 Manchester and District Challenge Cup Fourth Round Replay
Hyde Road
                    Ardwick   0   v   Denton   1

Ardwick team: Leather, Bennett and Heald; O'Brien McKenzie © and Watmough; Callagan Woodacre Hodgetts Howarth and Schofield.

These teams met to play off this undecided tie. The first meeting resulted in a draw of one goal each. Ardwick won the toss and played with the wind behind them. There was a large crowd which increased as time went on. Ardwick were first to the front and from a corner, SCHOFIELD kicked over. Holt for Denton made a good run and Plant sent in a shot but LEATHER cleared easily. Ardwick again pressed and from a corner play became very exciting in the Denton goalmouth but CALLAGAN finally kicked over. Denton had chances in the Ardwick goalmouth but the ball was eventually cleared and SCHOFIELD with the goal at his mercy kicked over. Even play followed up to half-time when there was no score.

The second-half opened evenly with each end being visited whilst long kicking by both teams took the place of the passing game. At last Denton pressed and a corner from Clarke was nearly rushed through, whilst Seddon sent a lightening shot just past the upright. O'BRIEN for the home team sent the ball well up into the Denton half and HODGETTS shot dropped on the bar. Denton now made a rush and were several times checked but from a throw in the ball was rushed through the Ardwick goal amidst great cheering. The rest of the game, which was played in semi-darkness, was all in favour of Ardwick who made strenuous efforts to equalise but failed. Denton won a good game by 1 goal to 0.

19th April 1890   Ardwick   1   v   Bolton Wanderers Reserve   3
Hyde Road

Bolton Wanderers Reserve started well scoring immediately. Play then became fast and even both ends being visited. At length HOWARTH equalised from a good pass by HODGETTS. Bolton then had slightly the best of the play and Rushton (who later in April went on trial to Ardwick) placed them in front and R. Turner also scored. At half-time the score was three goals to one in favour of Bolton Wanderers Reserve.

In the second-half, neither team scored. The final result was Bolton Wanderers Reserve 3 goals Ardwick 1.

21st April 1890   Ardwick 4 v Halliwell 3
Hyde Road 3,000
Ardwick team: Leather, Bennett and Heald; O'Brien 1 McKenzie © and Watmough; Callagan Woodacre Hodgetts 1 Howarth 2 and Schofield.

Play opened very fast and both ends were visited. A corner to Ardwick was cleared. The right wing of Halliwell then came away with the ball and Clark sent in a stinging cross shot from touch, which rebounded off the upright. Clark again shot, but LEATHER saved. After Fairclough had successfully kept out shots from HOWARTH and O'BRIEN, HODGETTS passed quickly to HOWARTH who scored. Again, Ardwick came and a shot from HODGETTS struck the upright and rebounded but HOWARTH was nearby and quickly popped the ball into the Halliwell goal. STANLEY next tried a long shot but Fairclough easily cleared. LEATHER gave a corner which Clark sent in and Mullin headed over. A spurt by the Ardwick right resulted in Hood kicking behind but nothing came of the corner. Considerable pressure was brought on the Ardwick goal, but the Ardwick defence was splendid. At half-time Ardwick were leading by two goals to nil.

On resuming, play was again exceedingly fast and Clark scored for Halliwell with a cross shot. Ardwick returned the assault, but Hood relieved and some passing by Halliwell ended in Mullin equalising the score. Still Halliwell forced matters and Ardwick conceded several corners which were all cleared. Ardwick then pressed and a capital shot by O'BRIEN just skimmed the bar. From a free kick by BENNETT, HOWARTH passed to HODGETTS who scored the third goal for Ardwick amidst cheers. From the kick off Ardwick again pressed and from a capital centre by WOODACRE, O'BRIEN scored the fourth goal. This roused Halliwell and Chadwick from mid-field sent in a long shot which just went under the bar, LEATHER failing in his attempt to reach it. A fast and exciting game finally ended in a win for Ardwick by 4 goals to 3.

26th April 1890   Ardwick 2 v Buxton 1
Hyde Road 2,000

The match was played in splendid weather. From a good run by Ardwick, HOWARTH put in a good shot which the Buxton goalkeeper saved. Buxton attacked but the ball went over. O'BRIEN had a shot at the other end but the goalkeeper fisted out. The Buxton forwards were now playing well and had slightly the best of it. The Buxton centre had a splendid chance to score but shot outside. The Ardwick forwards then brightened up and JOHNSON scored. Ardwick continued to have the best of matters but the game was rather slow. Buxton had a chance from hands in front of goal but shot badly. At half-time Ardwick were leading by one goal to nil.

In the second-half Buxton scored. Towards the finish Ardwick played a strong game and scored another goal. Ardwick won by 2 goals to 1.

In the last three weeks of the season, Ardwick played three further matches against Football League opponents: Burnley, Derby County and Blackburn Rovers. Ardwick also played two matches against local teams, West Manchester and Longsight.

28th April 1890   Ardwick 0 v Burnley 2
Hyde Road 1,500

The game was played in wet weather. Ardwick played two or three recruits and were also assisted by JONES McNEE and PATTON of Bolton Wanderers. A fairly even game resulted in a win for Burnley by 2 goals to nil.

The Ardwick committee, by way of experiment, gave trials to four new players: RUSHTON and McWHIRTER from Bolton Wanderers, WHITTLE from Halliwell and MACDONALD for the match against West Manchester.

Much excitement was caused by the meeting with West Manchester for they had not met before during the season and the last meeting, which took place in May 1889, was brought to an abrupt end owing to several of the players coming into contact with spectators. The score then stood at four goals to one in favour of West Manchester.

3rd May 1890   Ardwick 5 v West Manchester 1
Hyde Road 5,000
At the commencement, the play of Ardwick was of a decidedly superior character to their opponents and had it not been for the West Manchester goalkeeper they would have scored on several occasions. At length, West Manchester got in front of the Ardwick goal and they rushed the ball through and scored the first goal. The playing combination of the Ardwick team was superior to West Manchester but the goalkeeping of Richards was such that they were unable to score. At half-time West Manchester led by one goal to nil.
On resuming Ardwick continued to press and Richards effectively saved a swift high shot from MACDONALD. Then the services of both defences were required after which Ardwick continued with their aggressive tactics but their efforts were unrewarded. At length, the West Manchester forwards got away with a fine attack but Williams was unfortunate to head the ball over the Ardwick cross bar. Ardwick then dominated and MACDONALD equalised matters with a grand shot. Eventually McWHIRTER placed Ardwick ahead and a third goal was scored by RUSHTON shortly afterwards. West Manchester for a few minutes invaded the Ardwick end but with no success after which Ardwick completely disconcerted their opponents and WATMOUGH and McWHITER added fourth and fifth goals respectively. An appeal for an infringement against a sixth goal was answered in the affirmative. Ardwick won by 5 goals to 1.

12th May 1890   Ardwick 2 v Derby County 4
Hyde Road
This match was played on Monday evening before a good attendance. Derby County won by 4 goals to 2.

17th May 1890   Ardwick 8 v Longsight 2
Hyde Road

19th May 1890   Ardwick 1 v Blackburn Rovers 8
Hyde Road 4,000
Ardwick team: Leather; Bennett and Wilson; Stanley Whittle and Pearson; Rushton O'Brien 1 Hodgetts, Howarth and Moore.
Mr S. Chesters Thompson J.P. started the ball for Ardwick and the Rovers soon showed their superiority. Dewar put in a good shot which was saved; but Lofthouse scored shortly afterwards. Ardwick then ran down and HOWARTH put in a good shot which resulted in a corner, from which HODGETTS shot over. Ardwick continued to play well and HOWARTH had a good shot which just missed. Dewar then added a second goal for Rovers by heading through from a corner. At half-time the score was two goals to nil in favour of Blackburn.
In the second-half Ardwick attacked and from a foul in front of goal O'BRIEN scored with a fast shot. This was followed by a goal each for Campbell and Southworth for the Rovers. Ardwick then had hard lines, Lowe falling on the ball in goal. The Rovers were now playing a good game with their passing and shooting being superb. Walton, Southworth and Whitehead all scored. At the close, Ardwick who played remarkably well gave Lowe several strong shots to save, especially one from STANLEY. Blackburn won the game by 8 goals to 1.

Ardwick had continued to improve the team and had arranged matches against better opponents including several Football League teams: Everton, Burnley, Derby County and Blackburn Rovers.

Ardwick had played the majority of matches at Hyde Road and the club had been very well supported. As the Club gained in popularity, there were more detailed match reports with the team line-ups being published, particularly after the end of November 1889.

The club was becoming more ambitious and steps were taken towards the end of the season to strengthen the team with the signing of Rushton and McWhirter from Bolton Wanderers and Whittle from Halliwell.

Ardwick had made good progress during the 1889-90 Season in their efforts to become a leading club. Forty four matches were reported and Ardwick had won twenty eight; drawn two and lost fourteen of the games.

The team line-up was given in twenty one of the matches, excluding the matches with Everton (where some players from other clubs made guest appearances for Ardwick) and Blackburn Rovers (where a number of the players were on trial). In one of the matches against Hooley Hill, Ardwick only had ten players and in the match against Newton Heath Central the goalscorers are not known. Leather and Bennett played in all of the twenty one matches.

The players who had made the most recorded appearances for Ardwick in the twenty one matches were:

RECORDED APPEARANCES 1889-90	
Leather, F.	21
Bennett, P.	21
Heald, J.	20
Watmough, W.	20
McKenzie, K.	20
O'Brien, J.	20
Howarth, J.W.	20

The leading goalscorers were:

GOALSCORERS	
O'Brien, J.	16
Hodgetts, J.	14
Howarth, J.W.	12

There follows a summary of the season with details, where known, of reported matches, attendances, appearances and goal scorers. Ardwick entered the Manchester and District Senior Cup (MC) and the Lancashire Junior Cup (LJC).

SUMMARY
ARDWICK A.F.C. 1889-90

DATE		OPPONENT	RES	1	2	3	4	5	6
1889				7	8	9	10	11	
07-Sep	H	Darwen Rovers	L 3-5		P. Bennett				
14-Sep	A	Hurst	W 4-3		Bennett				
				J. O'Brien 2	J.Hodgetts 2	Hennefer			
21-Sep	H	Bacup	W 6-2				Watmough		
							J Howarth 2		4 goals *
28-Sep	H	Denton	W 4-2						J. Stanley
LJC 1			4000	O'Brien1	Hodgetts 1	H.Schofield1	Howarth 1		
05-Oct	A	Irwell Springs	L 0-3	F. Leather					9 players
12-Oct	A	Manchester Welsh	W 5-1	Leather	Bennett 1	McKenzie©			
LJC 2				O'Brien1	Hodgetts 2	Schofield 1	Gregson		
19-Oct	H	Rochdale Clifford	W 6-2						6 goals *
26-Oct	H	Farnworth Par. Church	W 8-1	O'Brien 1	Hodgetts 1	Schofield3	Howarth 1	Gregson 2	
			1500						
02-Nov	A	Manchester Clifford	W 6-1	O'Brien 2		Schofield 3	Howarth 1		J. Stanley
09-Nov	H	Heywood	D 1-1						
LJC 3		Central							
16-Nov	A	Marple	W 5-0						
23-Nov	H	Derby St. Luke's	W 3-2	Hodgetts	O'Brien	Hennefer 3			
30-Nov	H	Chester St. Oswald's	W 3-2	Leather	Bennett	J. Heald	Watmough	McKenzie ©	Stanley
			2000	Hodgetts 2	O'Brien	A.Booth	Howarth 1	Schofield	
07-Dec	H	Hooley Hill	W 7-1	Leather	Bennett	Heald	Watmough	J.Manning	Hart
				Hodgetts 1	O'Brien 3	Booth 2	Howarth 1	Gregson ©	
14-Dec	H	Royton	CANC.						
21-Dec	A	Newton HeathCentral	W 2-0	Leather	Bennett	Heald	Watmough	McKenzie ©	Stanley
				Hodgetts	O'Brien	W. Tait 1	Howarth	Schofield 1	
25-Dec	H	Derby Junction	L 2-5	Leather	Bennett	McKenzie©	Watmough	Hart	Stanley
			4000	Hodgetts	O'Brien 1	Walker	Hennefer 1	W. Tait	
26-Dec	H	Hyde	L 2-3		Bennett				
			4000	Hodgetts		W. Tait		Schofield 2	
30-Dec	H	Hurst	W 7-0	Leather	Bennett	Heald	Watmough	McKenzie ©	Stanley 2
				O'Brien 1	Hodgetts 3	W. Tait 1	Howarth	Gregson	
01-Jan	H	Rawtenstall	W 4-3	Leather	Bennett	Heald	Watmough	McKenzie ©	Stanley
1890				O'Brien 1	Hodgetts	W. Tait 3	Howarth	Schofield	
04-Jan	H	Marple	W 4-0	Leather	Bennett	Heald	Watmough	McKenzie ©	Stanley
				O'Brien 1	Hodgetts 3	Walker	Howarth	Schofield	
11-Jan	H	Gorton Villa	W 5-2						
MC 2			8000						
18-Jan	H	Witton	W 4-3	Leather	Bennett	Heald	Watmough	McKenzie ©	Stanley
			4000	Hodgetts	O'Brien	W. Tait 2	Howarth 1	Schofield 1	
25-Jan	A	Newton HeathCentral	W 6-1	Leather	Bennett	Heald	Watmough	McKenzie ©	J. Stanley
				J.Hodgetts 1	J. O'Brien	W. Tait 1	Howarth	Schofield	4 goals*
01-Feb	H	Newton Heath	L 0-3	Leather	Bennett	Heald	Watmough	McKenzie ©	Stanley
				Hodgetts	O'Brien	W. Tait	Howarth	Schofield	

Date	H/A	Opponent	Result						
08-Feb 1890	H	Irwell Springs	W 2-0	Leather O'Brien 1	Bennett W. Tait	Heald Schofield	Watmough Howarth	McKenzie©1 Gregson	R. Walker
15-Feb	A	Hooley Hill	L 0-4	Leather W. Tait	Bennett O'Brien	Heald Hennefer	Watmough Howarth	McKenzie©	Stanley 10 players
22-Feb MC 3	H	Hooley Hill	W 5-1	Leather Hodgetts	Bennett O'Brien 1	Heald Gregson	Watmough 1 Howarth 2	McKenzie© Schofield 1	Stanley
01-Mar	H	Manchester	W 6-4	Leather Hodgetts 1	Bennett O'Brien3	Heald Callagan	Watmough Howarth 1	McKenzie© Schofield1	Stanley
08-Mar	H	Welsh Druids	W 13-1	Leather Callagan 1	Bennett O'Brien 3	Heald Hodgetts 2	Watmough Schofield 3	McKenzie© Howarth 2	Stanley 1 1 own goal
10-Mar	H	Everton	L 0-3 5000	Leather Bakewell #	Bennett Lea	Heald Hodgetts	Watmough Stanley	McKenzie© Daft #	Edwards (# guests)
15-Mar	A	Bolton W. Reserves	L 0-6 5000	Leather Hodgetts	Bennett O'Brien	Heald Howarth	Watmough Schofield	McKenzie© Callagan	Stanley
22-Mar MC 4	A	Denton	D 1-1	Leather Hodgetts	Bennett O'Brien	Heald Howarth	Watmough Schofield	McKenzie© Callagan 1	Stanley
29-Mar	H	Heywood	W 2-0 4000	Leather Callagan	Bennett Woodacre 1	Heald Hodgetts	Watmough Howarth 1	McKenzie© Schofield	Manning
05-Apr	H	Royton	W 1-0	Leather R. Walker	Bennett Woodacre	Heald Hodgetts 1	O'Brien Howarth	McKenzie© Fergus	Manning
07-Apr	A	Chester St. Oswald's	L 1-3						
12-Apr MC4 R	H	Denton	L 0-1 4000	Leather Callagan	Bennett Woodacre	Heald Hodgetts	O'Brien Howarth	McKenzie© Schofield	Watmough
19-Apr	H	Bolton W. Reserves	L 1-3			Hodgetts	Howarth 1		
21-Apr	H	Halliwell	W 4-3 3000	Leather Callagan	Bennett Woodacre	Heald Hodgetts 1	O'Brien 1 Howarth 2	McKenzie© Schofield	Watmough
26-Apr	H	Buxton	W 2-1				O'Brien Johnson 1	Howarth	1 goal*
01-May	H	Burnley	L 0-2 1500						
03-May	H	West Manchester	W 5-1 5000	Rushton 1		McWhirter 2	Macdonald 1		Watmough1
12-May	H	Derby County	L 2-4						
17-May	H	Longsight	W 8-2						
19-May	H	Blackburn Rovers	L 1-8	Leather Rushton	Bennett O'Brien 1	Wilson Hodgetts	Stanley Howarth	Whittle Moore	Pearson

Captain: ©   Scorer(s) not known: *

RECORDED MATCHES 1889-90						
	P	W	D	L	F	A
Home	33	22	1	10	120	72
Away	11	6	1	4	30	23
Total	44	28	2	14	150	95

The Recorded Appearances Table is based upon the twenty one matches where the full team line-up was given and does not include the matches against Everton and Blackburn

RECORDED APPEARANCES 1889-90		
PLAYER	APPS.	GOALS
1. LEATHER,F	21	
2. BENNETT,P	21	
3. HEALD,J	20	
4. WATMOUGH,W	20	1
5. McKENZIE, K	20	1
6. O'BRIEN	20	16
7. HOWARTH,J.W.	20	12
8. HODGETTS,J	19	15
9. SCHOFIELD,H	16	7
10. STANLEY,J	15	3
11. TAIT,W	9	8
12. CALLAGAN,J	7	2
13. GREGSON,W.J.	4	
14. WALKER,R	4	
15. WOODACRE,W	4	1
16. MANNING,J	3	
17. HENNEFER,J	2	1
18. BOOTH,A	2	2
19. HART	2	
20. FERGUS,M	1	
Own goal		1

CHAPTER 14

ARDWICK ASSOCIATION FOOTBALL CLUB
1890-1891

Lawrence Furniss continued as Honorary Secretary.

Stephen Chesters Thompson, JP continued as President and John Allison was on the Committee.

Walter Chew

Walter Chew resigned from the Ardwick Committee in November 1890.

Walter Chew was there at the very beginning as a member of the St. Mark's Junior Cricket team in 1879. He played in the first football match against Macclesfield Baptist Church in 1880, when he was just fifteen years of age. He played for St. Mark's; West Gorton; Gorton and Ardwick. He was involved in the merger with Belle Vue Rangers and also played for that team prior to the merger. He led the negotiations for the Hyde Road Ground. He was involved in the administration of the Club and was Secretary of both Gorton and Ardwick.

Walter Chew still remained a supporter of the Club for the rest of his life. He devoted much of his life to football and served on the Committee of the Manchester and District Football Association (later the Manchester County Football Association) for sixty years from 1888 until the time of his death in 1948. He was Treasurer of the Association for forty six years.

In 1900, he was alloted shares in the Football Association which was a great honour.

In 1909, he was the recipient of the first long service medal issued by the Manchester County Football Association after completing twenty one years continuous service.

On 25th October 1934, at the Jubilee Banquet of the Manchester County Football Association, he proposed the toast to the clubs.

In June 1948, he was presented with a silver cigarette case to mark sixty years service with the Manchester County Football Association. This was regarded as one of the longest periods of service given by a Council member to any County Association.

In September 1948, Walter Chew died. In his obituary Walter Chew was described as one of the founders of Manchester City, but he was much more than that. In their book on the "History of the Lancashire Football Association" published in 1928, C.E. Sutcliffe and F. Hargreaves described Walter Chew as the "father" of the Club.

Walter Chew was certainly the most important member of the club during the first ten years from 1880 to 1890 and deserves the title of "Father of the Club"

The Football League which had been formed in 1888 was a great success. The Football Alliance and Lancashire League had followed in 1889.

In 1890 Ardwick had the opportunity of joining a new league "The Combination". Ardwick were proposed for membership but decided to withdraw. The Combination was formed and the first winners in 1890-91 were Gorton Villa. The other teams in The Combination were Macclesfield; Chester; Burton Swifts; Denton; Northwich Victoria; Hyde; Wrexham; and Leek. Burton Swifts and Northwich Victoria were later to be elected to the Football League.

Ardwick decided to continue to play friendly games and cup-ties. However they were now looking to build a much stronger side and were looking for sterner opposition.

In May 1890 Lawrence Furniss and John Allison, a prominent member of the Ardwick Committee, went to Scotland in search of talent. They were very successful and secured five Scottish players:

William Douglas	Goalkeeper	Dundee Old Boys

William Douglas

William Douglas was a very fine goalkeeper who was the first choice goalkeeper for Ardwick from September 1890 until 26th January 1894 when he was transferred to Newton Heath after Ardwick got into financial difficulties.

David Robson	Full-back	Ayr United
B. Campbell	Forward	Ayr United
Walter McWhinnie	Forward	Ayr United
Young	Forward	Glasgow Northern

Lawrence Furniss and John Allison were also able to sign eight other players from Lancashire clubs including six players from Bolton Wanderers:

J. Haydock	Full-back	Bolton Wanderers
John Milne	Half-back	Bolton Wanderers
A. McWhirter	Half-back	Bolton Wanderers
J. Pearson	Half-back	Bolton Wanderers
William McColl	Forward	Burnley
Walter Rushton	Forward	Bolton Wanderers
Daniel Whittle	Forward	Halliwell

David Weir	Forward	Bolton Wanderers

David Weir

David "Davie" Weir was one of the best forwards in the Football League and was an England International having played against Scotland and Northern Ireland in 1889. It seemed very strange that he should want to leave Bolton Wanderers who were one of the original members of the Football League in 1888 to play for Ardwick who were still playing friendly matches and cup-ties.

However, the following report appeared in a local newspaper on 25th May 1890:

"It is said that Weir, of the Bolton Wanderers, one of the most useful all-round players in the North of England, thinks of transferring his allegiance to Ardwick. A public house is said to be the bait with which this fish has been landed. He played for them last Wednesday, and managed to get injured."

David Weir was appointed captain.

Ardwick expended a sum of £600/£700 in buying a new team. The club had signed thirteen players (a goalkeeper; two full-backs; three half-backs and seven forwards).

The players from the previous season were all retained. Ardwick's players at the outset of the season were:

ARDWICK PLAYERS 1890-91
Goalkeepers:
Douglas, Leather and Warman;
Full-backs:
Robson, Haydock, Bennett and Heald;
Half-backs:
Milne, McWhirter, Whittle, J. Pearson and Watmough;
Forwards:
David Weir (captain), Rushton, Campbell, McWhinnie,
Young, McColl, Howarth, Hodgetts and O'Brien

Ardwick's colours were blue and white halved shirts with navy blue knickers (knee length shorts).

ARDWICK A.F.C. 1890-91
The players are not named on this photograph, but it is believed that the player in the centre of the three players on the back row is William Douglas, the goalkeeper, and that the player with the ball at his feet is the captain, David Weir.

Wonderful improvements had been made to the ground since the previous season. Twelve months previously the playing area was a miserable mixture of mud and filth. A sum of £600 had been expended in re-turfing and draining the pitch and in carrying out other improvements. The ground was now described as a green area in a wilderness of bricks, mortar and railway arches. Ardwick's Secretary, Lawrence Furniss, had arranged a very good fixture list although the great majority of the games were at home. The 1890-91 Season was to establish Ardwick as a leading club and at the end of the season they only just failed with an application to join the Football League.

Ardwick's first match of the season could not have been more difficult for it was against the Football League champions Preston North End. The match took place on Monday evening 1st September 1890 at Hyde Road Ardwick before a very good attendance of 6,000 spectators.

1st September 1890   Ardwick   0   v   Preston North End   6
Hyde Road 6,000
Ardwick team: Douglas; Bennett and Robson; Whittle Milne and McWhirter; Rushton McWhinnie Campbell Weir © Howarth

    Ardwick inaugurated the season at Hyde Road last evening against the Football League champions. The Mayor of Manchester got the ball "rolling" for Preston. After five minutes play, Brandon who was playing at centre scored the first goal. A few minutes later, Brandon scored a second goal, the ball going in off DOUGLAS, the Ardwick goalkeeper. Ardwick tried to attack but their efforts were to no avail. J. Drummond scored the third goal for Preston and at half-time Preston led by three goals to nil.

    On resuming WEIR rushed the ball downfield but shot behind. Preston again attacked the Ardwick goal and D. Ross scored the fourth goal. This was then followed by G. Drummond scoring a fifth goal and before the call of time Brandon added a sixth goal. Preston North End won by 6 goals to 0.

    The result drew the following comments:

"From the way Preston North End easily whipped Ardwick on Monday it does not look as if Ardwick has got such an incomparably superior team as the result of their summer's piratical efforts and expenditure of hard cash. The League champions of last season had no great amount of difficulty in winning by six goals to nil and what Ardwick may do against Witton and Bolton Wanderers will be awaited with considerable curiosity."

    The next match was on Saturday 6th September 1890 at Hyde Road against Witton, a Lancashire Club.

    Witton were to join the Lancashire League in the 1891-92 Season.

    Howarth lost his place in the Ardwick team to McColl. Campbell was replaced by Young. Only Bennett remained in the first team from the previous season.

6th September 1890   Ardwick   8   v   Witton   0
Hyde Road 3,000
Ardwick team: Douglas; Bennett and Robson; Whittle Milne and McWhirter; Rushton 2 McWhinnie 1 Young 1 Weir © 3 and McColl (1 own goal)

    WEIR kicked off for Ardwick in extremely hot weather. Witton were the first to attack but nothing resulted. Gradually Ardwick gained the upper hand but were unable to score principally through the excellent goalkeeping of Forrest. Eventually, however, McWHINNIE succeeded in scoring Ardwick's first goal. After the Ardwick backs had stopped a Witton attack WEIR McCOLL RUSHTON McWHINNIE and YOUNG tested Forrest with stinging shots. A clever piece of play by McCOLL enabled WEIR to score the second goal and RUSHTON scored a third goal. At half-time Ardwick led by three goals to nil.

    For some time after the resumption the game was evenly contested but eventually from a corner Ardwick scored a fourth goal when one of the visitors backs put the ball through his own goal. After McWHINNIE had struck the Witton upright with a terrific shot some clever play by MILNE RUSHTON and WEIR resulted in WEIR scoring Ardwick's fifth goal. RUSHTON then added the sixth goal YOUNG a seventh goal and WEIR an eighth goal for Ardwick who won by 8 goals to 0.

    The draw for the Lancashire Football Association Senior Cup and Junior Cup took place on 8th September 1890. Ardwick were in the Junior Cup Competition and drew a bye in the first round.

    On 8th September 1890, Ardwick played another Football League team when Bolton Wanderers were the visitors to Hyde Road.

8th September 1890   Ardwick 1 v Bolton Wanderers 5
Hyde Road 2,000
Ardwick team: Douglas; Haydock and Robson; Whittle Milne and Young; Rushton McColl McWhirter Weir © 1 and McWhinnie

   This match took place at Hyde Road on Monday afternoon in very warm weather. Ardwick started the game and the play was not very interesting until a magnificent run down the wing by WEIR resulted in him scoring the first goal. This roused the Wanderers and play became exceedingly fast without either side having an advantage. The Wanderers eventually equalised through Cassidy. WEIR and McWHINNIE then went close for Ardwick. At half-time the score was one goal each.
   In the second half despite the Wanderers playing with the sun in their eyes, Jarrett scored and then followed up with a third goal. The Wanderers had matters much their own way and from a scrimmage in front of the Ardwick goal Brogen scored the fourth goal and Cassidy followed with a fifth goal. Bolton Wanderers won by 5 goals to 1.

   The newspapers were still critical of Ardwick *"in thinking that it was possible to get a first-rate team together by the mere expenditure of money. It needed something more – labour, practice, patience, training, and coaching being as necessary as hard cash before they could compete with Preston North End and Bolton Wanderers."*

   On 13th September 1890 Ardwick played against Lancashire League opponents in Heywood Central at Hyde Road.

13th September 1890   Ardwick 7 v Heywood Central 0
Hyde Road 5,000
Ardwick team: Douglas; Haydock and Robson; Whittle Milne and Simon; Rushton 1 McWhinnie 3 McColl Weir © 3 and Jarrett

   WEIR kicked off but Heywood were soon on the attack and WHITTLE cleared with a long kick. Hands against Heywood proved fatal and after a scrimmage McWHINNIE scored. The Heywood forwards then pressed and sent in several stiff shots which DOUGLAS saved well. JARRETT and McWHINNIE by good passing put the Heywood goal in danger, and keeping up the attack RUSHTON scored the second goal for Ardwick. A minute later some good combined play by the Ardwick forwards resulted in WEIR scoring the third goal. Just before the interval WEIR scored again and at half-time Ardwick led by four goals to nil.
   Central restarted but Ardwick were soon in the ascendancy and McWHINNIE scored a fifth goal. WEIR supplemented this with the sixth goal. Central then held the upper hand for some time and after several unsuccessful attempts to score Horsefield shot but DOUGLAS saved well. Again, Ardwick proved to be masters of the situation, McCOLL sending in a lofty shot which Briscoe only partially cleared, McWHINNIE rushing up headed through the Central goal to score the seventh goal. Shortly afterwards McCOLL was compelled to retire having received a kick in the face and Ardwick were deprived of his services for the last 25 minutes of the game. Nevertheless, although playing in these adverse circumstances Ardwick clearly held their own and retired the winners by 7 goals to 0.

   On Monday 15th September 1890 Ardwick played Manchester at Hyde Road.

15th September 1890   Ardwick 2 v Manchester 0
Hyde Road 1,200
Ardwick team: Douglas; Robson and Bennett; Simon McWhirter Milne; Allen McColl Weir © 2 Jarrett and McWhinnie

   Manchester started the game and, for a time, interesting play ensued, but gradually Ardwick were careless and allowed Manchester to take advantage on several occasions but they did not score. After thirty minutes play WEIR scored for Ardwick. This seemed to enliven the proceedings somewhat and at half-time Ardwick led by one goal to nil.
   On restarting, Ardwick went off with a rush and would have scored several times but for the splendid goalkeeping of Earp. The Manchester backs played a grand game and several times repulsed the Ardwick attacks. WEIR eventually got in one of his express shots and notched the second goal. Loose play followed in front of Manchester's goal, but although shot after shot was sent in quick succession Earp kept his goal in tact. Ardwick won by 2 goals to 0.

On 20th September 1890 a local newspaper reported that *"Ardwick had an excellent list of fixtures and had a fine chance of making a name for themselves. Ardwick only play away from home half a dozen times, whilst they have twenty first and second class fixtures to be played at Ardwick. Today they are to be visited by Blackburn Rovers whilst next Saturday they go to West Manchester and if they win the latter match it will be "war to the knife" between the two Clubs".*

It was also reported that the Manchester and District Football Association had become affiliated to the Lancashire Football Association which strengthened their position for inflicting penalties for breach of rules.

The senior clubs in the Manchester Association included Ardwick, Denton, Eccles, Farnworth Parish Church, Heaton Park, Hooley Hill, Hurst, Hyde, Manchester, Newton Heath, Royton, West Manchester, Cheetham Hill and Stockport County.

The junior clubs included Ardwick Reserves.

20th September 1890   Ardwick   1   v   Blackburn Rovers   5
Hyde Road 7,000
Ardwick team: Douglas; Robson and Haydock; Milne Whittle and Simon; Weir © Rushton McColl McWhinnie 1 and Jarrett.

Blackburn Rovers were the FA Cup holders and they paid a visit to Hyde Road. During the morning rain had fallen heavily making the ground rather slippery. Southworth started the ball for Blackburn who took the ball into the Ardwick half but WHITTLE cleared with a good kick. A good run by JARRETT and McWHINNIE ended in Pennington fisting out. JARRETT then gave WEIR a splendid opportunity of scoring which opportunity was lost. After some good play by the Blackburn players Southworth scored the first goal for the Rovers. A good run by Campbell ended in that player shooting over the Ardwick goal. Good combined play by the Rovers forwards resulted in Campbell scoring the second goal with a lightening shot. A foul against the Rovers transferred play to the Blackburn end but MILNE shot over. Play was even for a time, but after some judicious play by the Ardwick forwards, the ball was brought down to the Rovers end and McWHINNIE with a swift shot scored the first goal for Ardwick. A long shot from McCOLL nearly added a second goal for Ardwick but the ball went just out. A free kick for the Rovers looked dangerous and Southworth scored the third goal for Blackburn. The Rovers then had a corner and with the aid of a strong wind Rovers added a fourth goal. DOUGLAS was kept busy for a time but proved equal to the occasion. At half-time Blackburn Rovers led by four goals to one.

WEIR started the second half and McCOLL sent in a splendid shot which just grazed the crossbar. A missed kick by ROBSON let in Lofthouse who scored with a beautiful shot giving DOUGLAS no chance. DOUGLAS was applauded for saving a swift shot from Walton. Ardwick then took the ball to the Blackburn end but when JARRETT had nobody to beat but the goalkeeper he unfortunately stumbled and the ball went out. A minute later WEIR had a good chance of scoring but missed. WEIR McWHINNIE and JARRETT ran the ball down to the Rovers end but JARRETT shot wide. A grand rush by WEIR and McCOLL looked dangerous but WEIR was pulled up almost under the posts. Blackburn Rovers won by 5 goals to 1.

In the match against Blackburn Rovers two of the Ardwick players, SIMON and JARRETT played as amateurs, but the others were all professionals.

In the first three weeks of the season Ardwick had played three Football League teams, Preston North End (League Champions); Bolton Wanderers and Blackburn Rovers (FA Cup holders). Whilst Ardwick had lost all three games, the Club was very ambitious. Ardwick next played West Manchester in the first game to be played away from Hyde Road.

27th September 1890 West Manchester 1 v Ardwick 3
Brooks' Bar 5,000
Ardwick team: Douglas; Haydock and Robson; Milne Whittle Simon; Weir © McWhinnie 2 Rushton 1 McColl and Jarrett.

    The match was played at the Hullard Hall Ground, Brooks' Bar. This is the first time the teams had met this season and there was a very large attendance of spectators, both sides being strongly represented. Ardwick kicked off but West Manchester were soon attacking and gave the Ardwick backs plenty of work, DOUGLAS saving in fine style. The Ardwick forwards finally came forward with some neat passing. WEIR put in a good centre which resulted in RUSHTON gaining the first goal. West were not to be denied and attacked the Ardwick goal but failed to equalise, Jarmen missing a good chance. O'BRIEN was next conspicuous with the ball at his toes, he made a good run down the wing and placed the ball in the goalmouth, but WEIR missed a golden opportunity. At half-time Ardwick led by one goal to nil.

    On resuming, WEIR blocked a kick by Jeffrey which gave Ardwick a chance and McWHINNIE notched the second goal. Ardwick still held the upper hand and sent in several shots but West's backs managed to save. McWHINNIE then scored with a lofty shot. West now played better and for the last few minutes sent in several shots with one from Gotheridge proving successful. Ardwick won by 3 goals to 1.

Ardwick now had a team which was too strong for most of the local junior teams. In October 1890, Ardwick signed:

W. Harvie	Full-back	Glasgow Northern

The next match was in the qualifying round of the FA Cup against Liverpool Stanley.

4th October 1890   FOOTBALL ASSOCIATION CUP   Qualifying Round
Hyde Road 3,000

Ardwick 12 v Liverpool Stanley 0

Ardwick team: Douglas; Harvie and Robson; Milne Whittle 1 Simon; McWhinnie 2 Hodgetts 2 Weir © 3 Campbell 2 and Rushton 2

    Ardwick showed good form and CAMPBELL scored with a splendid shot. There was some fine work by the right wing of RUSHTON and McWHINNIE which resulted in RUSHTON scoring the second goal. A third goal was then scored by McWHINNIE after some grand play. A clever shot by WHITTLE resulted in a fourth goal and a fifth goal was scored by McWHINNIE after the Stanley goalkeeper was out of his goal. Some clever play was put in by WEIR and a good attempt by HODGETTS just failed to score. At the interval Ardwick led by five goals to nil.

    On resuming a beautiful effort by WEIR resulted in a sixth goal. RUSHTON was then conspicuous and added a seventh goal. After more pressing by the Ardwick team and occasional spurts by Stanley, WEIR added an eighth goal and HODGETTS a ninth goal, both of these being gained in scrimmages. A tenth goal was gained by HODGETTS from a magnificent centre by McWHINNIE. The eleventh goal was scored by CAMPBELL and the last goal by WEIR. Ardwick won by 12 goals to 0.

Ardwick's next opponents were Bury who were the holders of the Lancashire Junior Cup and who finished as champions of the Lancashire League in 1890-91.

11th October 1890   Ardwick 1 v Bury 3
Hyde Road 6,000
Ardwick team: Douglas; W.P. Jones and Robson; Milne Whittle 1 and J. Pearson; Weir © Rushton Hodgetts Campbell and McWhinnie.

    CAMPBELL kicked off for Ardwick but the Bury forwards gained possession and with the Ardwick goal in imminent danger, Bourne shot rashly over the bar. After DOUGLAS had fisted out a good shot, RUSHTON and McWHINNIE were conspicuous with a fine run but on passing to HODGETTS he lost a fine chance by shooting wildly. Bury next took up the attack and after some smart play in front of the Ardwick goal, Fielding scored for Bury. Play was very open for some time. Eventually the Ardwick forwards got well away but WEIR missed a splendid opening at a critical moment. Bury then pressed and had it not been for ROBSON DOUGLAS and MILNE they would have scored on several occasions. RUSHTON was then compelled to leave the field for a few minutes having sprained his knees. Playing with only ten men, Ardwick were at once placed on the defensive and Fielding scored the second goal for Bury. Ardwick had attacks which were dangerous but Sharrocks cleared grandly. ROBSON performed similarly on behalf of Ardwick immediately afterwards. However the Bury forwards came again towards the Ardwick goal and Conway scored the third goal. At half-time Bury led by three goals to nil.

On resuming, Conway started for Bury who at once attacked and Ardwick were compelled to concede a couple of corners, following which DOUGLAS saved a terrific shot which was well cleared by JONES. At length the Bury forwards appeared like scoring but Conway headed over the bar. A good run by RUSHTON resulted in a corner to Ardwick and some smart play ended near the Bury goal with WHITTLE scoring for Ardwick. Subsequently play was greatly in favour of Ardwick but the superb defensive tactics of the Bury backs prevented any further score. Bury won by 3 goals to 1.

18th October 1890   Lancashire Junior Cup   Second Round
Hyde Road

Ardwick 6 v Heywood Central 2

Ardwick team: Douglas; Haydock and Robson; Milne 1 Whittle and J. Pearson; Weir © O'Brien McWhinnie McColl and McWhirter (scorers of 5 goals not known).

Ardwick had a bye in the first round. Ardwick had earlier beaten Heywood Central in a friendly by seven goals to nil. Ardwick were slightly handicapped by the absence of RUSHTON who was suffering from an injury. Ardwick won by 6 goals to 2.

The newspapers commented that *"Ardwick could now take the shine out of any Club of the calibre of Heywood Central (who were to finish in third place in the Lancashire League in 1890-91). Some of the Ardwick players seem to be able to play in almost any part of the field. McWHIRTER was removed from centre half to left wing for the match against Heywood Central and played a sterling game, whilst the forwards seemed to do well either in the centre or on the right or left wing as they are needed. MILNE played a capital game at half back and has not been in anything but first class form during the season. MILNE gained about the best goal ever seen on the Ardwick ground against Heywood Central."*

On 25th October 1890 Ardwick were due to play away at Halliwell in the next qualifying round of the FA Cup, but Ardwick decided to scratch. Instead, Ardwick played a home fixture against Higher Walton, who had achieved great success by becoming the first winners of the Lancashire League in 1889-90.

During October 1890, Ardwick also signed:

A. Pearson	Forward	Dundee Old Boys

A. Pearson played on the right wing with Weir.

25th October 1890   Ardwick 3 v Higher Walton 2
Hyde Road

Ardwick team: Douglas; Harvie and Robson; Milne J. Pearson and Whittle; Weir © 1 A. Pearson McWhinnie 1 McColl 1 and Rushton.

These teams met to decide their only engagement this season. McWHINNIE commenced play for Ardwick. After the home team had pressed, Higher Walton's forwards resisted all opposition and Fielding beat DOUGLAS with a good shot. At length, however, RUSHTON passed grandly to McWHINNIE, who headed a fine goal, thus equalising the scores. WEIR then almost scored after good work by MILNE and WHITTLE, and following this, McWHINNIE shot just over the cross bar. Ardwick were placed on the defensive by good work from J. Mather and Fielding but J PEARSON came to the rescue with a timely kick. For about ten minutes afterwards Higher Walton played with only ten men one of their players having sustained a kick on the ankle. Ardwick dominated up to the interval hitting the post on several occasions but at half-time the score remained at one goal each.

W. Mather restarted the game for Higher Walton and after DOUGLAS had saved his charge RUSHTON McWHINNIE and McCOLL tested the capabilities of the Higher Walton goalkeeper with express shots. Higher Walton attacked and W. Mather scored to give Higher Walton a lead of two goals to one. This unexpected reverse stimulated Ardwick who attacked severely but their opponents likewise defended stubbornly, conceding corner after corner and then packing their goal. As the game was drawing to a close McCOLL after a grand run dropped the ball under the Higher Walton bar thus equalising the scores. Higher Walton had a goal disallowed for some reason which was not apparent after which WEIR scored the third goal for Ardwick who won by 3 goals to 2.

On 1st November 1890 Ardwick had a home match against Warwick County who had been members of the Midland League in 1889-90.

1st November 1890   Ardwick 7 v Warwick County 0
Hyde Road
Ardwick team: Douglas; Harvie and Robson; Milne Whittle and J. Pearson; Weir © A. Pearson McWhinnie 2 McColl and Rushton 1 (4 other goals)

Hyde Road was in a very sodden condition following heavy rain. McWHINNIE started for Ardwick. Warwick's goal was put under pressure and from a grand centre by RUSHTON, A. PEARSON put the ball over the bar. Warwick mounted several attacks and Hall sent in a splendid shot which DOUGLAS saved. For a time play was chiefly confined in the centre but on Stanley obtaining possession the ball was taken down to the Ardwick end and Warwick had hard lines in not scoring. After some good combination play on the part of the Ardwick forwards, RUSHTON and McCOLL sent in some good shots which Hollis, the Warwick goalkeeper cleared. However, after a general scrimmage in the goalmouth McWHINNIE scored. A minute later RUSHTON headed through for Ardwick. At half-time Ardwick led by two goals to nil.

Restarting Warwick tried hard to score but a few minutes after the restart McWHINNIE notched the third goal for Ardwick. Warwick then made a determined attempt to score but the Ardwick defence proved equal to the occasion. Some uninteresting play followed with each side showing a lack of combination. The Ardwick team continued to have the better of the game and when time was called Ardwick won by 7 goals to 0.

On 3rd November 1890 Ardwick played away to Sheffield United, who were then in the Midland League.

3rd November 1890   Sheffield United 4 v Ardwick 2
Bramall Lane Sheffield
Ardwick team: Douglas; Harvie and Robson; Milne 1 Whittle and J. Pearson; Weir © A. Pearson McWhinnie McColl and Rushton (I own goal)

Ardwick with the disadvantage of a bright sun kicked off before a good attendance of spectators. In the first half Howell, Robertson and Watson each scored for United whilst a fourth goal accrued from a foul. In attempting to centre Groves put the ball through his own goal, and at half-time Sheffield United led by four goals to one.

After crossing over Ardwick pressed and were very unlucky in not scoring as WEIR kicked a goal which was disallowed on the grounds of offside. Midway through the second half ROBSON had to retire owing to a player falling upon him. Ardwick were then left with ten men but MILNE scored a second goal for Ardwick. The final score was Sheffield United 4 goals Ardwick 2.

On Saturday 8th November 1890, Ardwick played against Hyde who had been founder members of the Lancashire League in the 1889-90 Season. Hyde had decided to change leagues and became founder members of The Combination in the 1890-91 Season.

8th November 1890   Ardwick 4 v Hyde 2
Hyde Road 4,000
Ardwick team: Douglas; Harvie and H. Golding; Milne J. Pearson and Weir ©; Rushton McColl 2 McWhinnie 1 A. Pearson 1 and McWhirter.

RUSHTON was injured within a few minutes of the start. DOUGLAS was beaten by McNab with a swift shot from the right baffling him. At half-time Hyde led by one goal to nil.

In the second half, WEIR put in good work for Ardwick and from his pass McWHINNIE equalised. McCOLL kicked a splendid goal to put Ardwick in front but Hargreaves equalised for Hyde. A. PEARSON scored to put Ardwick ahead and within two minutes of the end of the game McCOLL added a fourth goal. Ardwick won by 4 goals to 2.

Ardwick now had the first of three fixtures against Newton Heath. This was the first occasion during the season that Newton Heath opposed a local Club and much interest was manifested in the match as Ardwick had already met and beaten both Manchester and West Manchester. Ardwick had been doing very well during the year but had been playing friendly and cup matches whereas Newton Heath were members of the Football Alliance.

15th November 1890   Newton Heath   4   v   Ardwick   1
North Road, Newton Heath 10,000
Ardwick team: Douglas; Harvie and Robson; J. Pearson Whittle and Milne 1; Rushton McColl O'Brien McWhinnie and A. Pearson

The ground was in a rather sodden condition owing to recent rain. Evans kicked off for Newton Heath and Ardwick were at once on the attack. An exciting scrimmage took place in the Newton Heath goal but Clements cleared. Newton Heath had several shots at DOUGLAS and Farman opened the scoring for Newton Heath with a shot close in the goalmouth. Ardwick came into the Newton Heath half with some neat passes and a corner kick resulted but came to nothing. Newton Heath's right wing was again to the fore and Farman put in a grand run and centred finely but Evans missed a good opportunity. Ardwick were now being pressed and corner kicks were taken but WHITTLE changed the attack to the other end. Newton Heath returned to the attack and Ramsey scored with a long shot which DOUGLAS was unable to reach. The play was then mostly in mid-field until Newton Heath again got through the Ardwick defence with Stewart easily putting the ball through the posts when DOUGLAS was out of position. This reverse aroused Ardwick who rushed away with some neat passing by McWHINNIE and McCOLL. The ball afterwards was transferred to the left where O'BRIEN passed to MILNE who scored Ardwick's only goal. At half-time Newton Heath led by three goals to one.

Ardwick started the second half and DOUGLAS had at once to save a shot from Farman. The Ardwick forwards were not to be denied and made determined efforts but the Newton Heath backs were in fine form and prevented any scoring. Play was again taken into Newton Heath half but Doughty relieved. Stewart then gave DOUGLAS a shot which he failed to clear properly and Sharpe rushed up and scored the fourth goal for Newton Heath. Newton Heath won by 4 goals to 1.

Ardwick played Heywood of the Lancashire League, having earlier in the season played and beaten Heywood Central, also members of the Lancashire League.

22nd November 1890   Ardwick   7   v   Heywood   3
Hyde Road 2,000
Ardwick team: Douglas; D. McCarthy and Harvie; J. Pearson Whittle and Weir © 2; McWhinnie 3 McColl McWhirter A. Pearson and O'Brien 2

The above teams met for the first time this season. Ward started the ball for Heywood who at once carried the ball into the Ardwick quarter but McWHINNIE repelled the attack. The Heywood goal was put in danger but O'BRIEN'S kick was misdirected and the ball went wide. From the subsequent goal kick play was transferred into the Ardwick half but HARVIE cleared. WHITTLE was next conspicuous with some fine play and after some lively proceedings had taken place in the Heywood goal the ball was kicked out. Ardwick continued to press but failed to break through due to the good defence of Heywood. On Dunn getting possession he made a splendid sprint and after gaining a couple of corners Dunn scored the first goal. From the re-start Chadwick and Langham were called upon to defend and WEIR lost a good opportunity of scoring when he had the goal practically at his mercy. Ardwick now tried hard to gain a goal and obtained a couple of corners which did not prove beneficial. At this point of the game rain came down in torrents and Ardwick who wore white shirts, were almost black with the mud. The Ardwick forwards were able to press the ball dangerously near the Heywood goal and WEIR scored but the goal was disallowed for off-side. Just before half-time McWHINNIE equalised and when half-time was called the score was one goal each.

WEIR restarted and the home team at once assailed the Heywood goal and before five minutes had elapsed O'BRIEN gained the lead amidst cheers. WEIR scored the third goal and a good attempt by O'BRIEN added a fourth goal. Still Ardwick pressed and McWHINNIE added the fifth and six goals. Heywood got a look in and obtained their second goal. WEIR scored the seventh goal for Ardwick and Heywood scored again. Ardwick won by 7 goals to 3.

On 29th November 1890, Ardwick played a cup-tie against Skerton.

29th November 1890　　　　Lancashire Junior Cup　　　　Third Round
Hyde Road

Ardwick   3   v   Skerton   0

Ardwick team: Douglas; Bennett and Harvie; Milne Whittle and J. Pearson; Weir © McWhinnie McColl 1 A. Pearson and O'Brien 2

Ardwick started the match before a poor attendance. Skerton had to work hard to keep their goal in tact and seldom invaded Ardwick territory. Eventually, O'BRIEN managed to score for Ardwick from a clever pass by McWHINNIE. McWHINNIE worked hard and shot very cleverly as did RUSHTON. Before the interval McCOLL added a second goal for Ardwick who led at half-time by two goals to nil.

In the second half, WEIR almost scored on resuming play. McWHINNIE distinguished himself by clever shooting. O'BRIEN was responsible for the third goal after some smart work at both ends. Whiteside had to save repeatedly. Play was taken to the Ardwick end for a time and HARVIE and BENNETT cleared well. DOUGLAS too had to use his fists when Skerton attacked. Ardwick had all the best of the play at the finish and the final score was Ardwick 3 goals Skerton 0.

In December 1890, Ardwick signed:

William Lambie	**forward**	**Queen's Park**

William Lambie

William Lambie played for Ardwick during the 1890-91 Season and also for a short time in 1892. He was a very good centre forward and whilst with Queen's Park he played for Scotland on nine occasions between 1892 and 1897:
　　Northern Ireland 1892, 1895, 1896 and 1897
　　Wales 1893
　　England 1894, 1895, 1896 and 1897

William Lambie made his debut for Ardwick in the next match against Darwen who were members of the Football Alliance.

6th December 1890   Ardwick 2 v Darwen 2
Hyde Road
Ardwick team: Douglas; Harvie and J. Pearson; Milne Weir © and Whittle; Rushton McColl W. Lambie1 A. Pearson and O'Brien 1.

LAMBIE, Ardwick's new centre forward, kicked off. Darwen were the first to attack and a good run by Entwistle was stopped by WEIR who carried the ball into the Darwen half. Some combined play on the part of the Ardwick forwards gave O'BRIEN a chance but he shot outside. A minute later LAMBIE got possession and made a splendid spurt and after passing to RUSHTON the ball was rushed through the goal by LAMBIE, amidst cheers. From the restart, Darwen attacked and after a neat run Entwistle equalised with a splendid shot which DOUGLAS did not have the slightest chance of stopping. Keeping up the pressure, Darwen continued to attack and DOUGLAS was called to save a hot shot from Nightingale. Entwistle then had a good run and on centring DOUGLAS mulled the ball and Marsden rushed the ball through for Darwen to put them in the lead. Ardwick put Darwen under pressure and Walton in the Darwen goal saved a splendid shot by WEIR. This was followed by Ardwick putting further shots at the Darwen goalkeeper which were fisted out. Ardwick continued to have the best of matters and after a combined run O'BRIEN equalised. At half-time the score was two goals each.

In the second half, Ardwick took up the attack and experienced hard lines in not scoring on several occasions, the ball either striking the upright or rolling into touch. A missed kick by Leech almost let in RUSHTON but he was charged into touch. A minute later Darwen pressed and the ball was placed through the goal posts but it was disallowed. When time was called the score stood at Ardwick 2 goals Darwen 2.

On Saturday 13th December 1890 Ardwick played a home match against Derby Junction who played in the Midland League.

13th December 1890   Ardwick 5 v Derby Junction 0
Hyde Road 2,000
Ardwick team: Douglas; J. Pearson and Harvie; Weir © Milne and Whittle; Rushton 1 McColl Lambie 2 A. Pearson 1 and O'Brien (1 own goal)

During the first fifteen minutes Ardwick played without the services of RUSHTON and WHITTLE, but despite this they forced Derby on the defensive. O'BRIEN and A. PEARSON, the Ardwick left wing forwards played superbly and they troubled the Derby defence. At length O'BRIEN passed to RUSHTON who scored the first goal. Ardwick continued to press and Brommage the Derby goalkeeper was continually fisting away shots. Derby rarely crossed the centre line. LAMBIE was tripped and Ardwick were awarded a free kick which was well placed by MILNE enabling A. PEARSON to score the second goal for Ardwick who led at half-time by two goals to nil.

On the resumption Derby took up the attack but Miller shot rashly over the cross bar. McCOLL and RUSHTON then gave Brommage two shots to save. Ardwick continued to attack and RUSHTON gave LAMBIE a pass and he hit a terrific shot under the Derby crossbar. O'BRIEN on receiving a pass from LAMBIE struck the post with at good shot. Later Ardwick were awarded a free kick and Brommage was rushed through his goal with the ball in his possession, the referee allowing Ardwick a goal. Shortly afterwards some splendid passing between the home forwards resulted in LAMBIE scoring the fifth goal for Ardwick. Towards the end of the game Derby Junction did have several attacks but they were repulsed by WEIR and HARVIE. The only occasion DOUGLAS handled the ball was within a few minutes of time being called. Ardwick won by 5 goals to 0.

On Christmas Day, Ardwick played at Hyde Road against Stoke who had not been re-elected by the Football League after finishing bottom in the 1889-90 Season and who were now playing in the Football Alliance.

Stoke were to be champions of the Football Alliance in the 1890-91 Season and were re-elected to the Football League for the following season.

25th December 1890   Ardwick 0 v Stoke 0
Hyde Road 5,000
Ardwick team: Douglas; Weir © and Harvie; Whittle McWhirter and J. Pearson; McWhinnie McColl Lambie A. Pearson and O'Brien.

    Stoke kicked off at 11:30am. Ardwick immediately obtained a corner but Dunn getting possession ran down the field and put in a good shot which WEIR cleared well. Play became very fast and another corner to Ardwick was unproductive. Baker then rushed through and when close to goal, he tried hard to score but the ball hit the post and rebounded into play. The Stoke forwards through erratic shooting failed to take advantage on several occasions and from a long scrimmage in the home goal McWHIRTER cleared well. Each side strove hard to get the lead but the backs on both sides played well. Just before half-time, Stoke put the ball through the Ardwick goal but it was clearly off-side and the goal was disallowed. At half-time there was no score.

    In the second half there was some fast play but the game ended in a goalless draw.

On Boxing Day, Ardwick played Blackpool South Shore at Hyde Road.

26th December 1890   Ardwick 0 v Blackpool South Shore 4
Hyde Road 2,000
Ardwick team: Douglas; Weir © and Harvie; Whittle McWhirter and J. Pearson; McWhinnie McColl Lambie A. Pearson and O'Brien.

    South Shore started the game and immediately attacked but when they looked like scoring McWHIRTER came to the rescue and cleared. Keeping up the pressure South Shore again attacked the Ardwick goal, and from a scrimmage in the Ardwick goal the ball was rushed through. Roused by this reverse, Ardwick attacked the South Shore goal but without result. Ardwick continued to press and through the efforts of McWHINNIE, the ball was transferred to the South Shore end, but McWHINNIE shot wide. South Shore forced DOUGLAS to concede a corner which was unproductive. After DOUGLAS had fisted out a couple of shots the ball was again rushed through the Ardwick goal. From the restart McWHINNIE obtained possession and brought the ball well down but shot outside. South Shore continued to have much the best of matters and DOUGLAS had to work hard but acquitted himself creditably, saving repeatedly. At this point Ardwick had the great misfortune to lose two of their players who were disabled and could not take any further part in the game. At half-time South Shore were leading by two goals to nil.

    WEIR restarted the game for Ardwick and A. PEARSON took the ball to the South Shore end but the ball was cleared. With two men short Ardwick during the latter portion of the game were outplayed and South Shore scored two further goals. South Shore won by 4 goals to 0.

The next day, Ardwick played Southport Central of the Lancashire League.

27th December 1890   Ardwick 2 v Southport Central 0
Hyde Road 2,000
Ardwick team: Douglas; Harvie and Robson; Milne Whittle J. Pearson; McWhinnie McColl 1 Lambie A. Pearson 1 and Rushton.

    Following some very exciting play, Ardwick gained a corner and McCOLL scored. No further goals were gained prior to the interval when Ardwick led by one goal to nil.

    On restarting Central attacked but ROBSON defended well and cleared the ball to RUSHTON who very nearly scored. ROBSON checked another attack by Central, but in doing so he fell hurting his leg and had to retire. A. PEARSON added a second goal following fine play by McCOLL. The final score was Ardwick 2 goals Southport Central 0.

On New Years Day, Ardwick arranged a home match against West Bromwich Albion of the Football League and there was a very good attendance. **W. Milarvie** at full back made his debut for Ardwick against West Bromwich Albion (he is not to be confused with Robert Milarvie who played on the left wing for Newton Heath and who later joined Ardwick)

1st January 1891   Ardwick 2 v West Bromwich Albion 2
Hyde Road 7,000
Ardwick team: Douglas; Milarvie and Robson; McWhirter J. Pearson and Whittle; O'Brien A. Pearson Lambie 1 Weir © and Rushton 1.

    The Hyde Road ground was in good condition and Groves started the game for the Albion before a very good attendance. From a neat run by Bassett and Woodall, DOUGLAS had to save. The

Ardwick forwards then attacked but LAMBIE and A. PEARSON shot outside. Groves was noticeable with some nice play for the Albion but McWHIRTER robbed him of the ball on several occasions. Ardwick attacked and J. PEARSON put in a long shot from half-back which Reader fisted out but RUSHTON met the ball and scored the first goal for Ardwick amidst tremendous applause. Soon afterwards Woodall equalised for Albion and Groves gave Albion the lead with a fast low shot which struck the upright and went through. Reader was called upon to save a shot from LAMBIE and Reader had to concede a corner from a good shot by O'BRIEN. O'BRIEN was prominent with a good run from which LAMBIE equalised. The score at half-time was two goals each.

Ardwick restarted and O'BRIEN caused Reader to kick out. RUSHTON tried hard to screw the ball through but Reader and Horton saved luckily. Albion then attacked and Woodall had a shot which went outside. The Ardwick forwards were now playing a spirited game and Reader had to save a stinging shot from O'BRIEN. After some even play in midfield Groves got through but MILARVIE robbed him beautifully. The Albion forwards now tried to force the game but WEIR was very safe. LAMBIE was next conspicuous with a shot which went just over. A fine game ended in a draw with each side scoring 2 goals.

The following day Ardwick had a home match against Newton Heath and **H.Davidson** made his debut.

2nd January 1891   Ardwick 1 v Newton Heath 1
Hyde Road
Ardwick team: Douglas; Weir © and Milarvie; J. Pearson Whittle and Davidson; McColl Lambie O'Brien McWhinnie and A. Pearson (goal scorer not known)

Stewart started the ball for Newton Heath, and early in the game Newton Heath had several attacks DOUGLAS being applauded for saving a hard shot from Ramsey. Ardwick then pressed and Slater repelled a hot shot from LAMBIE. For a short time Newton Heath besieged the Ardwick goal but without any tangible result. RUSHTON and McWHINNIE were instrumental in carrying play to the Newton Heath end but Clements relieved the pressure. Shortly afterwards Newton Heath forwards caused some anxiety to the Ardwick backs and after a severe tussle in the Ardwick goalmouth Farman scored amidst cheers. Newton Heath continued to attack and DOUGLAS was applauded for some fine goalkeeping saving a splendid shot from Stewart. Just before half-time a thick mist gathered over the ground and it was difficult for the spectators to distinguish the players. At half-time Newton Heath led by one goal to nil.

LAMBIE restarted for Ardwick. The fog at this point was so dense that it was nearly impossible to see across the ground and it was only at intervals that the spectators could see any play. Ardwick then scored. However when the mist continued to thicken time was called owing to the fog, the score being 1 goal each.

The next day Ardwick had a home match against Paisley St. Mirren. Ardwick kept the same team save that McCOLL replaced RUSHTON.

3rd January 1891   Ardwick 0 v Paisley St Mirren 1
Hyde Road 2,500
Ardwick team: Douglas; Weir © and Milarvie; J. Pearson Whittle and Davidson; McColl Lambie O'Brien McWhinnie and A. Pearson.

This was St. Mirren's first match at Hyde Road. St Mirren attacked and DOUGLAS had to deal with a good shot from McBean. The St Mirren forwards treated the spectators to some fine passing and obtained a corner, but this came to nothing. From a goal kick, Ardwick pressed and WEIR was applauded for a fine long shot which Cameron, the St Mirren goalkeeper just saved. McWHINNIE and McCOLL were conspicuous with a good run and just before half-time O'BRIEN had the goal practically at his mercy but missed his kick and the ball went into touch. Half-time was called with no goals having been scored.

LAMBIE restarted and the ball was given to O'BRIEN who made a splendid sprint finishing with a good shot which was headed out. St Mirren pressed severely and DOUGLAS was deservedly applauded for the fine manner in which he kept the St. Mirren forwards from scoring. LAMBIE made a good run along the centre and Cameron had to fist out a couple of shots. A corner fell to Ardwick and DAVIDSON who had been playing a good game throughout experienced hard lines in not scoring, the ball going just out. With only a few minutes to go, St Mirren were let in by WEIR and scored a decisive goal. St Mirren won by 1 goal to 0.

On 10th January 1891, Ardwick played against Chirk who were the Welsh Cup holders.

10th January 1891   Ardwick 2 v Chirk 1
Hyde Road 3,000
Ardwick team: Douglas; Milarvie and Weir ©; J. Pearson Whittle and McWhirter; O'Brien1 A. Pearson Lambie 1 Milne and McWhinnie.

Chirk attacked but MILARVIE was prominent with a good kick and he cleared his lines. McWHINNIE got possession and running along the right wing he got within scoring distance but without result. Chirk then had a turn in attacking and caused the home defence some anxiety but DOUGLAS saved in fine style. LAMBIE had a good run and passed to A. PEARSON who had a chance of scoring but he waited too long and one of the Chirk backs came to the rescue. At half-time neither side had scored.

Ardwick re-started and at the commencement Chirk had to play with ten men as G. Griffiths had been injured. There was then some good combined play from the Ardwick forwards and after a general scrimmage in the Chirk goal O'BRIEN scored the first goal for Ardwick. A. Griffiths was applauded for some tricky work which resulted in him equalising for Chirk. The Chirk forwards kept up the pressure on the Ardwick defence and WEIR and MILARVIE defended stubbornly and cleared all kinds of shots. LAMBIE was then to the fore with a good run and a missed kick by one of the Chirk backs gave him an easy opening to score the second goal for Ardwick. There was some good work by A. Griffiths for Chirk but DOUGLAS fisted out a missed kick by WEIR. When the whistle sounded Ardwick had won an evenly contested game by 2 goals to 1.

On 12th January 1891, the Football League passed a resolution that none of the affiliated clubs should play against Ardwick, because they had "poached" J. Walker from Burnley. The matter was resolved by Ardwick signifying their willingness to re-transfer Walker to his former club Burnley and the boycotting notice was rescinded by the League on 13th February 1891.

Ardwick's next opponents were Derby Midland from the Midland League.

17th January 1891   Ardwick 4 v Derby Midland 2
Hyde Road
Ardwick team: Douglas; Milarvie and Robson; J. Pearson Whittle and McWhirter; Weir © 3 Milne McWhinnie 1 A. Pearson and Rushton.

Midland kicked off and Storer got in a long shot which DOUGLAS was unable to cope with to give Midland the lead. From a free kick for Ardwick taken by MILNE, McWHINNIE headed through and equalised. WEIR added a second goal for Ardwick with a splendid low shot and followed it with a third goal from a fine pass by WHITTLE. Before the interval Ardwick scored two other goals but they were disallowed for off-side. At half-time Ardwick led by three goals to one.

Immediately after restarting DOUGLAS had to make a save. Midland continued to attack and Rose after many tries succeeded in scoring Midland's second goal. Some clever work by McWHINNIE resulted in WEIR scoring for Ardwick. Nothing further took place and Ardwick won by 4 goals to 2.

There were reports in the newspapers of a threatened split in the Football League and the following report appeared on 24th January 1891:

"Blackburn correspondent to the Sporting Contemporary Newspaper reports the recent ruling of the Football League, and more particularly the decisions of that body with respect to the games to be replayed and the division of gate money have caused the greatest dissatisfaction in football circles. The vagaries of the League Executive have undoubtedly given rise to much adverse criticism and a rumour is afloat which emanated from a most reliable source – that the Lancashire Clubs may possibly secede and form a league of their own. It would not be difficult to do this for out of Preston North End, Everton, Blackburn Rovers, Bolton Wanderers, Accrington, Burnley, Sunderland, Bootle, Darwen, Newton Heath, Ardwick, Bury and one or two other clubs which are rapidly coming to the front a

Northern League could be made almost immediately which would create as much interest as the present Football League does. The question is, we understand under consideration, and in the event of certain circumstances taking place a meeting of Lancashire Clubs in the League will be held to decide on what course of action to take. The secession of the Lancashire Clubs from the League would be a serious blow to the Midland Clubs for it is generally accepted that the Northern teams are the ones which draw the money."

Whilst nothing came of the suggested "Northern League" it must have been very encouraging for Ardwick that they were now being regarded as a senior club. This justified the decision of the Ardwick Committee to build a new and much stronger team during the season and to play friendly matches against the bigger and more established Clubs in the North and in the Midlands. If Ardwick had joined The Combination they would have only been playing against local teams of a lesser standing.

Ardwick played Burslem Port Vale from the Midland League.

24th January 1891   Ardwick   3   v   Burslem Port Vale   2
Hyde Road 1,000
Ardwick team: Douglas; Milarvie and Robson; J. Pearson Whittle and McWhirter; Weir © 1 Milne McWhinnie A. Pearson 1 and Rushton 1.

After heavy showers which had prevailed during the previous few days the ground was exceedingly difficult for the players. McGuinnis kicked off for Port Vale who took up the attack. McGuinnis got the ball and made a good sprint. After a series of passes McGuinnis scored the first goal for Port Vale. From the restart McWHINNIE made a good run along the right and centring WEIR put in a good shot which the Port Vale goalkeeper only partially saved and WEIR ran in to equalise. RUSHTON was then prominent with a good run but when he had the opportunity of scoring he put the ball over the bar. Port Vale attacked but DOUGLAS was equal to the Port Vale efforts and a shot from Ash was cleverly dealt with by DOUGLAS. At half-time the score was one goal each.

In the second half there was a heavy shower. The Ardwick players were first to attack and after McWHINNIE and RUSHTON had indulged in some judicious passing RUSHTON gave Ardwick the lead. Ardwick kept up the pressure and after several unsuccessful attempts A. PEARSON scored Ardwick's third goal. Port Vale retaliated and after a good run by Ditchfield, McCalton scored Port Vale's second goal. Ardwick forwards attacked and both RUSHTON and McWHINNIE had good shots. McGuinnis got possession of the ball and after a good run his shot beat DOUGLAS but it was disallowed for an off-side infringement. Ardwick won by 3 goals to 2.

A week later Ardwick had a return match against Blackpool South Shore who were to join the Lancashire League at the end of the 1890-91 Season.

31st January 1891   Ardwick   4   v   Blackpool South Shore   1
Hyde Road 3000
Ardwick team: Douglas; Milarvie and Robson; J. Pearson Whittle and Milne; Weir © 3 A. Pearson Lambie 1 McColl and McWhinnie.

LAMBIE started the ball and after a few minutes play WEIR scored a splendid goal. Roused by this reverse South Shore made a spirited attack but their efforts were spoiled by Wilson who shot outside when he had the goal practically at his mercy. Not to be denied South Shore were again to the fore, and after a combined run, the Ardwick goal was again placed in danger and a misunderstanding by the Ardwick backs allowed South Shore to equalise. McCOLL made a neat run and after a series of passes WEIR added another goal. At half-time Ardwick led by two goals to one.

On resumption of play, South Shore pressed but could not score. Some lively proceedings then took place near to the South Shore goal and Ardwick obtained three consecutive free kicks within five yards of the goalmouth, all of which proved abortive. Nelson for South Shore sent in a splendid shot which hit the crossbar and rebounded into play. Ardwick attacked and WEIR after receiving a pass from A. PEARSON scored the third goal. Shortly afterwards WEIR centred to LAMBIE who added the fourth goal. Ardwick won by 4 goals to 1.

On 7th February 1891, Ardwick played Bury in the Fourth Round of the Lancashire Junior Cup Competition. Bury were the holders of the Cup.

7th February 1891   Lancashire Junior Cup   Fourth Round
Ardwick   4   v   Bury   3

Hyde Road 10,000

Ardwick team: Douglas; Milarvie and Robson; J. Pearson Whittle and Milne; Weir © 1 A. Pearson Lambie 1 McWhinnie 1 and McColl 1.

There was a very big attendance which included a large number from Bury who had arranged three special trains for their supporters. LAMBIE kicked off and WEIR missed a fine opening. McCOLL when he had the Bury goal at his mercy shot wildly over the crossbar. Almost immediately afterwards taking advantage of a throw in at the Bury end McCOLL made amends for this mistake by scoring the first goal for Ardwick amidst tremendous cheering. Ardwick maintained a decided advantage for some time and MILNE crossed to McWHINNIE, who scored the second goal for Ardwick. A couple of minutes later LAMBIE passed to WEIR who added the third goal with a grand cross shot. At half-time Ardwick led by three goals to nil.

Bury kicked off in the second half. McCOLL dribbled and then centred to LAMBIE who shot a few feet outside the upright. Scowcroft sent in a lofty shot for Bury which DOUGLAS just managed to clear. Following this DOUGLAS had to concede a corner from a shot by Flint. N. Conway scored Bury's first goal from the corner. Bury then had a free-kick which was well taken and Whiteside rushed the ball through the Ardwick goal. The Cup holders continued to attack and from a corner Bury equalised, amidst tremendous cheering. Five minutes from time, amidst a scene of the wildest excitement, Ardwick forwards took the ball down to the Bury goal and LAMBIE scored the fourth goal which proved to be the winning goal for Ardwick. Thus ended the most exciting game ever witnessed in the Ardwick enclosure with Ardwick wining by 4 goals to 3.

On 14th February 1891, Ardwick were drawn away to Denton (who were members of The Combination) in the first round of the Manchester Cup.

14th February 1891   Manchester Senior Cup   First Round
Denton   1   v   Ardwick   5

Denton 3,000

Ardwick team: Douglas; Milarvie and Robson; Milne 1 Whittle and J. Pearson; Weir © 2 A. Pearson Lambie 2 McWhinnie and McColl.

LAMBIE kicked off before a good attendance of 3000 spectators, 2000 of whom had come from Ardwick. After some pressure from Ardwick, LAMBIE scored from a pass by WEIR. Play remained in the Denton half for most of the time. From a corner, WEIR scored again for Ardwick and MILNE added a third with Ardwick thoroughly outplaying Denton. At half-time Ardwick were leading by three goals to nil.

On restarting Denton played down hill and put in more effort but it was to no avail. LAMBIE scored a fourth goal for Ardwick. Denton then obtained their first corner and struck the post. Plant was playing well for Denton but the forwards were very weak. Grand passing by LAMBIE and McCOLL resulted in WEIR scoring the fifth goal. The Denton team were outclassed and were seldom dangerous but towards the end Brown rushed through for Denton and scored. The final result was Ardwick 5 goals Denton 1.

On 21st February 1891 Ardwick played in the Semi-Final of the Lancashire Junior Cup against Hindley. The match was played at West Manchester's ground at Whalley Range before a very good attendance.

21st February 1891   **Lancashire Junior Cup**   Semi-Final
Ardwick   1   v   Hindley   0

Whalley Range 5,000

Ardwick team: Douglas; Milarvie and Robson; Milne J. Pearson and Whittle; Weir © 1 A. Pearson Lambie McWhinnie and McColl.

In the first half neither side scored. On restarting Hindley almost scored. McCOLL distinguished himself a little later with a splendid centre. WEIR then shot the ball through for Ardwick but the goal was disallowed for off-side. LAMBIE gave McWHINNIE a fine chance but he missed. From a fine shot by McWHINNIE, Howcroft conceded a corner but nothing came of it. A corner on the right was well put in for Ardwick but Prendagast cleared. PEARSON caused Howcroft to handle the ball and he came within an ace of scoring. Eight minutes from time, PEARSON gave WEIR a chance and WEIR scored the only goal of the game. Ardwick won by 1 goal to nil.

Whilst Ardwick were beating Hindley in the Lancashire Junior Cup, the Ardwick Reserves were playing away at Hyde and lost by four goals to two. The reserves contained many of the players who had been in the Ardwick first team in the previous season and the team was: Leather; Bennett and Golding; Davidson, McWhirter, Watmough; Hodgetts, Rushton, Campbell, Hennefer and Anderson. Davidson and Hodgetts scored for the Reserves. Rushton (24), McWhirter (18), Davidson (15) and Bennett (8) played many matches for the first team during the season.

On 19th February 1891 Ardwick signed:

Joseph Davies	Forward	Chirk

Joseph Davies

Joseph Davies was the first Ardwick player to play international football whilst an Ardwick player and played for Wales against England and Scotland in 1891. He made eleven international appearances for Wales between 1889 and 1900 including an appearance against England in 1896 whist a Manchester City player. He played in several positions in the forward line for Ardwick from October 1891 until January 1894.

Joseph Davies made his debut in the match against Newton Heath on 28th February 1891 and he took the place of A. Pearson.

28th February 1891   Ardwick   1   v   Newton Heath   3
Hyde Road   11,000
Ardwick team: Douglas; Milarvie and Robson; Whittle H. Davidson and Milne 1; Weir © J. Davies Lambie McWhinnie and Rushton.

From the kick-off Ardwick had the better of matters but after ten minutes Farman scored for Newton Heath. Later in the first half Craig and Stewart forced the ball through the Ardwick goal after McWHINNIE had scored an off-side goal for Ardwick. MILNE shot a splendid goal for Ardwick, LAMBIE accounting for Slater. At half-time Newton Heath led by two goals to one.

Resuming Ardwick pressed but could not score. Ramsey scored a good goal for Newton Heath. LAMBIE scored for Ardwick but this was not allowed for off-side. Towards the finish Ardwick made desperate attempts to score but Newton Heath won by 3 goals to 1.

On 7th March 1891, Ardwick played against Birmingham St Georges.

7th March 1891   Ardwick   4   v   Birmingham St Georges   1
Hyde Road
Ardwick team: Douglas; Milarvie and Robson; Whittle 1, Davidson and Milne 1; Weir © 1 McWhinnie Lambie 1 McColl and Rushton

    The game opened in a most exciting fashion for almost immediately after the kick-off LAMBIE ran the ball down the field and after a series of passes LAMBIE beat Kenyon in the Saints goal at close quarters. The Saints produced some good play with Shore at centre forward, in particular doing some fine work and when close in Daley equalised. The Saints forwards were now playing a fine combined game and DOUGLAS and the Ardwick backs were frequently troubled. McWHINNIE received the ball from MILARVIE, in a good position for scoring, but shot high over the bar. Ardwick continued in the Saints half and WHITTLE, who was playing a splendid game, scored the second goal for Ardwick. DOUGLAS then defended the Ardwick goal in fine fashion. At half-time Ardwick led by two goals to one.

    After the interval the Saints were first to press and a brilliant run by Shore was only stopped by DOUGLAS throwing the ball away. Shortly afterwards both WEIR and DAVIDSON nearly scored. Ardwick then headed by WEIR made a determined attack and LAMBIE after some good work gave the ball to WEIR who beat Kenyon to score Ardwick's third goal. WEIR was again to the fore with a good run but his shot went wide. Some exciting scrimmages next ensued in the Saints goalmouth but Ardwick were unable to break through the Saints defence. Just before time MILNE added a fourth goal for Ardwick who won the game by 4 goals to 1.

On 7th March 1891 Joseph Davies played at outside right for Wales who lost to England by 4 goals to 1.

On 13th March 1891 a Football League sub-committee meeting was held in Birmingham and it was decided to recommend that for the next season the league should consist of thirty six clubs to compete in three "classes" of twelve each. The league thus constituted would be governed by a committee composed of two representatives from the clubs in class 1 and one from each of the other classes. The competition would be a Cup for the first class and Shields for each of the other two. At the end of the season the bottom team in class 1 would play off with the top team of class 2 and the bottom of class 2 with the top of class 3. The last four clubs in the league would retire each year but would be eligible for re-election. The scheme met with the general approval of the representatives and was to be recommended to the Football League at an early meeting. This recommendation was not taken up by the Football League but if it had, there was a possibility that Ardwick would have become a Football League Club in 1891.

On 14th March 1891 Ardwick played against their local rivals West Manchester in the semi-final of the Manchester & District Senior Cup. West Manchester were members of the Lancashire League.

14th March 1891   Manchester and District Cup   Semi-final
Manchester Athletic Ground, Old Trafford
                             Ardwick   4   v   West Manchester   1
Ardwick team: Douglas; Milarvie and Robson; Whittle Davidson and Milne; Weir © 1 McWhinnie 1 Lambie McColl and Rushton (2 other goals)

    The semi-final of the Manchester Senior Cup was played before a good muster of spectators. LAMBIE kicked off for Ardwick. West were the first to attack but WHITTLE relieved. MILNE getting possession ran the ball well down but the ball went over the bar. Ardwick continued to have the best of matters and Ardwick scored (the scorer was not recorded). West's goal was again in danger and after a severe struggle in the goalmouth McWHINNIE added the second goal. From the kick-off Ardwick again troubled their opponents but Stones (the West Manchester goalkeeper who was later to play for Ardwick) proved himself a good custodian and cleared all kinds of shots. WEIR was prominent with a good run and after a series of passes WEIR beat Stones with a lightening shot. This did not discourage the West team, Shore running along the left wing centred and the ball hit the cross bar and rebounded away. At half-time Ardwick led by three goals to nil.

In the second half, West Manchester were first to press but bad luck and the strong Ardwick defence prevented them from scoring. Ultimately, J. Angus (who later played for Ardwick) ran down with the ball and after a severe scrimmage in the goalmouth Shore scored the first goal for West, amidst cheers. This seemed to encourage West Manchester and Allison had hard lines with a shot which hit the crossbar. Siddeley then got the ball and sent in a nice shot. DOUGLAS in trying to fist it out was charged by Siddeley and blows were exchanged, a scene which was speedily stopped by the referee. Ardwick scored a fourth goal and won by 4 goals to 1.

On Saturday 21st March 1891 Ardwick appeared in the final of the Lancashire Junior Cup which was played at Preston. There was a great deal of interest in the final, and an excursion was run by the Railway Company to enable a large number of the Ardwick supporters to travel.

21st March 1891   Lancashire Junior Cup Final
Deepdale, Preston

Ardwick   1   v   Blackpool   3

Ardwick team: Douglas; Milarvie and Robson; J. Pearson Whittle and Davidson; Weir © Milne Lambie1 McWhinnie and McColl.

Pittaway kicked off for Blackpool before a large number of spectators. Ardwick were the first to press but it was only for a short time. Stanley of Blackpool cleared well to Tyrer who ran the ball down the field and after a series of passes Barrow scored amidst enthusiasm. Ardwick now pressed and LAMBIE equalised to loud cheers. Blackpool made a regular bombardment of the Ardwick goal, but they were met with a strong defence. Ultimately, Robson cleared and at the other end Ardwick nearly scored. Blackpool made strenuous efforts to score and eventually Tyrer got his second goal to put Blackpool in the lead. A short stoppage was caused in consequence of Tyrer being injured. He soon recovered and the game was resumed. Blackpool scored another goal and at half-time Blackpool were leading by three goals to one.

In the second half LAMBIE restarted but no goals were scored and Blackpool won by 3 goals to 1.

The local newspapers were not impressed with Ardwick's performance in the final. They commented that Blackpool had been far too clever for them and had been carefully trained for the event. Blackpool had played the better football and the Ardwick defence had not been satisfactory. There was also criticism that Ardwick had so often played on their own ground that they suffer when playing away and that they did not do themselves justice by a long way in the final. This was the last season Ardwick were to play in the Lancashire Junior Cup for they were now an established club and from 1891-92 they played in the Lancashire Senior Cup

In March 1891, Ardwick signed:

Hugh Morris	Forward	Chirk

Hugh Morris played for Ardwick from March 1891 until 1st December 1893. He was later to play for Wales when he was with Sheffield United, Manchester City and Grimsby Town. He played for Wales on three occasions between 1894 and 1897 (he was a Manchester City player when he played against England in1896). He played at outside left for Ardwick but later moved to insde right.

Hugh Morris made his debut on the left wing in the match against Crewe Alexandra of the Football Alliance on Good Friday 27th March 1891.

27th March 1891   Ardwick   6   v   Crewe Alexandra   5
Hyde Road 5,000
Ardwick team: Douglas; Bennett and Robson; McWhirter Weir © 2 and Davidson; J. Davies McWhinnie 1 Lambie 2 Milne and Morris (1 other goal)

    LAMBIE kicked off and Ardwick immediately went on the attack, Gee the Crewe goalkeeper fisting out a shot from MILNE. From a throw in, DOUGLAS gave Crewe a corner but Cartwright kicked wide. McWHIRTER twice stopped Crewe attacks. McDuff passed well and Crewe scored their first goal when the ball rebounded off BENNETT. Shortly afterwards, McWHIRTER got possession and centred to LAMBIE, who equalised. Lewis then ran right through the Ardwick defence but DOUGLAS took the ball from his toes. Not to be denied Lewis put Crewe ahead with a beautiful shot. Even play followed until LAMBIE again equalised. At half-time the score was two goals each.

    Price restarted for Crewe who played well and added two goals very quickly. Ardwick aroused much enthusiasm by smart play in which McWHINNIE scored. BENNETT then missed his kick and let in McDuff who added the fifth goal for Crewe who led by five goals to three. From now on up to the close, the Crewe goal was heavily bombarded, Ardwick scoring from a scrimmage and WEIR scoring two goals afterwards to put Ardwick ahead amidst loud applause. Ardwick won by 6 goals to 5.

    On Easter Saturday, 28th March 1891 Ardwick played against the very famous Glasgow Celtic who were visiting Manchester for the first time. Ardwick engaged a brass band for the occasion and there was a very good attendance.

28th March 1891   Ardwick   2   v   Glasgow Celtic   7
Hyde Road 6,000
Ardwick team: Douglas; Milarvie and Robson; McWhirter 1; Weir © and Davidson; J. Davies, McWhinnie, Lambie, Milne and Morris (1 other goal)

    Ardwick kicked off and Celtic soon forced a corner from DOUGLAS which was cleared by MILNE. Bell then had to fist out and McWHINNIE headed just outside. After a good run by McCOLL, LAMBIE missed an easy chance. The ball was then taken to the Ardwick end by Campbell and Dowds scored. Some good passing by the Celtic forwards was heartily cheered. From a grand centre by DAVIES, McWHITER equalised. Celtic soon added a couple of goals, one from a scrimmage and the other by Dowds. At half-time Celtic led by three goals to one.

    On restarting Celtic soon showed their superiority in every part of the game, their passing being beyond description. Dowds added the fourth and from a corner ROBSON put the ball through his own goal. A most one sided game finally ending Celtic 7 goals Ardwick 2.

    After the defeat at the hands of Celtic, Ardwick's next Easter match was against Partick Thistle.

    The Ardwick Committee made several alterations in their team, the most noticeable being that DAVIES was moved from the right wing to centre.

30th March 1891   Ardwick   3   v   Partick Thistle   3
Hyde Road
Ardwick team: Douglas; W. Milarvie and Robson; H. Davidson Weir © 1 and McWhirter; Rushton Davies 1 Morris McWhinnie and J. Milne. (1 other goal)

    Ardwick were the first to press McWHINNIE heading in beautifully, but Marshall was there and threw away splendidly. A combined run by the Partick forwards resulted in the ball being taken in close proximity to the Ardwick goal and DOUGLAS was deservedly applauded for fisting out a low shot when severely pressed. For a time play was chiefly confined to mid-field but ultimately Marshall was called upon to defend his goal. A neat run by RUSHTON brought the ball well down and a good centre was well met by WEIR who banged the ball through the Partick goal, a feat which was loudly cheered. DOUGLAS was for a long time kept busy with all kind of shots being well negotiated. Marshall was now called upon to save a stinging shot from DAVIES. Partick made strenuous efforts to equalise and after a combined run, Partick drew level. For some time play continued to remain in the Ardwick half but without any further result. At half-time the score was one goal each.

DAVIES restarted for Ardwick and only a few minutes had elapsed when DAVIES scored a second goal. Patrick now tried hard to rub off this reverse but they were met with a strong defence and their numerous attempts were for a long time useless. Eventually the game resulted in a draw Ardwick 3 goals Partick Thistle 3.

The match against Glasgow Celtic showed how far Ardwick had progressed. They were now able to arrange a fixture with one of the leading Clubs in Britain and whilst they had been heavily beaten, they did well against Partick Thistle who were one of the founder members of the Second Division of the Scottish League in 1893-94.

On 4th April 1891, Ardwick played Bury who were champions of the Lancashire League in 1890-91.

4th April 1891   Bury   2   v   Ardwick   4
Bury
Ardwick team: Douglas; Weir © and Robson; J. Pearson Whittle and Davidson; J. Davies 1 McWhinnie 2 Lambie 1 Milne and Morris.

    DAVIDSON placed a free kick finely and DAVIES scored a grand goal for Ardwick. Bury pressed strongly and Plant equalised through a misunderstanding between DOUGLAS and ROBSON. At half-time the score was one goal each.

    On resuming, Ardwick pressed and McWHINNIE headed through the Bury goal from a corner kick. Lowe the Bury goalkeeper then saved a good shot from DAVIES but LAMBIE headed the ball through. The Bury forwards ran down and after a scrimmage in front of the Ardwick goal the ball was forced through. Ardwick then scored a fourth goal through McWHINNIE. Ardwick won by 4 goals to 2.

Two days later Ardwick had a home match against Sheffield United and **T. Warman** made his debut in goal for Ardwick.

6th April 1891   Ardwick   4   v   Sheffield United   1
Hyde Road
Ardwick team: Warman; Robson and Weir ©; Davidson Milne and McWhirter; McWhinnie 1 Davies 1 Lambie 1 McColl and Morris 1.

    United were the first to attack and were immediately driven back. This however did not prevent United from coming again and Watson scored. MORRIS then equalised. United attacked and had hard lines in not getting through but there was no denying the fact that the ground was all against good play. Ardwick appeared to revel in the mud and LAMBIE scored a second goal. After Crawford and Watson had shots at the other end McWHINNIE scored the third goal for Ardwick. Ardwick were having all the best of the game and at half-time Ardwick led by three goals, to one.

    In the second half DAVIES got a fourth goal. Ardwick continued to attack but nothing further resulted. Ardwick won by 4 goals to 1.

A few days later Ardwick played a return match against Heywood Central of the Lancashire League.

11th April 1891   Heywood Central   3   v   Ardwick   0
Heywood
Ardwick team: Warman; P. Bennett and Robson; Milne Whittle and Davidson; Davies McWhinnie Lambie McColl and Morris.

    The Central commenced up the incline and had hard lines in not scoring. They promptly got a couple of corners which yielded nothing. Soon afterwards however Webster scored with a brilliant shot. Mackay recorded a second goal and Critchley a third. At half-time Heywood Central led by three goals to nil.

    In the second half play was very evenly divided. Both teams were repeatedly within an ace of scoring. Both goalkeepers defended finely and their performances were enthusiastically applauded. About fifteen minutes from time one of the Ardwick players was hurt and had to retire. The game resulted in a win for Heywood Central by 3 goals to 0.

On 18th April 1891 Ardwick played their great rivals Newton Heath in the Final of the Manchester and District Cup. The final was at West Manchester's Ground at Whalley Range. The crowds poured in for the final and there were probably 10,000 assembled even though there had been a rugby match earlier in the day. Ardwick made some positional changes with WEIR going to centre forward and BENNETT to full back.

18th April 1891 **MANCHESTER & DISTRICT CUP FINAL**
Whalley Range 10,000

ARDWICK 1 v NEWTON HEATH 0

Ardwick team: Douglas; Bennett and Robson; Milne Whittle and Davidson; J. Davies McWhinnie Weir © 1 Lambie and McColl.

WEIR kicked off for Ardwick and they at once raced away, Felton stopping a good shot from LAMBIE at the expense of a corner which was then cleared. Neat play by Sharpe and Milarvie for Newton Heath resulted in Milarvie gaining a foul against BENNETT but nothing resulted. WEIR then passed wide to DAVIES who sharply returned the ball. WEIR got in a lightening shot which completely beat Slater in the Newton Heath goal. Deafening cheers greeted the Ardwick goal. Play now slackened. Ardwick had somewhat the best of matters and both teams indulged in rough play until the referee called all the players together and severely cautioned them. Some good combined play by Ardwick nearly resulted in DAVIES scoring on two occasions. Ramsey spoiled a grand chance for Newton Heath by shooting over. DOUGLAS neatly handled a good shot from Sharpe and when WHITTLE transferred play to the other end LAMBIE and McCOLL were pressing until the referee blew the whistle for half-time. At half-time Ardwick led by one goal to nil.

On resuming play, Stewart went to centre forward and Newton Heath tried hard to equalise, but a corner was easily got away by MILNE. LAMBIE was noticeable with two shots in succession grazing the bar. WEIR repeatedly robbed Stewart before he could shoot and all the efforts of Newton Heath were unavailing. The Ardwick men played a capital combination and at full-time Ardwick had beaten Newton Heath by 1 goal to nil to win the Manchester Cup for the first time.

The Manchester Senior Cup was still a prestigious cup competition and it was a very good achievement on the part of Ardwick to win the cup for the first time, particularly against their local rivals, who had won the Manchester Cup on four occasions. Two days later Ardwick played Nelson at Ardwick.

20th April 1891   Ardwick 1 v Nelson 1
Hyde Road 2000

Ardwick team: Douglas; Bennett and Robson; Milne McWhirter and Davidson; Davies McWhinnie Hodgetts Lambie 1 and McColl.

The match was played on a Monday evening. HODGETTS set the ball rolling for the home team who at once began to press. DAVIES and McWHINNIE put in some good play and the Nelson goalkeeper saved the danger. The game was fairly fast but some of the Ardwick team were completely off colour. DAVIES was again prominent and from his centre LAMBIE headed the first goal. This seemed to rouse Nelson who put in some spirited play and Squire equalised. The game was pretty even but at half-time the score was one goal each.

In the second half, Nelson began to press and gained two corners but nothing resulted. The Ardwick forwards attacked and McWHITER almost scored, Fletcher saving at the expense of a corner, but nothing resulted. When time was called the game ended in a draw with each side scoring 1 goal.

This match was **HODGETTS** last appearance for Ardwick. He had first played for Gorton in the 1886-87 Season and had played for Ardwick in the following four seasons, becoming Ardwick's first professional. He was the last of the Gorton players to play for Ardwick

Ardwick had started the season with a home match against Preston North End which they had lost by six goals to nil. Ardwick arranged another match with Preston, again at Ardwick. The Preston team was fully represented. The Ardwick Brass Band was in attendance and on stepping onto the ground the Preston players were very well received.

25th April 1891   Ardwick 0 v Preston North End 2
Hyde Road
Ardwick team: Douglas; Weir © and Robson; J. Pearson Whittle and Davidson; Davies Milne Lambie McWhinnie and McColl.

In the first half Ardwick were pressed severely by Preston and WEIR scored an own goal. At the interval Preston North End led by one goal to nil.

In the second half DAVIES had a brilliant run and his final shot was well meant, but it skimmed the cross bar. Keeping up the pressure DAVIES again experienced hard lines when the Preston goalkeeper just managed to save his shot. After Ardwick had had several unsuccessful attempts to score they gained a corner and LAMBIE placed the ball grandly through the Preston goal but the goal was disallowed. Ardwick were awarded a free kick but all danger was averted by Ross, Holmes and Trainer. Preston then scored again. Shortly afterwards time was called with Preston North End being winners of a poor exhibition of football by 2 goals to nil.

The final match of the season was a home match against Gorton Villa who were champions of the Combination. The Villa had tried hard to get a fixture against Ardwick and the match was played at Hyde Road before a good attendance. Ardwick were without Weir and **Roberts**, a new player from Wales, took his place.

27th April 1891   Ardwick 2 v Gorton Villa 2
Hyde Road 5,000

The Ardwick forwards got hold of the ball and two shots from DAVIES and LAMBIE were beautifully fisted out by the Gorton Villa goalkeeper. Play for some time afterwards was of a more open nature. At length Armitt and Bennett for Villa made a grand dribble along the left wing and when the ball was centred Pickford shot at DOUGLAS who cleared, but Hickson pounced on the ball and scored with a well judged shot. On re-starting Ardwick played with more determination, and at length, DAVIES scored when he managed to put in a long shot which hit Cope's head and bounced through out of Jenkinson's reach. At half-time the score was one goal each.

In the second half play was quite rough. Ardwick played up better and from a scrimmage in front of the Villa goal the ball was put in and knocked out again until an appeal for a goal was allowed by the referee. Villa then pressed and were rewarded following some smart play by Armitt, Bennett, Pickford and Myatt which resulted in Bennett putting the ball safely through the Ardwick goal out of the reach of DOUGLAS. The game was a scorcher from start to finish. For Ardwick, DOUGLAS, ROBERTS and DAVIDSON played a hard and determined game in defence and DAVIES, LAMBIE and McCOLL in the forward division were most conspicuous. The game finished in a draw with each side scoring 2 goals.

There were reports of forty six matches played throughout the season and the team line-ups were given for all the matches with the exception of the last match against Gorton Villa. Ardwick won twenty six of the recorded matches, drawing seven and losing thirteen. Ardwick scored one hundred and thity six goals

Thirty one players played for the first team and the eleven who made twenty appearances or more were:

RECORDED APPEARANCES 1890-91				
William Douglas	43	William McColl	33
David Weir	41	J. Pearson	27
Walter McWhinnie	41	William Lambie	25
John Milne	39	Walter Rushton	24
Daniel Whittle	38	A. Pearson	22
David Robson	35		

The leading goalscorers were:

GOALSCORERS 1890-91	
David Weir	32
Walter McWhinnie	23
William Lambie	16
Walter Rushton	10
John Milne	6
J. O'Brien	6
William McColl	6

On Wednesday 29th April 1891, Manchester and District Football Association held a Committee Meeting at the Spread Eagle Hotel Manchester, when £20 was awarded to the clubs in the Final of the Senior Cup. It was also mentioned that the radius of the association would be extended to twelve miles which would enable several strong Clubs to enter the Senior Cup next season.

At the close of the Committee Meeting, the presentation of the Manchester Cup to the Ardwick Football Club as well as the medals to the winners and runners up was made. Mr Nall in handing over the Cup complimented the Ardwick Club upon their victory and paid testimony to the Newton Heath team for having held the honour of appearing in the final each year since the competition was inaugurated.

Mr Allison of the Ardwick Committee in accepting the Cup on behalf of his Club took credit for his Club having won the Cup by dint of good play and invited members of the Committee to the Club's presentation on Friday night.

At the end of the season William Lambie returned to Scotland to play for Queen's Park but he came back to play for Ardwick for a short time in 1892.

On 4th May 1891 the Football League held its third annual meeting in Liverpool and took the important step of increasing the number of Clubs in the Football League from twelve to fourteen thus securing a full programme of matches right up to the end of April. The four clubs at the bottom of the Football League had to apply for re-election and with two additional clubs, there were six places available. Ardwick applied for election.

The voting was as follows:

Aston Villa	8 votes	Re-elected
Accrington	8 votes	Re-elected
Darwen	7 votes	Elected
Stoke	7 votes	Elected
Derby County	6 votes	Re-elected
West Bromwich Albion	6 votes	Re-elected
ARDWICK	4 votes	
Nottingham Forest	1 vote	
Sunderland Albion	1 vote	
Newton Heath	none	

The result of the voting was that Aston Villa, Accrington, Derby County and West Bromwich were all re-elected and the two new Clubs who were elected to the League were Darwen and Stoke.

Ardwick finished seventh in the vote and were so close to being elected. Newton Heath received no votes on their application for election.

On 27th May 1891 James Moores died aged 52. Although there was no mention in his obituary of any connection with St. Mark's Cricket and Football Clubs nor with Gorton Football Club, he attended the early fund raising events of the St Mark's Cricket Club when mention was made of the football section and he was Chairman of Gorton Association Football Club when this came into being in October 1884.

At the beginning of the 1890-91 Season, the Ardwick Committee had taken a very brave decision to spend £600/£700 in buying a new team and the team had been considerably strengthened during the season.

In the side were two Internationals - David Weir (England) and Joseph Davies (Wales). There were also two players who were soon to become Internationals - William Lambie (Scotland) and Hugh Morris (Wales).

Ardwick came very close to being elected to the Football League.

It was a good decision not to join *The Combination* for they were able to arrange a very good fixture list including matches against some of the leading clubs in England and Scotland - Preston North End, Blackburn Rovers, Bolton Wanderers and Glasgow Celtic.

The winning of the Manchester Cup had been a significant achievement and in one season Ardwick had become a senior club.

After just failing to be elected into the Football League, Ardwick applied to join the Football Alliance and were successful.

There follows a summary of the season with details, where known, of reported matches, attendances, appearances and goalscorers.

Ardwick had played friendly matches during the season but had entered three cup competitions: Football Association Cup (FAC), Manchester and District Senior Cup (MC) and the Lancashire Junior Cup (LJC).

SUMMARY
ARDWICK A.F.C. 1890-91

DATE		OPPONENT	RES	1	2	3	4	5	6
				7	8	9	10	11	
01-Sep	H	Preston	L 0-6	W.DOUGLAS	Bennett	D.ROBSON	D.WHITTLE	J.MILNE	A.McWHIRTER
1890		North End	6000	W.RUSHTON	W.McWHINNIE	B.CAMPBELL	D.WEIR ©	Howarth	
06-Sep	H	Witton	W 8-0	Douglas	Bennett	Robson	Whittle	Milne	McWhirter
			3000	Rushton 2	McWhinnie 1	YOUNG 1	Weir © 3	W.McCOLL	1 own goal
08-Sep	H	Bolton	L 1-5	Douglas	J.HAYDOCK	Robson	Whittle	Milne	Young
		Wanderers	2000	Rushton	McColl	McWhirter	Weir © 1	McWhinnie	
13-Sep	H	Heywood	W 7-0	Douglas	Haydock	Robson	Whittle	Milne	SIMON
		Central	5000	Rushton 1	McWhinnie 3	McColl	Weir © 3	JARRETT	
15-Sep	H	Manchester	W 2-0	Douglas	Robson	Bennett	Simon	McWhirter	Milne
			1200	ALLEN	McColl	Weir © 2	Jarrett	McWhinnie	
20-Sep	H	Blackburn	L 1-5	Douglas	Robson	Haydock	Milne	Whittle	Simon
		Rovers	7000	Weir ©	Rushton	McColl	McWhinnie1	Jarrett	
27-Sep	A	West	W 3-1	Douglas	Haydock	Robson	Milne	Whittle	Simon
		Manchester	5000	Weir ©	McWhinnie2	Rushton 1	McColl	Jarrett	
04-Oct	H	Liverpool	W 12-0	Douglas	W. HARVIE	Robson	Milne	Whittle 1	Simon
FACQ		Stanley	3000	McWhinnie2	Hodgetts 2	Weir © 3	Campbell 2	Rushton 2	
11-Oct	H	Bury	L 1-3	Douglas	W.P.JONES	Robson	Milne	Whittle 1	J. PEARSON
			6000	Weir ©	Rushton	Hodgetts	Campbell	McWhinnie	
18-Oct	H	Heywood	W 6-2	Douglas	Haydock	Robson	Milne 1	Whittle	J. Pearson
		Central		Weir ©	O'Brien	McWhinnie	McColl	McWhirter	5 goals *
25-Oct	A	Halliwell	Ardwick scratched						
FACQ									
25-Oct	H	Higher	W 3-2	Douglas	Harvie	Robson	Milne	J. Pearson	Whittle
		Walton		Weir © 1	A.PEARSON	McWhinnie 1	McColl 1	Rushton	
01-Nov	H	Warwick	W 7-0	Douglas	Harvie	Robson	Milne	Whittle	J. Pearson
		County		Weir ©	A. Pearson	McWhinnie 2	McColl	Rushton 1	*4 goals
03-Nov	A	Sheffield	L 2-4	Douglas	Harvie	Robson	Milne 1	Whittle	J. Pearson
		United		Weir ©	A. Pearson	McWhinnie	McColl	Rushton	1 own goal
08-Nov	H	Hyde	W 4-2	Douglas	Harvie	H. GOLDING	Milne	J. Pearson	Weir ©
			4000	Rushton	McColl 2	McWhinnie1	A.Pearson1	McWhirter	
15-Nov	A	Newton	L 1-4	Douglas	Harvie	Robson	J. Pearson	Whittle	Milne 1
		Heath	10,000	Rushton	McColl	O'Brien	McWhinnie	A. Pearson	
22-Nov	H	Heywood	W 7-3	Douglas	D. McCARTHY	Harvie	J. Pearson	Whittle	Weir © 2
			2000	McWhinnie3	McColl	McWhirter	A. Pearson	O'Brien 2	
29-Nov	H	Skerton	W 3-0	Douglas	Bennett	Harvie	Milne	Whittle	J. Pearson
LJC 3				Weir ©	McWhinnie	McColl 1	A. Pearson	O'Brien 2	
06-Dec	H	Darwen	D 2-2	Douglas	Harvie	J. Pearson	Milne	Weir ©	Whittle
				Rushton	McColl	W.LAMBIE1	A. Pearson	O'Brien1	
13-Dec	H	Derby	W 5-0	Douglas	J. Pearson	Harvie	Weir ©	Milne	Whittle
		Junction	2000	Rushton 1	McColl	Lambie 2	A. Pearson1	O'Brien	1 own goal
25-Dec	H	Stoke	D 0-0	Douglas	Weir ©	Harvie	Whittle	McWhirter	J. Pearson
			5000	McWhinnie	McColl	Lambie	A. Pearson	O'Brien	
26-Dec	H	South	L 0-4	Douglas	Weir ©	Harvie	Whittle	McWhirter	J. Pearson
		Shore	2000	McWhinnie	McColl	Lambie	A. Pearson	O'Brien	
27-Dec	H	Southport	W 2-0	Douglas	Harvie	Robson	Milne	Whittle	J. Pearson
		Central	2000	McWhinnie	McColl 1	Lambie	A.Pearson1	Rushton	
01-Jan	H	West Brom.	D 2-2	Douglas	W. MILARVIE	Robson	McWhirter	J. Pearson	Whittle
1891		Albion	7000	O'Brien	A. Pearson	Lambie 1	Weir ©	Rushton 1	
02-Jan	H	Newton	D 1-1	Douglas	Weir ©	Milarvie	J. Pearson	Whittle	H.DAVIDSON
		Heath		McColl	Lambie	O'Brien	McWhinnie	A. Pearson	1 goal *
03-Jan	H	Paisley	L 0-1	Douglas	Weir ©	Milarvie	J. Pearson	Whittle	Davidson
		St Mirren	2,500	McColl	Lambie	O'Brien	McWhinnie	A. Pearson	

Date	H/A	Opponent	Result						
10-Jan	H	Chirk	W 2-1	Douglas	Milarvie	Weir ©	J. Pearson	Whittle	McWhirter
1891			3,000	O'Brien 1	A. Pearson	Lambie 1	Milne	McWhinnie	
17-Jan	H	Derby	W 4-2	Douglas	Milarvie	Robson	J. Pearson	Whittle	McWhirter
		Midland		Weir © 3	Milne	McWhinnie1	A. Pearson	Rushton	
24-Jan	A	Port Vale	W 3-2	Douglas	Milarvie	Robson	J. Pearson	Whittle	McWhirter
			1,000	Weir © 1	Milne	McWhinnie	A.Pearson1	Rushton 1	
31-Jan	H	Blackpool	W 4-1	Douglas	Milarvie	Robson	J. Pearson	Whittle	Milne
		SouthShore	3,000	Weir © 3	A. Pearson	Lambie 1	McColl	McWhinnie	
07-Feb	H	Bury	W 4-3	Douglas	Milarvie	Robson	J. Pearson	Whittle	Milne
LJC 4			10,000	Weir © 1	A. Pearson	Lambie 1	McWhinnie1	McColl 1	
14-Feb	A	Denton	W 5-1	Douglas	Milarvie	Robson	Milne 1	Whittle	J. Pearson
MC 1			3,000	Weir © 2	A. Pearson	Lambie 2	McWhinnie	McColl	
21-Feb	N	Hindley	W 1-0	Douglas	Milarvie	Robson	Milne	J. Pearson	Whittle
SF	LJC		5,000	Weir © 1	A. Pearson	Lambie	McWhinnie	McColl	
28-Feb	H	Newton	L 1-3	Douglas	Milarvie	Robson	Whittle	Davidson	Milne 1
		Heath		Weir ©	J. DAVIES	Lambie	McWhinnie	Rushton	
07-Mar	H	Birmingham	W 4-1	Douglas	Milarvie	Robson	Whittle 1	Davidson	Milne 1
		St. Georges		Weir © 1	McWhinnie	Lambie 1	McColl	Rushton	
14-Mar	N	West	W 4-1	Douglas	Milarvie	Robson	Whittle	Davidson	Milne
SF	MC	Manchester		Weir © 1	McWhinnie1	Lambie	McColl	Rushton	2 goals *
21-Mar	N	Blackpool	L 1-3	Douglas	Milarvie	Robson	J. Pearson	Whittle	Davidson
FINAL	LJC			Weir ©	Milne	Lambie 1	McWhinnie	McColl	
27-Mar	H	Crewe	W 6-5	Douglas	Bennett	Robson	McWhirter	Weir © 2	Davidson
		Alexandra	5,000	J. Davies	McWhinnie 1	Lambie 2	Milne	H.MORRIS	1 goal *
28-Mar	H	Glasgow	L 2-7	Douglas	Milarvie	Robson	McWhirter1	Weir ©	Davidson
		Celtic	6,000	J. Davies	McWhinnie	Lambie	Milne	Morris	1 goal *
30-Mar	H	Partick	D 3-3	Douglas	Milarvie	Robson	Davidson	Weir © 1	McWhirter
		Thistle		Rushton	Davies 1	Morris	McWhinnie	Milne	1 goal *
04-Apr	A	Bury	W 4-2	Douglas	Weir ©	Robson	J. Pearson	Whittle	Davidson
				J. Davies 1	McWhinnie2	Lambie 1	Milne	Morris	
06-Apr	H	Sheffield	W 4-1	T. WARMAN	Robson	Weir ©	Davidson	Milne	McWhirter
		United		McWhinnie1	J. Davies 1	Lambie 1	McColl	Morris 1	
11-Apr	A	Heywood	L 0-3	Warman	P.Bennett	Robson	Milne	Whittle	Davidson
		Central		Davies	McWhinnie	Lambie	McColl	Morris	
18-Apr	N	Newton	W 1-0	Douglas	Bennett	Robson	Milne	Whittle	Davidson
FINAL	MC	Heath	10,000	Davies	McWhinnie	Weir © 1	Lambie	McColl	
20-Apr	H	Nelson	D 1-1	Douglas	Bennett	Robson	Milne	McWhirter	Davidson
			2,000	Davies	McWhinnie	Hodgetts	Lambie 1	McColl	
25-Apr	H	Preston	L 0-2	Douglas	Weir ©	Robson	J. Pearson	Whittle	Davidson
		North End		Davies	Milne	Lambie	McWhinnie	McColl	
27-Apr	H	Gorton Villa	D 2-2	Douglas	Roberts				Davidson
			5000	Davies 1			Lambie	McColl	*1 goal

Captain: ©   Scorer(s) not known: *   Player debut: CAPITALS

REPORTED MATCHES 1890-91						
	P	W	D	L	F	A
Home	35	19	7	9	111	70
Away	11	7	0	4	25	21
Total	46	26	7	13	136	91

The team line-up was given in forty five of the forty six matches. The recorded appearances and goals are taken from those forty five matches.

RECORDED APPEARANCES 1890-1891		
PLAYER	APPS.	GOALS
1. DOUGLAS,W	43	
2. McWHINNIE, W	42	23
3. WEIR,D	41	32
4. MILNE,J	39	6
5. WHITTLE,D	38	3
6. ROBSON,D	35	
7. McCOLL, W	33	6
8. PEARSON,J	27	
9. LAMBIE,W	25	16
10. RUSHTON,W	23	10
11. PEARSON,A	22	4
12. McWHIRTER,A	18	1
13. MILARVIE,W	16	
14. DAVIDSON,H	15	
15. HARVIE,W	13	
16. O'BRIEN,J	12	6
17. DAVIES,J	10	3
18. BENNETT,P	8	
19. MORRIS,H	6	1
20. HAYDOCK,J	5	
21. SIMON	5	
22. JARRETT	4	
23. CAMPBELL,B	3	2
24. HODGETTS,J	3	2
25. WARMAN,T	2	
26. YOUNG	2	1
27. JONES,W.P.	1	
28. GOLDING,H	1	
29. McCARTHY, D	1	
30. HOWARTH,J.W	1	
31. ALLEN	1	
Own goals		3
Not known		15

CHAPTER 15

ARDWICK ASSOCIATION FOOTBALL CLUB
1891-1892

Ardwick were elected to the Football Alliance which had been formed in 1889. The other teams in the Alliance were: Birmingham St. George's, Bootle, Burton Swifts, Crewe Alexandra, Grimsby Town, Lincoln City, Newton Heath, Nottingham Forest, Sheffield Wednesday, Small Heath and Walsall Town Swifts.

At the end of August the Manchester Courier reported that there was great excitement at the beginning of the season that both Ardwick and Newton Heath would be seen to "better advantage" than was the case in the previous year, both having considerably strengthened their teams. Only two matches had been arranged between Ardwick and Newton Heath and they would fall in the ordinary course in the Alliance but as the season advances it was thought that a third fixture would be arranged. Ardwick, who were the Manchester Cup holders and who were making their debut in the Football Alliance, had been working hard to get a strong team together.

Lawrence Furniss continued as Secretary. John Allison, who with Lawrence Furniss was instrumental in attracting so many good players to the Club, resigned from the Committee. The Chairman was Mr Stephenson.

The Hyde Road ground had been described as being in splendid condition with three stands (one covered to hold over 3500 spectators).

David (Davie) Weir continued as captain but when he was not playing, Robert (Bob) Milarvie stood in as captain.

The club colours were white shirts with navy blue knickers (knee length shorts).

It was announced that the club had been working hard to get a strong team and that the Alliance team in the first four weeks of the season would be selected from:

ARDWICK PLAYERS 1891-92		
Player		Position
Goalkeeper		
William	Douglas	retained
Full-backs		
Archibald	Ferguson	signed from Heart of Midlothian
David	Robson	retained
Half-backs		
H.	Davidson	retained
John	Milne	retained
J.	Pearson	retained
Daniel	Whittle	retained
Forwards		
Joseph	Davies	retained
Walter	McWhinnie	retained
Robert	Milarvie	signed from Newton Heath
Hugh	Morris	retained
David	Weir	retained

Ardwick also signed three players who did not play in the Alliance team but did play for the club in other matches.

J. Campbell	Forward	Glasgow Celtic

D. Lafferty	Forward	Glasgow Celtic

J. McCarthy	Forward	

The following players were signed during the season and played for the Alliance team:

Player		Position
	Cooke	Full-back
John	McVickers	Full-back
	Baker	Half-back
William	Hopkins	Half-back
S.	Jackson	Half-back
Harry	Middleton	Half-back
Charles	Parry	Half-back
John	Angus	Forward
Alex	Boggie	Forward
	Powery	Forward
William	Sharpe	Forward.

In addition to the Alliance matches, a good list of friendly matches had been arranged including several against League Clubs. Taking all things into account a good season was to be expected.

SEPTEMBER 1891

Ardwick started the season with a friendly match against West Manchester (Lancashire League) at Hyde Road on 1st September 1891 which ended in a draw with each side scoring 2 goals. Ferguson, Lafferty and Milarvie made their first appearances for Ardwick. The Ardwick goal scorers were Lafferty and Davies. In the West Manchester side were two players who were later to play for Ardwick, Stones in goal and Angus, a forward.

On 5th September 1891, Ardwick beat Gainsborough Trinity (Midland League) by 2 goals to 1 before an attendance of 5,000 at Hyde Road. The Ardwick goal scorers were Davies and Robson.

During the week the Football Association Challenge Cup draw for the qualifying round of the competition took place and Ardwick were drawn away to Newton Heath.

The draw also took place for the Manchester & District Association Senior Cup and Ardwick were granted a bye.

On Saturday 7th September 1891, Ardwick played Rossendale (Lancashire League) at Hyde Road and lost by 4 goals to 1.

The Football Alliance fixtures commenced on 12th September 1891 and Ardwick started with a home match against Bootle.

12th September 1891   FOOTBALL ALLIANCE
                    Ardwick   3   v   Bootle   3

6,000

Ardwick team: Douglas; Ferguson and Robson; Milne Whittle 1 and Davidson; Davies 1 McWhinnie Weir © Morris 1 Milarvie

Bootle started the match in glorious weather and Montgomery shot over the bar. Some good work by the Bootle halves gave them a good chance but their shots at goal were weak. MILARVIE got in a good centre but Lamont fouled McWHINNIE, the referee giving Ardwick a free-kick, which was kicked over. Subsequently, WHITTLE scored for Ardwick. Bootle then had a free-kick and forced a corner from DOUGLAS, but FERGUSON cleared well. At half-time Ardwick led by one goal to nil.

WEIR restarted and within a few minutes of resuming Mooney passed to Montgomery who equalised. Ardwick forwards then missed a ridiculously easy chance of scoring and ROBSON sustained an injury to his leg during a scramble. ROBSON lay on the ground for over a minute and no notice was taken by the referee. Bootle played the ball and Montgomery shot through the Ardwick goal. Ardwick strongly protested but the goal was allowed. The decision aroused Ardwick and from a pass by MILARVIE, DAVIES scored Ardwick's second goal. DAVIES then passed to MORRIS who ran the ball through the Bootle goal to give Ardwick the lead but Grearson equalised a few minutes from time for Bootle. The final score was Ardwick 3 goals Bootle 3.

Ardwick's next Alliance match was away at Lincoln City.

19th September 1891   FOOTBALL ALLIANCE
                    Lincoln City   3   v   Ardwick   0

2,000

Ardwick team: Douglas; Ferguson and Robson; J. Pearson, Whittle and Davidson; Davies McWhinnie Weir © Morris and Milarvie.

At the beginning, play was even, but when the teams settled down City had the best of the exchanges. After fifteen minutes play Lincoln scored the first goal, when Smallman headed through from a pass by Moore. City had the best of matters for a long time. At half-time, Lincoln led by one goal to nil.

In the second half, Ardwick pressed and a smart run ended in an off side decision. Lincoln scored a second goal after thirty minutes play. Ardwick then obtained two corners but were slow to take up chances. Smallman scored a third goal for Lincoln with a fast oblique shot. The final score was Lincoln City 3 goals Ardwick 0.

On Monday 21st September 1891, Ardwick played Denton at Hyde Road and won by 3 goals to 1 before an attendance of 700 spectators. The Ardwick goal scorers were Anderson, Lafferty and McWhinnie.

On 26th September 1891, Burton Swifts paid their first visit to the Hyde Road ground. Burton Swifts played with their full strength team. David Weir, the Ardwick captain, missed the game with a knee injury. Morris went to centre. Ardwick wore white jerseys and black bands in memory of the late Councillor Chesters.

26th September 1891   FOOTBALL ALLIANCE
                    Ardwick   1   v   Burton Swifts   0

3,000

Ardwick team: Douglas; Ferguson and Robson; J. Pearson Whittle and Davidson; Davies McWhinnie Morris 1 Milne and Milarvie.

Ardwick gained two corners very quickly but nothing resulted. Swifts' forwards then attacked but ROBSON relieved with a big kick. The Swifts backs had to concede another corner to MILNE but nothing resulted. The Swifts attacked and Emey put in a good shot which DOUGLAS saved well. Ardwick were doing most of the pressing and McWHINNIE just headed by the post from a corner. Worrall, the Swifts centre forward, led a rush by the Swifts forwards but WHITTLE cleared the danger. DAVIDSON put in some good play at half back. Ardwick obtained a number of free kicks but the Swifts packed their goal and prevented any score. MILARVIE sent in a splendid shot which the Swifts goalkeeper Horne managed to push over the bar. Ardwick had much the best of matters and MILARVIE raced away and sent in a fine centre which was cleared. Ardwick then returned to the attack and MORRIS almost scored. DAVIES put in a fast shot which just went outside. There was no score at half-time.

In the second half MILARVIE had a grand shot which Horne saved but gave away a corner. DAVIES MORRIS and McWHINNIE had a grand run and forced a corner but again nothing resulted. Play became very exciting with both teams straining every nerve to score. May had a splendid opening but shot badly. WHITTLE came through and passed to MILARVIE who centred well but one of the Swifts backs McDermott relieved the pressure. At length from a grand run and pass by MILARVIE, MORRIS ran the ball through the Swifts goal to give Ardwick the lead, amidst great cheering. The Ardwick team played up very well and almost scored again. Ardwick won an exciting game by 1 goal to 0.

The next fixture was a friendly against Football League opponents, Blackburn Rovers. The game was played at Hyde Road on Monday, 28th September 1891 before a good attendance of 2,000 spectators. Blackburn were short of some of their regular players. The Ardwick team included a well known Scotsman who played under the assumed name of "Thompson". Ardwick played well and the game ended in a draw each side scoring one goal. McWhinnie scored Ardwick's goal.

OCTOBER 1891

On 3rd October 1891, Ardwick played Newton Heath in the Football Association Cup at Newton Heath. During the match, an unfortunate accident occurred. Mr. Allison, of the Ardwick Club was standing outside the press box talking to the reporters, when the staple of the shutter of the press box came out and the shutter came with considerable force upon Mr Allison who was carried into the press box in a fainting condition.

3rd October 1891   FOOTBALL ASSOCIATION CUP   Qualifying Round
Newton Heath   5   v   Ardwick   1
11,000
Ardwick team: Douglas; Ferguson and Robson; J. Pearson 1 Whittle and Davidson; Davies Morris McWhinnie Dewar and Milarvie.

McWHINNIE started the game. Newton Heath were the first to attack, Farman and Edge forcing DOUGLAS to fist out a couple of shots. The game was even for a time and then Sneddon shot wide and when Newton Heath next attacked ROBSON kicked out. Stewart had hard lines in not scoring from a pass by Edge, DOUGLAS saving at the expense of a corner. DOUGLAS and ROBSON next made two grand saves. Ardwick were then awarded a penalty kick which was taken by DAVIES but Slater saved the shot in grand style. Newton Heath attacked and Henries put the ball over the bar. Newton Heath again went away and Sneddon put the ball through the Ardwick goal thus putting Newton Heath ahead. At half-time Newton Heath led by one goal to nil.

After the interval Newton Heath had several attacks and Farman went away and rounding the Ardwick half-backs had a good chance, but ROBSON kicked out. A rush by the Ardwick forwards was well stopped by Clements. DAVIES and MORRIS were conspicuous for Ardwick but a corner was the only result of their efforts. After some give and take play the Ardwick goal was again reached, and Sharpe sent the ball across to Edge but that player missed the ball and Farman rushing up sent the ball past DOUGLAS. On the restart, Sharpe was again at the front and putting in a high shot Doughty made the score three goals to nil in favour of Newton Heath. On commencing again Ardwick went away and gained a free kick just outside the twelve yards mark. J. PEARSON took the kick and the ball went through off Stewarts hands. This rapid scoring seemed to put more life into the game and Farman shot the ball through the top right hand corner of the Ardwick goal. Edge put in a fine shot which DOUGLAS just touched but failed to hold. Newton Heath took it very easy after this being four goals to the good. Farman however put in a good shot which went wide. The final score was Newton Heath 5 goals Ardwick 1.

Following the FA Cup defeat, Ardwick had two friendly matches which were both away, against Denton and West Manchester.

On 5th October 1891, Ardwick beat Denton by 2 goals to 0 at Denton with the goals being scored by Davies and "Thompson".

In October 1891, Ardwick signed two Scottish players:

S. Jackson	Half-back

Alex Boggie	Forward

On 8th October 1891, Ardwick played at Brooks' Bar against West Manchester. Ardwick played a strong team including the two new players S. Jackson and A. Boggie. Ardwick won by 3 goals to 0 with the goals being scored by Boggie, Powery and Milarvie.

A week after being defeated in the FA Cup, Ardwick again played Newton Heath at North Road in an Alliance match. Whilst there was not the same interest in the Alliance match a fair crowd turned up to see whether Ardwick could retrieve themselves. Ardwick left out Ferguson with Weir taking his place whilst Milne and Powery took the places of McWhinnie and Dewer.

10th October 1891   FOOTBALL ALLIANCE
                  Newton Heaton   3   v   Ardwick   1
4,000.
Ardwick team: Douglas; Weir © and Robson; J. Pearson Whittle and Davidson; Davies Morris 1 Milne Powery and Milarvie.

The game was started by MILNE and Ardwick were the first to get away, but Clements stopped the Ardwick right wing. The Newton Heath forwards then had a chance and DOUGLAS had to concede a corner from a shot by Sneddon. Newton Heath attacked on several occasions and the Ardwick defence was severely tested. Sharpe and Sneddon next made a good run, and Sharpe shot but the ball was headed over after DOUGLAS had saved twice. MILARVIE and POWERY attacked for Ardwick but McFarlaine was too good for them. After some neat play on the Ardwick left DAVIES shot, but the ball went out. Ardwick began to play better and Newton Heath had to defend for some time. Ardwick had a good attack and MILARVIE shot in but an appeal for off side was allowed. POWERY had a grand shot for Ardwick but it went over. Newton Heath attacked and Edge after a good run put in a grand shot which DOUGLAS fisted out, but Donaldson then headed past the Ardwick goalkeeper. Each side had turns in attacking. A penalty kick was given against WEIR for deliberately stopping the ball with his hands. Farman took the kick and although DOUGLAS touched the ball, he could not stop it going in. At half-time Newton Heath led by 2 goals to nil.

On resuming Ardwick gained two fruitless corners. Afterwards MORRIS scored the first goal for Ardwick. DAVIES and MORRIS were prominent with several good runs but found the Newton Heath defence was too good for them. Donaldson made a grand run but his pass was badly missed by Sharpe. Edge was next prominent with a neat run but the Ardwick backs were now playing strongly and gave nothing away. Newton Heath attacked the Ardwick goal and after several shots had been grandly saved by DOUGLAS, Farman beat him with a low shot. The final score was Newton Heath 3 goals Ardwick 1.

On 17th October 1891, Ardwick played at home against Birmingham St Georges and **S. Jackson** and **A. Boggie** made their first appearances in the Alliance.

17th October 1891   FOOTBALL ALLIANCE
                  Ardwick   4   v   Birmingham St Georges   3
6,000
Ardwick team: Douglas; Weir © and Robson; Jackson Milne and Davidson; Davies McWhinnie 1 Boggie 2 Morris 1 and Milarvie.

St Georges were the first to show up and DOUGLAS was called upon to save an awkward shot, and then Harrison shot over the bar. St Georges continued the pressure and after some nice passing Matthews scored the first goal. After several attempts W. Shore from a scrimmage succeeded in beating DOUGLAS for a second goal. Ardwick did not show up well in the absence of FERGUSON and WHITTLE. St George's second goal roused Ardwick and Kenyon in the St Georges goal had a warm time of it for about quarter of an hour, MORRIS and McWHINNIE scoring for Ardwick and thus drawing level. At half time the score was two goals each.

In the second half, play was very fast but somewhat more even. BOGGIE worked his way through the St Georges defence and scored with a splendid shot. St Georges now pressed and Shore scored what seemed to be an off-side goal but the referee allowed the goal to stand. DAVIES sent in a splendid shot and Kenyon was lucky in saving. Ardwick had a chance from a free kick and WEIR put the ball in goal and it was rushed through by BOGGIE. Ardwick continued the pressure and McWHINNIE headed over. The final score was Ardwick 4 goals Birmingham St Georges 3.

Ardwick now had three friendly matches against good opposition.

On Saturday, 24th October 1891, Ardwick played against Sunderland Albion of the Northern League at Hyde Road. The game attracted an attendance of 5,000. Ardwick won by 2 goals to 1 with both goals being scored by Milne.

On Saturday, 31st October 1891, Ardwick played at Hyde Road against Stoke who had regained their place in the Football League. Ardwick won by 5 goals to 2 before an attendance of 4,000. The Ardwick scorers were Boggie (2), Morris (2) and McWhinnie.

NOVEMBER 1891

On Monday 2nd November 1891, Ardwick played at Chirk before a large crowd of spectators. Ardwick defeated Chirk by 3 goals to 2 and the Ardwick scorers were Milarvie (2) and Morris.

Ardwick had played ten friendly matches most of them at home and had only lost one match. However, in the Alliance and F.A.Cup, Ardwick had played six matches and had lost three. This was very disappointing particularly as the Ardwick Committee thought they had built a team which could compete in the Football League. In early November 1891, Ardwick signed a half-back:

Charles Frederick Parry	Half-back	Everton

Charles Frederick Parry

Charles "Charlie" **Parry** had played for Chester St. Oswald's before joining Everton. Whilst at Everton he played for Wales against England and Scotland in 1891. He made his debut in the next match against Walsall Town Swifts.

7th November 1891　　　　　　FOOTBALL ALLIANCE
　　　　　　　　　　　Ardwick　6　v　Walsall Town Swifts　0
4,500
Ardwick team: Douglas; Weir © and Robson; Jackson Whittle and Parry; Davies Milne 1 Boggie 1 Morris 3 and Milarvie 1.

　　　Ardwick pressed from the start and DAVIES almost scored from a good pass by MILARVIE, Edge the Walsall goalkeeper conceding a corner. Ardwick maintained the pressure and MORRIS headed through the Walsall goal after Edge had fisted out. MILARVIE again shot the ball through the Walsall goal, but off-side was successfully claimed. However, shortly afterwards MILARVIE sent in a fast shot which gave Edge no chance. Ardwick continued the pressure and MILNE rushed through the third goal. MORRIS headed a fourth goal for Ardwick from a well placed corner by DAVIES. The Ardwick forwards were playing in grand form, and could not be stopped. Walsall had several attacks but ROBSON and the other defenders defended well. At half-time the score was Ardwick four goals Walsall nil.

　　　In the second half play quietened down. Walsall had a chance from a free kick but DAVIES relieved the pressure. The Ardwick forwards again attacked and MORRIS almost scored with a grand high shot. Edge scooped out a shot by DAVIES. The Ardwick forwards continued to press and MILNE put the ball over the bar from a corner. After some good play in the Walsall goalmouth MORRIS scored a fifth goal. DOUGLAS saved a good shot by Wood. MILARVIE put in some good work and BOGGIE scored a sixth goal. Ardwick won by 6 goals to 0.

　　　Ardwick now had home and away matches against the Alliance leaders, Nottingham Forest.

14th November 1891　　　　　　FOOTBALL ALLIANCE
　　　　　　　　　　　Ardwick　1　v　Nottingham Forest　3
8,000
Ardwick team: Douglas; Weir © and Robson; Jackson Whittle and Parry; Davies McWhinnie Boggie Morris and Milarvie 1.

　　　Forest kicked off and play from the start was exceedingly fast and even. WEIR dallied with the ball. Pike robbed him and easily rushed the ball past DOUGLAS. MILARVIE shot in at the other end to equalise, BOGGIE taking care of the goalkeeper and making way for the ball. Forest appealed for off-side but the appeal was not allowed. Higgins then sent in a shot between the post and DOUGLAS which put Forest in front again. At the interval Forest were leading by two goals to one.

　　　On the restart Forest got away and DOUGLAS had a busy time. Ardwick transferred play to the other end and BOGGIE MILARVIE and DAVIES made capital attempts to defeat Brown the Forest goalkeeper. Higgins threw away a good chance for Forest by shooting over. Play was transferred from end to end, being if anything faster at the finish than at the start. Pike added a third goal for Forest. The final score was Nottingham Forrest 3 goals Ardwick 1.

　　　A few days later, on Thursday 19th November 1891, Ardwick played at Nottingham. Ardwick kept the same team and both sides were fully represented.

19th November 1891　　　　　　FOOTBALL ALLIANCE
　　　　　　　　　　　Nottingham Forest　4　v　Ardwick　0
2,000
Ardwick team: Douglas; Weir © and Robson; Jackson Whittle and Parry; Davies McWhinnie Boggie Morris and Milarvie.

　　　Forest kicked off against the sun and wind. The game was very fast, both sides pressing in turn. Forest, by superior combination, had hard lines on several occasions with DOUGLAS saving well. Forest were awarded a penalty for a foul by PARRY and Russell scored. Ardwick now played much better and MILARVIE put in some pretty play. Forest again attacked and kept the Ardwick backs fully employed, their passing being very good. Russell was playing grandly. From a free-kick, Norris kicked the ball over the Ardwick bar. Following good play by the Ardwick half-backs, MILARVIE shot twice, Smith saving one and the other going over the cross bar. From a good run by the Forest left wing Pike shot outside and then DOUGLAS saved in splendid style a shot from the right. Higgins hit the post with a splendid shot. At half-time the score was Nottingham Forest one goal Ardwick nil.

In the second half, Forest forced two corners in succession and from the second corner Russell scored. Forest pressed and DOUGLAS saved splendidly on several occasions. Forest then scored from another corner. Ardwick now had a chance but MORRIS shot miserably when he had an open goal. Towards the close of the game Forest had the best of the play and added a fourth goal. The game ended in an easy victory for Nottingham Forrest by 4 goals to 0.

Ardwick had been well beaten by Nottingham Forest who went on to win the Alliance. Two days later, Ardwick played Burton Swifts in an Alliance fixture at Burton.

21st November 1891   FOOTBALL ALLIANCE
Burton Swifts 4 v Ardwick 4

1,000
Ardwick team: Douglas; Weir © and Robson; Jackson Milne and Parry; Davies McWhinnie Boggie 3 Morris and Milarvie 1.

The Swifts started and the game opened most sensationally. McWHINNIE got hold of the ball and working forward passed to DAVIES who centred to BOGGIE, who scored within half a minute of the start. A short time later, Worrall by smart play equalised. Splendid work by MILARVIE and BOGGIE gave Ardwick the lead with both scoring. Worrall then scored two goals for the Swifts. At half-time the score was Ardwick three goals Burton Swifts three.

In the second half BOGGIE restarted. The Swifts attacked and DOUGLAS made a good save. Each goalkeeper was then put under pressure. Berry kept off MILARVIE at a critical moment and MORRIS was heavily charged down. A corner to the Swifts was smartly cleared but from a scrimmage they scored a fourth goal. The Swifts kept the lead until approximately five minutes from the end, when BOGGIE shot past Hadley, thus equalising. MILARVIE and McWHINNIE shone most conspicuously for Ardwick. The final score was Ardwick 4 goals Burton Swifts 4.

The next Alliance match was against Lincoln City who had easily beaten Ardwick in their first encounter on 19th September 1891.

28th November 1891   FOOTBALL ALLIANCE
Ardwick 2 v Lincoln City 3

1,000
Ardwick team: Douglas; Parry and Robson; Jackson Weir © and Milne; Davis 1 McWhinnie 1 Boggie Morris and Milarvie.

The match was played in miserable weather. There was only a poor attendance when Lincoln kicked off against the wind. Ardwick were the first team to show up, MILARVIE sending the ball over the line. Hodder got away for Lincoln with a fast run but PARRY just managed to rob him. The Lincoln right wing attacked and ROBSON and PARRY relieved. MILARVIE put in a good shot but was given off-side. MILARVIE again shot well but the ball was worked away. Parsons in the Lincoln goal was showing grand form and saved three stiff shots in fine style. Ardwick continued to attack and McWHINNIE forced the ball through the Lincoln goal. Lincoln then did all the pressing and after good work Walker equalised. Lincoln kept up the pressure and after some loose play Hodder gave Lincoln the lead. At half-time Lincoln led by two goals to one.

Ardwick restarted the game and at once gained a corner, MILNE landing the ball on top of the goal net. Ardwick continued to attack and DAVIES shot by the post. MILARVIE got the ball and dribbled nicely before passing to DAVIES who equalised. This put new life into Ardwick, but it was not sustained. Lincoln attacked and ROBSON gave a corner, but nothing resulted. Lincoln continued to press and WEIR and ROBSON kept them from scoring. It was now almost dark and it was difficult to follow the play. WEIR missed his kick and Moore scored the third goal for Lincoln. The final score was Lincoln City 3 goals Ardwick 2.

In the first three months of the season, Douglas in goal, Robson at full-back and three forwards: Davies, Morris and Milarvie had played in all of Ardwick's ten Alliance fixtures. Weir (9), McWhinnie (8), Whittle (7), Milne (7), Jackson (6) and Boggie (6) had played in most of the Alliance matches.

Ferguson at full-back had been replaced by Weir moving to full-back and Boggie had become the regular centre forward. J. Pearson and Davidson at half-back had been replaced by Jackson and Parry respectively. Morris (7) and Boggie (6) were the leading goal scorers.

The League Table with the results up to Saturday 28th November 1891 showed Ardwick in sixth place with 8 points from ten games. Nottingham Forest led the Alliance with 20 points from twelve games.

FOOTBALL ALLIANCE 28th November 1891							
	P	W	D	L	F	A	Pts.
Notts Forest	12	9	2	1	40	11	20
Newton Heath	9	7	1	1	33	10	15
Sheffield Wednesday	10	6	2	2	29	15	14
Burton Swifts	11	5	1	5	25	31	11
Small Heath	9	4	2	3	18	14	10
ARDWICK	10	3	2	5	22	26	8
Bootle	9	3	1	5	17	18	7
Lincoln City	6	3	0	3	12	21	6
Birmingham St Georges*	11	3	1	7	22	27	5
Grimsby Town	6	1	2	3	12	13	4
Walsall Town Swifts	9	2	0	7	9	33	4
Crewe Alexandra	6	1	0	5	10	22	2

*Birmingham St Georges had 2 points deducted for playing ineligible men

DECEMBER 1891

On 5th December 1891, Sheffield Wednesday made their first appearance at Hyde Road and a special train from Sheffield brought a good number of their supporters. After their defeat by Lincoln City the previous Saturday the Ardwick supporters were not at all confident of their chances.

5th December 1891   FOOTBALL ALLIANCE
Ardwick   0   v   Sheffield Wednesday   4
6,000
Ardwick team: Douglas; Weir © and Robson; Jackson Whittle and Parry; Davies McWhinnie Boggie Morris and Milarvie.

Ardwick kicked off but Wednesday were the first to show with a good run by Gemmell. DAVIES replied for Ardwick and put in a fine shot from which Smith, the Wednesday goalkeeper, conceded a corner, but after a severe tussle the ball was worked away. MILARVIE then had a chance but his final shot went over. WHITTLE was noticeable for some good defensive work. DAVIES was knocked over when about to shoot. After a good run by Thompson, DOUGLAS fumbled the ball and Woolhouse rushed up and scored for Wednesday. DAVIES again put in a fast shot which Smith had difficulty in saving. The Wednesday forwards showed good combination and severely taxed the Ardwick defence. Wednesday again scored from a free kick, DOUGLAS not parting with the ball quick enough. Ardwick then got down to the Wednesday end but MILARVIE shot over. WHITTLE was cheered for some good defensive work. Ardwick had a chance but JACKSON shot by the goal post. Wednesday attacked again and DOUGLAS was again at fault and a third goal was added. The Ardwick forwards put in a splendid run but had hard lines. DAVIES was very prominent but Ardwick were unable to score. At half-time Sheffield Wednesday led by three goals to nil.

Wednesday restarted the game and were soon pressing but DOUGLAS saved well. The home forwards attacked but McWHINNIE shot outside. Wednesday now began to show rough tactics and the game seemed likely to become very rough. Wednesday attacked and in a scrimmage DOUGLAS was beaten by Gemmell, who scored Wednesday's fourth goal. The final score was Sheffield Wednesday 4 goals Ardwick 0.

On 8th December 1891, it was reported that a complaint had been made to the Glasgow Football Association by Ardwick. Carson and Diamond of Cowlairs (Cowlairs had finished bottom of the Scottish League in the 1890-91 Season) had on 16th September 1891 played a match for Ardwick against Kirkmanshulme, and had thereby bound themselves for the season to Ardwick.

The story was that Ardwick had engaged Carson and Diamond for £25 down and a nice weekly salary. After playing in a single match, Carson and Diamond had returned to Cowlairs and helped them in a Glasgow cup-tie, thus they were ineligible to play for Ardwick again during the season.

Carson and Diamond admitted having registered for Ardwick and receiving money but denied having played in the match for them. Affidavit evidence had been given by officials and players of Ardwick and Kirkmanshulme that Carson and Diamond had played for Ardwick. This was read to the Glasgow Football Association who unanimously agreed that Carson and Diamond had played for Ardwick against Kirkmanshulme on 16th September 1891; that the case be reported to the Scottish Football Association and that in the event of that body wishing to take action they would be given all the evidence in the possession of the Glasgow Football Association.

The Scottish Football Association later "convicted" Carson and Diamond of professionalism with the result that they were both suspended for a year. There does not appear to be a published record of the Ardwick and Kirkmanshulme match on 16th September 1891.

On Saturday, 12th December 1891, Ardwick played against a Canadian XI and won by 3 goals to 1. The Ardwick goal scorers were Morris (2) and Milne. The Canadian goal was scored by Walter Bowman who was later to play for Ardwick and Manchester City.

On Wednesday, 16th December 1891 Ardwick played Old Reptonians and won by 1 goal to 0.

In December 1891, Ardwick signed:

Cooke	Full-back
W.Sharpe	Forward

On 19th December 1891 Ardwick had an Alliance fixture at home against Newton Heath who had beaten Ardwick on two occasions earlier in the season. There was great excitement with a large crowd expected. **Cooke** and **W. Sharpe** played their first games for Ardwick at right back and inside left respectively. Milarvie captained the side in the absence of Weir.

19th December 1891   FOOTBALL ALLIANCE
Ardwick 2 v Newton Heath 2
10,000
Ardwick team: Douglas; Cooke and Robson; Jackson Whittle and Parry; Davies Morris Milne 2 W. Sharpe and Milarvie ©.

Ardwick kicked off but from the first Newton Heath had the best of matters and only good goal keeping by DOUGLAS and poor shooting stopped the Newton Heath attacks. Ardwick were the first to score with a fine run by MORRIS and DAVIES ending in MILNE scoring with a good shot. A series of mistakes on the Ardwick left let in Newton Heath and Farman equalised with a long low shot. Before long Farman with a good shot scored a second goal for Newton Heath. Some very rough play by Farman and PARRY resulted in several free kicks but nothing resulted. At the interval Newton Heath led by two goals to one.

On resuming, Ardwick came within an ace of scoring. PARRY was badly injured in the face and retired in a fainting condition but returned later. Ardwick had, if anything, the best of matters in the second half and the Newton Heath goalkeeper was worthy of all praise for keeping the Ardwick forwards at bay. Ten minutes from the end a corner to Ardwick resulted in MILNE equalising. The final score was Ardwick 2 goals Newton Heath 2.

On Christmas Day 1891, Ardwick had a home Alliance fixture against Grimsby Town.

Before starting, there was a consultation between the officials as to whether fog would prevent the match from being played. However, it was decided to commence the game. Boggie returned as centre forward.

25th December 1891   FOOTBALL ALLIANCE
Ardwick   3   v   Grimsby Town   1
6,000
Ardwick team: Douglas; Cooke and Robson; Jackson Milne and Parry; Davies Morris 1 Boggie Sharpe and Milarvie © 2.

BOGGIE started the game for Ardwick, who gained a corner but it was put behind. The fog began to clear away. Ardwick worked the ball down field and obtained a free kick against Frith, but PARRY placed the ball badly. MILARVIE and MILNE led some strong attacks but a sudden burst away by Grimsby enabled Riddoch to get a good shot past DOUGLAS at close quarters. Still keeping the Grimsby backs on the defensive Ardwick failed to score and at half-time Grimsby led by one goal to nil.

On changing ends, Ardwick again pressed, obtaining a corner, but Grey, the Grimsby full back, cleared. A moment later DAVIES centred and MILARVIE equalised with a swift shot. Grimsby tried in vain to stop MILARVIE and DAVIES, and DAVIES sent in a terrific shot which was glanced into the Grimsby goal by MORRIS. Akroyd and Riddoch, for Grimsby then got down the field but were well tackled by PARRY who was playing finely. A combined run started by MILNE ended in MILARVIE scoring the finest goal of the day. Ardwick won easily by Ardwick 3 goals to 1.

On Boxing Day, Ardwick played against Sheffield Wednesday at the Olive Grove Ground Sheffield.

The Sheffield ground was very heavy. Weir was still absent for Ardwick and Milarvie continued as captain.

26th December 1891   FOOTBALL ALLIANCE
Sheffield Wednesday   2   v   Ardwick   0
7,000
Ardwick team: Douglas; Cooke and Robson; Jackson Whittle and Parry; Davies Morris Milne Sharpe and Milarvie ©.

MILNE started the ball. Wednesday were soon pressing and some energetic work by Gemmell and Betts forced COOKE to concede a corner which was finely cleared by WHITTLE. The Ardwick forwards then ran the length of the field but Brandon at full back, forced MILARVIE off the ball at a critical moment. DOUGLAS then saved splendidly, but Wednesday kept up the pressure and Thomson scored for them. MILARVIE and SHARPE put in some good play but the Wednesday defence was very strong. Gemmell got away with a fast run but his final shot went outside. Wednesday gained a corner which DOUGLAS saved. DAVIES tried a long shot which just went by the post. The score at half-time was Sheffield Wednesday one goal Ardwick nil.

Thomson restarted the game for Wednesday who pressed and Richardson missed a good chance. DOUGLAS then saved a shot from Woolhouse. Wednesday were having the better of the game and DOUGLAS saved in a marvellous manner. Ardwick broke away and DAVIES put in a grand shot, which resulted in a corner but this came to nothing. DAVIES again put in a fine shot which

Smith saved. Wednesday gained a corner from which Hall scored a second goal. Ardwick pressed and should have scored but Smith in the Wednesday goal made a good save. The final score was Sheffield Wednesday 2 goals Ardwick 0.

The results up to Saturday 26th December 1891, showed Ardwick still in sixth position with 11 points having won 4 games drawn 3 and lost 7.

On 28th December 1891, Ardwick played a friendly against Sunderland at Hyde Road. The game resulted in a no score draw.

JANUARY 1892

On 1st January 1892, Ardwick had another home friendly against West Bromwich Albion. The game was played at Hyde Road before 5,000 spectators. Ardwick won by 4 goals to 2. The Ardwick goal scorers were Morris (2), Milarvie and McWhinnie.

On 2nd January 1892, Ardwick played an Alliance match against Small Heath Alliance at Ardwick. The previous week Small Heath had drawn with Newton Heath and there was speculation as to how Small Heath would fare against the rival Manchester Alliance team.

2nd January 1892　　　　　　　FOOTBALL ALLIANCE
　　　　　　　　　　　　　　Ardwick   2   v   Small Heath   2
5,000
Ardwick team: Douglas; Cooke and Robson; Weir © Whittle and Milne; Davies Morris 2 Boggie McWhinnie and Milarvie.

The weather was dull and showery. Harrison started the game for Small Heath. For a long time the game was of a very even nature. Unfortunately DAVIES got injured and for a long time was of little use. Ardwick mounted strong attacks and McWHINNIE and WEIR did some good work. Hallam came away for Small Heath with a neat dribble but COOKE cleared. Ardwick again pressed and WEIR, WHITTLE and McWHINNIE had shots which were well saved. There was some nice play by the Small Heath forwards in front of the Ardwick goal and DOUGLAS saved miraculously. DAVIES then sent in a fast shot which the Small Heath goalkeeper only just saved. Ardwick were the first to score through MORRIS who put a good centre from MILARVIE very cleverly past Charsley the Small Heath goalkeeper. A grand dribble by MILARVIE resulted in MORRIS scoring a second goal immediately afterwards. Ardwick kept up the pressure and MORRIS put in some good shots but only a corner resulted. Small Heath attacked and Weldon after a fine dribble scored for Small Heath. MILARVIE and MORRIS gave the Small Heath goalkeeper a lot to do, but at half-time the score was Ardwick two goals Small Heath one.

In the second half Ardwick restarted and Small Heath began to attack. For a considerable time the Ardwick full backs COOKE and ROBSON worked very hard. Some good passing between WEIR, McWHINNIE and MILARVIE confused the Small Heath goalkeeper but the ball was cleared and rushed up field resulting in Warton equalising for Small Heath. Ardwick had now the best of matters and for a time the Small Heath goal was totally besieged. A good run by DAVIES with a fine centre gave MILARVIE a chance but Charsley cleared splendidly. WEIR, DAVIES and WHITTLE then came away with the ball and DAVIES just missed scoring. Hallam had a good shot which DOUGLAS saved well. Play was very exciting for both teams were working hard to gain the lead. DAVIES sent in two splendid shorts but Charsley saved them both. The final score was Ardwick 2 goals Small Heath 2

Ardwick then played three friendly matches at Hyde Road.

On 4th January 1892, Ardwick lost to Airdrieonians by 2 goals to 1. The Ardwick goal scorer was Milarvie.

On 9th January 1892, Ardwick lost to Bolton Wanderers of the Football League by 3 goals to nil.

A week later, Ardwick should have played an Alliance fixture against Crewe Alexandra, but Crewe had to play Wolverhampton Wanderers in the F.A. Cup.

On 16th January 1892, Ardwick arranged a match against Heywood Central of the Lancashire League. Ardwick won by 4 goals to nil with the goals being scored by Davies (2) Morris and Robson.

On 23rd January 1892, Ardwick played an away fixture in the Alliance against Bootle. Parry was moved to centre forward.

23rd January 1892 FOOTBALL ALLIANCE
Bootle 2 v Ardwick 1

4,000
Ardwick team: Douglas; Cooke and Robson; J. Pearson Whittle and Milne; Davies Morris Parry 1 Weir © and Sharpe

Bootle started the game but Ardwick were the first to make headway, Dunning having to make good saves. Bootle attacked and DOUGLAS saved splendidly. Even play followed but the Bootle forwards then set about the Ardwick defence in some style. A shot from Hughes was saved and then Davies shot and Montgomery headed a pretty goal. Play continued in favour of Bootle and Clarkin struck the upright. Ardwick played up, and PARRY equalised with a lightening shot. Even and exciting play followed, and at half-time the score was Bootle one goal Ardwick one.

In the second half PARRY restarted and immediately shot over. Ardwick pressed heavily having a goal disallowed. WEIR and PARRY were very prominent and COOKE behind very safe. Grierson tried a long shot for Bootle which went just wide and in averting a charge DOUGLAS upset Kilner. A long dispute ensued on account of a penalty kick being awarded to Bootle, the ball certainly appearing to have been out of play when the foul occurred. From the penalty kick Bootle added a second goal. Ardwick tried hard to get level but failed. The final score was Bootle 2 goals Ardwick 1.

On 30th January 1892, Ardwick played away against Grimsby Town who were bottom of the League.

Grimsby were well represented and gave a performance which was much better than expected.

30th January 1892 FOOTBALL ALLIANCE
Grimsby Town 4 v Ardwick 0

2,000
Ardwick team: Douglas; Cooke and Robson; Weir © Whittle and Milne; Davies Morris Parry Boggie and Sharpe.

PARRY started for Ardwick and MORRIS was at once pulled up for off side. Devlin put in a grand shot for Grimsby and scored. Hands to Ardwick made Ogilvie clear but Grimsby obtained a second goal from a corner when the wind carried the ball through the Ardwick goal. WHITTLE nearly scored for Ardwick. At half-time Grimsby were leading by two goals to nil.

Devlin restarted and obtained a corner but nothing resulted. Ardwick now pressed severely and DAVIES shot over. WEIR went forward and Ardwick gained a couple of free kicks but nothing resulted. A swift shot by WEIR then struck the bar. After DOUGLAS made a good save Smalley added a third goal for Grimsby and shortly afterwards Grimsby scored a fourth goal. The final score was Grimsby Town 4 goals Ardwick 0.

Up to the end of January 1892, Douglas, Robson, Davies and Morris had played in all seventeen of the Alliance matches. Morris was the leading goal scorer with ten goals.

Ardwick were now seventh in the League with twelve points. Nottingham Forest continued to lead the Alliance followed by Newton Heath and Sheffield Wednesday.

FOOTBALL ALLIANCE 30th January 1892							
	P	W	D	L	F	A	Pts
Notts Forest	15	11	3	1	49	14	25
Newton Heath	15	9	5	1	49	22	23
Sheffield Wednesday	16	10	2	4	51	26	22
Burton Swifts	17	9	2	6	39	40	20
Small Heath	14	6	4	4	31	27	16
Bootle	17	6	2	9	30	50	14
ARDWICK	17	4	4	9	30	43	12
Walsall Town Swifts	14	5	0	9	34	41	10
Lincoln City	11	4	1	6	20	35	9
Birmingham St Georges*	14	4	2	8	30	34	8
Crewe Alexandra	12	2	2	8	19	36	6
Grimsby Town*	12	2	3	7	21	24	5

* Birmingham St Georges and Grimsby Town have had 2 points deducted for playing ineligible men.

FEBRUARY 1892

On 6th February 1892, Ardwick played a friendly match at home against Fairfield and won by 8 goals to 1. The Ardwick goal scorers were Lafferty (4), Morris, Weir, Davies and Campbell.

Ardwick were now involved in cup competitions.

On 10th February 1892, Ardwick played away at Accrington in the first round of the Lancashire Senior Cup and lost by 6 goals to 0.

On 13th February 1892, Ardwick played away against Heywood Central in the first round of the Manchester Senior Cup and won by 3 goals to 1. The Ardwick goal scorers were Weir, Morris and Davies.

The next Alliance fixture was away at Small Heath Alliance on 20th February 1892. The match was played at Coventry. Milarvie who had missed the previous two Alliance fixtures returned for Ardwick. **W. Hopkins** who had joined Ardwick in the 1891 closed season made his first appearance and he was to keep his place in the team for the Alliance matches for the rest of the season.

20th February 1892   FOOTBALL ALLIANCE
Small Heath Alliance   4   v   Ardwick   0
1,000
Ardwick team: Douglas; Cooke and Robson; Milne Whittle and W. Hopkins; Davies Weir © Morris McWhinnie and Milarvie.

The ground was in fair condition after a lot of snow had been removed. Small Heath, who were strongly represented, started the game. HOPKINS hit a long shot which Hollies cleared. Ardwick forced a corner which went out. WHITTLE and MILNE kept out the Small Heath forwards although Waldon hit a good shot which DOUGLAS saved very coolly. WEIR got in a splendid position but the whistle went for off side. The game became very fast and Ardwick had the best of the exchanges. Small Heath forced a corner, but ROBSON cleared. A swift shot by WEIR was fisted out by Hollies. The Ardwick defence was then put under pressure. Waldon missed a good opening but Hallam opened the scoring easily beating DOUGLAS. A moment later the Small Heath forwards rushed up strongly and Waldon made amends for his earlier miss by scoring the second goal for Small Heath. At half-time Small Heath led by two goals to nil.

In the second half Ardwick, seemed to be handicapped by the state of the ground and made a gallant attempt to score but they were not to succeed. The Small Heath forwards broke away and scored a third goal and shortly before the end of the game Small Heath added a fourth goal. Ardwick played well but frequently experienced hard lines. The final score was Small Heath 4 goals Ardwick 0.

Following the defeat, Ardwick went on a good run for they were undefeated in the remaining four Alliance matches, and in three Cup and ten friendly matches, they only lost one game. Why Ardwick had not played much better earlier in the season in the Alliance was not clear. Ardwick had good, experienced players in Weir, Davies, Morris, Milarvie, Milne, Whittle, Robson and Douglas who had played in most of the Alliance fixtures and they should have been capable of challenging the leaders of the Alliance.

On 27th February 1892, Ardwick played a friendly at Hyde Road against Blackpool and won by 4 goals to 0. The Ardwick goal scorers were Morris (2), Weir and Milarvie.

MARCH 1892

On 1st March 1892, Ardwick played against Crewe Alexandra at Hyde Road. The attendance was only 2,000 even though there was a large contingent of apprentices in the crowd who were taking advantage of a holiday.

1st March 1892   FOOTBALL ALLIANCE
Ardwick   4   v   Crewe Alexandra   0
2,000

Ardwick team: Douglas; Cooke and Robson; Milne 1 Whittle and Hopkins; Davies 2 Weir © 1 Morris Milarvie and Sharpe

The ground was in good condition. Ardwick were the first to show up when WEIR obtained possession but MORRIS missed a good chance. Ardwick attacked again and DAVIES scored the first goal. Ardwick repeatedly went very close. WEIR broke through the Crewe defence and with a grand shot added a second goal. Crewe worked the ball up to the Ardwick end and DOUGLAS had to fist out. Two free kicks for Ardwick placed the Crewe goal in danger again and good combination by MORRIS, WEIR and DAVIES resulted in DAVIES scoring a third goal for Ardwick. One of the Crewe backs then fouled an Ardwick player and the referee awarded Ardwick a penalty kick from which MILNE had no difficulty in scoring the fourth goal for Ardwick just before half-time. At half-time Ardwick led by four goals to nil.

Immediately on the restart, Crewe went away and nearly scored but Ardwick returned to the attack very smartly and WEIR shot just over. Burrough had a good run for Crewe which was well stopped by WHITTLE. When the Crewe forwards did get into dangerous positions they shot wretchedly. SHARPE for Ardwick shot over from a good pass by MORRIS. ROBSON had to retire having wrenched his back. WEIR fell back to full back and Ardwick were forced to defend but the Crewe forwards could not get past COOKE and WEIR. The final score was Ardwick 4 goals Crewe Alexandra 0

On 2nd March 1892, Ardwick played a friendly against Heywood Central at Hyde Road and drew 2 goals each

The next Alliance match was against Birmingham St Georges. Robson was still injured and Hopkins took his place at full back with **Baker** making his debut and playing at half back. Sharpe moved from the forward line to half back and McWhinnie took his place in the forward line.

5th March 1892   FOOTBALL ALLIANCE
                Birmingham St George's   0   v   Ardwick   1

1,000

Ardwick team: Douglas; Cooke and Hopkins; Baker Sharpe and Milne 1; Davies Weir © Morris Milarvie and McWhinnie.

Ardwick were poorly represented whilst St Georges had their full strength side. St Georges played a good game at the beginning but Ardwick soon started to attack but their shooting was poor. St Georges gained the first corner and MILNE cleared the ball. Ardwick attacked again and after Coulton and Roberts stopped several shots MILNE eventually succeeded in scoring the first goal of the match. HOPKINS, who was playing at full back in place of ROBSON, was a tower of strength for Ardwick and had a very fine game. At half-time, Ardwick led by one goal to nil.

On resuming, a very fast game was witnessed, both sides working hard to score. Unfortunately shooting on the part of both teams' forwards was poor. St Georges made bold efforts to equalise. The score at full time was Ardwick 1 goal Birmingham St Georges 0

On 12th March 1892, Ardwick played Fairfield at West Manchester's ground in the semi-final of the Manchester Senior Cup and lost by 3 goals to 1. However, the match was ordered to be re-played.

On 16th March 1892, Ardwick played Third Lanark from the Scottish League at Hyde Road and drew 1 goal each.

On 19th March 1892, Ardwick played Preston North End at Hyde Road before an attendance of 6,000. The match ended in a draw, each side scoring 2 goals, the Ardwick goal scorers being Milne and Weir.

In March 1892, Ardwick made six new signings:

John McVickers	Full-back	Accrington
Harry Middleton	Half-back	Derby Junction
James Cairns	Half-back	
John W. Angus	Forward	Third Lanark
Hugh Angus	Forward	West Manchester
Adam Carson	Forward	Newton Heath

McVickers, **Middleton** and **John Angus** were all to make their first appearances in the match against Walsall Town Swifts on 26th March 1892.

26th March 1892   FOOTBALL ALLIANCE
                Walsall Town Swifts   2   v   Ardwick   2

2,000

Ardwick team: Douglas; McVickers and Middleton; Milne Whittle and Hopkins; Davies 1 Weir © 1 Morris J. Angus and Milarvie.

The ground was in good condition and the weather fine. Pangborn started the game for Walsall. A nice return by MIDDLETON was stopped by Stokes and Grey shot over the crossbar. At the Walsall end, Hawkins charged MORRIS and in doing so, let a shot from DAVIES go through the posts for Ardwick's first goal. Play was very fast. DOUGLAS saved very neatly a shot from the Walsall right wing. MORRIS was applauded for some really grand play. Ardwick pressed heavily and MORRIS shot over the cross bar. The first corner fell to Ardwick, but Grey headed away and MORRIS again shot over. HOPKINS had two shots at goal but both went wide and MIDDLETON again stopped grandly a sudden break away by the home right wing. Following a Walsall corner, DOUGLAS cleared well. WEIR scored a second goal for Ardwick very easily. Walsall then gained a free kick and scored their first goal. At half-time Ardwick led by two goals to one.

On resuming Walsall pressed and their forwards showed better combination than in the first half, but they could not score. As the game progressed Walsall tried desperately hard to draw level but the Ardwick defence was very strong, MIDDLETON especially being conspicuous whilst DOUGLAS in goal was very sure. Eventually, from a scrimmage Dixon equalised for Walsall amidst cheers. After this, both sides tried hard to get the winning goal and the excitement ran high. The final score was Walsall Town Swifts 2 goals Ardwick 2.

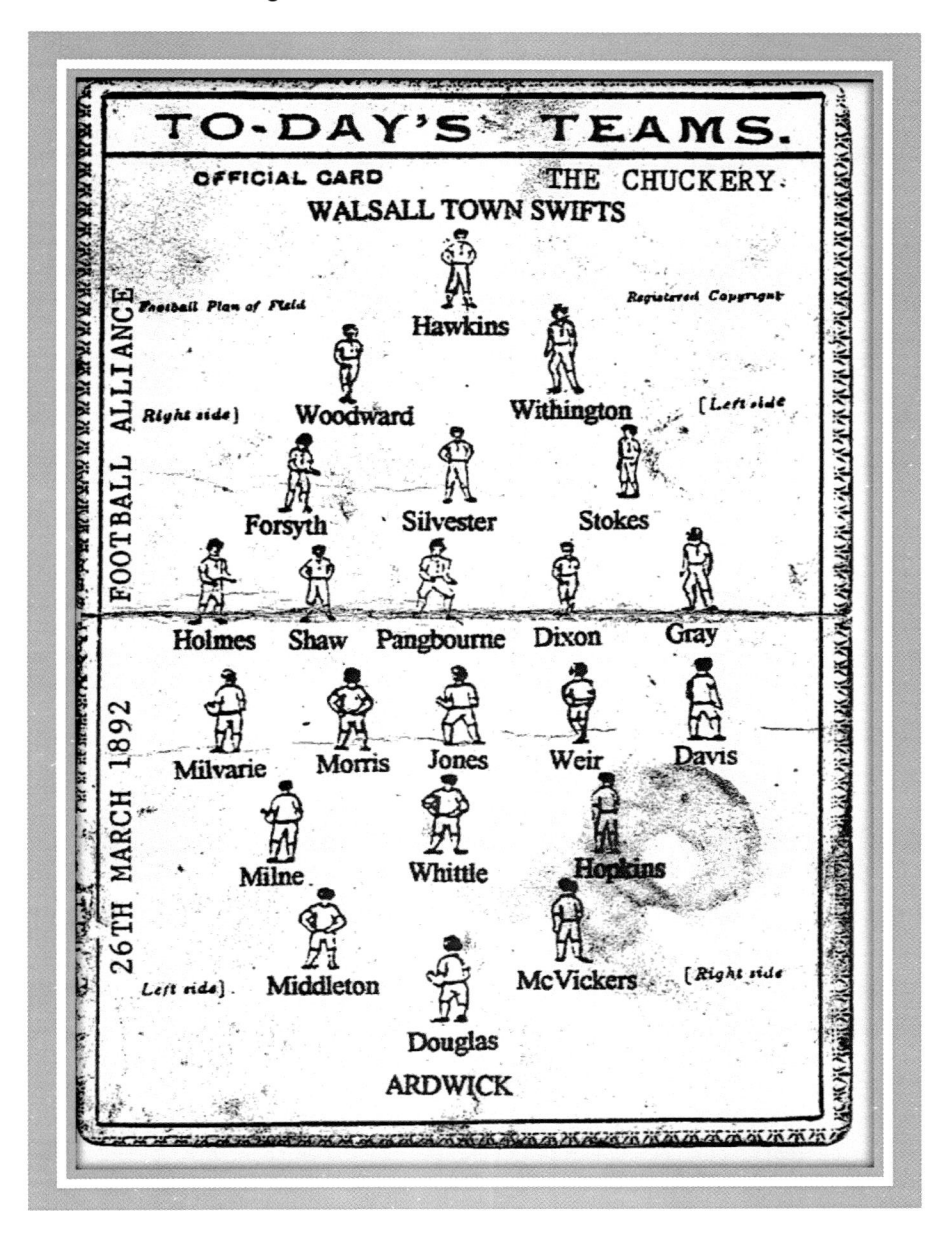

A very rare official card for the match.
The Ardwick team is correctly shown save that John Angus played and not Jones.

On 30th March 1892, Ardwick played Accrington from the Football League at Hyde Road and drew 3 goals each. The Ardwick goal scorers were J. Angus, Morris and an own goal.

APRIL 1892

On 2nd April 1892, Ardwick re-played the semi-final of the Manchester Senior Cup against Fairfield at Newton Heath's ground. On this occasion, Ardwick won by 4 goals to nil, the Ardwick goal scorers being Davies (2), McWhinnie and Milne.

147

Ardwick's last Alliance fixture was against Crewe Alexandra. Ardwick needed to win to finish above Crewe.

6th April 1892   FOOTBALL ALLIANCE
             Crewe Alexandra   2   v   Ardwick   2
2,000.
Ardwick team: Douglas; McVickers and Robson; Milne Middleton and Hopkins; Davies1 Weir © Morris J. Angus 1 and Milarvie.

From the kick off, Crewe had an advantage over Ardwick and after a good run, Lindop scored Crewe's first goal. Ardwick soon equalised through J. ANGUS. At half-time the score was Crewe Alexandra one goal Ardwick one.

In the second half, Ardwick took the lead through DAVIES but Crewe were not to be denied and Roberts headed through the Ardwick goal to equalise. The final score was Crewe Alexandra 2 goals Ardwick 2.

Ardwick finished the season in seventh position in the Football Alliance.

FOOTBALL ALLIANCE 1890-1891							
	P	W	D	L	F	A	Pts
Notts Forest	22	14	5	3	59	22	33
Newton Heath	22	12	7	3	69	33	31
Small Heath	22	12	5	5	29	15	29
Sheffield Wednesday	22	12	4	6	65	35	28
Burton Swifts	22	12	2	8	54	52	26
Crewe Alexandra	22	7	4	11	44	49	18
ARDWICK	22	6	6	10	39	51	18
Bootle	22	8	2	12	40	61	18
Lincoln City	22	6	5	11	37	65	17
Grimsby Town*	22	6	6	10	40	39	16
Walsall Town Swifts	22	6	3	13	33	59	15
Birmingham St Georges*	22	5	3	14	34	64	11

* Birmingham St Georges and Grimsby Town had 2 points deducted for playing ineligible men.

On 9th April 1892, Ardwick arranged a Benefit Match for David Weir against a team of Internationals. Ardwick had Poole from Glasgow Celtic playing for them and Weir played for the Internationals. The game ended in a draw with each side scoring 2 goals, Milarvie scoring both of Ardwick's goals.

Ardwick arranged five friendly matches in April.

On 12th April 1892, Ardwick lost by 2 goals to 1 against local rivals Gorton Villa at Hyde Road. Middleton scored for Ardwick.

On 16th April 1892, Ardwick beat Renton from the Scottish League by 5 goals to 1 at Hyde Road. Morris, H. Angus (2), J. Angus and Davies scored for Ardwick.

On 18th April 1892, Ardwick beat Notts County from the Football League by 3 goals to 1 at Hyde Road. Hugh Morris, John Angus and Hugh Angus scored for Ardwick.

Ardwick, who were the current holders of the Manchester Senior Cup, again got to the Final, after having beaten Heywood Central by 3 goals to 1 and Fairfield by 4 goals to 0.

The final of the Manchester Senior Cup against Bolton Wanderers took place on 23rd April 1892 on the ground of Newton Heath.

23rd April 1892　　　　**MANCHESTER SENIOR CUP FINAL**
　　　　　　　　　　　Ardwick　4　v　Bolton Wanderers　1

Newton Heath 5,000

Ardwick team: Douglas; McVickers and Robson; Middleton Whittle and Hopkins; Davies Morris 1 Weir © 2 Milne 1 and Milarvie.

There was a strong cross wind blowing which was slightly in favour of Ardwick. Ardwick attacked and DAVIES caused the Bolton goalkeeper to save. MORRIS then shot and the Bolton goalkeeper again saved. Bolton raced away but Cassidy was given off side. WEIR passed nicely to DAVIES who had hard lines with a fast shot which only just missed the goal. The game was then stopped for a short time as MIDDLETON received a kick in the face. When the game resumed, Wanderers attacked and DOUGLAS just managed to save. Gardiner then came through for Wanderers and gave Munro a grand opening but his final shot was poor. However, he made amends soon after by scoring after some loose play by ROBSON. MILARVIE made a grand run beating Somerville and putting the ball across for MORRIS to dash it through the Wanderers goal. At half-time the score was Ardwick one goal Bolton one.

In the second half MILNE restarted for Ardwick. The Wanderers had the wind slightly in their favour and attacked but McVICKERS relieved. WEIR then fastened onto the ball in midfield and went right through the Wanderers defence to score a grand goal amidst great cheers. The Wanderers had a chance to equalise but Gardiner's final shot went just over the cross bar. Wanderers gained a corner which MORRIS brought away. Paton tried a long shot which just went wide. Ardwick again broke away and gained a free kick from which MILNE scored. MILARVIE broke away and sent in a good shot which WEIR forced through the Wanderers goal. The Wanderers pressed but their shooting was wide of the mark. ROBSON and McVICKERS defended finely whilst WHITTLE was always in the thick of the fray. The final score was Ardwick 4 goals Bolton Wanderers 1.

To win the Manchester Senior Cup so convincingly against such good opposition was a very significant achievement.

On 26th April 1892, Ardwick played Everton from the Football League at Hyde Road and drew 1 goal each. Weir scored for Ardwick.

Ardwick's final game of the season took place on 30th April 1892, when Ardwick played Stoke from the Football League at Hyde Road before 5,000 spectators. Ardwick won by 5 goals to 1, with Weir (3), J. Angus and Milarvie scoring for them.

Ardwick had finished the season well but overall the season was disappointing. After a victory on 7th November 1891 against Walsall Town Swifts, Ardwick only won one of the next twelve Alliance matches.

Twenty three players played for the Alliance team and the twelve who made ten appearances or more were:

RECORDED APPEARANCES 1891-92	
William Douglas	22
Joseph Davies	22
Hugh Morris	22
David Robson	20
Robert Milarvie	20
David Weir	18
John Milne	18
Daniel Whittle	16
Walter McWhinnie	12
Charles Parry	11
S. Jackson	10
Alex Boggie	10

The leading goalscorers in the previous season had been: David Weir (32), Walter McWhinnie (23) and William Lambie (16). William Lambie had returned to Queen's Park. David Weir had played much of the season at full-back or half-back and only scored two goals. Walter McWhinnie had made twelve appearances and scored two goals.

The leading goalscorer in the 1891-92 Season was Hugh Morris with ten goals.

GOALSCORERS	
Hugh Morris	10
Joseph Davies	6
Alex Boggie	6
Robert Milarvie	5
John Milne	5
Walter McWhinnie	2
David Weir	2

In the closed season Cooke, J. Pearson, Powery and W. Sharpe left the club

On 6th May 1892, Ardwick were formally presented with the Manchester Senior Cup at the Spread Eagle Hotel, Manchester by Alderman Stephen Chesters Thompson, who was President of both Ardwick and the Manchester & District Football Association.

There was a large attendance, the company including Mr Stevenson (Chairman of Ardwick), Mr Cairns (Ardwick), Mr J.J. Bentley (Secretary of Bolton Wanderers) and Messrs. Furniss and Leech (Secretaries of Ardwick).

The presentation was made by Alderman Chesters Thompson to David Weir the Captain of the Ardwick team. The presentation was acknowledged in suitable terms by David Weir.

J.J. Bentley made some complimentary remarks observing that the victory of the Ardwick Club was rendered more creditable because whilst they were simply attached to the Alliance their opponents stood third in the Football League.

Later in the evening the annual dinner of the Ardwick Football Club took place at the Hyde Road Hotel, Ardwick.

On Friday, 13th May 1892, the Annual Meeting of the Football League was held at the Queen's Hotel, Sunderland. Ardwick applied to join the First Division and Mr Cairns spoke for Ardwick on their application. Ardwick were not successful but were elected to the Second Division. West Bromwich Albion, Accrington and Stoke were re-elected to the First Division. Nottingham Forest, Newton Heath and Sheffield Wednesday from the Alliance were also elected to the First Division.

Ardwick, Bootle, Burton Swifts, Crewe Alexandra, Grimsby Town, Lincoln City, Small Heath and Walsall Town Swifts from the Alliance were elected to the Second Division (Birmingham St. George's did not apply). Burslem Port Vale, Darwen, Northwich Victoria and Sheffield United were also elected to the Second Division.

SUMMARY

FOOTBALL ALLIANCE 1891-92

DATE		OPPONENT	RES	1	2	3	4	5	6
1891				7	8	9	10	11	
12-Sep	H	Bootle	D 3-3	W.DOUGLAS	A.FERGUSON	D.ROBSON	J.MILNE	D.WHITTLE1	H.DAVIDSON
			6000	J.DAVIES1	W.McWHINNIE	D.WEIR ©	H.MORRIS1	R.MILARVIE	
19-Sep	A	Lincoln City	L 0-3	Douglas	Ferguson	Robson	J.PEARSON	Whittle	Davidson
			2000	Davies	McWhinnie	Weir ©	Morris	Milarvie	
26-Sep	H	Burton	W 1-0	Douglas	Ferguson	Robson	Pearson	Whittle	Davidson
		Swifts	3000	Davies	McWhinnie	Morris 1	Milne	Milarvie ©	
10-Oct	A	Newton	L 1-3	Douglas	Weir ©	Robson	Pearson	Whittle	Davidson
		Heath	4000	Davies	Morris 1	Milne	POWERY	Milarvie	
17-Oct	H	Birmingham	W 4-3	Douglas	Weir ©	Robson	S.JACKSON	Milne	Davidson
		St.Georges	6000	Davies	McWhinnie1	A.BOGGIE 2	Morris 1	Milarvie	
07-Nov	H	Walsall	W 6-0	Douglas	Weir ©	Robson	Jackson	Whittle	C.PARRY
		Town Swifts	4500	Davies	Milne 1	Boggie 1	Morris 3	Milarvie 1	
14-Nov	H	Nottingham	L 1-3	Douglas	Weir ©	Robson	Jackson	Whittle	Parry
		Forest	8000	Davies	McWhinnie	Boggie	Morris	Milarvie 1	
19-Nov	A	Nottingham	L 0-4	Douglas	Weir ©	Robson	Jackson	Whittle	Parry
		Forest	2000	Davies	McWhinnie	Boggie	Morris	Milarvie	
21-Nov	A	Burton	D 4-4	Douglas	Weir ©	Robson	Jackson	Milne	Parry
		Swifts	1000	Davies	McWhinnie	Boggie 3	Morris	Milarvie 1	
28-Nov	H	Lincoln City	L 2-3	Douglas	Parry	Robson	Jackson	Weir ©	Milne
			1000	Davies 1	McWhinnie1	Boggie	Morris	Milarvie	
05-Dec	H	Sheffield	L 0-4	Douglas	Weir ©	Robson	Jackson	Whittle	Parry
		Wednesday	6000	Davies	McWhinnie	Boggie	Morris	Milarvie	
19-Dec	H	Newton	D 2-2	Douglas	COOKE	Robson	Jackson	Whittle	Parry
		Heath	10000	Davies	Morris	Milne 2	W.SHARPE	Milarvie©	
25-Dec	H	Grimsby	W 3-1	Douglas	Cooke	Robson	Jackson	Milne	Parry
		Town	6000	Davies	Morris 1	Boggie	Sharpe	Milarvie© 2	
26-Dec	A	Sheffield	L 0-2	Douglas	Cooke	Robson	Jackson	Whittle	Parry
		Wednesday	7000	Davies	Morris	Milne	Sharpe	Milarvie ©	
02-Jan	H	Small Heath	D 2-2	Douglas	Cooke	Robson	Weir ©	Whittle	Milne
1892		Alliance	4000	Davies	Morris 2	Boggie	McWhinnie	Milarvie	
23-Jan	A	Bootle	L 1-2	Douglas	Cooke	Robson	Pearson	Whittle	Milne
			2500	Davies	Morris	Parry 1	Weir ©	Sharpe	
30-Jan	A	Grimsby	L 0-4	Douglas	Cooke	Robson	Weir ©	Whittle	Milne
		Town	2000	Davies	Morris	Parry	Boggie	Sharpe	
20-Feb	A	Small Heath	L 0-4	Douglas	Cooke	Robson	Milne	Whittle	W.HOPKINS
		Alliance	1000	Davies	Weir ©	Morris	McWhinnie	Milarvie	
01-Mar	H	Crewe	W 4-0	Douglas	Cooke	Robson	Milne 1	Whittle	Hopkins
		Alexandra	2000	Davies 2	Weir © 1	Morris	Milarvie	Sharpe	
05-Mar	A	Birmingham	W 1-0	Douglas	Cooke	Hopkins	BAKER	Sharpe	Milne1
		St.Georges	1000	Davies	Weir ©	Morris	Milarvie	McWhinnie	
26-Mar	A	Walsall	D 2-2	Douglas	J.McVICKERS	H.MIDDLETON	Milne	Whittle	Hopkins
		Town Swifts	2000	Davies 1	Weir © 1	Morris	J.ANGUS	Milarvie	
06-Apr	A	Crewe	D 2-2	Douglas	McVickers	Robson	Milne	Middleton	Hopkins
		Alexandra	2000	Davies 1	Weir ©	Morris	Angus 1	Milarvie	

FOOTBALL ASSOCIATION CUP 1891-92

DATE		OPPONENT	RES	1	2	3	4	5	6
03-Oct	A	Newton	L 1-5	Douglas	Ferguson	Robson	J.Pearson 1	Whittle	Davidson
1891	Q	Heath	11000	Davies	Morris	McWhinnie	DEWAR	Milarvie ©	

Captain: ©   Alliance Debut: CAPITALS

FOOTBALL ALLIANCE 1891-92

	P	W	D	L	F	A	Pts
Notts Forest	22	14	5	3	59	22	33
Newton Heath	22	12	7	3	69	33	31
Small Heath	22	12	5	5	29	15	29
Sheffield Wednesday	22	12	4	6	65	35	28
Burton Swifts	22	12	2	8	54	52	26
Crewe Alexandra	22	7	4	11	44	49	18
ARDWICK	22	6	6	10	39	51	18
Bootle	22	8	2	12	40	61	18
Lincoln City	22	6	5	11	37	65	17
Grimsby Town*	22	6	6	10	40	39	16
Walsall Town Swifts	22	6	3	13	33	59	15
Birmingham St Georges*	22	5	3	14	34	64	11

* Birmingham St Georges and Grimsby Town had 2 points deducted for playing ineligible men.

ARDWICK A.F.C. 1891-1892 — FOOTBALL ALLIANCE APPEARANCES 1891-1892

	Player	Pos	Arrival	Previous Club	Apps	Goals	Departure
W.	Douglas	G	May 1890	Dundee Old Boys	22		Retained
	Cooke	FB	Dec 1891		9		C.S. 1892
A.	Ferguson	FB	C.S. 1891	Hearts	3		Oct 1891 Preston N.E.
J.	McVickers	FB	25 Mar 1892	Accrington	2		Retained
D.	Robson	FB	May 1890	Ayr United	20		Retained
	Baker	HB			1		
H.	Davidson	HB	C.S. 1891		5		Retained
W.	Hopkins	HB	C.S. 1891	Derby County	5		Retained
S.	Jackson	HB	Oct 1891		10		
J.	Milne	HB/F	May 1890	Bolton Wanderers	18	5	Retained
H.	Middleton	HB	9 Mar 1892	Derby Junction	2		Retained
C.	Parry	HB	Nov 1891	Everton	11	1	
J.	Pearson	HB	May 1890	Bolton Wanderers	4		C.S. 1892
D.	Whittle	HB	C.S. 1890	Halliwell	16	1	Retained
J.	Angus	F	Mar 1892	Third Lanark	2	1	Retained
A.	Boggie	F	Oct 1891		10	6	Jan 1892 West M/c.
J.	Davies	F	17 Feb 1891	Chirk	22	6	Retained
W.	McWhinnie	F	May 1890	Ayr United	12	2	Retained
R.	Milarvie	F	C/S 1891	Newton Heath	20	5	Retained
H.	Morris	F	Mar 1891	Chirk	22	10	Retained
	Powery	F			1		C.S.1892
W	Sharpe	F	Dec 1891		7		C.S. 1892
D.	Weir	F/FB	May 1890	Bolton Wanderers	18	2	Retained

ARDWICK A.F.C. 1890-1892   F.A.CUP APPEARANCES

Player		Pos.	1890-91 Apps	1890-91 Goals	1891-92 Apps	1891-92 Goals	TOTAL Apps	TOTAL Goals
William	Douglas	G	1		1		2	
	Harvie	FB	1				1	
David	Robson	FB	1		1		2	
Archibald	Ferguson	FB			1		1	
John	Milne	HB	1				1	
Daniel	Whittle	HB	1	1	1		2	1
	Simon	HB	1				1	
	Davidson	HB			1		1	
J.	Pearson	HB			1	1	1	1
Walter	McWhinnie	F	1	2	1		2	2
J.	Hodgetts	F	1	2			1	2
David	Weir	F	1	3			1	3
	Campbell	F	1	2			1	2
W	Rushton	F	1	2			1	2
Joseph	Davies	F			1		1	
Hugh	Morris	F			1		1	
Robert	Milarvie	F			1		1	
	Dewar	F			1		1	

LANCASHIRE SENIOR CUP 1891-92

DATE		OPPONENT	RES	1	2	3	4	5	6
1891				7	8	9	10	11	
10-Feb	A	Accrington	L 0-6						
1892	R1								

MANCHESTER SENIOR CUP 1891-92

13-Feb	A	Heywood	W 3-1	Douglas	Hopkins	Robson	J. Pearson	Whittle	Milne
1892	R1	Central		Weir © 1	Davies 1	Morris 1	Lafferty	McWhinnie	
12-Mar	N	Fairfield	L 1-3	Douglas	Cooke	Hopkins	Milne	Whittle	Baker
Semi Final		Replay Ordered		Davies	McWhinnie	Morris 1	Sharpe	Milarvie ©	
02-Apr	N	Fairfield	W 4-0	Douglas	Cooke	Robson	Milne 1	Whittle	Hopkins
Semi Final Rep.				Davies 2	Weir ©	Morris	McWhinnie 1	Milarvie	
23-Apr	N	Bolton	W 4-1	Douglas	McVickers	Robson	Middleton	Whittle	Hopkins
FINAL		Wanderers	5000	Davies	Morris 1	Weir © 2	Milne 1	Milarvie	

FRIENDLY MATCHES 1891-92

01-Sep	H	West	D 2-2	Douglas	Ferguson	Robson	"Horsborth"	Milne	Davidson
1891		Manchester		Davies 1	McWhinnie	Lafferty 1	Milarvie ©	Morris	
05-Sep	H	Gainsborough	W 2-1	Douglas	Ferguson	Robson 1	Milne	Whittle	Davidson
		Trinity	5000	Davies 1	McWhinnie	Lafferty	Milarvie ©	Morris	
07-Sep	H	Rossendale	L 1-4						
21-Sep	H	Denton	W 3-1	Douglas	Ferguson	Robson	Milne	Whittle	Davidson
			700	Anderson 1	McWhinnie 1	Lafferty 1	Milarvie ©	Smith	
28-Sep	H	Blackburn	D 1-1	Douglas	Ferguson	Robson	Milne	Whittle	Davidson
		Rovers	2000	Davies	Morris	McWhinnie 1	Thompson	Milarvie ©	
05-Oct	A	Denton	W 2-0	Douglas	Ferguson	Robson			
				Davies 1			Thompson 1	Milarvie	
08-Oct	A	West	W 3-0	Douglas	Ferguson	Robson	Jackson	Weir ©	Milne
		Manchester		Davies	Morris	Boggie 1	Powery 1	Milarvie 1	
24-Oct	H	Sunderland	W 2-1	Douglas	Weir ©	Robson	Jackson	Whittle	Milne 2
		Albion	5000	Davies	McWhinnie	Boggie	Mackay	Milarvie	
31-Oct	H	Stoke	W 5-2	Douglas	Weir ©	Robson	Jackson	Whittle	Milne
			4000	Davies	McWhinnie 1	Boggie 2	Morris 2	Milarvie	
02-Nov	A	Chirk	W 3-2						
							Morris 1	Milarvie 2	

Date	H/A	Opponent	Result						
12-Dec	H	Canadian XI	W 3-1	Douglas	Weir ©	Robson	Jackson	Whittle	Parry
				Davies	Morris 2	Milne 1	Milarvie	Baker	
16-Dec	H	Old Reptonians	W 1-0						
28-Dec	H	Sunderland	D 0-0	Douglas	Robson	Cooke	Boggie	Milne	Jackson
				Davies	Morris	Sharpe	McWhinnie	Milarvie ©	
01-Jan 1892	H	WestBromwich Albion	W 4-2 5000	Douglas Davies	Weir © Morris 2	Sharpe	Boggie McWhinnie1	Milarvie 1	
04-Jan	H	Airdrieonians	L 1-2	Stones	Cooke	Robson	Weir ©	Whittle	Milne
				McWhinnie	Morris	Boggie	Sharpe	Milarvie 1	
09-Jan	H	Bolton Wanderers	L 0-3	Douglas Davies	Cooke Morris	Robson Milne	J. Pearson Milarvie	Whittle Sharpe	Weir ©
16-Jan	H	Heywood Central	W 4-0	Douglas Davies 2	Cooke Morris 1	Robson1 Parry	Milne Milarvie	Whittle Sharpe	Weir ©
06-Feb	H	Fairfield	W 8-1 3000	Douglas Davies1	Hopkins Morris 1	Robson Campbell1	J.Pearson Weir © 1	Milne Lafferty 4	Parry
27-Feb	H	Blackpool	W 4-0 4000	Douglas Davies	Cooke Weir © 1	Robson Morris 2	Milne Milarvie 1	Whittle Sharpe	Hopkins
02-Mar	H	Heywood Central	D 2-2 1000	Douglas Davies	Cooke McWhinnie1	Weir Morris	Milne Milarvie	Whittle Sharpe 1	Rushton
16-Mar	H	Third Lanark	D 1-1 1000	Douglas Davies	McVickers Weir ©	Middleton Morris 1	Cooke J.Angus	Milne Milarvie	Hopkins
19-Mar	H	Preston North End	D 2-2 6000	Douglas Davies	McVickers Weir © 1	Middleton Morris	Milne 1 J. Angus	Whittle Milarvie	Hopkins
30-Mar	H	Accrington	D 3-3 2000	Douglas Davies	McVickers Morris 1	Robson Bostock	Milne J.Angus 2	Middleton Milarvie ©	Hopkins
09-Apr	H	Internationals Weir's Benefit	D 2-2	Douglas Davies	McVickers Morris	Robson Poole	Milne J. Angus	Whittle Milarvie © 2	Middleton
12-Apr	H	Gorton Villa	L 1-2 3000	Stones H.Angus	McVickers Davied	Robson Morris	Hopkins J. Angus	Middleton1 Milarvie	Cooke
16-Apr	H	Renton	W 5-1	Douglas Davies1	McVickers Morris 1	Robson J.Angus 1	Middleton H.Angus 2	Whittle Milarvie ©	Hopkins
18-Apr	H	Notts County	W 3-1	Douglas Davies	McVickers Morris 1	Robson J.Angus 1	Middleton H.Angus 1	Whittle Milarvie ©	Hopkins
26-Apr	H	Everton	D 1-1 2000	Douglas Morris	McVickers Davies	Robson J.Angus	Middleton Weir © 1	Milne Milarvie	Hopkins
30-Apr	H	Stoke	W 5-1 2500	Douglas Morris	McVickers Davies	Robson J.Angus 1	Middleton Weir © 3	Milne Milarvie 1	Hopkins

CHAPTER 16

ARDWICK ASSOCIATION FOOTBALL CLUB
1892-1893

SEPTEMBER 1892

Lawrence Furness continued as Hon Secretary in 1892.

Joshua Parlby assisted in an ex-officio capacity.

The previous season in the Football Alliance had not been a financial success. However, election to the Second Division of the Football League was enthusiastically received by the Ardwick supporters and a good number of season tickets were sold.

In March 1892, it was possible to improve the team by bringing in several experienced players: John McVickers, Harry Middleton, John Angus, Adam Carson and Hugh Angus

On 21st July 1892 Ardwick signed:

David Russell	Centre Half	Nottingham Forest

David Russell was born in Beith, Scotland in 1862. He was a famous centre half who played for the "invincible" Preston North End team in 1888-89 and 1889-90 making thirty nine League appearances and scoring four goals. He then joined Nottingham Forest and signed for Ardwick on 21st July 1892 when he was thirty.

On 5th August 1892, Ardwick signed:

Walter Bowman	Centre Half Right Half Inside Left	Accrington

Walter Bowman was born in Ontario, Canada in 1862 and was a Canadian International. He was a versatile player and could play as a half-back and forward.

He played for Accrington in 1891-92 and made five League appearances scoring three goals.

The players who were with Ardwick at the beginning of the season and who played in the league team were:-

ARDWICK PLAYERS 1892-93		
Player	Arrival	Previous Club
Goalkeepers		
William Douglas	May 1890	Dundee Old Boys
Full-backs		
David Robson	May 1890	Ayr United
John McVickers	25 Mar 1892	Accrington
Half-backs		
John Milne	C/S 1890	Bolton Wanderers
Daniel Whittle	C/S 1890	Halliwell
William Hopkins	C/S 1891	Derby County
Harry Middleton	19 Mar 1892	Derby Junction
David Russell	21 Jul 1892	Nottingham Forest
Forwards		
David Weir	May 1890	Bolton Wanderers
Joseph Davies	17 Feb 1891	Chirk
Hugh Morris	Mar 1891	Chirk
Robert Milarvie	C/S 1891	Newton Heath
John Angus	Mar 1892	Third Lanark
Hugh Angus	Mar 1892	West Manchester
Adam Carson	15 Mar 1892	Newton Heath
Walter Bowman	5 Aug 1892	Accrington
William Lambie	C/S 1892	Queen's Park

The team colours were white shirts with navy blue knickers

David Russell was appointed captain.

Ardwick's Reserve team joined the Lancashire Combination which had been formed in 1891-92.

The Ardwick first team at the beginning of the season was:-

    Douglas
    McVickers   Robson
    Middleton   Russell   Hopkins
Davies   Morris   J. Angus   Weir   Milarvie

The following players joined Ardwick during the season and played in the league team.

Player	Arrival	Previous Club
Goalkeeper		
H. Stones	22 Sep 1892	West Manchester
Full-back		
F. Steele	11 Oct 1892	
Forwards		
Thomas Forrester	5 Oct 1892	Stoke St. Peter's
Felix Mooney	15 Nov 1892	Bootle
James Yates	15 Nov 1892	Burnley
Wilmot Turner	26 Jan 1893	Stoke
G. Armitt	11 Feb 1893	Blackburn Rovers

Ardwick started the season on 1st September 1892 with a friendly match at Hyde Road against First Division opponents, Nottingham Forrest. The game ended in a very creditable draw with each side scoring two goals. J. Angus scored both goals for Ardwick.

On 3rd September 1892, the first league match in the Second Division of the Football League took place at Hyde Road against Bootle.

3rd September 1892   FOOTBALL LEAGUE   SECOND DIVISION
Ardwick   7   v   Bootle   0

4,000

Ardwick Team: Douglas; McVickers and Robson; Middleton Russell © and Hopkins; Davies 3 Morris 2 J. Angus 1 Weir 1 and Milarvie.

Notwithstanding the damp surroundings 4000 spectators assembled at Hyde Road to witness the first meeting of these teams under league rules. The visitors won the toss and J.ANGUS started for Ardwick. WEIR took the ball along the left but Arridge brought about a clever save and Grearson helped the ball up the field. RUSSELL returned and DAVIES racing away a goal seemed certain but with only the goalkeeper in front of him he shot wretchedly. From the goalkick, M. Lafferty had a chance and McVICKERS, was compelled to give a corner which however went behind. Owing to the wind and a missed kick by HOPKINS the ball was again taken to the Ardwick goal but Montgomery shot the ball over the bar. Some nice play by the Ardwick halves followed and DAVIES was loudly applauded for a fine bit of dribbling and a splendid shot. A foul by Hutchinson gave Ardwick a penalty kick which RUSSELL took, but he put in rather a poor shot and McLaughlin was able to save. Arridge came up to the front and the ball was dashed up to Law, but his shot was saved by DOUGLAS. Bootle's right wing now got away, but HOPKINS stopped them. WEIR rushed the ball along the left wing sending it across the field for MORRIS to score the first goal of the season. Law, a new addition to the Bootle team was playing a splendid game and repeatedly beat RUSSELL. The ball was again put into the Bootle half and DAVIES scored with the ball hitting the upright and rebounding through. From the restart, MIDDLETON got the ball and rounding his opponents, scored the third goal. Ardwick were now having all the game, completely penning Bootle in their own quarters. DAVIES and J.ANGUS quickly scored the fourth and fifth goals. At the interval Ardwick were leading by five goals to nil.

After the interval the game was resumed and Ardwick again assumed the offensive. For a time, Bootle kept their goal in tact but with a splendid high shot MORRIS scored the sixth goal. The Bootle halves were weak and as a consequence, the Ardwick forwards centred the ball as they liked. However, the Bootle players pulled themselves together, but the Ardwick defence did not have much difficulty in keeping them at bay. Finlayson had a grand chance of scoring for Bootle but shot too high. Ardwick gradually worked the ball up field but HOPKINS took the ball out. After some interesting play, DAVIES was responsible for scoring Ardwick's seventh goal. All the interest had now gone out of the game and with the rain falling heavily, the game ended with Ardwick wining by 7 goals to 0.

Ardwick could not have started their league season in a better manner and a week later they were away to Northwich Victoria.

10th September 1892   FOOTBALL LEAGUE   SECOND DIVISION
Northwich Victoria   0   v   Ardwick   3

3,000

Ardwick Team: Douglas; McVickers and Robson; Middleton Russell © 2 and Hopkins; Davies Morris 1 J. Angus Weir and Milarvie.

A good number of Ardwick supporters accompanied the team which was exactly the same as against Bootle. Northwich were short of their captain Crosier. RUSSELL, the Ardwick captain, won the toss and played against the wind. The game was very even and each goalkeeper was tested by MILARVIE and Macbeth respectively. With an easy chance of scoring Burrows hit a poor shot and a corner to the Victorians was badly put in. Finnerhan accidentally twisted his leg and had to be carried from the field but by strong defence and long kicks Ardwick were kept at bay so that at half-time there was no score.

Gow, the Northwich goalkeeper, did some grand work immediately after the game was restarted, J.ANGUS sending in a smart shot. Gradually asserting their superiority Ardwick scored the first goal, RUSSELL, giving Gow no chance of saving a high shot from the centre. MILARVIE got well down the left wing and passed to MORRIS who scored the second goal. DOUGLAS was then given some work to do and saved in marvellous fashion. RUSSELL scored Ardwick's third goal after some smart play by ROBSON. Ardwick won the game by 3 goals to 0.

Two days later Ardwick played Burslem Port Vale at Hyde Road.

12th September 1892   FOOTBALL LEAGUE   SECOND DIVISION
Ardwick   2   v   Burslem Port Vale   0

2,000
Ardwick Team: Douglas; McVickers and Robson; Middleton Russell © and Hopkins; Davies Morris J. Angus 1 Weir 1 and Milarvie.

Ardwick kept exactly the same team as played in the first two matches, whilst the visitors were short of Farrington their captain. J. ANGUS started the game for Ardwick. The opening stages were not exciting, each end being visited in turn, but the backs on both sides seemed able to cope with the attacks. Ardwick began to press and WEIR made three good attempts at scoring but without success. The Vale forwards returned and gained two corners in succession but ROBSON and DOUGLAS prevented any score. Ardwick continued to press and from a good centre by MORRIS, WEIR put in a good shot which completely beat Frail. Ardwick continued the pressure and MILARVIE and MORRIS both missed chances. The Vale forwards took up the running and tried hard to score but they were driven back and Ardwick were leading at half-time by one goal to nil.

Bliss re-started the game for Vale which was now slow and uninteresting with both sets of forwards being very loose. The Vale forwards did some neat passing, but when called upon DOUGLAS saved well. WEIR then got away but J. ANGUS missed an easy chance. The Vale forwards then returned on the attack but Walker shot over the bar. Ardwick attacked and MILARVIE almost scored. WEIR again got the ball and centring well, J. ANGUS managed to get the ball through the goal. The Vale forwards now tried hard to score but the Ardwick defence was too strong. Ardwick won by 2 goals to 0.

Ardwick had won the first three matches of the seaon and the team had remained unchanged. The next match was against Walsall Town Swifts at Walsall. Weir was injured and Lambie took his place.

17th September 1892   FOOTBALL LEAGUE   SECOND DIVISION
Walsall Town Swifts   2   v   Ardwick   4

2,000
Ardwick Team: Douglas; McVickers and Robson; Middleton, Russell © and Hopkins; Davies 2, Morris J. Angus 1 Lambie 1 and Milarvie

Ardwick were fully represented with the exception of WEIR, whose place was taken by LAMBIE. J.ANGUS started the match against the sun and a slight wind. DAVIES had a smart shot. A neat run by the Walsall forwards was stopped by ROBSON, but the ball went to Marshall who scored the first goal for Walsall. When close to the Walsall goal RUSSELL was fouled but nothing resulted from the free-kick. Ardwick pressed heavily and LAMBIE missed a glorious chance of equalising. A corner kick to Ardwick followed by a free-kick resulted in DAVIES shooting high over. Some pretty passing by Ardwick followed and J. ANGUS taking a pass from RUSSELL equalised. Walsall forced a corner off ROBSON but this came to nothing. J.ANGUS put the ball through the Walsall goal again but this was disallowed by the referee. Play was now chiefly in the Walsall half and both DAVIES and LAMBIE each scored. Walsall tried to penetrate the Ardwick defence but without avail. MILARVIE tried to get through but Hawkins safely negotiated the shot. At half-time Ardwick were leading by three goals to one.

On continuing, both Marlow and LAMBIE respectively had chances of scoring. ROBSON stopped Marlow very well. At this period of the game only the really fine defence of the Walsall team prevented a series of disasters. MIDDLETON did some good work and Shore and Robinson were equally effective. MILARVIE did some very tricky work on the wing. A foul relieved the Walsall goal and Walsall then attacked and Turner headed through to score Walsall's second goal. Walsall tried desperately hard to equalise, but failed, and with five minutes remaining DAVIES scored the fourth goal for Ardwick who won by 4 goals to 2.

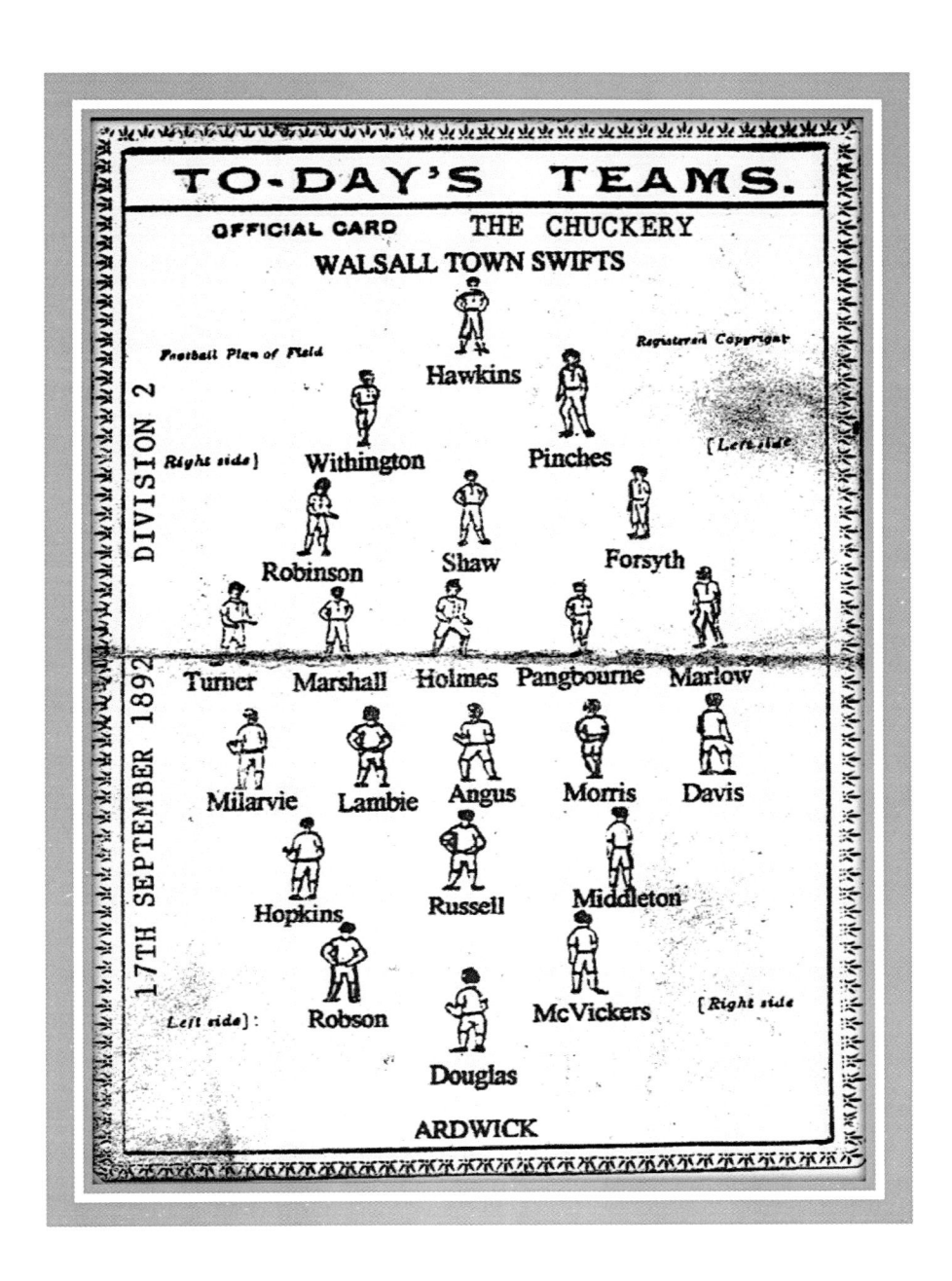

The Official Card of the match

    Ardwick had made a very good start to the season and were leading the Second Division by four points from Burton Swifts, Small Heath, Sheffield United, Darwin and Crewe Alexandra.

    There was some respite from the league and Ardwick's next match was against Fleetwood Rangers in a qualifying round of the Football Association Cup. This match should have been played at Fleetwood but after Ardwick made a tempting offer to their opponents, Fleetwood agreed to play the match at Ardwick. Ardwick were able to play their strongest team with the exception of Weir who was still absent and his place on this occasion was taken by Bowman. The match took place on Thursday, 22nd September 1892.

22nd September 1892   FOOTBALL ASSOCIATION CUP   Qualifying Round
                        Ardwick   1   v   Fleetwood Rangers   1

600

Ardwick Team: Douglas; McVickers and Robson; Middleton Russell © and Hopkins; Davies Morris J.Angus Bowman 1 and Milarvie.

J. ANGUS kicked off before very few spectators. Both DAVIES and J. ANGUS had shots which went over the upright. Ardwick pressed again and BOWMAN headed a splendid goal from a good corner kick by MILARVIE. Fleetwood had a chance and forced a corner but could not break through the Ardwick defence which was very good. Ardwick's forwards attacked and DAVIES hit the post with a good shot. RUSSELL gave the Rangers a corner but nothing resulted. A doubtful free kick was given against BOWMAN and the Rangers equalised. After the equaliser Ardwick played up but off side was given against them on two occasions when they appeared to be dangerous. Brogan shot over for the Rangers and MIDDLETON did likewise at the other end. ROBSON let in Hogan for the Rangers but his final shot went wide. At half-time the score was one goal each.

Rangers restarted the game and were the first to attack but ROBSON relieved. MILARVIE got away and J.ANGUS tried a long shot which went wide. J. ANGUS then passed to DAVIES who put in a fast shot which just skimmed the bar. Ardwick continued to have much the best of matters but could not score. The Ardwick forwards worked the ball down and J.ANGUS put the ball across but there was nobody there. The Rangers goalkeeper next gave a corner from a shot by RUSSELL but nothing resulted. Ardwick gained two further corners but no score resulted from either. After some even play the Ardwick forwards came down but J. ANGUS shot wildly over the bar. The Rangers forwards next broke away and put in a fine shot which DOUGLAS saved. At the call of time the score was Ardwick 1 goal Fleetwood Rangers 1. The Rangers refused to play extra time.

On 22nd September 1892, Ardwick signed:

H. Stones	Goalkeeper	West Manchester

H. Stones had no previous League experience

Ardwick had a return league match against Northwich Victoria at Hyde Road. Weir returned to the Ardwick forward line but Davies was absent and Lambie took his place.

24th September 1893   FOOTBALL LEAGUE   SECOND DIVISION
                             Ardwick   1   v   Northwich Victoria   1

6000

Ardwick Team: Douglas; McVickers and Robson; Middleton 1 Russell © and Hopkins; Morris Weir J. Angus Lambie and Milarvie.

Ardwick kicked off. WEIR played a fine game for Ardwick but he was unable to break through the Northwich defence. Bailey, with a shot from close in beat DOUGLAS and gave Northwich the lead. At half-time Northwich led by one goal to nil.

In the second half Ardwick, with the wind at their backs, strove hard to get through but could not. Ramsey was injured and the game was stopped for a minute or two. The ball burst and a fresh one had to be procured. Several corners fell to Ardwick but the visitors packed their goal and Ardwick could not score. However, with three minutes to go to the finish, MIDDLETON found an opening and scored. The game finished in a draw, Ardwick 1 goal Northwich Victoria 1.

The draw at home against Norwich Victoria was disappointing but nevertheless Ardwick remained at the top of the Second Division.

On 28th September 1892, Ardwick played a friendly game in Middlesborough against Middlesborough Ironopolis who were members of the Northern League and who were to be elected to the Second Division of the Football League in 1893-94. Before an attendance of 1,000, Ardwick played all their first team players and lost by 3 goals to 2 with both goals being scored by J. Angus.

At the end of September 1892, Ardwick were leading the Second Division with Burton Swifts in second place and Small Heath third.

FOOTBALL LEAGUE Second Division 30th September 1892							
	P	W	D	L	F	A	Pts
1.ARDWICK	5	4	1	0	17	3	9
2.Burton Swifts	3	3	0	0	12	4	6
3.Small Heath	4	3	0	1	12	5	6

OCTOBER 1892

On Saturday 1st October 1892, Ardwick had a return match at home against Walsall Town Swifts.

Ardwick were able to turn out their full team except that Milne took the place of Hopkins at half-back.

1st October 1892   FOOTBALL LEAGUE   SECOND DIVISION
Ardwick   2   v   Walsall Town Swifts   0

4000
Ardwick Team: Douglas; McVickers and Robson; Middleton Russell © and Milne; Davies 1 Morris J.Angus Weir 1 and Milarvie.

Ardwick kicked off in dull weather and did all the pressing for the first quarter of an hour. Hawkins had to save time after time, MORRIS DAVIES and MILNE all sending in shots. WEIR scored for Ardwick but the referee disallowed the goal. Later, however WEIR scored with a magnificent shot. Ardwick continued to have the best of matters and at half-time Ardwick led by one goal to nil.

Resuming, Ardwick severely taxed the Walsall defence. MILNE was playing finely and he sent shot after shot at the Swifts goalkeeper. DAVIES finally scored with a shot which gave the Walsall goalkeeper no chance to save. The latter portion of the game was very tame. A thunderstorm burst over the ground in the last ten minutes. Ardwick won by 2 goals to 0.

On 5th October 1892, Ardwick signed:

Tom Forrester	Centre Forward	Stoke St. Peter's

Tom Forrester had played for Stoke and then Stoke St. Peter's but had no previous League experience.

On Wednesday, 5th October 1892, Ardwick and Fleetwood Rangers met to replay the drawn F.A. Cup tie. Fleetwood had refused to play extra time and the Football Association ordered the match to be replayed at the Ardwick ground.

5th October 1892   FOOTBALL ASSOCIATION CUP   Qualifying Round Replay
Ardwick   0   v   Fleetwood Rangers   2

2,000
Ardwick Team: Douglas; McVickers and Robson; Middleton Russell © and Milne; Davies Morris Bowman Weir and Milarvie.

The weather was showery and only a moderate number of spectators had assembled when Craven commenced the game for Rangers. Ardwick were the first to show up, gaining a corner but nothing resulted. Hands against Rangers followed a good fist away by DOUGLAS. Weir transferred play and MILNE struck the bar with a grand shot. Chapman was forced to concede another corner to Ardwick, but again nothing came of it. The Rangers pressed but the Ardwick defence beat them off. Ardwick took another corner which Chapman smartly put out of danger and no score had been recorded at half-time.

Crossing over, Craven for Fleetwood made a desperate attempt to score without avail. A free kick for Ardwick close in was somewhat luckily cleared. Some rough play took place on both sides and the players were cautioned by the referee following a foul charge on DOUGLAS. Free kicks were frequent, but Fleetwood took the lead from a corner, the ball being scrimmaged through after a hard struggle. Each end was again visited but Brogan got clear of the Ardwick backs and notched a second goal for Rangers. When the final whistle blew the score was Fleetwood Rangers 2 goals Ardwick 0.

On Saturday, 8th October 1892, Ardwick lost their unbeaten league record.

8th October 1892   FOOTBALL LEAGUE   SECOND DIVISION
Darwen 3 v Ardwick 1

6,000

Ardwick Team: Douglas; McVickers and Robson; Middleton Russell © and Hopkins; Davies 1 Morris Milne Weir and Milarvie.

Great interest was taken in the meeting of the above teams at Darwen which was reflected in the large attendance. MILNE took the centre position for Ardwick in place of J.ANGUS. Ardwick losing the toss started against the wind. Following good passing WEIR obtained possession and placed the ball across smartly where DAVIES put it past Kenyon to score the first goal in less than a minute from the start. The Darwen forwards immediately dashed away and forced an abortive corner off ROBSON. MILARVIE got well down and Leach cleared at a critical moment. Sutherland and Lofhouse for Darwen were prominent, Douglas throwing out the ball from a swift shot by Sutherland. A well placed kick by Maxwell equalised the score. MILNE ably assisted by WEIR was very dangerous and Kenyon was forced to concede Ardwick several unproductive corners. However, before the interval arrived McKennie had put Darwen ahead. At half-time Darwen led by two goals to one.

A couple of showers fell and the ground got very holding but on resuming Ardwick attacked strongly without result. Wade made several fine runs for Darwen, and a desperate scrimmage close under Ardwick's goal was eventually cleared. WEIR was applauded for a straight run through and MORRIS brought Kenyon to his knees with a stinging shot. Immediately afterwards, WEIR put the ball through the Darwen goal but the referee would not allow the goal to be registered. Still keeping up the attack DAVIES shot and Leach with a long kick transferred play. MILARVIE let in McKennie who scored again for Darwen. Darwen won by 3 goals to 1.

Despite the defeat Ardwick still led the Second Division. On Monday 10th October 1892, Ardwick went to Cobridge to play a return league game against Burslem Port Vale.

10th October 1892   FOOTBALL LEAGUE   SECOND DIVISION
Burslem Port Vale 1 v Ardwick 2

1,000

Ardwick Team: Douglas; McVickers and Robson; Middleton Russell © and Hopkins; Davies Morris Milne Weir 2 and Milarvie.

Although defeated by Darwen last Saturday, Ardwick played the same team again. MILNE started the game for Ardwick against a stiff wind and McVICKERS and ROBSON showed good play against a strong attack by Bliss and Walker. Working the ball back again WEIR and MILNE were prominent for Ardwick but a smart return by Clutton gave Walker an opening and he promptly put the ball past DOUGLAS to give Port Vale the lead. There was good play by the Ardwick half-backs and a neat pass to DAVIES by HOPKINS enabled the former to smartly centre to WEIR who equalised. A free kick near Ardwick's goal was dangerous but MIDDLETON relieved. Several rushes by the Port Vale forwards next occurred but McVICKERS played a grand defensive game. At half-time the score was one goal each.

Crossing over Bliss tried to get through, but MIDDLETON checked him and the Vale goal had one or two narrow escapes. WEIR eventually gave Ardwick the lead with a magnificent shot. DOUGLAS saved well from Walker and Dean. Frail at the other end saved his side from a severe defeat with shots being rained in upon him by DAVIES, WEIR and HOPKINS. A free kick was taken by the Vale close on time but the Ardwick defence was too strong. The game ended with a victory for Ardwick by 2 goals to 1.

On 11th October 1892, Ardwick signed:

F. Steele	Right Back Centre Forward

On 22nd October 1892, Ardwick played Small Heath Alliance at Hyde Road.

22nd October 1892   FOOTBALL LEAGUE   SECOND DIVISION
Ardwick 2 v Small Heath Alliance 2

3,000
Ardwick Team: Douglas; McVickers and Robson; Middleton Russell © and Hopkins; Davies Morris 1 Lambie Weir 1 and H. Angus.

    Mobley started the game for Small Heath, who at once began to press. ROBSON was cheered for fine play. The Ardwick forwards went away and after a fine cross from H.ANGUS, MORRIS scored a grand goal. The Ardwick forwards pressed and WEIR gave Ollis a testing shot to save. Two fruitless corners to Ardwick followed and DAVIES tried a long shot which went wide. "Hands" near the Small Heath goal looked dangerous but Bailey cleared. Ardwick gained a corner and RUSSELL just headed past the post. Play was very even in mid-field, both sets of backs showing up well. A foul against ROBSON gave Small Heath a chance but the ball was put over the bar. The Ardwick forwards again ran down and WEIR scored with a well-judged shot. The visitors now had a chance but shot badly. WEIR played grandly and passed the backs but LAMBIE missed the centre. Ollis saved several good shots and at half-time the score was Ardwick two goals Small Heath nil.

    On resuming it was raining heavily and the game progressed in a fearful storm of hail and rain. Small Heath pressed and Whelden got the ball into the net, and soon afterwards Small Heath equalised. Both teams worked hard to get the lead and LAMBIE was unlucky when heading against the cross bar. The final score was a draw, Ardwick 2 goals Small Heath 2.

The match against Small Heath Alliance was William Lambie's last appearance for Ardwick and he returned to Queen's Park

FOOTBALL LEAGUE Second Division 22nd October 1892	P	W	D	L	F	A	Pts
ARDWICK	9	6	2	1	24	9	14
Darwen	8	6	0	2	20	9	12
Small Heath	8	5	1	2	25	12	11
Burton Swifts	6	4	0	2	18	10	8
Sheffield United	6	4	0	2	10	5	8
Burslem Port Vale	8	3	1	4	14	18	7
Grimsby Town	7	3	0	4	9	10	6
Northwich Victoria	6	2	1	3	11	13	5
Walsall Town Swifts	7	2	0	5	9	18	4
Crewe Alexandra	7	2	0	5	10	27	4
Bootle	7	1	1	5	6	19	3
Lincoln City	5	1	0	4	8	14	2

On 29th October 1892, Ardwick played a home friendly against Middlesborough and won by 6 goals to 3. The Ardwick goal scorers were Weir 3, Morris 2 and Russell.

NOVEMBER 1892

Ardwick were still Second Division leaders. The next game was at Grimsby

5th November 1892   FOOTBALL LEAGUE   SECOND DIVISION
Grimsby Town 2 v Ardwick 0

2,000
Ardwick team: Douglas; McVickers and Robson; Middleton Russell © and Hopkins; Davies Morris Weir Milne and H. Angus.

    Each side was well represented. WEIR kicked off against the wind. MIDDLETON frustrated a well meant attack by Riddoch and Walker. A run to the other end was nearly fatal to Grimsby as WEIR only just failed to reach the ball after Lundie had misjudged it. MILNE led another attack and forced Whitehouse to come out of goal to save. Long kicks by Lundie and Frith gave the home forwards a chance but after DOUGLAS had saved and Riddoch had missed an easy chance of scoring, Murrell gave Grimsby the lead when close up. A second goal fell to Grimsby but Higgins was near to being given off-side. Though HOPKINS fed his forwards untiringly, Ardwick failed to beat Lundy and Frith. At half-time Grimsby led by two goals to nil.

On the resumption, from a backward pass, HOPKINS with a long shot forward put the ball right in the goalmouth and it found its way into the net but the referee failed to allow the goal. A corner was then forced off VICKERS but he cleared well. Shots were put in by WEIR, MILNE and RUSSELL, but the Grimsby backs played confidently and kept forcing them back. An off-side goal was scored by Henderson. Energetic play by MILNE gave Ardwick another chance but H. ANGUS failed badly. Though the ball was kept in the Grimsby half up to the finish Ardwick could not penetrate the strong defence and retired beaten by 2 goals to 0 thus losing top place in the Second Division of the League.

On 12th November 1892, Ardwick played a friendly against Bolton Wanderers at Hyde Road and won by 3 goals to 0 with Milarvie, Morris and Davies all scoring. At that time Bolton were eighth in the First Division and the match attracted a good attendance of 5,000 spectators.

The Ardwick Committee decided to strengthen the team and signed two players on 15th November 1892:-

Felix Mooney	Inside Left Centre Forward	Bootle

Felix Mooney was an inside left or centre forward. He was signed from Bootle and had no previous League experience

James Yates	Outside Right	Burnley

James "Jimmy" Yates

James Yates was born in Sheffield in 1871. In 1891-92 he played for Burnley but made no League appearances. He signed for Ardwick on 15th November 1892. He was a fast and clever outside right and became a firm favourite with the Ardwick supporters.

On 19th November 1892, Ardwick played a friendly away to Middlesborough and lost by 6 goals to 3 with Weir, Middleton and Mooney scoring for Ardwick.

On 26th November 1892, Ardwick had a League fixture against Burton Swifts. Two new forwards, **Tom Forrester** and **Felix Mooney** made their first league appearances in place of Morris and Milarvie respectively.

26th November 1892   FOOTBALL LEAGUE   SECOND DIVISION
Ardwick   1   v   Burton Swifts   1

1,000

Ardwick team: Douglas; McVickers and Robson; Middleton Russell © 1 and Hopkins; Davies Forrester Weir Morris and Mooney.

These close rivals (Ardwick were third and Burton Swifts fourth in the Second Division) met at Ardwick and the ground was in a very heavy state but the referee ruled it was fit for a league match. Worrall started for the Swifts but WEIR forced the play. Accurate passing was impossible but Ardwick took the lead from a penalty kick awarded for a foul against FORRESTER. RUSSELL took the kick and scored. From a return by Furniss, Perry obtained the ball in an apparently off-side position but no whistle blew and it was rushed through by Worrall who equalised the score. FORRESTER, WEIR and RUSSELL worked strenuously to find an opening and several corners were taken by Ardwick but to no avail. At half-time the score was one goal each.

WEIR restarted and by dashing and determined play the Swifts goal had numerous lucky escapes. The assaults upon DOUGLAS were only spasmodic and hardly ever dangerous but in spite of brilliant individual play on the part of the Ardwick team they could not beat Hadley, although they worked extremely hard up to the last minute. Two apparently certain goals were missed by DAVIES and WEIR through the treacherous state of the ground. The result was Ardwick 1 goal Burton Swifts 1.

Ardwick had played one half of their League fixtures and had fifteen points. They were now third in the League, behind Small Heath and Darwen, who both had seventeen points.

FOOTBALL LEAGUE Second Division 26th November 1892						
	P	W	D	L	F	A	Pts
1.Small Heath	11	8	1	2	34	17	17
2.Darwen	12	8	1	3	30	14	17
3.ARDWICK	11	6	3	2	25	12	15

DECEMBER 1892

In December 1892, **John Angus** was transferred to Southampton St. Marys.

Ardwick's next two fixtures were friendly matches against two First Division sides Notts County and Stoke

On 3rd December 1892, Ardwick drew 3 goals each with Notts County at Hyde Road, with Forrester (2) and Hopkins scoring for Ardwick.

On 10th December 1892, Ardwick lost by 6 goals to 2 against Stoke at Hyde Road, with Weir and Davies scoring for Ardwick.

On 17th December 1892, Ardwick resumed their league campaign with an excellent victory against Darwen who were leading the Second Division.

17th December 1892   FOOTBALL LEAGUE   SECOND DIVISION
Ardwick   4   v   Darwen   2

3,000

Ardwick team: Douglas; McVickers and Robson; Middleton Russell © and Hopkins; Davies Morris Weir 2 Mooney 1 and Milarvie 1.

WEIR started the game and Ardwick at once attacked but MILARVIE shot wide. Darwen returned and gained a fruitless corner. WEIR almost got clear but Orr just relieved in time. Darwen swarmed around the Ardwick goal, and after a short struggle the ball was forced through. Ardwick now strove hard and WEIR, beating both full-backs, scored with a magnificent shot. Soon afterwards

WEIR forced Kenyon to concede a corner from which the ball was forced through the goal by MOONEY. The cheering was deafening. Ardwick continued to press but Leach and Orr were safe. Darwen attacked and had hard lines. The game was then stopped through an accident to Fish who had to be carried from the field. Soon after the restart Darwen were dangerous but DOUGLAS saved in a wonderful manner. Ardwick attacked and MOONEY put in a good long shot which Kenyon saved. The Ardwick forwards continued to press and a second corner was forced off Kenyon. MORRIS took the kick and MILARVIE scored Ardwick's third goal. When half-time arrived the score was Ardwick three goals Darwen one.

Soon after the re-start WEIR added an excellent goal for Ardwick. Entwistle then almost scored a second goal for Darwen forcing DOUGLAS to thrust the ball over the bar. The game continued hard and exciting. From a corner to Darwen the ball passed under the bar but as nobody had touched it the goal was not allowed. McKennie after half an hour's play added a second for Darwen and reduced Ardwick's lead to two. The game was hard fought to the end. The Ardwick defence played well and they gained a popular victory winning by 4 goals to 2.

On 24th December 1892, Ardwick had an away match against Lincoln City who were bottom of the League. Tom Forrester and **James Yates** (who was making his debut) played in place of Davies and Milarvie.

24th December 1892   FOOTBALL LEAGUE   SECOND DIVISION
Lincoln City   2   v   Ardwick   1
1,000

Ardwick team: Douglas; McVickers Robson; Middleton Russell © Hopkins; Morris Forrester 1 Weir Mooney and Yates.

The first league match between these teams was played on John-o'-Gaunt's ground. Ardwick started the game and were the first to press but the ball was carried over the touchline by FORRESTER. Aided by a couple of useful kicks by Neil and Roberts, the Lincoln forwards got well down, and after DOUGLAS had saved very smartly, Smallman beat him with a difficult shot thus scoring the first goal for Lincoln. Later on WEIR put the ball high over the bar. Corners were taken by each side but the score remained unaltered when half-time arrived with Lincoln City leading by one goal to nil.

After half an hours play in the second half a corner was conceded by RUSSELL, from which Richardson rushed the ball past DOUGLAS. A little more dash was then shown by Ardwick's wing forwards, who were well assisted by the halves, and FORRESTER headed through very smartly for them. Although Ardwick were dangerous towards the end of the game Lincoln eventually won by 2 goals to 1.

Ardwick remained in third place.

FOOTBALL LEAGUE Second Division 24th December 1892							
	P	W	D	L	F	A	Pts
Darwen	16	11	1	4	45	25	23
Small Heath	15	10	2	3	57	22	22
ARDWICK	13	7	3	3	30	16	17
Sheffield United	11	7	1	3	34	12	15
Burton Swifts	12	6	1	5	27	22	13
Grimsby Town	11	6	0	5	20	13	12
Northwich Victoria	10	4	1	5	21	25	9
Burslem Port Vale	14	3	2	9	16	43	8
Walsall Town Swifts	11	3	1	7	21	44	7
Lincoln City	9	3	1	5	15	21	7
Bootle	13	2	3	8	19	41	7
Crewe Alexandra	11	3	0	8	23	44	6

On 26th December 1892, Ardwick played Glasgow Celtic at Hyde Road, Ardwick. The match was played for the benefit of the Catholic Charities of Manchester and though the weather was bitterly cold and the ground was most unmistakably hard, no fewer than 8500 spectators assembled. Glasgow Celtic played their strongest possible eleven but Ardwick were weakened by the absence of Russell, Weir (who could not play due to a sudden domestic bereavement) and Davies (who had suffered an injury in the match against Darwen). Ardwick were no match for Celtic and Glasgow Celtic won by 5 goals to nil.

Ardwick then played friendly matches against Glasgow Thistle, Newton Heath and Blackpool South Shore.

On 31st December 1892, Ardwick lost by I goal to nil against Glasgow Thistle at Hyde Road.

JANUARY 1893

On 2nd January 1893, Ardwick lost by 5 goals to 3 against Newton Heath before an attendance of 10,000 spectators at Hyde Road, with Weir (2) and Morris scoring for Ardwick.

On 7th January 1893, Ardwick beat Blackpool South Shore by 5 goals to 1 before an attendance of 1,000 spectators at Hyde Road, with Milne (2), Milarvie, Morris and Davies scoring for Ardwick.

On 11th January 1893, Ardwick played a team of Internationals at Hyde Road, the match being arranged for the benefit of the Ardwick Club. The match was played with the aid of Wells lights. Rain threatened during the day but fortunately held off. Nevertheless the ground was described as being very bad and pools of water lay about in all directions. There was an attendance of 2,000 spectators. WEIR played for the team of Internationals who beat Ardwick by 5 goals to 0.

On 14th January 1893, Ardwick played at Burton-on-Trent against Burton Swifts. Ardwick were short of John McVickers and Joe Davies whose places were taken by Daniel Whittle and John Milne.

14th January 1893   FOOTBALL LEAGUE   SECOND DIVISION
Burton Swifts 2 v Ardwick 0
1,000
Ardwick team: Douglas; Hopkins and Robson; Middleton Russell © and Whittle; Milne Morris Weir Mooney and Milarvie.

WEIR commenced the game and MILNE got away at once but was forced over the line by Berry. A strong attack by Worrall Emery and Dewey was cleverly diverted by WHITTLE and HOPKINS before they could get within shooting range. From a long kick, MILARVIE got possession and nearly scored with a high shot, but the chance was missed. Neat passing in the open by the Swifts brought them up to the Ardwick end. Two corners were forced, but both were unproductive. A rough scrimmage in which five or six players were locked together ended in favour of Ardwick. Berry again transferred play but there was a smart return by RUSSELL which gave WEIR a chance, Hadley running far out to save a dangerous shot. West forced another abortive corner off DOUGLAS and RUSSELL headed away. Sutherland robbed MORRIS and let in Worrall. After some close passing in front of goal Worrall gave Burton the lead from close quarters, DOUGLAS being covered and unable to reach the ball. A dangerous run was made by MILARVIE and WEIR the latter shooting in hard, the ball luckily cannoning off Furniss. The interval arrived with Burton Swifts leading by one goal to nil.

Emery started the second half and the Swifts were soon dangerous but HOPKINS and ROBSON were very steady. Keeping up a strong series of attacks the Swifts forwards were at last successful as RUSSELL interfered with HOPKINS giving Worrall a splendid chance and he scored. The Ardwick wing forwards especially MILARVIE occasionally made splendid spurts, but with little assistance their efforts were easily checked by Furniss and Berry. The final score was Burton Swifts 2 goals Ardwick 0.

On 21st January 1893, Ardwick played at Bootle. The match against Bootle was Weir's last appearance for Ardwick.

21st January 1893   FOOTBALL LEAGUE   SECOND DIVISION
Bootle 5 v Ardwick 3

800

Ardwick team: Douglas; Hopkins and Robson; Middleton 1 Russell © and Whittle; Milne Davies Mooney 2 Weir and Milarvie.

The second meeting of these two Clubs took place at Bootle. The Cup Tie at Everton spoiled the "gate". Starting against a strong wind Ardwick were called upon very early to defend and STEELE, ROBSON and RUSSELL soon showed good defensive play. Some even play followed but RUSSELL then conceded a corner from which Grearson headed through to score the first goal for Bootle. Montgomery scored a second goal for Bootle. Hughes caused DOUGLAS to save brilliantly. Pretty work by MILNE and DAVIES was spoiled by MIDDLETON kicking rashly and a free kick to Ardwick was grandly put in by HOPKINS but was successfully headed away. After some good passing Clarkin scored the third goal for Bootle who led at half-time by three goals to nil.

Better play was seen at the commencement of the second half, both WEIR and MOONEY troubling Whitehead, whilst MILARVIE shot across the goal in splendid fashion. Montgomery added the fourth and fifth goals for Bootle, the tricky passing of Hughes and Grierson defeating the Ardwick halves Ardwick improved and after MOONEY had missed a grand chance he made up for the mistake by scoring a good goal. A moment later MIDDLETON added a second and in the last few minutes MOONEY got another goal. Time was called and Bootle won by 5 goals to 3.

On 26th January 1893, **David Weir** returned to Bolton Wanderers. Weir had been Ardwick's leading player and could play equally well in defence as in the forward line. His departure was a great loss and probably arose because the club's financial position was causing the Ardwick Committee some concern.

On 26th January 1893, Ardwick signed:

Wilmot Turner	Centre Forward	Stoke

Wilmot Turner was a centre forward who had scored 8 goals in 32 league appearances for Stoke.

On Saturday 28th January 1893, Ardwick played a first round Lancashire Senior Cup tie against Rossendale before an attendance of 3,000 spectators at Hyde Road. After extra time, Ardwick won by 3 goals to 2 with their goals being scored by Russell (2) and Milarvie.

On Monday 30th January 1893, Ardwick played a return League match against Grimsby Town at Hyde Road. Owing to the firm stand taken by the Ardwick Committee (which was believed to relate to player's wages and bonuses), the Ardwick team was not as strong as it might have been but the visitors were well represented.

30th January 1893   FOOTBALL LEAGUE   SECOND DIVISION
Ardwick 0 v Grimsby Town 3

1000

Ardwick team: Douglas; Steele and Robson; Middleton Whittle and Hopkins; Yates Forrester Russell © Mooney Milarvie.

Mullen started the game for Grimsby and MILARVIE at once got well down, Lundie however forcing him over the line. A bad pass by RUSSELL let in Higgins, and though DOUGLAS fell in saving his shot Riddoch placed the ball between the posts, the goal being allowed after an appeal. A couple of corners were gained by Ardwick but Lundie clearing splendidly. With a beautiful chance from a centre by MILARVIE, MOONEY put the ball out. DOUGLAS was again called upon to save from Mullen and Fletcher. STEELE kicking rashly let Riddoch get past, but HOPKINS intervened just as Fletcher reached the centre. Two free kicks for fouls against RUSSELL and MOONEY gave Ardwick no tangible advantage and at half-time the score was Grimsby one goal Ardwick nil.

The opening play in the second half was in favour of Ardwick, RUSSELL causing Whitehouse to save grandly and another scrimmage close in again gave the goalkeeper an opportunity of showing marvellous form. Lundie and Reid then gained the upper hand with the Ardwick forwards and more combined play was shown by the Grimsby front rank, Fletcher scoring twice very cleverly from good work by Akroyd and Higgins. Ardwick were beaten for the first time on their own ground in a League match this season by 3 goals to 0.

FOOTBALL LEAGUE Second Division 30th January 1893						
	P	W	D	L	F	A	Pts
4. ARDWICK	16	7	3	6	33	26	17

FEBRUARY 1893

Ardwick were in fourth place but the defeat at Hyde Road was bitterly disappointing. On 4th February 1893, Ardwick played a league match against the amateurs of Crewe Alexandra. Hopkins failed to turn up and Middleton went to full back for Ardwick, with Milne moving to half-back. **Wilmot Turner** who had recently been signed from Stoke made his debut at centre forward

4th February 1893   FOOTBALL LEAGUE   SECOND DIVISION
Crewe Alexandra   4   v   Ardwick   1
1,000
Ardwick team: Douglas; Middleton and Robson; Milne Russell © and Whittle; Yates 1 Forrester Turner Mooney and Milarvie.

TURNER started the game on the very soft Crewe ground and MILARVIE at once got away but Cope allowed his final shot to go into touch. From the goal kick, Roberts troubled the Ardwick defence eventually forcing a corner and Williams headed the ball past DOUGLAS after six minutes play. Good combined play by Ardwick resulted in shots from FORRESTER MOONEY and MILARVIE being cleverly saved by Hickton but weak play by RUSSELL let in Macduff who scored a second goal for the Cheshire team. YATES next got in a beautiful centre which TURNER just failed to reach but a series of strong attacks by Ardwick at last proved successful, and YATES scored. ROBSON was beaten by the right wing just before the interval, Barnett meeting a good centre from a doubtful position, scored Crewe's third goal. The half-time score was Crewe Alexandra three goals Ardwick one.

Fast play was seen upon resuming the game, Roberts and Barnett being very prominent, MIDDLETON, however, checked them neatly. For a long time Ardwick had considerably the better of the game YATES especially doing good work, but with RUSSELL showing poor form, the smart tackling of the home halves prevented any score. A magnificent centre from FORRESTER was unluckily missed by MILARVIE and Hickton gave a splendid exhibition of goalkeeping successfully dealing with shots from all quarters. A burst away by Williams gave Macduff an opportunity and he scored a fourth goal after Barnett had struck the post. The game ended Crewe Alexandra 4 goals Ardwick 1.

With the defeat by Crewe Alexandra, Ardwick had lost five consecutive league games and had not won a league match since their good victory over Darwen on 17th December 1892. Ardwick's two most experienced players had been WEIR who had already returned to Bolton Wanderers and RUSSELL who showed poor form in the game against Crewe Alexandra. RUSSELL did not play any further league games for Ardwick, although he did play in a friendly against Middlesborough Ironopolis on 11th February 1893 as well as in a Manchester Senior Cup Match against Bury on 25th February 1893.

On 9th February 1893, Ardwick signed:

J. Hargreaves	Outside Left	Northwich Victoria

J.Hargreaves, was an outside left from Northwich Victoria who did not play in the league team until the following season.

On 11th February 1893, Ardwick signed:

G. Armitt	Outside Left	Blackburn Rovers

G. Armitt, was also an outside left. He had not made any League appearances for Blackburn Rovers.

On 11th February 1893, Ardwick played Middlesborough Ironopolis in a friendly at Hyde Road and lost by 3 goals to 1, with YATES scoring for Ardwick.

On Tuesday 14th February 1893, Ardwick played a friendly against Blackpool at Hyde Road and lost by 7 goals to 2.

On Tuesday 18th February 1893, Ardwick played a return league match against Crewe Alexandra at Hyde Road. Steele, Morris and Bowman were included in the Ardwick team in place of Russell, Forrester and Turner. At last, Ardwick were successful!

18th February 1893　　　　FOOTBALL LEAGUE　　　　SECOND DIVISION
Ardwick　3　v　Crewe Alexandra　1

1,000
Ardwick team: Douglas ©; Hopkins and Robson; Middleton Steele and Whittle; Yates 1 Morris Milne Bowman 1 and Milarvie 1.

DOUGLAS (who appears to have been Captain) decided choice of ends and Crewe started the game. Crewe soon obtained a corner and BOWMAN cleared the ball. After good work by MILNE and WHITTLE, BOWMAN scored the first goal for Ardwick with a grand shot. From a free kick, MIDDLETON banged the ball through but with no other player intervening nothing resulted. Working cleverly down the centre MILNE forced his way past Cope and Stafford, beating Hickton with his final shot. The referee however disallowed the goal amidst shouts of disapproval. After smart individual play by Barnett and Williams, the Ardwick forwards continually kept Crewe on the defensive and at half-time, Ardwick led by one goal to nil

MILNE restarted the game and though the heavy ground prevented accurate passing, each team was cheered for determined work. A centre from the right on the touch line by Roberts enabled Pickard and Payne to equalise the score and but for the smartness of DOUGLAS a second would have been added. Ardwick scored a second goal through a magnificent piece of work by YATES. After several fine runs by YATES he gave the ball to MILARVIE who scored a third goal. Playing steadily up to the finish, ROBSON and HOPKINS kept off the Crewe forwards and Ardwick were close to the Crewe goal when the whistle blew. YATES was carried from the field by the enthusiastic spectators. The final score was Ardwick 3 goals Crewe Alexandra 1.

On 25th February 1893 Ardwick played Bury in the first round of the Manchester Senior Cup before a large attendance of 6,000 at Bury and lost by 3 goals to 0.

MARCH 1893

On 4th March 1893, Ardwick played a league match against Sheffield United at Hyde Road. **G. Armitt** who had been signed from Blackburn Rovers in February made his debut at outside left for Ardwick. John McVickers who had not played a league match for Ardwick since the game against Lincoln City on 24th December 1892 returned after injury. The Ardwick team was regarded as a "very weak eleven" and the Sheffield United team was regarded as a "very fine team".

4th March 1893   FOOTBALL LEAGUE   SECOND DIVISION
Ardwick   2   v   Sheffield United   3
3,000

Ardwick team: Douglas ©; McVickers and Robson; Middleton Whittle 1 and Hopkins; Yates Morris Bowman 1 Mooney and Armitt.

    This important match was played at Hyde Road on a beautifully fine afternoon. Hill commenced the game for Sheffield against a moderate wind. A little hesitation by McVICKERS at the commencement appeared to give Sheffield a chance, but WHITTLE stepped in to clear. Dashing away on the right wing, YATES initiated a series of attacks on Whittam and Cain, the Sheffield full-backs, and though they struggled hard to keep him at bay United were at last completely beaten by a well judged shot by BOWMAN which gave Ardwick the lead. A couple of minutes later loud cheers greeted a grand run by WHITTLE who scored a second goal for Ardwick in a brilliant manner, and his play throughout gave great satisfaction. Drummond and Hammond were persistent in their efforts to gain a footing in the Ardwick half and after Drummond had caused DOUGLAS to save smartly the Sheffield inside men rushed the ball past him and the score was two goals to one in favour of Ardwick at the interval.

    More combination was shown by Hill and his wing players on resuming and the equalising goal for Sheffield was obtained by Drummond after the ball had been passed back and rebounded from the post. Keen play followed and free-kicks were frequent. A throw by Whittam was penalised and ARMITT failed to get the ball past Howlett when right in the goalmouth. A long high shot from Cain which appeared to be going over, gave Sheffield the lead. On every appearance of danger afterwards the Sheffield backs did not hesitate to kick the ball out of play, though two or three chances were allowed to slip by the Ardwick forwards hesitating too long in front of goal. A finely contested game ended in favour of Sheffield United by 3 goals to 2.

FOOTBALL LEAGUE Second Division 4th March 1893						
	P	W	D	L	F	A	Pts
5. ARDWICK	19	8	3	8	39	34	19

On 5th March 1893, Ardwick signed:

J. Baker	Half-back

J. Baker was a left half who did not play in the first team until the following season.

On 11th March 1893, Ardwick played Blackpool in the second round of the Lancashire Senior Cup and won by 3 goals to 1 before an attendance of 6000. The scorers were Milarvie, Morris and Mooney. Ardwick had reached the semi-final of the Lancashire Senior Cup for the first time.

On 18th March 1893, Ardwick played Fairfield in a friendly before an attendance of 2,000 at Fairfield and won by 2 goals to 1, with the Ardwick goals being scored by Mooney and an own goal by a Fairfield player.

On 20th March 1893, Ardwick played Rotherham Town in a friendly before an attendance of 1,000 at Hyde Road and drew, each side scoring 2 goals, with Mooney and Milarvie scoring for Ardwick.

On 25th March 1893 Ardwick returned to league action with a match against Sheffield United at Bramall Lane.

Adam Carson (signed on 15th March 1892) and **H. Stones** (signed on 22nd September 1892) made their league debuts in this match.

25th March 1893   FOOTBALL LEAGUE   SECOND DIVISION
Sheffield United   2   v   Ardwick   1
2000
Ardwick team: Stones; McVickers and Robson; Middleton Whittle and Hopkins; Yates 1 Morris Steele Carson and Milarvie.

    Ardwick made a first appearance at Bramall Lane in glorious weather. STEELE started the game for Ardwick and short pressure by YATES and MORRIS was relieved by Cain. At the other end Gallagher shot into touch. A foul immediately afterwards fell to United but ROBSON cleared. Some very even exchanges followed. STONES, the Ardwick goalkeeper, cleared very finely from Gallagher and a corner to United brought no result. Hands against Sheffield gained Ardwick some ground. YATES centred finely and MILARVIE nearly headed through. Another foul for hands relieved the Ardwick lines and STEELE shot grandly. Ardwick were pressing in this period but MORRIS kicked over the line. Drummond forced another abortive corner for the United. A good attack by the Sheffield forwards was again well cleared by STONES. Howlett the United goalkeeper was severely tested by STEELE and CARSON. Watson missed a fine opportunity from a pass by Hill and good play was shown by MORRIS and CARSON. MILARVIE took a corner kick which was headed out. At half-time neither side had scored.

    After changing ends Ardwick attacked. Howlett repulsed good shots from MILARVIE and YATES. Play now became much faster than previously with United attacking in force. STONES beat away several shots in quick succession. After twenty minutes play, MILARVIE passed to YATES who scored for Ardwick. Five minutes later Needham equalised and towards the close the Sheffield forwards pressed. The Ardwick backs and goalkeeper warded off the attacks until nearly time when Needham scored a second goal for United. The final score was Sheffield United 2 goals Ardwick 1.

Ardwick had played well against Sheffield United in both matches but suffered two close defeats. Sheffield United would finish the season in second place in the Second Division and were promoted to the First Division following a Test Match when they beat Accrington by 1 goal to 0.

On 31st March 1893, Ardwick played West Manchester in a friendly before a large attendance of spectators at Brooks' Bar and lost by 2 goals to 0.

APRIL 1893

On 1st April 1893 Ardwick played the penultimate league match against Small Heath Alliance at Small Heath. There was one change in the Ardwick team with Douglas returning in goal for Stones.

1st April 1893   FOOTBALL LEAGUE   SECOND DIVISION
Small Heath Alliance   3   v   Ardwick   2
2,000
Ardwick team: Douglas ©; McVickers and Robson; Middleton Whittle and Hopkins; Yates 1 Morris Steele Carson 1 and Milarvie.

Ardwick started the game against a slight wind and at once threatened danger, MILARVIE getting a good shot at Charlsley (the Small Heath goalkeeper). Jenkins, a Small Heath half back, saved at a critical moment when the Ardwick forwards were very close up. Small Heath obtained a free kick which was shot outside. Ardwick had a prolonged attack on the Small Heath goal and YATES took a pass from CARSON and scored the first goal for Ardwick. After twenty minutes play Small Heath obtained a corner, which came to nothing, but DOUGLAS was then called upon to save very smartly on several occasions. Two corners were taken by Small Heath and from the second corner Small Heath rushed the ball through. At half-time the score was one goal each.

    The game in the second half was fiercely contested around the Ardwick goal and Small Heath playing in grand form added two further goals very quickly. CARSON then scored for Ardwick. The final score was Small Heath Alliance 3 goals Ardwick 2.

On 3rd April 1893, Ardwick played Blackpool in a friendly match at Blackpool and lost by 6 goals to 1.

On 8th April 1893, Ardwick played in the Semi-Final of the Lancashire Senior Cup against Bolton Wanderers.

The match was played at Bolton before an attendance of 4000 spectators. Bolton Wanderers won the game by 5 goals to 1 with Mooney scoring for Ardwick. David Weir was playing in the Bolton Wanderers side and scored three goals.

On 10th April 1893, Ardwick played Newton Heath in a friendly match before an attendance of 3000 at Newton Heath and lost by 2 goals to 1, with Mooney scoring for Ardwick.

On Monday evening, 17th April 1893 Ardwick played their last league match of the season against Lincoln City, the game being played at Hyde Road.

17th April 1893   FOOTBALL LEAGUE   SECOND DIVISION

Ardwick   3   v   Lincoln City   1

2,000
Ardwick team: Stones; McVickers and Robson; Middleton Whittle and Hopkins; Yates 1 Morris 1 Mooney 1 Carson and Milarvie.

Irving started for Lincoln against the wind and Ardwick pressed at once, YATES forcing a corner off Neill, which was kicked against the post. Moore got down the Lincoln left wing and finished with a good shot which STONES turned through his own goal, giving Lincoln the lead. Two further corners were taken by Ardwick but to no avail. Neat work by CARSON and MOONEY ended in MOONEY equalising. The Lincoln halves were repeatedly beaten by the Ardwick forwards, Richardson alone proving a stumbling block. After Graham had saved a rapid shot from MILARVIE, a free kick fell to WHITTLE and two corners resulted. The visiting goalkeeper only half saved a swift attempt from CARSON and MORRIS rushed up to give Ardwick the lead. Raby at the Ardwick end was beaten by McVICKERS. Ardwick were soon attacking again and a fee kick was nearly headed through by YATES. Just before the interval a grand shot from the Lincoln centre half nearly scored. At half-time Ardwick were leading by two goals to one.

From the re-start the Lincoln defence was on the defensive. MOONEY got through and scored but the goal was disallowed for offside. A pass to YATES resulted in Ardwick's third goal. Close work between CARSON and MORRIS nearly produced another goal. Towards the close Lincoln put more energy into their play and took a flag kick which MOONEY headed out of danger. A foul in favour of Lincoln under the home posts caused some anxiety, the ball eventually going into touch, whilst Moore and Raby shot just wide of the posts. Morris kicked over at the Galloway's end. Ardwick finally won by 3 goals to 1 taking fifth position in the Second Division.

Ardwick finished the season in fifth position in the Second Division of the Football League. In the first eleven league matches, Ardwick had won six, drawn three and lost two, gaining fifteen points and were third in the League. In the last eleven league matches Ardwick won three and lost eight, gaining only six points to finish the season with twenty one points.

FOOTBALL LEAGUE SECOND DIVISION 1892-93	P	W	D	L	F	A	Pts
1. Small Heath	22	17	2	3	90	35	36
2. Sheffield United	22	16	3	3	62	19	35
3. Darwen	22	14	2	6	60	36	30
4. Grimsby Town	22	11	1	10	42	41	23
5. ARDWICK	22	9	3	10	45	40	21
6. Burton Swifts	22	9	2	11	47	47	20
7. Northwich Victoria	22	9	2	11	42	58	20
8. Bootle	22	8	3	11	49	63	19
9. Lincoln City	22	7	3	12	45	51	17
10. Crewe Alexandra	22	6	3	13	42	69	15
11. Burslem Port Vale	22	6	3	13	30	57	15
12. Walsall Town Swifts	22	5	3	14	37	75	13

The Ardwick Reserve team finished in eighth position in the Lancashire Combination.

The season finished with four friendly matches.

On 20th April 1893, Ardwick drew 1 goal each with Gorton Villa at Hyde Road.

On 22nd April 1893, Ardwick beat Northwich Victoria by 1 goal to nil before an attendance of 3,000 at Hyde Road with Morris scoring for Ardwick.

On 24th April 1893, Ardwick lost to Rotherham Town by 1 goal to nil at Rotherham.

On 29th April 1893, in the very last match of the season, Ardwick recorded a victory by 3 goals to nil against Newton Heath at Hyde Road, the attendance being described as "very moderate". The Ardwick scorers were Morris, Hopkins and an own goal by a Newton Heath player.

At the end of the season, David Russell moved to Heart of Midlothian and H. Angus, H. Turner and G. Armitt all left the Club.

Although Ardwick had played twenty two league matches, two F.A. Cup ties; three Lancashire Senior Cup ties; one Manchester Senior Cup tie and twenty five friendly matches, they were already in financial difficulty owing to lack of capital and also high wages and travelling costs.

FINANCIAL PROBLEMS

At the end of the 1892-93 season, Ardwick and many first and second division teams were experiencing financial difficulties and there was great concern that the income of the clubs was insufficient to meet player's wages and bonuses and also travelling expenses by rail. The Sunday Chronicle reported on these problems during the summer months of 1893 and campaigned for reforms.

Sunday Chronicle on 21st May 1893 commented:

The General Meeting of the League, which takes place in Manchester next Friday, is perhaps one of the most important in the history of the organisation. There is the question as to sharing gates raised by Sunderland and Preston North End whilst a vital matter for Notts County and Accrington involves the proposal to increase the number of clubs to 18.

The clubs left in the Second Division must be exceedingly anxious as to their possible future. It is no secret that the experiment, owing to the high rate of wages paid and the cost of railway travelling, has been a comparative failure, several clubs concerned being saddled with the serious weight of debt. If the League delegates only legislate in the right direction a remedy may be found but it is very clear that relief must be found not in trying to increase receipts but in a steady reduction of expenses.

With the exception of some highly favoured and popular clubs such as Everton and Sheffield Wednesday, it is plain enough that the wages of professionals have reached a level which cannot be maintained. Relief therefore must be sought in this direction, and if a standard wage is established in conjunction with a strict adherence to the rule as regards the bonus limit, there may be a more comfortable state of things in the future than at present prevails.

The following Sunday **28th May 1893** the **Sunday Chronicle** commented on the Football League meeting which had taken place on 26th May 1893:

The Football League at their all important Annual Meeting on Friday got through a lot of work, but with the exception that the number of clubs in the Second Division be increased to 16, matters practically remain as they were in the 1892-1893 Season. Sunderland's efforts to secure a division of gates were fruitless as were all attempts to either increase or diminish the teams in the First League.

What Notts County and Accrington will do under the circumstances has not been made clear but the Lancashire League have given Accrington an opportunity to come in out of the cold, and many will question whether that is the best step they could take. The committee of the club have a very difficult question to settle.

Now that the plan of two Divisions of the League is to be tried for another season, possibly the Leagues will just waken up to a sense of their own strength and make a determined effort to reduce the expenses of club existence by persuading the Railway Companies to give special concessions to football teams and also try to establish a fixed standard of wages for professionals. If something of this sort is not done, it will be impossible for the clubs in the Second Division to live and pay their way.

On **4th June 1893** the **Sunday Chronicle** commented:

The League held a meeting in London on Thursday to arrange the fixtures for next season. So far as the 16 clubs in the First Division are concerned the prospects for the future look bright and hopeful but what about the second 16 (Second Division)? Are they to struggle on in the same miserable fashion as last winter running into debt and vainly trying to compete with their seniors in securing good players at all cost? Is there to be no help or direction in the matter of wages which have unquestionably reached a level that cannot be maintained?

*What sort of story must some of the teams in the Second Division have to tell? It is suggested that very few appear to have issued balance sheets at all, **though a correct financial statement for such a club as Ardwick** would I imagine have been singularly interesting. If the leading clubs have to use up their capital in a successful season, something badly wants altering or else there will be a big smash before long, which will do the game a considerable amount of harm.*

Plainly therefore wages must come down to a rate which can be paid without having to resort to all sorts of financial tricks and dodges. The League now includes so many of the big clubs in the North and Midlands that anything decided on in the shape of a standard wage could, I feel sure, be carried into effect, especially if the stern powers of the boycott were tried on such as broke the rule. A reasonable rate of payment will give the Second Division a chance of living which is by no means their prospect at the present time.

On **11 June 1893** the **Sunday Chronicle** further commented:

Despite the apparent indifference of the teams in the Senior League (First Division) the question of a lower rate of wages and reduced expenses is a matter of vital importance to 14 out of the 16 teams at least. If they (the teams in the First Division) cannot pay their way, how are the second 16 (Second Division) to exist, as most of them are now suffering from the disagreeable and ignominious pressure of pecuniary embarrassment. How is the Second League (Division) to exist if nearly all the Clubs have to face next season with loads of debt hanging around their necks? This state of affairs is thoroughly dangerous for the continued welfare of the sport and 3 or 4 of the "wisest heads" should endeavour to find a happy solution for the troubles that are now threatening association football in the North and Midlands".

Speaking with all plainness what is there to hinder the big professional clubs in a proper endeavour to keep their expenses within reasonable limits by establishing a standard wage for players which should not be exceeded, even by such a wealthy organisation as Everton? The League passed a rule as to a £10 bonus and if it has been evaded the clubs have done so at their own risk and the others owe it to themselves that the first offenders against whom a conviction can be obtained should be treated with the utmost severity. If a bonus can be fixed why not wages? There is no earthly reason why any player should be paid more than £3 a week during the season, and possibly a smaller sum, as a limit would give not a few of the clubs a better and healthier chance of existence.

Even Preston North End who had been the most successful club in the first five years of the League's existence were having financial difficulties and the Sunday Chronicle commented:

"The affairs of Preston North End were laid before a General Meeting of the Club on Thursday evening. According to the statement of the Chairman the total expenditure of the past 4 years has been £18,129 and the receipts £17,083. The deficit however is actually more than that, for a sum of £700 is owing to tradesmen and the bank and £443 to Mr Sudells. These figures are of a very serious character especially when Mr Sudells ventured onto the further statement that he thought "there was no first class club in existence that owed so little.

It has been decided to form a limited liability company to work the club in the future and though these debts seem a big incumbrance, Preston are well worth supporting on account of their past history. There is a fine ground at Deepdale and some excellent players so that with economy, especially in the matter of salaries, the organisation might in the course of time be worked out of its present difficulties."

On **30 July 1893**, the **Sunday Chronicle** commented on the difficulties of Accrington Football Club:

"The Committee of the Accrington Football Club imagined that they had got out of their troubles by breaking their word. After pledging themselves to compete in the Second Division of the League they have crawled out, and the Lancashire League on Thursday evening admitted them as members and promptly proceeded to re-arrange all their fixtures. Whether these steps will be of any particular use to Accrington remains to be seen."

Accrington played in the Lancashire League finishing fourth in 1893-94 and twelfth in 1894-95. Accrington then joined the Lancashire Combination but their record in 1895-96 was excluded when they failed to complete their fixtures.

Another Football Club in difficulty at this time was Bootle Football Club and the **Sunday Chronicle** commented on **20 August**:

Those who are responsible for the management of the Bootle Football Club have had to "throw in the sponge". They held a public meeting on Monday night but derived no encouragement from the tone of the proceedings and it seems clear that the local enthusiasm in the game has, for a time at least, been sucked dry. As the cost of the clubs existence has been in no way diminished, the committee have withdrawn from the Second Division of the League.

Despite the risk of riding a hobby to death, we must again point out that the League could have given relief to the weaker clubs by prudent legislation in the way of reducing expenses. Possibly the end of last April was the more appropriate moment for such a reform, as the wild extravagance of a summer wage for men, who were well paid in the thirty five weeks of the winter season might have been made a nominal evil, or what would have been better, abolished altogether. Nothing was done, however, but that is no reason why wages should not be fixed at a reasonable maximum especially for clubs in the Second Division. Why clubs should run into debt merely to pay professionals an extravagant sum for Saturday afternoon services passes all comprehension. It was never intended that men would get wages to keep them well all week for less than 2 hours work once every 7 days. If the players were remunerated on a basis which would compel them to supplement their pay by labour on other days they would be none the worse for having their leisure time properly occupied, and the clubs might be able to pay their way and possibly accumulate a useful reserve. The present method of doing things leads to the Bankruptcy Court and promises to do a deadly injury to the game.

Following Bootle's late withdrawal, the Second Division in 1893-94 was reduced to fifteen teams.

The very strong words in the Sunday Chronicle foretold the problems which Ardwick (and many other clubs) were to experience in the next twelve months. Clearly, by referring specifically to Ardwick in the paper's comments on 4th June 1893, the Chronicle was aware that Ardwick already had financial problems.

SUMMARY

FOOTBALL LEAGUE SECOND DIVISION 1892-93

DATE		OPPONENT	RES	1	2	3	4	5	6
				7	8	9	10	11	
03-Sep	H	Bootle	W 7-0	W.DOUGLAS	J.McVICKERS	D.ROBSON	H.MIDDLETON	D.RUSSELL©	W.HOPKINS
1892			4000	J.DAVIES 3	H.MORRIS 2	J.ANGUS 1	D.WEIR 1	R.MILARVIE	
10-Sep	A	Northwich	W 3-0	Douglas	McVickers	Robson	Middleton	Russell© 2	Hopkins
		Victoria	3000	Davies	Morris 1	J. Angus	Weir	Milarvie	
12-Sep	H	Burslem	W 2-0	Douglas	McVickers	Robson	Middleton	Russell ©	Hopkins
		Port Vale	2000	Davies	Morris	J. Angus 1	Weir 1	Milarvie	
17-Sep	A	Walsall	W 4-2	Douglas	McVickers	Robson	Middleton	Russell ©	Hopkins
		Town Swifts	2000	Davies 2	Morris	J. Angus 1	W.LAMBIE 1	Milarvie	
24-Sep	H	Northwich	D 1-1	Douglas	McVickers	Robson	Middleton 1	Russell ©	Hopkins
		Victoria	6000	Morris	Weir	J. Angus	Lambie	Milarvie	
01-Oct	H	Walsall	W 2-0	Douglas	McVickers	Robson	Middleton	Russell ©	J.MILNE
		Town Swifts	4000	Davies 1	Morris	J. Angus	Weir 1	Milarvie	
08-Oct	A	Darwen	L 1-3	Douglas	McVickers	Robson	Middleton	Russell ©	Hopkins
			6000	Davies 1	Morris	Milne	Weir	Milarvie	
10-Oct	A	Burslem	W 2-1	Douglas	McVickers	Robson	Middleton	Russell ©	Hopkins
		Port Vale	1000	Davies	Morris	Milne	Weir 2	Milarvie	
22-Oct	H	Small Heath	D 2-2	Douglas	McVickers	Robson	Middleton	Russell ©	Hopkins
		Alliance	3000	Davies	Morris 1	Lambie	Weir 1	H.ANGUS	
05-Nov	A	Grimsby	L 0-2	Douglas	McVickers	Robson	Middleton	Russell ©	Hopkins
		Town	2000	Davies	Morris	Weir	Milne	H. Angus	
26-Nov	H	Burton	D 1-1	Douglas	McVickers	Robson	Middleton	Russell© 1	Hopkins
		Swifts	1000	Davies	T.FORRESTER	Weir	Morris	F.MOONEY	
17-Dec	H	Darwen	W 4-2	Douglas	McVickers	Robson	Middleton	Russell ©	Hopkins
			3000	Davies	Morris	Weir 2	Mooney 1	Milarvie 1	
24-Dec	A	Lincoln	L 1-2	Douglas	McVickers	Robson	Middleton	Russell ©	Hopkins
		City	1000	Morris	Forrester 1	Weir	Mooney	J.YATES	
14-Jan	A	Burton	L 0-2	Douglas	Hopkins	Robson	Middleton	Russell ©	D.WHITTLE
1893		Swifts	1000	Milne	Morris	Weir	Mooney	Milarvie	
21-Jan	A	Bootle	L 3-5	Douglas	Hopkins	Robson	Middleton 1	Russell ©	Whittle
			800	Milne	Davies	Mooney 2	Weir	Milarvie	
30-Jan	H	Grimsby	L 0-3	Douglas ©	F.STEELE	Robson	Middleton	Whittle	Hopkins
		Town	1000	Yates	Forrester	Russell©	Mooney	Milarvie	
04-Feb	A	Crewe	L 1-4	Douglas ©	Middleton	Robson	Milne	Russell ©	Whittle
		Alexandra	1000	Yates 1	Forrester	W.	Mooney	Milarvie	
18-Feb	H	Crewe	W 3-1	Douglas ©	Hopkins	Robson	Middleton	Steele	Whittle
		Alexandra	0.1	Yates 1	Morris	Milne	W.BOWMAN 1	Milarvie 1	
04-Mar	H	Sheffield	L 2-3	Douglas ©	McVickers	Robson	Middleton	Whittle 1	Hopkins
		United	3000	Yates	Morris	Bowman 1	Mooney	C.ARMITT	
25-Mar	A	Sheffield	L 1-2	H.STONES	McVickers	Robson	Middleton	Whittle	Hopkins
		United	2000	Yates 1	Morris	Steele	A.CARSON	Milarvie	
01-Apr	A	Small Heath	L 2-3	Douglas ©	McVickers	Robson	Middleton	Whittle	Hopkins
		Alliance	2000	Yates 1	Morris	Steele	Carson 1	Milarvie	
17-Apr	H	Lincoln	W 3-1	Stones	McVickers	Robson	Middleton	Whittle	Hopkins
		City	2000	Yates 1	Morris 1	Mooney 1	Carson	Milarvie	

FOOTBALL ASSOCIATION CUP 1892-93

22-Sep	H	Fleetwood	D 1-1	Douglas	McVickers	Robson	Middleton	Russell ©	Hopkins
Q.		Rangers	600	Davies	Morris	J. Angus	Bowman 1	Milarvie	
05-Oct	H	Fleetwood	L 0-2	Douglas	McVickers	Robson	Middleton	Russell ©	Milne
Q. ®		Rangers	2000	Davies	Morris	Bowman	Weir	Milarvie	

Captain: ©   League Debut: CAPITALS

178

FOOTBALL LEAGUE SECOND DIVISION 1892-93							
	P	W	D	L	F	A	Pts
1. Small Heath	22	17	2	3	90	35	36
2. Sheffield United	22	16	3	3	62	19	35
3. Darwen	22	14	2	6	60	36	30
4. Grimsby Town	22	11	1	10	42	41	23
5. ARDWICK	22	9	3	10	45	40	21
6. Burton Swifts	22	9	2	11	47	47	20
7. Northwich Victoria	22	9	2	11	42	58	20
8. Bootle	22	8	3	11	49	63	19
9. Lincoln City	22	7	3	12	45	51	17
10. Crewe Alexandra	22	6	3	13	42	69	15
11. Burslem Port Vale	22	6	3	13	30	57	15
12. Walsall Town Swifts	22	5	3	14	37	75	13

LANCASHIRE COMBINATION 1892-93								
		P	W	D	L	F	A	Pts
1	Blackburn Rovers Res.	20	14	1	5	59	30	29
2	Darwen Res.	20	11	3	6	84	42	25
3	Newton Heath Res.	20	10	5	5	47	30	25
4	Bolton Wanderers Res.	20	12	0	8	42	42	24
5	Turton	20	9	3	8	50	41	21
6	North Meols	20	8	4	8	44	42	20
7	Royton	20	8	4	8	44	42	20
8	ARDWICK RES	20	8	3	9	49	46	19
9	Preston North End Res.	20	6	4	10	40	44	16
10	Skelmersdale United	20	5	2	13	28	78	12
11	Tranmere Rovers	20	4	1	15	30	81	9

ARDWICK A.F.C.
FOOTBALL LEAGUE APPEARANCES 1892-93

	Player	Pos	Arrival	Previous Club	Apps	Gls	Departure
William	Douglas	G	May 1890	Dundee Old Boys	20		Retained
H.	Stones	G	22 Sep 1892	West Manchester	2		Retained
David	Robson	FB	May 1890	Ayr United	22		Retained
John	McVickers	FB	25 Mar 1892	Accrington	17		Retained
F.	Steele	FB/G	11 Oct 1892		4		Retained
John	Milne	HB/F	C.S. 1890	Bolton W.	8		Retained
Daniel	Whittle	HB	C.S. 1890	Halliwell	9	1	Retained
William	Hopkins	HB	C.S. 1891	Derby County	20		Retained
Harry	Middleton	HB	19 Mar 1892	Derby Junction	22	2	Retained
David	Russell	HB	21 Jul 1892	Nottm. Forest	17	3	C/S Hearts
David	Weir	F	May 1890	BoltonWanderers	14	8	26 Jan 1893 BoltonW.
Joseph	Davies	F	17 Feb 1891	Chirk	12	7	Retained
Hugh	Morris	F	Mar 1891	Chirk	19	5	Retained
Robert	Milarvie	F	C.S. 1891	Newton Heath	17	2	Retained
John	Angus	F	Mar 1892	Third Lanark	6	3	Dec1892 Southampton St M
Hugh	Angus	F	Mar 1892	West Manchester	2		C.S.1893
Walter	Bowman	HB/F	5 Aug 1892	Accrington	2	2	Retained
William	Lambie	F	C.S. 1892	Queens Park	3	1	Oct 1892 Queens Park
Thomas	Forrester	F	5 Nov 1892		4	1	Retained
Felix	Mooney	F	5 Nov 1892	Bootle	9	4	Retained
James	Yates	F	5 Nov 1892	Burnley	8	5	Retained
Wilmot	Turner	F	26 Jan 1893	Stoke	1		C.S.1893
C.	Armitt	F	11 Feb 1893	BlackburnRovers	1		C.S.1893
Adam	Carson	F	15 Mar 1893	Newton Heath	3	1	Retained

ARDWICK A.F.C. F.A.CUP APPEARANCES

	Player	Pos	1890-1891 Apps	1890-1891 Goal	1891-1892 Apps	1891-1892 Goal	1892-1893 Apps	1892-1893 Goal
W.	Douglas	G	1		1		2	
	Harvie	FB	1					
D.	Robson	FB	1		1		2	
A.	Ferguson	FB			1			
J.	McVickers	FB					2	
J.	Milne	HB	1				1	
D.	Whittle	HB	1	1	1			
	Simon	HB	1					
H.	Davidson	HB			1			
J.	Pearson	HB			1	1		
H.	Middleton	HB					2	
D.	Russell	HB					2	
W.	Hopkins	HB					1	
W.	McWhinnie	F	1	2	1			
J.	Hodgetts	F	1	2				
D.	Weir	F	1	3			1	
	Campbell	F	1	2				
W.	Rushon	F	1	2				
J.	Davies	F			1		2	
R.	Milarvie	F			1		2	
H.	Morris	F			1		2	
	Dewar				1			
J.	Angus	F					1	
W.	Bowman	F					2	1

LANCASHIRE SENIOR CUP 1892-93

28-Jan	H	Rossendale	W 3-2	Douglas	Steele	Robson	Whittle	Middleton	Hopkins
R.1		extra time	3000	Milne	Forrester	Russell© 2	Mooney	Milarvie 1	
11-Mar	H	Blackpool	W 3-1	Douglas	McVickers	Robson	Middleton	Whittle	Hopkins
R.2			6000	Yates	Morris 1	Bowman	Mooney 1	Milarvie 1	
08-Apr	N	Bolton	L 1-5	Stones	McVickers	Robson	Middleton	Whittle	Hopkins
S.F.		Wanderers	4000	Yates	Morris	Steele	Mooney 1	Milarvie	

MANCHESTER SENIOR CUP 1892-93

25-Feb	A	Bury	L 0-3	Douglas	Hopkins	Robson	Middleton	Russell ©	Whittle
R.1			6000	Yates	Morris	Milne	Mooney	Milarvie	

FRIENDLY MATCHES 1892-93

01-Sep	H	Nottingham	D 2-2	Douglas	McVickers	Robson	Middleton	Russell ©	Hopkins
1892		Forest		Davies	Morris	J. Angus 2	Weir	Milarvie	
28-Sep	A	Middlesbrough	L 2-3	Douglas	McVickers	Robson	Middleton	Russell ©	Hopkins
		Ironopolis	1000	Davies	Morris	J. Angus 2	Weir	Milarvie	
15-Oct	H	West	L 2-3	Douglas	McVickers	Robson	Middleton	Russell ©	Hopkins
		Manchester	3000	Davies	Morris	Forrester 1	Weir 1	Milarvie	
29-Oct	H	Middlesbrough	W 6-3	Douglas	Steele	Robson	Middleton	Russell© 1	Hopkins
			2500	Davies	Morris 2	Weir 3	J. Angus	Milne	
12-Nov	H	Bolton	W 3-0	Douglas	McVickers	Robson	Middleton	Russell ©	Hopkins
		Wanderers	5000	Davies 1	Forrester	Weir	Morris 1	Milarvie 1	
19-Nov	A	Middlesbrough	L 3-6	Douglas	McVickers	Robson	Middleton1	Russell ©	Hopkins
			2000	Davies	Forrester	Weir 1	Morris	Mooney 1	
03-Dec	H	Notts County	D 3-3	Douglas	McVickers	Robson	Middleton	Russell ©	Hopkins 1
			2000	Davies	Forrester 2	Weir	Morris	Mooney	

Date	H/A	Opponent	Result						
10-Dec	H	Stoke	L 2-6	Douglas	McVickers	Robson	Middleton	Russell ©	Hopkins
			2000	Davies 1	Forrester	Weir 1	Morris	Mooney	
26-Dec	H	Glasgow Celtic	L 0-5	Douglas	McVickers	Robson	Middleton	McGregor	Hopkins
			8500	Yates	Morris	Forrester	Mooney	Milarvie	
31-Dec	H	Glasgow Thistle	L 0-1	Douglas	Hopkins	Robson	Middleton	Russell ©	Milne
				Forrester	Morris	Weir	Mooney	Milarvie	
02-Jan 1893	H	Newton Heath	L 3-5 10000	Douglas Milne	Hopkins Morris 1	Robson Weir 2	Middleton Mooney	Russell © Milarvie	Whittle
07-Jan	H	Blackpool South Shore	W 5-1 1000	Steele Milne 2	Hopkins Davies 1	Robson Weir	Middleton Morris 1	Russell © Milarvie 1	Whittle
11-Jan	H	Internationals	L 0-5 2000	Douglas Davies	Steele Milne	Robson Morris	Middleton Mooney	Hopkins Milarvie	Lumsden
11-Feb	H	Middlesbrough Ironopolis	L 1-3 2000	Douglas Yates 1	Hopkins Forrester	Robson Turner	Middleton Mooney	Russell © Milarvie	Whittle
14-Feb	H	Blackpool	L 2-7						
18-Mar	A	Fairfield	W 2-1 2000	Stones Yates	McVickers Morris	Robson Steele	Middleton Mooney 1	Whittle Milarvie	Hopkins 1 own goal
20-Mar	H	Rotherham Town	D 2-2 1000		McVickers Carson	Robson Steele	Mooney 1	Milarvie 1	
27-Mar	A	Newton Heath	L 2-3 2000	Stones Yates	McVickers Morris	Robson Carson	Middleton Mooney 1	Steele Milarvie 1	Hopkins
31-Mar	A	West Manchester	L 0-2 5000	Douglas Yates	McVickers Morris	Robson Steele	Middleton Carson	Whittle Milarvie	Hopkins
03-Apr	A	Blackpool	L 1-6						
10-Apr	A	Newton Heath	L 1-2 3000	Stones Yates	McVickers Morris	Robson Mooney 1	Bowman Carson	Regan Milarvie	Hopkins
20-Apr	H	Gorton Villa	D 1-1						
22-Apr	H	Northwich Victoria	W 1-0 3000	Steele Yates	McVickers Morris 1	Robson Mooney	Middleton Carson	Whittle Milarvie	Hopkins
24-Apr	A	Rotherham Town	L 0-1						
29-Apr	H	Newton Heath	W 3-0	Steele Yates	McVickers Morris 1	Robson Mooney	Middleton Carson	Whittle Bowman	Hopkins 1 1 own goal

CHAPTER 17

ARDWICK ASSOCIATION FOOTBALL CLUB
1893-1894

SEPTEMBER 1893

Joshua Parlby became the Club's first paid secretary at a wage of two pounds ten shillings per week.

Joshua Parlby was described as a burly figure with a boisterous manner. He was also described as a past master in the art of "wangling" which no doubt would have assisted Ardwick in getting through the 1893-94 Season, for the club had financial difficulties. Joshua Parlby was also a member of the Football League Management Committee.

Lawrence Furniss, who had been Honorary Secretary in the previous season, was on the list of Football League Referees.

Ardwick's reserve team continued to play in the Lancashire Combination.

During the closed season Ardwick signed:-

Frank Dyer	Left Back/Left Half	Woolwich Arsenal
A. McDowell	Right Back	
E. Regan	Left Half	
H. Saddington	Outside Left	
Robert Robinson	Inside Left	
A. Jones	Inside Right	Small Heath

Frank Dyer was a Left Back or Left Half and was the most experienced of all the players signed by Ardwick during the closed season.

Frank Dyer had played for West Bromwich Albion in 1890 and 1891 making forty one Football League appearances and scoring two goals. He had then joined Woolwich Arsenal before signing for Ardwick on 15th August 1893. He was one of only three Ardwick players to join Manchester City soon after the club's formation.

A. Jones was an Inside Right signed by Ardwick from Small Heath in July 1893 but he had no previous league experience.

A. McDowell, Right Back, **E.J. Regan,** Left Half, **H. Saddington,** Outside Left, and, **Robert Robinson,** Inside Left, were all signed during the closed season and had no previous League experience.

The players who were with Ardwick at the beginning of the season and who played in the Football League team were:-

Player		Pos.	Arrival	Previous Club
Goalkeepers				
William	Douglas	G	May 1890	Dundee Old Boys
H.	Stones	G	22 Sep 1892	
F.	Steele	G/RB/CF	11 Oct 1892	
Full-backs				
Frank	Dyer	LB/LH	15 Aug 1893	Woolwich Arsenal
David	Robson	LB	May 1890	Ayr United
John	McVickers	RB	25 Mar 1892	Accrington
A.	McDowell	RB	28 Jul 1893	
Half-backs				
Walter	Bowman	CH/RH/IL	25 Aug 1892	Accrington
E.	Regan	LH	May 1893	
Daniel	Whittle	CH	C/S 1890	Halliwell
Harry	Middleton	RH/CH	19 Mar 1892	Derby Junction
John	Milne	IL/CH/IR	C/S 1890	Bolton Wanderers
J.	Baker	LH	5 Mar 1893	
William	Hopkins	LH/RB	C/S 1891	Derby County
James	Cairns	RH/LB	16 Mar 1892	
Forwards				
Robert	Milarvie	OL	C/S 1891	Newton Heath
James	Yates	OR	5 Nov 1892	Burnley
Hugh	Morris	IR/OL	Mar 1891	Chirk
J.	Hargreaves	OL	9 Feb 1893	Northwich Victoria
H.	Saddington	OL	C/S 1893	
Adam	Carson	IL/CF	15 Mar 1892	Newton Heath
Thomas	Forrester	CF/IR	5 Oct 1892	
Joseph	Davies	OR/IR/IL	19 Feb 1891	Chirk
Robert	Robinson	IL	C/S 1893	
A.	Jones	IR	Jul 1893	Small Heath

The following players were signed by Ardwick during the 1893-94 Season and played for the league team.

Player		Position	Arrival	Previous Club
E.	Pickford	Outside Right	13 Sep 1893	
Joseph	O'Brien	Outside/Inside Left	15 Sep 1893	
James	Stenson	Right Back	21 Sep 1893	
Arthur	Spittle	Inside Right	27 Sep 1893	
A.	Bennett	Inside Right	6 Oct 1893	
D.	Robertson	Centre Forward	18 Oct 1893	
William	Egan	Centre Forward /IR	15 Nov 1893	Fairfield
William	Willey	Centre Forward	22 Dec 1893	
Alfred	Edge	Inside /Outside Left	15 Jan 1894	Northwich Victoria
John	Hughes	Outside Left	20 Mar 1894	

Ardwick continued to play in their colours of white shirts and navy blue knickers.

The Football League Second Division fixtures commenced on 2nd September 1893 and Ardwick's first match was at Burslem Port Vale. **Frank Dyer** and **Robert Robinson** made their debuts.

2nd September 1893   FOOTBALL LEAGUE   SECOND DIVISION
Burslem Port Vale   4   v   Ardwick   2
2,500
Ardwick team: Douglas; Dyer and Robson; Middleton Bowman and Hopkins; Yates Morris Carson 1 Robinson 1 and Milarvie.

Beats started the game for Vale in beautiful weather. The first action was when MIDDLETON forced Frail (the Vale goalkeeper) to save smartly. Beats got away but overran the ball. DOUGLAS conceded a corner but nothing came of the corner. ROBSON got the better of several well meant attacks. ROBINSON was applauded for a grand shot. Ardwick scored a fine goal when CARSON shot through the corner of the goal from long range. Vale next attacked and Campbell passed across to Sands who scored. A free kick for Vale was forced through by Beats. ROBINSON for Ardwick scored a goal which was disallowed for off-side. Scarratt then scored for Vale. At half-time Port Vale were leading by three goals to one.

The second half was more evenly contested with each side scoring once, the Ardwick goal being scored by ROBINSON. Burslem Port Vale had the best of the game and won by 4 goals to 2.

On 4th September 1893, Ardwick played a friendly at Hyde Road against Bolton Wanderers of the First Division before an attendance of 2000 spectators. Ardwick lost by 5 goals to 0.

The next league match was on Saturday 9th September 1893 at Hyde Road against Middlesbrough Ironopolis. **A. Jones** made his first appearance.

9th September 1893   FOOTBALL LEAGUE   SECOND DIVISION
Ardwick   6   v   Middlesbrough Ironopolis   1
4,000
Ardwick team: Douglas; Dyer and Robson; Middleton Bowman 1 and Hopkins; Yates Jones 1 Morris 2 Carson 1 and Robinson 1.

Ardwick were the first to press but HOPKINS shot wide when he had a good opening. Ardwick were not to be denied and JONES scored the first goal. Ardwick, who were assisted by the wind, were doing all the pressing. MORRIS and ROBINSON had hard lines but BOWMAN then scored with a splendidly judged shot. The visitors raised an attack but ROBSON relieved with a good kick. The visitors seemed altogether at sea and CARSON again shot over when in a good position. The Ironopolis goalkeeper, Nixon, came in for a round of applause as he saved several splendid shots in quick succession. Nixon again saved a splendid shot from CARSON. Ironopolis visited the Ardwick end, but the ball went harmlessly wide. After a tussle in the visitors goalmouth MORRIS managed to push the ball through to score Ardwick's third goal. Ardwick gained another corner but good defence prevented any score. From a grand centre by YATES, ROBINSON scored the fourth goal. Ironopolis then got clean away but DOUGLAS just managed to save. Ardwick put the ball through again but the goal was not allowed. Ironopolis again got away and DOUGLAS was easily beaten. At half-time Ardwick were leading by four goals to one.

In the second half, MORRIS restarted and Ardwick at once gained two corners but no score resulted. Ardwick were very aggressive but the visitors defence was very sturdy. YATES put in a grand centre but CARSON missed the ball. The visitors now pulled together and DOUGLAS had one or two nasty shots to save. Ardwick worked the ball down and JONES headed outside from a good centre by YATES. Ardwick played very slowly and the spectators repeatedly called on them to play up. YATES got through and put in a good shot which was grandly saved. At last MORRIS just got through from a pass by ROBINSON to score the fifth goal. During the game the crowd had greatly increased and there must have been fully 5000 spectators present. Ironopolis seemed to be greatly hampered through only having ten men and Ardwick should certainly have scored more goals. Ironopolis got away and with only DOUGLAS to beat they made a wretched attempt. Ardwick next pressed and Nixon gave a corner but nothing resulted. CARSON then shot the ball through to score the sixth goal for Ardwick from a good cross by JONES. Ardwick won by 6 goals to 1.

On Monday 11th September 1893, Ardwick played their third league match in nine days against Burton Swifts.

11th September 1893   FOOTBALL LEAGUE   SECOND DIVISION
Ardwick 1 v Burton Swifts 4

1,000
Ardwick team: Douglas; Dyer and Robson; Middleton Bowman and Hopkins; Yates Jones Morris 1 Carson and Robinson.

Ardwick made no change from the team which played on the previous Saturday and the Swifts were very strongly represented. MORRIS commenced the game and after BOWMAN and ROBSON had repelled a determined rush, play for some minutes was kept in front of the Burton goal but a fine bit of work by Jones removed the danger. Ardwick then forced Furness and Bury to kick out. After corners had been taken by each side, BOWMAN got hold of the ball in the centre, and trickily passing the halves, he passed to MORRIS to notch the first goal for Ardwick. At half-time Ardwick led by one goal to nil.

During the second half an unfortunate accident to HOPKINS handicapped Ardwick who played with only ten men until the end. Taking advantage of this the Swifts forced the pace and Elkins equalised at close quarters. Dewey with a swift ground shot added a second goal a moment later. A fine attempt to get on level terms again was made by YATES without success. Towards the close the strong play of the Swifts wore down the weakened defence and they scored two more goals from scrimmages. The final score was 4 goals to 1 in favour of Burton Swifts.

The next day, Tuesday 12th September 1893, Ardwick played a friendly away to Darwen of the First Division and lost by 7 goals to 0.

Ardwick needed to strengthen the team.

On 13th September 1893, Ardwick signed:

E. Pickford	Outside Right

On 15th September 1893, Ardwick signed:

Joseph O'Brien	Outside Left/Inside Left

Neither Pickford nor O'Brien had previous league experience. However, Joseph O'Brien had played for Ardwick previously and had been very successful scoring 6 goals in 3 appearances in 1888-89 (the full team was only recorded on four occasions); 16 goals in 20 appearances in 1889-90 and 6 goals in 12 appearances in 1890-91.

On 16th September 1893, Ardwick played a home league match against Liverpool. **Regan** at left half and **Saddington** at inside right both made their first appearances.

16th September 1893   FOOTBALL LEAGUE   SECOND DIVISION
Ardwick 0 v Liverpool 1

6,000
Ardwick team: Douglas; Steele and Robson; Middleton Whittle and Regan; Yates Saddington Bowman Carson and Robinson.

Liverpool, who had not previously played at Hyde Road, attracted a large attendance. A very evenly contested game marked with accurate passing and sterling defence elicited enthusiastic cheering. CARSON started play for Ardwick, who had four reserves playing, two of them Regan and Saddington both making their debuts. Ardwick were the first to press obtaining a corner which was not converted. McOwen, the Liverpool goalkeeper saved shots from CARSON and WHITTLE. Liverpool attacked and DOUGLAS saved. BOWMAN and YATES were conspicuous and the Liverpool goal was again in jeopardy, CARSON just failing to take a splendid pass. McOwen was again troubled and was almost beaten by CARSON. Ardwick were now having much the best of matters and YATES put a grand shot just on the outside of the post. The Liverpool right wing tried hard to get away but ROBSON was in splendid form, his kicking being clean and sure. WHITTLE also put in good work and repeatedly robbed his opponents of the ball. A good run and centre by YATES was well saved by Hannah. There was no score a half-time.

McQueen restarted the game. Ardwick obtained a free kick which was placed over the line. A bit of loose play by WHITTLE almost let in Liverpool but McQueen shot outside with the goal at his mercy. Both teams tried hard to score but the defence on both sides was superb. McQueen put in a hot shot which just went over. Another corner to the visitors resulted in a hot tussle in the goalmouth but the defence prevailed. From a missed kick by STEELE Liverpool got through and Stott beat DOUGLAS with a fast shot. Ardwick then came very close to scoring. The game was stopped through ROBINSON being charged down and having to be taken off. The final score of a hard fought game was a victory for Liverpool by 1 goal to 0.

On 18th September 1893, Ardwick played away against Stoke of the First Division and lost by 4 goals to 0 before an attendance of 1,000 spectators.

On 20th September 1893, Ardwick played a return match against Burton Swifts at Burton. In the earlier match on 11th September, Ardwick had been leading by one goal to nil until they were reduced to ten players with Hopkins injury and they had then lost by four goals to one.

20th September 1893　　　FOOTBALL LEAGUE　　　SECOND DIVISION
Burton Swifts　5　v　Ardwick　0

3,000

Ardwick team: Douglas; Steele and Robson; Middleton Whittle and Dyer; Yates Forrester Bowman Carson and Milarvie.

The return league match was played at Peel Croft, Burton. Ardwick had their full strength side. Ardwick kicked off but the Swifts speedily attacked, their left wing playing grandly. Boggie (formerly of Ardwick) shot the first goal for the Swifts after seven minutes play. Ekins followed with a second goal a few minutes afterwards. Ardwick tried hard to get on equal terms, YATES doing grand service on the right wing but the Burton defence was magnificent, West at centre half playing superbly. Tricky work by Munroe and Ekins, who played a fine game all through, enabled Ekins to score the third goal. At the interval the Swifts led by three goals to nil.

On resuming Ardwick went away and Stokes cleared nicely. The Ardwick goal was then severely bombarded. DOUGLAS did his work in fine style and was well supported by ROBSON, but after about twenty minutes play Boggie got in again with a grand cross shot which DOUGLAS had no chance of saving. With the exception of flying visits the Ardwick men were rarely out of their own half, the Swifts half-backs keeping them well in check. Shortly before the finish Jones had a couple of grand shots to stop from YATES. Dewar then finished a splendid sprint by beating DOUGLAS for the fifth goal. The Swifts continued to have the best of it, although Ardwick's right wing continued to play in grand form and several times Jones was tested to his utmost capacity but he proved equal to the occasion and kept Ardwick from scoring. The game ended Burton Swifts 5 goals Ardwick 0.

On 21st September 1893, Ardwick signed:

James Stenson	Right Back

James Stenson had no previous league experience. The next League game was on 23rd September 1893 away to Middlesbrough Ironopolis and **Joseph O'Brien** made his debut in the Ardwick forward line at inside left.

23rd September 1893　　　FOOTBALL LEAGUE　　　SECOND DIVISION
Middlesbrough Ironopolis　2　v　Ardwick　0

800

Ardwick team: Douglas; Steele and Robson; Middleton Whittle and Regan; Yates Bowman Carson O'Brien and Milarvie.

O'BRIEN took the centre position for Ardwick. When play started rain was falling heavily and a stiff breeze blew across the ground. Very few spectators were present when Mooney opened the game, Hunter putting the ball over the line. Hand ball against MIDDLETON was well cleared by

ROBSON. O'BRIEN failed to reach a centre by MILARVIE. MILARVIE and BOWMAN tried to get through but without success. Neither side could become dangerous on the slippery ground. Hunter got through and passed across to Alport who opened the scoring. At the other end WHITTLE put the ball over. There was an abortive corner taken by CARSON. MILARVIE ran down very finely and Ord saved with great difficulty. The half-time score was Ironopolis one goal Ardwick nil.

On commencing the second half the rain eased. A corner kick was taken by Alport which YATES headed out of danger. YATES missed a cross from MILARVIE. Ord then threw away from MILARVIE and punched a shot from CARSON over the bar. Several openings were missed by the Ironopolis forwards, the Ardwick defence being severely taxed. Adams then got through and scored the second goal with DOUGLAS being hurt. The final score was Middlesbrough Ironopolis 2 Ardwick 0

On 25th September 1893, Ardwick played a friendly at Hyde Road against Darwen before 1,000 spectators. Darwen won the game by 5 goals to 2. The Ardwick scorers were Yates and O'Brien.

On Saturday 30th September 1893 Ardwick had a league match at home against Small Heath Alliance and **E .Pickford** made his debut at inside right.

30th September 1893   FOOTBALL LEAGUE   SECOND DIVISION
Ardwick   0   v   Small Heath Alliance   1

5,000
Ardwick team: Douglas; Steele and Robson; Middleton, Whittle and Bowman; Yates Pickford Morris O'Brien and Saddington.

Small Heath kicked off and after a few minutes scored a goal which was disallowed for off-side. Play was very even with both goalkeepers being tested. YATES, PICKFORD and SADDINGTON were very conspicuous for Ardwick. Hallam for Small Heath had a splendid opportunity but shot wide. Ardwick took several corners, but failed to score. When half-time arrived neither side had scored.

Ardwick restarted the second half and the game continued to be of an even character. After a neat run by Hands on the right wing, he passed to Wheldon who scored an easy goal for Small Heath. Ardwick tried hard to equalise, but the game ended with a victory for Small Heath by 1 goal to 0.

During the month of September, Ardwick had played 7 league matches and 4 friendly matches. Ardwick had lost 10 of these matches and the only victory was on 9th September against Middlesbrough Ironopolis when they won by 6 goals to 1. Ardwick.

Ardwick could hardly have had a worse start to the season and by the end of September they were next to bottom in the Second Division in fourteenth place.

FOOTBALL LEAGUE Second Division 30th September 1893	P	W	D	L	F	A	Pts
14. ARDWICK	7	1	0	6	9	18	2

OCTOBER 1893

On 6th October 1893, Ardwick signed:

A. Bennett	Inside Right

Bennett had no previous league experience.

On 7th October 1893, Ardwick had a home league match against the league leaders Burslem Port Vale, who had won their first seven games of the season. Ardwick made many changes with a view to improving the team and to stopping the long list of wins secured by the Staffordshire team.

McVickers came back at right back and Steele moved to centre forward. Middleton moved from right half to inside right. Dyer and Regan played as half backs. Few could have expected what was to happen in this game.

7th October 1893   FOOTBALL LEAGUE   SECOND DIVISION
Ardwick   8   v   Burslem Port Vale   1

4000

Ardwick team: Douglas; McVickers and Robson; Dyer Whittle and Regan; Yates 1 Middleton 1 Steele1 Morris 3 and Milarvie 1 (1 own goal)

STEELE started the ball for Ardwick. The game was very exciting, every inch of the ground being fiercely contested. MILARVIE was cheered for some tricky play on the left, his final shot going just over the bar. Port Vale went down the field and through a slip by ROBSON, Searatt came away, but DOUGLAS saved beautifully and play was again taken to the Port Vale end. MILARVIE put in some good work but MIDDLETON missed a great opening. A free kick brought relief for the Vale and the ball was put over the line. Another corner to Ardwick was got away and play veered from one end to the other in quick succession. The Vale attacked and McVICKERS gave a corner which came to nothing. The game was stopped for a few minutes through Searatt being hurt in a collision with ROBSON. When the game resumed, WHITTLE put in a nice pass to MORRIS who got clean away but he was too eager and his shot went wide. Searatt returned and from his pass Beats only just missed scoring. A splendid run by the Ardwick forwards deserved a goal but only a corner resulted. YATES took the corner and MORRIS headed the first goal for Ardwick. The Vale tried hard to equalise but the Ardwick backs were too strong. At half-time Ardwick led by one goal to nil.

On the restart MORRIS quickly made two grand runs which were futile. There then followed a regular bombardment by Ardwick of Frail in the Vale goal. YATES MILARVIE and MIDDLETON each scored in quick succession. These reverses demoralised the Vale defence and Yowds headed into his own goal to score Ardwick's fifth goal. In the next ten minutes, MORRIS and STEELE followed up excellent centres from YATES and three more goals were added with MORRIS scoring two of the goals and YATES the other goal. With only three minutes to play, Campbell and Wood evaded McVICKERS and Vale scored their only goal. Ardwick won by 8 goals to 1.

At the end of the match several of the Ardwick players were carried from the field amidst enthusiastic cheering from the spectators. Ardwick had beaten the league leaders in a very convincing manner. This was Ardwick's biggest league victory (beating the win by 7 goals to 0 against Bootle on 3 September 1892). Ardwick moved up the league from fourteenth place to tenth position.

The next match was against West Manchester in a qualifying round of the FA Cup. Ardwick played the same team which had been so successful against Burslem Port Vale. West Manchester were members of the Lancashire League.

14th October 1893   FOOTBALL ASSOCIATION CUP   QUALIFING ROUND
West Manchester   3   v   Ardwick   0

6000

Ardwick team: Douglas; McVickers and Robson; Dyer, Whittle and Regan; Yates Middleton Steele Morris and Milarvie.

The match was played at Brooks' Bar, the home of West Manchester. The state of the ground was against good football. Miller started play for West Manchester up the slight incline. MILARVIE at once gained much ground for Ardwick and Taylor cleared at close quarters. Clever tackling by H. Lee enabled West Manchester to work forward and Lee gave DOUGLAS a difficult shot to save. From a scrimmage the ball was put behind the Ardwick goalkeeper but the goal was disallowed for a foul. YATES was then prominent and twice got within a few yards of the West Manchester goal but was unable to score. WHITTLE missed an opening. Good play by Waring resulted in a corner. Waring took the corner kick which came to nothing but a second corner from the other wing was rushed into the Ardwick net the goal being allowed despite some strong appeals that the ball had been out of play. Five minutes later Waring evaded McVICKERS scoring a second goal with a swift cross shot.

Ardwick followed with a spell of clever work but this was marred by bad shooting. At the interval West Manchester led by two goals to nil.

For some time after resuming, Russell the West Manchester full-back was hotly pressed but a free kick to West Manchester afforded relief. Some weak tackling on the Ardwick right resulted in another goal, Walsh smartly working into the centre and placing the ball in the corner. A quarter of an hour afterwards Suggs goal was in danger from corners and close passing but West Manchester staved off disaster by energetic tackling and retained their lead to win by 3 goals to 0.

The Ardwick team which had beaten Port Vale should have been strong enough to beat a Lancashire League team.

Two days later on Monday 16th October 1893 Ardwick played a friendly match against First Division opponents, Everton, before an attendance of 2,000 spectators at Hyde Road. **Bennett** made his first appearance for the club and Stewart of Newton Heath made a guest appearance for Ardwick. Everton won by 3 goals to 2 with the Ardwick goals being scored by Yates and Morris.

On 18th October 1893, Ardwick signed:

D. Robertson	Centre Forward

Robertson had no previous league experience. On Saturday 21st October 1893 Ardwick played Newcastle United at home in a league match. **James Cairns** who had joined Ardwick on 16 March 1892 made his debut at left half.

21st October 1893   FOOTBALL LEAGUE   SECOND DIVISION
Ardwick   2   v   Newcastle United   3

3000
Ardwick team: Douglas; McVickers and Robson; Dyer Whittle and Cairns; Yates 1 Morris 1 Regan Bowman and Milarvie.

Newcastle started the game and shortly afterwards they gained a free kick in front of the Ardwick goal which looked dangerous but DOUGLAS fisted away. The Newcastle forwards again attacked but Robson cleared beautifully to MILARVIE who put the ball in front of MORRIS who scored Ardwick's first goal. YATES and MORRIS got the ball down to the Newcastle end and BOWMAN shot, MILARVIE putting the final touch to the second goal. YATES was cheered for a fine run and centre, Miller just clearing. The Newcastle forwards attacked and DOUGLAS saved in splendid fashion. At half-time Ardwick led by two goals to nil.

REGAN restarted the game and Ardwick at once began to attack but no score resulted. Newcastle returned and DOUGLAS was forced to concede a corner but the ball was headed over the bar. Newcastle were now having rather the better of the game and from a grand centre by Ingles, Crate headed through for Newcastle's first goal. Immediately on restarting ROBSON gave away a corner which was badly taken. YATES got away with a fast run forcing Miller to give a corner but nothing resulted. Another corner fell to Newcastle but nothing resulted. YATES and MORRIS made a nice run but the final shot of MORRIS was just wide of the mark. Newcastle ran down and from a throw in, the ball was headed through the Ardwick goal thus equalising the score. Ardwick made an effort but YATES shot wide. YATES got in a fine centre which MILARVIE headed into the goalkeepers hands. WHITTLE shot over the bar. Newcastle attacked and with DOUGLAS running out the ball was put through the Ardwick goal. Newcastle United won by 3 goals to 2.

There was more concern expressed in the newspapers about the financial state of the game. It was reported that most of the big clubs were brought to the verge of bankruptcy before the league system was inaugurated because the public felt little interest in the way that ordinary club matches (friendly matches) were played. The concern now was that if clubs were still unable to make both ends meet the cause was not to be traced back to the league but to recklessly extravagant management. The newspapers were advocating that the question of summer wages must be dealt with radically with a view to its total abolition and that a maximum weekly wage should be fixed.

In October it was also mentioned that the clubs had to come to the conclusion that something must be done in the way of economy if the clubs were not to go into bankruptcy. According to the Chairman of the Football League there were only three clubs out of sixteen in the First Division of the League which were out of debt at the commencement of the present season. In the Second Division it was mentioned that only two out of fifteen teams could pay "20 shillings in the pound " – and this after the league system had materially increased the interest in the game all-round.

During October, it was reported that Ardwick had got into "such low water" that it was found necessary to call a meeting of the ticket-holders to discuss the situation. They decided to carry on the club somehow or other until the end of the season when Ardwick would be allowed to die. The Ardwick Committee seemed to accept the position for there was no response from them.

Ardwick were in thirteenth place in the league with only two wins.

FOOTBALL LEAGUE Second Division 21st October 1893							
	P	W	D	L	F	A	Pts
Liverpool	8	6	2	0	22	6	14
Burslem Port Vale	9	7	0	2	33	18	14
Notts County	8	6	1	1	17	9	13
Burton Swifts	9	6	1	2	27	15	13
Small Heath	10	6	1	3	28	20	13
Grimsby Town	9	5	0	4	27	21	10
Royal Arsenal	6	2	2	2	12	13	6
Lincoln City	6	2	2	2	9	10	6
Walsall Town Swifts	9	3	0	6	12	23	6
Newcastle United	6	2	1	3	14	12	5
Crewe Alexandra	7	2	1	4	12	15	5
Rotherham Town	7	2	1	4	12	19	5
ARDWICK	9	2	0	7	19	22	4
Middlesbrough Ironopolis	7	1	0	6	3	24	2
Northwich Victoria	8	1	0	7	8	28	2

On 28th October 1893, Ardwick played a home fixture against Notts County who were then third in the Second Division. **Bennett** made his league debut.

28th October 1893   FOOTBALL LEAGUE   SECOND DIVISION
Ardwick   0   v   Notts County   0

4000
Ardwick team: Douglas; McVickers and Robson; Dyer Whittle and Regan; Yates Morris Bowman Bennett and Milarvie.

County started the game, the ground being very wet and slippery. Daft got away for Notts County and a good centre resulted in McVICKERS giving a corner and another one followed immediately afterwards but nothing resulted. MORRIS put in a good shot which the County goalkeeper Toone saved. BENNETT also had hard lines with a good shot. Ardwick were doing most of the pressing and YATES, BENNETT and ROBSON all had near misses. The County forwards got away but ROBSON was cheered for some fine defensive play. County again attacked and from a good centre by Daft, Watson shot over the bar. County gained a corner which was well placed but ROBSON kicked away after DOUGLAS had pushed the ball out. At half-time neither side had scored.

BOWMAN restarted the game and Ardwick were soon pressing. MILARVIE put in some tricky play and from his centres both MORRIS and YATES just missed getting the ball. Ardwick continued to press and MORRIS got the ball through the County goal but the goal was disallowed. WHITTLE was cheered for a good run but the ball was brought back and DOUGLAS was forced to save. MORRIS and MILARVIE worked the ball down and MILARVIE caused Toone to save. Both teams now strove hard to score, but the defences' generally prevailed, accurate shooting was almost impossible owing to the wet and heavy state of the ground. YATES tried hard on several occasions but Hendry was a great stumbling block. MORRIS got through and sent in a beautiful shot which Toone caught in his arms whilst falling and the ball was got away. Ardwick continued to press and REGAN shot wide. The game was very exciting but neither team could score and the game ended in a draw.

NOVEMBER 1893

At the beginning of November 1893 Ardwick signed:

William Egan	Centre Forward	Fairfield

William Egan was born in Chirk in 1872. He began his football career with Chirk and made his only appearance for Wales against Scotland in 1892 when he was twenty. He moved from Chirk to Fairfield, who were members of the Lancashire League, and then to Ardwick.

On Saturday 4th November 1893, Egan played in a friendly match against Fairfield at Hyde Road. The game ended in a draw with each side scoring 1 goal. The Ardwick goal scorer was Yates.

On Monday 6th November 1893, Ardwick played a friendly match at Hyde Road against Stoke who were mid-table in the First Division. Ardwick won by 6 goals to 3 before an attendance of 1,000, with Milarvie (3) Steele (2) and Davies scoring for Ardwick.

On 11th November 1893, Ardwick played Royal Arsenal at Manor Fields, Plumpstead.

11th November 1893   FOOTBALL LEAGUE   SECOND DIVISION
Royal Arsenal 1 v Ardwick 0
4000
Ardwick team: Douglas; McVickers and Robson; Middleton, Whittle and Regan; Yates, Morris, Steele, Davies and Milarvie.

Ardwick won the toss and played with a strong wind in their favour. Arsenal kicked off and although Ardwick pressed at first the play was fairly even. Ardwick had two good shots at goal but Jefferys in the Arsenal goal made good saves. Arsenal attacked, but the Ardwick backs defended well. YATES looked like scoring for Ardwick but the ball went too wide. ROBSON fouled Henderson and Arsenal were awarded a free kick but nothing resulted. Arsenal attacked again and Henderson at the second attempt scored a goal. Arsenal had a further chance when a few yards from the Ardwick goal "hands" was given against Ardwick. Although a good free kick was taken nothing resulted and at half-time Arsenal led by one goal to nil.

Resuming Arsenal pressed severely and several times the Ardwick goal was in danger. Play was better on both sides. On one occasion the ball was sent through the Ardwick posts but the goal was disallowed. Ardwick had several chances which they failed to take and were soon driven back. Arsenal's shooting was poor and there was no further score. Arsenal won by 1 goal to nil.

Ardwick then played against Walsall Town Swifts at Hyde Road.

18th November 1893　　　FOOTBALL LEAGUE　　　SECOND DIVISION
Ardwick　3　v　Walsall Town Swifts　0

3,000

Ardwick team: Stones; McVickers and Robson; Middleton Whittle and Regan; Yates 2 Morris Robertson 1 Davies and Milarvie.

There was a very strong wind blowing across the ground and snow had been falling for some time before the kick off. Copeland kicked off for Walsall who pressed immediately and gained several corners but good defensive play by ROBSON and McVICKERS held them in check. MILARVIE on the home left wing got clean away and centred accurately to ROBERTSON who scored. A run by YATES followed but his final shot went wide. There was then some good play by ROBSON. MILARVIE got possession and he centred to YATES who scored a second goal. Several chances then fell to Walsall through clever play by McWhinnie (formerly of Ardwick) and Holmes but weak shooting spoiled their efforts. At the interval Ardwick led by two goals to nil.

In the second half, MILARVIE got into a dangerous position but Baillie cleared his lines. This attack was followed by even exchanges. Holmes went close with a shot which rebounded off the crossbar and STONES threw away twice from Copeland and McWhinnie. The remainder of the game was played in a blinding snow storm. Ardwick were awarded a penalty kick with less than a minute to play and YATES beat Hawkins to score Ardwick's third goal. Ardwick won by 3 goals to 0.

This victory took Ardwick up to eleventh position in the Second Division.

FOOTBALL LEAGUE Second Division 18th November 1893	P	W	D	L	F	A	Pts
Liverpool	12	9	3	0	35	8	21
Small Heath	12	9	0	3	38	22	18
Notts County	13	8	2	3	27	14	18
Burton Swifts	12	8	1	3	39	21	17
Burslem Port Vale	11	8	0	3	35	24	16
Grimsby Town	11	6	0	5	35	27	12
Lincoln City	9	4	2	3	17	18	10
Royal Arsenal	10	4	1	5	18	27	9
Crewe Alexandra	8	3	1	4	15	15	7
Walsall Town Swifts	11	3	1	7	13	27	7
ARDWICK	12	3	1	8	22	23	7
Newcastle United	9	2	1	6	18	24	5
Rotherham Town	10	2	1	7	14	28	5
Northwich Victoria	10	2	0	8	13	34	4
Middlesbrough Ironopolis	10	2	0	8	7	34	4

On 25th November 1893, Ardwick played a friendly match against Derby County at Hyde Road. Derby County, who were in sixth position in the First Division, brought their full league team. The weather materially affected the attendance as there were only 1,000 spectators. A continuous downpour caused the game to be abandoned in the second half with Derby County leading by 2 goals to 1, the Ardwick goal scorer being Whittle.

In November 1893, **Joseph O'Brien** was transferred to Walsall Town Swifts.

DECEMBER 1893

Ardwick's financial position was becoming acute. On Friday 1st December 1893 the newspapers reported that "Ardwick were so hampered in money matters that they had to release for a consideration one or two of their better players. On Friday 1st December 1893 **James "Jimmy" Yates**, a dashing little wing player and always a pleasure to watch was transferred to Sheffield United and negotiations for the transfer of two other professionals were still in progress. Ardwick had no earthly chance when creditors from previous seasons were being paid out of the present winter's receipts. They simply could not manage to do so."

One of the other professionals referred to was **Hugh Morris** who was also transferred to Sheffield United on 1st December 1893.

On 2nd December 1893 Ardwick played at Anfield against Liverpool who were leading the Second Division. As a result of the transfer of the Ardwick right wing (Yates and Morris), Pickford and Saddington took their places. **Egan** made his League debut at centre forward.

2nd December 1893   FOOTBALL LEAGUE   SECOND DIVISION
Liverpool 3 v Ardwick 0
4,000

Ardwick team: Douglas; McVickers and Robson; Middleton Whittle and Regan; Pickford Saddington Egan Davies and Milarvie.

The match was played in rather foggy weather. Liverpool started the game and EGAN commenced a smart attack which McLean relieved. "Hand ball" against McVICKERS let in Liverpool but DOUGLAS threw out twice. Dick forced a corner and then a free kick but nothing resulted. Ardwick had several free-kicks for fouls and SADDINGTON had a good chance from a centre by MILARVIE but shot wide. Scott then beat DOUGLAS at close quarters from a pass by Henderson, after some very effective work. After Liverpool's goal, EGAN and WHITTLE gained much ground and DAVIES forced a corner off Hannah but Liverpool cleared. EGAN again got close but failed with his final shot. At the interval Liverpool led by one goal to nil.

The play in the second half was more in favour of Liverpool. DOUGLAS was often called upon and responded well. Liverpool's second goal was scored by McQueen and a third goal by Henderson. SADDINGTON then went close for Ardwick. The final score was Liverpool 3 goals Ardwick 0.

On 9th December 1893 Ardwick played against Grimsby Town at Hyde Road.

9th December 1893   FOOTBALL LEAGUE   SECOND DIVISION
Ardwick 4 v Grimsby Town 1
4000

Ardwick team: Douglas; McVickers and Robson; Middleton 1 Whittle 1 and Regan; Pickford Bennett 1 Egan Davies 1 and Milarvie.

Ardwick kicked off and were soon swarming around the Grimsby goal, DAVIES shooting in hard and EGAN a trifle wide. Whitehouse was very lucky on several occasions and conceded an abortive corner. Jones and Fletcher spoiled an opening for Grimsby through getting off side and ROBSON headed away a free kick. The game continued at a very fast pace and Ardwick had the best of matters. EGAN again got away but his final shot just skimmed the bar. Ardwick continued to attack and from a good pass by MILARVIE, MIDDLETON scored the first goal. At half-time Ardwick led by one goal to nil.

In the second half Ardwick continued to press and EGAN, who was playing well, passed to WHITTLE who scored a second goal. Grimsby did not give way in the least and made strenuous efforts to draw level but they were beaten back and DAVIES missed a grand opening. EGAN put in some splendid touches and caused a lot of problems to the Grimsby backs. The Ardwick backs then gave an opening to Grimsby and the ball was rushed through the Ardwick goal by McCairns. Ardwick appealed against the goal but the referee allowed it. Ardwick then, if anything improved, and DAVIES scored the best goal of the match with a fast curling shot which Whitehouse failed to hold. DAVIES almost scored again with a long shot and Whitehouse was called upon to throw out a good shot by BENNETT. Ardwick continued to play well, and their improved form gave great satisfaction to the spectators. A splendid run and shot by BENNETT was saved with difficulty and then MIDDLETON put in a grand shot which was only partially saved and BENNETT put the ball through the Grimsby goal. Ardwick won by 4 goals to 1.

This victory took Ardwick to tenth place in the league.

The newspapers reported that the Football League would be holding a meeting on 15th December 1893 to consider the proposals of a sub-committee to deal with the whole question of professional wages. There were reports of many clubs still unable to pay "20 shillings in the pound". The scheme which was being suggested was to debate and adopt a maximum wage with the clubs retaining from the wage a sum of £17 and for this money to be paid during the summer months. There was also a suggestion that no club should be allowed to pay a bonus of more than £10.

Whilst the Football League subsequently debated the financial issues, no decision was made and it was suggested that the Football League should draw up a series of questions which all thirty one clubs in the First and Second Divisions would be compelled to answer.

On 22nd December 1893 Ardwick signed:

William Willey	Centre Forward

On 23rd December 1893 Ardwick played a friendly match at Hyde Road against Liverpool before an attendance of 3,000 spectators. Ardwick lost by 6 goals to 2, the Ardwick scorers being Bennett and Whittle.

On 25th December 1893 Ardwick played a friendly match against Newton Heath at Bank Lane, Clayton before an attendance of 6,000 spectators. Ardwick lost by 2 goals to 1, the Ardwick scorer being Bennett.

On the following day, 26th December 1893, Ardwick had a league match at Hyde Road against Rotherham Town.

Ardwick were short of Douglas, Milarvie and Davies who were replaced by Steele, Dyer and Hargreaves.

26th December 1893   FOOTBALL LEAGUE   SECOND DIVISION
Ardwick 3 v Rotherham Town 2
4000
Ardwick team: Steele; McVickers and Robson; Middleton Whittle and Regan; Bennett 1 Pickford 2 Dyer Egan and Hargreaves.

Play was started by DYER. Rotherham at once attacked and a pass from Hill enabled Fairburn to work the ball forward. ROBSON checked the attack for a moment but Sylvester opened the scoring for Rotherham after less than a minutes play. Only steady play kept out Rae and Hill. Rotherham were a much heavier team and at intervals they were penalised for rough play. HARGREAVES was the first Ardwick forward to get in a shot but this went slightly wide. Ardwick kept up the pressure and Wharton made several good saves. After half an hours play, PICKFORD equalised the score with a fine dropping shot. WHITTLE forced Wharton to concede a corner but nothing resulted. BENNETT then scored from a splendid pass by DYER to give Ardwick a lead of two goals to one at half-time.

On resuming, Ardwick gained a corner from which Wharton had to fist away a good attempt by BENNETT. Ardwick pressed and MIDDLETON put in a high shot which surprised Wharton and PICKFORD put the finishing touch to score Ardwick's third goal. More corners were gained by EGAN and HARGREAVES but nothing resulted. Hill took a pass from Turner, but was ruled off side as he shot into the Ardwick net. With only a minute to play Fairburn raced down the Rotherham left wing and from his accurate centre, Hill scored a second goal for Rotherham. The final score was Ardwick 3 goals Rotherham Town 2.

On 30th December 1893, Royal Arsenal were the visitors to Hyde Road. Douglas and Milarvie returned in place of Steele and Hargreaves.

30th December 1893   FOOTBALL LEAGUE   SECOND DIVISION
Ardwick   0   v   Royal Arsenal   1

4,000

Ardwick team: Douglas; McVickers and Robson; Bowman Whittle and Regan; Bennett Pickford Dyer Egan and Milarvie,

This was the first visit of the Londoners to Manchester and there was much interest in the game. Unfortunately, foggy weather kept down the attendance. At the beginning Arsenal were doing all the attacking. EGAN and BENNETT both got away for Ardwick but the Arsenal defence was sound. Arsenal attacked again and Howat spoilt a good chance by shooting wide. EGAN got an opening for Ardwick and tried a long shot which went wide of the mark. A good centre from the Ardwick right wing looked dangerous but EGAN shot badly. Arsenal attacked and DOUGLAS had to save twice. PICKFORD had a splendid opening but made a very poor attempt at goal. At half-time there was no score.

In the second half BOWMAN went to centre forward and restarted the game. Ardwick attacked but BENNETT was beaten when about to centre. Arsenal attacked and a run by Henderson followed by a dropping shot resulted in a goal for Arsenal. After scoring, Arsenal were rarely dangerous as they confined their efforts to preventing Ardwick from equalising. The Arsenal goal had many narrow escapes from DYER, EGAN and MILARVIE. Arsenal maintained their lead and the final score was a win for Royal Arsenal by 1 goal to 0.

Ardwick were now in eleventh place in the Second Division.

FOOTBALL LEAGUE Second Division 31st December, 1893							
	P	W	D	L	F	A	Pts
Liverpool	17	13	4	0	48	9	30
Small Heath	19	14	0	5	63	31	28
Notts County	19	11	3	5	42	21	25
Burslem Port Vale	18	11	1	6	48	38	23
Burton Swifts	17	8	2	7	43	35	18
Grimsby Town	16	8	0	8	44	40	16
Newcastle United	16	6	4	6	32	29	16
Lincoln City	14	6	3	5	34	31	15
Royal Arsenal	14	6	2	6	26	33	14
Middlesbrough Ironopolis	17	5	3	9	22	41	13
ARDWICK	16	5	1	10	29	30	11
Walsall Town Swifts	16	4	3	9	19	34	11
Crewe Alexandra	14	3	4	7	20	35	10
Rotherham Town	14	3	1	10	24	49	7
Northwich Victoria	15	2	1	12	20	58	5

JANUARY 1894

On 1st January 1894 Ardwick had a friendly match at home against Wolverhampton Wanderers who were the FA Cup holders and who were making their first appearance at the Hyde Road ground. There was a disappointing attendance of only 1,500 spectators and Wolverhampton Wanderers won the game by 2 goals to 1. The Ardwick scorer was Pickford.

The next day, Tuesday, 2nd January, Ardwick had a friendly match at Hyde Road against West Manchester who were members of the Lancashire League. There was an attendance of 1,500 spectators who saw Ardwick win by 1 goal to 0.

On Saturday 6th January 1894 Ardwick played away at St James Park against Newcastle United. Ardwick had a difficult journey to Newcastle on the Saturday morning and the ground was covered with three inches of snow. The reports indicated that Ardwick had a "very scratchy team". McVickers and Milarvie were missing from the Ardwick team and Robertson played at centre forward in place of Dyer, who moved to full back.

6th January 1894 FOOTBALL LEAGUE SECOND DIVISION
Newcastle United 2 v Ardwick 1
800
Ardwick team: Douglas; Dyer and Robson; Middleton Bowman and Regan; Bennett Pickford 1 Robertson Egan and Saddington.

Ardwick played in the first half with the incline in their favour. Both sides played hard, but Ardwick were the first to look really dangerous and from a good attack PICKFORD was successful in scoring the first goal for Ardwick. Newcastle then made some good attempts, their shooting being for the most part from long range. DOUGLAS saved repeatedly in splendid style. BENNETT did some good work for Ardwick and gave the NEWCASTLE goalkeeper a difficult time. Newcastle made several attempts at goal, and in one of these attacks, Thompson took advantage of a slip by DYER and put the ball past DOUGLAS to equalise. Considering the state of the ground the game was well contested. EGAN and PICKFORD made attempts at goal but at the interval the score was one goal each.

In the second half, both sides made attempts at goal. ROBERTSON and EGAN made good runs and only clever defence kept out the Ardwick forwards. From a foul against ROBSON, the ball cannoned off several players into the net thus giving Newcastle the lead. BENNETT broke away once or twice but Lowrie had little to do in the second half, although DOUGLAS and ROBSON aided by clever work by MIDDLETON kept the score down. Newcastle won by 2 goals to 1.

On 8th January 1894, **David Robson**, a very good left back who had been with the club since May 1890, was transferred to Wolverhampton Wanderers.

On Saturday 13th January 1894, Ardwick played a league match away at Abbey Park against Grimsby Town. **William Willey** who had signed for Ardwick on 22nd December 1893 made his debut at centre forward.

13th January 1894 FOOTBALL LEAGUE SECOND DIVISION
Grimsby Town 5 v Ardwick 0
1000
Ardwick team: Douglas; Bowman and Dyer; Regan Whittle and Milne; Bennett Pickford Willey Egan and Milarvie

WILLEY started the match and BENNETT went close immediately. An accident to MILARVIE caused his retirement. McCarns opened the scoring for Grimsby and Robinson scored a second goal. Good work by BENNETT and PICKFORD was spoiled by poor shooting. McCarns scored a third goal for Grimsby. At the interval Grimsby led by three goals to nil.

After changing over, BOWMAN and DYER were severely pressed and DOUGLAS had to make fine saves from the Grimsby forwards. Robinson scored Grimsby's fourth goal from a well placed corner. Fletcher added a fifth goal from a doubtful position. Whitehouse, the Grimsby goalkeeper then had to make saves from EGAN and PICKFORD. A quick return by Fletcher, after DOUGLAS had partially cleared his shot, was handled by DYER but DOUGLAS saved the penalty kick. Grimsby won by 5 goals to 0.

On 14th January 1894 it was reported:

"Ardwick F.C. are cutting down expenses as they are bound to do in the face of the gates they are getting this season. They published their receipts for the matches up to 30th December 1893 but they do not show any allowance for season ticket holders of which there used to be a great number. Though the team has played several good games notably against Notts County there has been no warrant for a weekly wage list of £34 and so retrenchment is the order of the day. For some time past rumours have been circulating as to the possible activities on the part of a

Brewery company against two old officials of the Club for money advanced to maintain Ardwick FC.

There is criticism that players could not be expected to live on a wage from solely out of the game and there was no need to work at any regular employment. Such an idea was bad for the game, the Club and the players. High salaries cannot be paid to 14 or 15 players as the experience of the last 2 or 3 seasons clearly teaches."

On 20th January 1894, Ardwick played a first round Lancashire Senior Cup tie against Rossendale who were near the bottom of the Lancashire League. Rossendale won the game by 4 goals to 2 before an attendance of 1000 spectators at Hyde Road. The Ardwick scorers were Pickford and Bennett. Douglas, who had been the Ardwick goalkeeper since 1890, made his last appearance in this game.

It was reported during the following week that Ardwick had sold two more of their players. **Joseph Davies** (Ardwick's Welsh International) was transferred to Sheffield United and **William Douglas** a fine goalkeeper was transferred to Newton Heath. These transfers were a case of necessity. It was reported that if Ardwick could get a good local team together they might get the support of the public, which the Club had so badly needed during the season and also during the previous season.

On 15th January 1894, Ardwick signed:

Alfred Edge	Centre Forward	Northwich Victoria

Alfred Edge was an experienced centre forward having made thirty league appearances (four goals) for Stoke in 1888 and 1889 and three league appearances for Northwich Victoria.

On 27th January 1894 Ardwick played Northwich Victoria at Hyde Road. **Alfred Edge** made his debut and William Meredith played for Northwich.

27th January 1894   FOOTBALL LEAGUE   SECOND DIVISION
Ardwick   4   v   Northwich Victoria   2
3,000
Ardwick team: Stones; Steele and Dyer 1; Bowman Whittle 1 and Regan; Bennett 2 Pickford Egan Edge and Milarvie.

The match was played in fine but windy weather. EDGE made his first appearance for Ardwick partnering his old comrade MILARVIE. EGAN started the game against the strong breeze. EDGE executed a nice run which ended in BENNETT heading the ball past Hornby for Ardwick's first goal. Northwich aided by the wind then pressed and the ball was put over the bar. A good centre by MILARVIE only just missed going through. Northwich attacked and from a corner the ball was headed through to give Northwich their first goal. Ardwick attacked and "hand ball" in front of the Northwich goal looked dangerous but STEELE put the ball over the bar. Northwich settled in the Ardwick half and gained numerous corners but were unable to score. Ardwick raced away and getting a free kick in front of goal, WHITTLE, put the ball in but Scanlan cleared. The ball was at once taken to the other end and a fine centre by Meredith was headed past STONES by Guest. Some nice combined play by the Ardwick forwards resulted in MILARVIE shooting over the top. At half-time Northwich Victoria were leading by two goals to one.

In the second half with the wind behind them Ardwick attacked but the Northwich defence was very sound. The rain now came down in torrents and the players had a very uncomfortable time of it. The ball was continually in the Northwich half and numerous corners fell to Ardwick. At length the ball was rushed through the Northwich goal from a corner nicely placed by BOWMAN, WHITTLE being the scorer. Ardwick were urged on by their supporters to get another goal and this came from a cross by EDGE which BENNETT headed through. Ardwick then scored a fourth goal through DYER and won the game by 4 goals to 2.

FEBRUARY 1894

In February 1894, **Harry Middleton**, a half-back was transferred to Loughborough Town.

On 3rd February 1894, Ardwick played in the first round of the Manchester Senior Cup against Bury at Hyde Road. There was an attendance of 6,000 spectators.

The match was reported: "Bury beat Ardwick by 6 goals to 3 but for Ardwick it must be urged that they are going through a period of regeneration owing to debts and want of support". The Ardwick goals were scored by Hargreaves (2) and Pickford.

On 10th February 1894, Ardwick played the return league match against Northwich Victoria at Northwich. Finnerhan and Meredith (who were both later to play for Manchester City) played for Northwich, who were at the bottom of the Second Division.

10th February 1894　　　FOOTBALL LEAGUE　　　SECOND DIVISION
Northwich Victoria　1　v　Ardwick　4
2,000
Ardwick team: Stones; Steele and Dyer; Bowman Whittle and Regan; Bennett Milne 1 Robertson 1 Milarvie 2 and Hargreaves.

The Victorians played with the breeze and in the first few minutes Ardwick had to defend some onslaughts from Bailey, Finnerhan and Meredith who were passing to perfection. At length, Ardwick broke away and BENNETT shot at goal, without result. MILARVIE made a pretty run along the left wing but he was foiled by Guest. MILNE and BENNETT worked the ball to the Northwich end where MILARVIE scored with a grand shot. STONES, the Ardwick goalkeeper, had to make several saves. The ball was taken to the Northwich end and Hornby the Northwich goalkeeper whilst negotiating a difficult shot was charged and whilst down the ball was headed into the Northwich goal by ROBERTSON. MILNE then added a third goal for Ardwick and at half-time Ardwick led by three goals to nil.

On resuming, play became fast and good runs were made by both sides. Twenty minutes from the restart MILARVIE scored the fourth goal for Ardwick. Northwich then bombarded the Ardwick goal with Scanlan and Gathmore playing like lions. Play continued in the Ardwick half and Northwich eventually scored. Ardwick won by 4 goals to 1.

On Saturday, 17th February 1894, Ardwick beat Stockport County by 3 goals to 0 at Hyde Road before an attendance of 1000 spectators, with Milne, Robertson and Bennett scoring for Ardwick.

On Saturday, 24th February 1894 Ardwick played at Crewe in a league match. Ardwick played with ten men as Whittle missed the train.

24th February 1894　　　FOOTBALL LEAGUE　　　SECOND DIVISION
Crewe Alexandra　1　v　Ardwick　1
1,000
Ardwick team: Stones; Steele and Dyer; Bowman and Regan; Bennett 1 Milne Robertson Hargreaves and Milarvie.

Ardwick playing with ten men forced the play and from a free kick by MILARVIE, BENNETT scored for Ardwick. DYER played well for Ardwick and prevented Barnett from scoring for Crewe. At half-time Ardwick led by one goal to nil.

In the second half, ROBERTSON restarted the game but after about five minutes Jones equalised for Crewe. DYER worked finely for Ardwick in defending several attacks but the Crewe centre forward had hard lines with a shot which struck the bar. MILARVIE played grandly for Ardwick who worked hard and the game resulted in a very creditable draw, Crewe Alexandra 1 goal Ardwick 1.

Following the match on 24th February 1894, Ardwick were in eleventh place in the Second Division with 16 points from 21 games. The teams below Ardwick were Crewe Alexandra, Walsall Town Swifts, Rotherham Town and Northwich Victoria. Ardwick had only won seven league matches during the season and had been knocked out of the F.A.Cup, the Manchester Senior Cup and the Lancashire Senior Cup. Many of the club's senior players had been transferred to other clubs and the team was now very weak. With mounting debts Ardwick were struggling to complete the season.

FOOTBALL LEAGUE Second Division 24[th]February, 1894	P	W	D	L	F	A	Pts
Liverpool	21	17	4	0	63	11	38
Notts County	23	15	3	5	60	25	33
Small Heath	22	16	0	6	76	37	32
Newcastle United	24	12	5	7	58	37	29
Burslem Port Vale	24	12	3	9	58	51	27
Grimsby Town	22	12	1	9	63	48	25
Burton Swifts	21	11	2	8	61	49	24
Lincoln City	21	9	5	7	46	43	23
Royal Arsenal	22	10	3	9	43	47	23
Middlesbrough Ironopolis	23	7	4	12	32	57	18
ARDWICK	21	7	2	12	39	41	16
Crewe Alexandra	21	4	6	11	32	58	14
Walsall Town Swifts	22	5	3	14	32	54	13
Rotherham Town	23	5	2	16	35	79	12
Northwich Victoria	22	2	1	19	23	84	5

On 28th February 1894, **Adam Carson**, centre forward, was transferred to Liverpool.

MARCH 1894

Ardwick were due to play Notts County early in March 1894 but the game had to be postponed as Notts County reached the final of the FA Cup. The postponed league fixture was then played at Trent Bridge Nottingham on Thursday 15th March 1894.

15th March 1894   FOOTBALL LEAGUE   SECOND DIVISION
Notts County 5 v Ardwick 0
2500
Ardwick team: Stones; Steele and Dyer; Saddington Bowman and Regan; Bennett Milne Forrester Milarvie and Hargreaves.

County received a good reception from the spectators as they had qualified for the FA Cup Final. The afternoon was fine and Ardwick started against the wind. Right from the commencement of play, County went away and Logan opened the scoring from a good pass by Daft. The Ardwick defence endeavoured to check the County forwards but without avail and Allsopp scored the second goal past STONES. Bruce headed through a third goal from a long throw in by Bramley. MILARVIE and FORRESTER visited the County end but Harper cleared well. Logan made a good run for County but BOWMAN robbed him of the ball. After some mid-field play Allsopp scored the fourth goal for

County at close range and just before the interval Kerr added a fifth goal. At half-time Notts County led by five goals to nil.

With the wind behind them Ardwick showed up much better in the second half but were weak in shooting, ROBERTSON missing two fine chances. A long kick by Hendry set up Daft, but though several shots were put in at STONES, he cleared brilliantly. County were apparently content with their substantial lead and did little beyond acting on the defensive to prevent Ardwick from scoring and though MILARVIE and FORRESTER had some pretty passing they failed to test County's goalkeeper. County won easily by 5 goals to 0.

On Saturday 17th March 1894, Ardwick suffered their biggest defeat.

17th March 1894   FOOTBALL LEAGUE   SECOND DIVISION
Small Heath Alliance 10 v Ardwick 2
2000
Ardwick team: Stones; Steele and Dyer; Bowman Whittle and Regan; Bennett 1 Milne Robertson 1 Hargreaves and Saddington.

Ardwick started the game with just ten players and Wheldon scored for Small Heath before STONES the absentee arrived. Hallam added a second goal for Small Heath. MILNE and HARGREAVES transferred play to the Small Heath end but HARGREAVES was injured and retired. The Small Heath forwards, by grand passing, enabled Mobley to score a third goal and Jenkins put on a fourth goal. At half-time Small Heath Alliance led by four goals to nil.

In the second half, the game was even more one sided and Small Heath added six further goals to two goals scored for Ardwick by BENNETT and ROBERTSON. The final score was Small Heath Alliance 10 goals Ardwick 2.

On 20th March 1894, Ardwick signed:

John Hughes	Outside Left

On 23rd March 1894, Ardwick played a friendly against West Manchester at Hyde Road before an attendance of 3,000 spectators. The game ended in a draw with each side scoring 2 goals. The Ardwick goals were both scored by Milne.

On Saturday 24th March 1894 Ardwick played a league match away at Lincoln City. **James Stenson** who had joined Ardwick in September 1893 made his debut at right back.

24th March 1894   FOOTBALL LEAGUE   SECOND DIVISION
Lincoln City 6 v Ardwick 0
1,000
Ardwick team: Stones; Stenson and Dyer; Bowman, Whittle and Regan; Milne, Milarvie, Forrester, Hargreaves and Saddington.

The match was played in lovely weather. Irvine and Chadburn both scored for Lincoln early on and SADDINGTON missed two chances of scoring for Ardwick. Lees got a third goal past STONES at close quarters and Raby with a long shot increased Lincolns lead. At half-time Lincoln led by four goals to nil.

In the second half, Ardwick played better but were never a match for the Lincoln team. Lincoln added two further goals and in a one sided match Lincoln won by 6 goals to 0.

In the space of nine days Ardwick had conceded twenty one goals in three very heavy defeats by Notts County, Small Heath Alliance and Lincoln City. Ardwick had lost most of their better players and with dwindling support and financial difficulties, the club was in a desperate position.

On Monday 26th March 1894, Ardwick played at Rotherham who were second from the bottom of the Second Division. **A. McDowell**, a right back who joined Ardwick in July 1893 and **J. Baker** a half-back who joined Ardwick in March 1893 both made their debuts.

26th March 1894   FOOTBALL LEAGUE   SECOND DIVISION
Rotherham Town   1   v   Ardwick   3
2000
Ardwick team: Stones; McDowell and Dyer; Baker 1 Bowman and Regan; Robertson Milne 1 Forrester Milarvie 1 and Hargreaves.

The match was played in sunny weather. Ardwick commenced the game and played uphill. At once Ardwick pressed but Wharton cleared a shot from FORRESTER. An attack at the Ardwick end was made by Ray and Cutts but STONES saved well. Both FORRESTER and ROBERTSON again tested the Rotherham goalkeeper. At the other end DYER conceded a corner to Rotherham but nothing came of it. From a free kick to Ardwick, DYER shot a shade too high and ROBERTSON was pulled up for offside. Ardwick then scored two splendid goals through MILNE and MILARVIE after very strong attacks. At the interval Ardwick led by two goals to nil.

Immediately after recommencing a free kick was awarded to Rotherham and Barr went very close but BAKER was able to clear. Wharton was then penalised for carrying the ball but nothing resulted. Broadhead and McComick from an off side position rushed the ball past STONES and the goal was allowed to stand. BAKER then added a third goal for Ardwick with a high shot which bounced over Wharton the Rotherham goalkeeper. BAKER continued to play a strong game and McDOWELL made a very successful debut. Ardwick won easily by 3 goals to 1.

On 31st March 1894, Ardwick played the return league match against Lincoln City at Hyde Road. **John Hughes**, who had recently joined Ardwick, made his debut in this match at outside left.

31st March 1894   FOOTBALL LEAGUE   SECOND DIVISION
Ardwick   0   v   Lincoln City   1
3000
Ardwick team: Stones; McDowell and Regan; Dyer, Bowman and Baker; Forrester Milne, Whittle, Milarvie and Hughes.

The match was played in beautiful weather. During the first half, the game was well contested. Ardwick experienced hard luck when a good shot from MILARVIE went over, whilst a similar one from REGAN went wide. The Lincoln defence was fine and cleared a strong attack from a corner. Towards half-time the Lincoln players played splendidly but McDOWELL, Ardwick's latest recruit showed fine form at full back and repulsed all the efforts made to get through. Just prior to the interval, however, a rather simple shot from the foot of Chadburn went through. At the interval Lincoln City led by one goal to nil.

In the second half, MILARVIE missed a grand opportunity for Ardwick just after the restart. From a free kick, the ball was put through the Lincoln goal but was disallowed because a second player had not touched it. Lincoln forwards got past the Ardwick backs and looked like scoring again but Raby hit the post and the ball rolled away. During the later stages Lincoln showed better form in front of goal and STONES had to save several good shots in quick succession which he did remarkably well. Ardwick made strenuous efforts to get through but there was always an obstacle and the game resulted in a win for Lincoln City by 1 goal to 0.

In the last three matches Ardwick had introduced four new players: Stenson McDowell, Baker and Hughes but the reports mentioned that only McDowell and Baker had played well.

APRIL 1894

On 2nd April 1894, it was reported that a new football club would be formed to play on the present ground of the Ardwick club. The name proposed for the club was Manchester City, but up to the present time it had been refused affiliation to the

Football Association. An application was to be made to the Lancashire F.A. on Wednesday, 4th April, and as far as could be seen there ought not to be any objection to the new organisation, although there may be to the name adopted.

However, there was some doubt about this claim, for the members of the Ardwick Committee had "taken up the reins of management" with John Allison at their head. The Committee, which had been lying dormant for about three months, announced their intention to make a determined effort to reconstruct and carry on the old concern. Therefore, there were two applications for the ground and the decision of the Lancashire F.A. would depend upon which party succeeded.

Joshua Parlby resigned as Secretary of Ardwick stating: "After having induced professionals to fulfil engagements by promises of payment from gates still to be drawn, I cannot be a party to their being dropped without those benefits". Mr Parlby thought that such a situation would prevent the club playing its strongest team in the remaining League matches and render doubtful the fulfilment of a Combination fixture.

The Ardwick Committee arranged a series of benefit matches with a view to clearing off old debts. The first of those matches would be against Sheffield United on 18th April.

The promoters of the Manchester City club held a public meeting on Thursday, 5th April in furtherance of their objectives.

The Athletic News commented that: "It is a pity that the leaders of these rival parties cannot put their heads together to see if some amicable settlement cannot be reached. United they may make football a paying concern. Division spells disaster".

Ardwick next had a home league match against Crewe Alexandra. **Arthur Spittle** who had joined Ardwick in September 1893 made his debut at inside right against Crewe. McDowell, Baker and Hughes retained their places.

7th April 1894   FOOTBALL LEAGUE   SECOND DIVISION
                    Ardwick   1   v   Crewe Alexandra   2
2500.
Ardwick team: Stones; McDowell and Dyer; Bowman Whittle and Baker; Milne Spittle1 Robertson Milarvie and Hughes.

The match was played in fine weather. In the first half Ardwick had the best of matters, MILNE sending in a grand shot which Hickton, the Crewe goalkeeper saved at the expense of a corner. Peak was next conspicuous with a good shot which was well saved by STONES. WHITTLE had a fine opportunity at the other end but shot badly. Both Hickton and STONES showed fine form in goal. Crewe however were the first to get through Wolff having little difficulty in placing the ball in the net. At half-time Crewe led by one goal to nil.

On the restart, Ardwick forced a corner which proved abortive. Ardwick had most of the play and a beautiful shot from MILNE was just turned onto the outside of the post by Hickton and the subsequent corner was cleared. After a most determined attack SPITTLE scored for Ardwick. ROBERTSON, the Ardwick centre, had many opportunities but was too slow. The game became exciting but the defence on both sides was very strong. Bryant got away on the left and put in a grand centre which was luckily saved by STONES. The game was in favour of Ardwick but from a break away Sandham with a beautiful single handed effort put Crewe ahead. The final score was Crewe Alexandra 2 goals Ardwick 1.

On 9th April 1894, Ardwick played a friendly match against Newton Heath at Hyde Road. The match was billed in the posters as the last match between the two clubs. There was only a poor attendance. Ardwick lost by 2 goals to 1 the Ardwick goal being scored by Bowman.

Ardwick's last league match was against Walsall Town Swifts at Walsall.

14th April 1894   FOOTBALL LEAGUE   SECOND DIVISION
Walsall Town Swifts   5   v   Ardwick   2
2000
Ardwick team: Steele; McDowell and Dyer; Bowman, Whittle and Stenson; Bennett Milne 1 Forrester 1 Milarvie and Hargreaves.

Ardwick were nearly 2 hours late. Walsall pressed strongly and scored four times after which Ardwick scored two goals through MILNE and FORRESTER. At half-time Walsall led by four goals to two.

On changing over, Walsall continued to press and McWhinnie (a former Ardwick player) added a fifth goal for Walsall. Both sides worked hard and Ardwick defended capitally. Walsall Town Swifts won by 5 goals to 2.

Ardwick finished in thirteenth position in the Second Division and Ardwick Reserves finished in ninth position in the Lancashire Combination.

	FOOTBALL LEAGUE SECOND DIVISION 1893-94						
	FINAL TABLE	P	W	D	L	F	A	Pts
1	Liverpool	28	22	6	0	77	18	50
2	Small Heath	28	21	0	7	103	44	42
3	Notts County	28	18	3	7	70	31	39
4	Newcastle United	28	15	6	7	66	39	36
5	Grimsby Town	28	15	2	11	71	58	32
6	Burton Swifts	28	14	3	11	79	61	31
7	Burslem Port Vale	28	13	4	11	66	64	30
8	Lincoln City	28	11	6	11	59	58	28
9	Woolwich Arsenal	28	12	4	12	52	55	28
10	Walsall Town Swifts	28	10	3	15	51	61	23
11	Middlesbrough Ironopolis	28	8	4	16	37	72	20
12	Crewe Alexandra	28	6	7	15	42	73	19
13	ARDWICK	28	8	2	18	47	71	18
14	Rotherham Town	28	6	3	19	44	91	15
15	Northwich Victoria	28	3	3	22	30	98	9

On 15th April 1894, it was reported that the opposition to the Manchester City Football Club had been abandoned and it was now clear for the new club to get a fair start. Ardwick still had to play two friendly matches.

On 18th April 1894 Ardwick played Sheffield United at Hyde Road before a poor attendance. Ardwick lost by 2 goals to 0. Both Sheffield United goals were scored by Hugh Morris, the former Ardwick player.

The Last Match

On 28th April 1894, Ardwick's last match took place against Stockport County at Stockport. Amongst the Ardwick players who played in this game were Steele in goal and the forwards included Milarvie, Milne, Spittle and Hughes.

28th April 1894   STOCKPORT COUNTY 0 v ARDWICK 0

Ardwick kicked off and were soon the aggressors SPITTLE and MILARVIE being cheered for good work. HUGHES and SPITTLE showed fine form but Chandley cleared all shots. Ardwick forced several corners, but were unable to score before the interval.

Upon resuming County had the best of matters, but could not defeat Steele who saved repeatedly. MILARVIE and MILNE passed well but time arrived without any score.

It was clear that Ardwick could not continue. The club's financial difficulties resulted in most of the better players leaving. In December 1893, James Yates and Hugh Morris had been transferred to Sheffield United. In January and February 1894, Ardwick had transferred William Douglas to Newton Heath; Joseph Davies to Sheffield United; David Robson to Wolverhampton Wanderers; Harry Middleton to Loughborough Town and Adam Carson to Liverpool.

The financial problems went back prior to the 1893-94 Season but when financial statements were issued in January 1894 it was clear that the Club's weekly wage bill of £34 could not be met from the gate receipts. Another problem was that Ardwick only had three league matches at Hyde Road in 1894, two of them being at the end of the season. Ardwick were not unique in having financial difficulties for the newspapers had highlighted the financial problems of the First Division Clubs, where it was thought that only two or three were making a profit, and also the difficulties of the Second Division Clubs where it was thought that most were running at a loss. Many newspapers continued to campaign for a maximum wage and for clubs not to pay summer wages. They also highlighted the increased cost of rail travel for the clubs were travelling longer distances.

In April 1894, Manchester City were affiliated to the Lancashire Football Association. On 29th April 1894 it was reported that the Manchester City Football Club Company Limited would take the place of Ardwick Football Club and that a big attempt would be made to gain admission to the Second Division of the Football League for which an application had already been made.

MAY 1894

The Football League meeting took place on 21st May 1894. Ardwick were now defunct and did not apply for membership of the Second Division.

It was sad to see the demise of Ardwick. Gorton had been formed in October 1884 and the name of the club was changed to Ardwick when the club moved to the Hyde Road Ground in 1887. The club had grown rapidly from the time Lawrence Furniss and John Allison had gone to Scotland in the summer of 1890 to recruit players, but the club lacked capital and support had dwindled with poor results. Manchester City came into being as the direct successor to Ardwick and Joshua Parlby, the last secretary of Ardwick, was to be the first secretary of Manchester City.

Fred Johnson in his book on "The History of Manchester City" remembers Lawrence Furniss informing him how he had to pay "the personal penalty of official responsibility". Lawrence Furniss was Secretary up to 1892-93 and personally met some of Ardwick's debts.

Joshua Parlby, when he was Secretary in 1893-94, gave some personal guarantees. On Wednesday, 12th September 1894, Manchester City played a friendly match against Burnley at Hyde Road with the proceeds to be used to pay off the debts of Ardwick which were guaranteed by Joshua Parlby and a few other members of the Committee. Joshua Parlby already had a Court Judgment against him for a debt of £18. There was criticism of the supporters when only about £20 was collected at the gate, for Joshua Parlby had worked very hard in keeping Ardwick alive until the end of the season.

The Ardwick players

Three Ardwick players were signed by Joshua Parlby, as Secretary of Manchester City:

Walter Bowman 24 league and 2 F.A.Cup appearances

Frank Dyer 21 league and 1 F.A.Cup appearances

Robert Milarvie 38 league and 4 F.A.Cup appearances

Joseph Davies, **Hugh Morris** and **David Robson** who had formerly played for Ardwick in the Football League were later signed by Manchester City.

Archibald Ferguson who had played for Ardwick in the Football Alliance in 1891-1892 was also signed by Manchester City.

Several Ardwick players joined other clubs:

Daniel Whittle, who had been with Ardwick since 1890 and had made 30 league and 3 F.A.Cup appearances, joined Bolton Wanderers.

William Hopkins, an Ardwick player since 1891 with 23 league and 1 F.A.Cup appearances, joined Burslem Port Vale.

John McVickers, who had made 26 league and 3 F.A.Cup appearances in his two years with Ardwick, joined Macclesfield in The Combination.

E. Regan (21 league and 1 F.A.Cup appearances) and James Cairns (1 league appearance) both joined Liverpool.

Felix Mooney (9 league appearances) joined Bury.

J. Hargreaves (8 league appearances) joined Blackburn Rovers.

H. Stones (12 league appearances) joined Newton Heath.

SUMMARY
FOOTBALL LEAGUE SECOND DIVISION 1893-94

DATE		OPPONENT	RES	1	2	3	4	5	6
1893				7	8	9	10	11	
02-Sep	A	Burslem	L 2-4	Douglas	F.DYER	Robson	Middleton	Bowman	Hopkins
		Port Vale	2500	Yates	Morris	Carson 1	R.ROBINSON1	Milarvie	
09-Sep	H	Middlesbrough	W 6-1	Douglas	Dyer	Robson	Middleton	Bowman 1	Hopkins
		Ironopolis	4000	Yates	A.JONES 1	Morris 2	Carson 1	Robinson 1	
11-Sep	H	Burton	L 1-4	Douglas	Dyer	Robson	Middleton	Bowman	Hopkins
		Swifts	1000	Yates	Jones	Morris 1	Carson	Robinson	
16-Sep	H	Liverpool	L 0-1	Douglas	Steele	Robson	Middleton	Whittle	E.REGAN
			6000	Yates	H.SADDINGTON	Bowman	Carson	Robinson	
20-Sep	A	Burton	L 0-5	Douglas	Steele	Robson	Middleton	Whittle	Dyer
		Swifts	3000	Yates	Forrester	Bowman	Carson	Milarvie	
23-Sep	A	Middlesbrough	L 0-2	Douglas	Steele	Robson	Middleton	Whittle	Regan
		Ironopolis	800	Yates	Bowman	Carson	J.O'BRIEN	Milarvie	
30-Sep	H	Small Heath	L 0-2	Douglas	Steele	Robson	Middleton	Whittle	Bowman
		Alliance	5000	Yates	E.PICKFORD	Morris	O'Brien	Saddington	
07-Oct	H	Burslem	W 8-1	Douglas	McVickers	Robson	Dyer	Whittle	Regan
		Port Vale	4000	Yates 1	Middleton 1	Steele 1	Morris 3	Milarvie 1	I own goal
21-Oct	H	Newcastle	L 2-3	Douglas	McVickers	Robson	Dyer	Whittle	J.CAIRNS
		United	3000	Yates 1	Morris 1	Regan	Bowman	Milarvie	
28-Oct	H	Notts County	D 0-0	Douglas	McVickers	Robson	Dyer	Whittle	Regan
			4000	Yates	Morris	Bowman	A.BENNETT	Milarvie	
11-Nov	A	Woolwich	L 0-1	Douglas	McVickers	Robson	Middleton	Whittle	Regan
		Arsenal	3000	Yates	Morris	Steele	Davies	Milarvie	
18-Nov	H	Walsall Town	W 3-0	Stones	McVickers	Robson	Middleton	Whittle	Regan
		Swifts	3000	Yates 2	Morris	D.ROBERTSON1	Davies	Milarvie	
02-Dec	A	Liverpool	L 0-3	Douglas	McVickers	Robson	Middleton	Whittle	Regan
			4000	Pickford	Saddington	W.EGAN	Davies	Milarvie	
09-Dec	H	Grimsby	W 4-1	Douglas	McVickers	Robson	Middleton 1	Whittle 1	Regan
		Town	4000	Pickford	Bennett 1	Egan	Davies 1	Milarvie	
26-Dec	H	Rotherham	W 3-2	Steele	McVickers	Robson	Middleton	Whittle	Regan
		Town	4000	Bennett 1	Pickford 2	Dyer	Egan	J.HARGREAVES	
30-Dec	H	Woolwich	L 0-1	Douglas	McVickers	Robson	Bowman	Whittle	Regan
		Arsenal	4000	Bennett	Pickford	Dyer	Egan	Milarvie	
06-Jan	A	Newcastle	L 1-2	Douglas	Dyer	Robson	Middleton	Bowman	Regan
1894		United	1000	Bennett	Pickford 1	Robertson	Egan	Saddington	
13-Jan	A	Grimsby	L 0-5	Douglas	Bowman	Dyer	Regan	Whittle	Milne
1894		Town	1000	Bennett	Pickford	W.WILLEY	Egan	Milarvie	
27-Jan	H	Northwich	W 4-2	Stones	Steele	Dyer 1	Bowman	Whittle 1	Regan
		Victoria	3000	Bennett 2	Pickford	Egan	A.EDGE	Milarvie	
10-Feb	A	Northwich	W 4-1	Stones	Steele	Dyer	Bowman	Whittle	Regan
		Victoria	2000	Bennett	Milne 1	Robertson 1	Milarvie 2	Hargreaves	
24-Feb	A	Crewe	D 1-1	Stones	Steele	Dyer	Bowman		Regan
		Alexandra	1000	Bennett 1	Milne	Robertson	Hargreaves	Milarvie	10 men
15-Mar	A	Notts County	L 0-5	Stones	Steele	Dyer	Saddington	Bowman	Regan
			2500	Bennett	Milne	Forrester	Milarvie	Hargreaves	
17-Mar	A	Small Heath	L 2-10	Stones	Steele	Dyer	Bowman	Whittle	Regan
		Alliance	2000	Bennett 1	Milne	Robertson1	Hargreaves	Saddington	
24-Mar	A	Lincoln City	L 0-6	Stones	J.STENSON	Dyer	Bowman	Whittle	Regan
			1000	Milne	Milarvie	Forrester	Hargreaves	Saddington	
26-Mar	A	Rotherham	W 3-1	Stones	A.McDOWELL	Dyer	J.BAKER 1	Bowman	Regan
		Town	2000	Robertson	Milne 1	Forrester	Milarvie 1	Hargreaves	

31-Mar	H	Lincoln City	L 0-1	Stones	McDowell	Regan	Dyer	Bowman	Baker
			3000	Forrester	Milne	Whittle	Milarvie	J.HUGHES	
07-Apr	H	Crewe	L 1-2	Stones	McDowell	Dyer	Bowman	Whittle	Baker
		Alexandra	2500	Milne	A.SPITTLE 1	Robertson	Milarvie	Hughes	
14-Apr	A	Walsall Town	L 2-5	Steele	McDowell	Dyer	Bowman	Whittle	Stenson
		Swifts	1700	Bennett	Milne 1	Forrester 1	Milarvie	Hargreaves	

FOOTBALL ASSOCIATION CUP 1893-94

14-Oct	A	West	L 0-3	Douglas	McVickers	Robson	Dyer	Whittle	Regan
1893	Q	Manchester	6000	Yates	Middleton	Steele	Morris	Milarvie	

ARDWICK A.F.C. 1893-94 FOOTBALL LEAGUE APPEARANCES

		Pos	Arrival	Previous Club	1893 Apps	1894 Goals	TOTAL Apps	Goals	Departure
William	Douglas	G	May 1890	Dundee Old Boys	16		36		26 Jan 1894 Newton Heath
H.	Stones	G	22 Sep 1892		10		12		C.S.1894 Newton Heath
David	Robson	FB	May 1890	Ayr United	17		39		8 Jan 1894 Wolverhampton
John	McVickers	FB	25 Mar 1892	Accrington	9		26		C.S.1894 Macclesfield Town
F.	Steele	FB/G	11 Oct 1892		13	1	17	1	C.S. 1894
A.	McDowell	RB	28 Jul 1893		4		4		C.S. 1894
Frank	Dyer	FB/HB	15 Aug1893	WoolwichArsenal	21	1	21	1	Manchester City
John	Milne	HB/F	C.S. 1890	Bolton W.	10	3	18	3	C.S. 1894
Daniel	Whittle	HB	C.S. 1890	Halliwell	21	2	30	3	Aug 1894 Bolton Wanderers
William	Hopkins	HB	C.S. 1891	Derby County	3		23		C.S.1894 Burslem Port Vale
James	Cairns	HB	16 Mar1892		1		1		C.S.1894 Liverpool
Harry	Middleton	HB	19 Mar 1892	Derby Junction	14	2	36	4	Feb 1894 Loughborough T.
Walter	Bowman	HB/F	5 Aug1892	Accrington	22	1	24	3	Manchester City
J	Baker	HB	5 Mar 1893		3	1	3	1	C.S. 1894
E	Regan	HB	May 1893		21		21		C.S.1894 Liverpool
James	Stenson	HB	21 Sep 1893		2		2		C.S.1894
Joseph	Davies	F	17 Feb 1891	Chirk	4	1	16	8	Retained
Robert	Milarvie	F	C/S 1891	Newton Heath	21	4	38	6	Manchester City
Hugh	Morris	F	Mar 1892	Chirk	9	7	28	12	1 Dec 1893 Sheffield United
Thomas	Forrester	F	5 Nov 1892		6	1	10	2	Retained
Felix	Mooney	F	5 Nov 1892	Bootle	0		9	4	C.S. 1894 Bury
James	Yates	F	5 Nov 1892	Burnley	12	4	20	9	1 Dec 1893 Sheffield United
J.	Hargreaves	F	9 Feb 1893	Northwich Vict.	8		8		C.S. 1894 Blackburn Rovers
Adam	Carson	F	15 Mar 1893	Newton Heath	6	2	9	3	28 Feb 1894 Liverpool
H.	Saddington	F	C.S.1893		7		7		C.S.1894
Robert	Robinson	F	C.S.1893		4	2	4	2	8 Jan 1894 Wolverhampton
A.	Jones	F	Jul 1893	Small Heath	2	1	2	1	C.S.1894
E.	Pickford	F	13 Sep 1893		8	3	8	3	C.S.1894
Joseph	O'Brien	F	15 Sep 1893		2		2		Nov1893 Walsall Town Swifts
Arthur	Spittle	F	27 Sep 1893		1	1	1	1	C.S.1894
A.	Bennett	F	6 Oct 1893		12	6	12	6	C.S.1894
D.	Robertson	F	18 Oct 1893		7	3	7	3	C.S.1894
William	Egan	F	15 Nov 1893	Fairfield	7		7		Mar 1894 Burnley
William	Willey	F	22 Dec 1893		1		1		C.S.1894
Alfred	Edge	F	15 Jan 1894	Northwich Vict.	1		1		C.S.1894
John	Hughes	F	20 Mar 1894		2		2		C.S.1894
Own	Goal					1		1	

FORMER ARDWICK PLAYERS 1892-93

David	Russell	HB	21 Jul 1892	Nottm. Forest			17	3	C.S.1893 Hearts
David	Weir	F	May 1890	BoltonWanderers			14	8	26 Jan 1893 Bolton W.
John	Angus	F	Mar 1892	Third Lanark			6	3	Dec 1892 Southampton St.M
Hugh	Angus	F	Mar 1892	West Manchester			2		C.S.1893
William	Lambie	F	C.S. 1892	Queens Park			3	1	Oct 1892 Queens Park
Wilmot	Turner	F	2 6 Jan 1893	Stoke			1		C.S.1893
C.	Armitt	F	11 Feb 1893	BlackburnRovers			1		C.S.1893

FOOTBALL LEAGUE SECOND DIVISION 1893-94

	FINAL TABLE	P	W	D	L	F	A	Pts
1	Liverpool	28	22	6	0	77	18	50
2	Small Heath	28	21	0	7	103	44	42
3	Notts County	28	18	3	7	70	31	39
4	Newcastle United	28	15	6	7	66	39	36
5	Grimsby Town	28	15	2	11	71	58	32
6	Burton Swifts	28	14	3	11	79	61	31
7	Burslem Port Vale	28	13	4	11	66	64	30
8	Lincoln City	28	11	6	11	59	58	28
9	Woolwich Arsenal	28	12	4	12	52	55	28
10	Walsall Town Swifts	28	10	3	15	51	61	23
11	Middlesbrough Ironopolis	28	8	4	16	37	72	20
12	Crewe Alexandra	28	6	7	15	42	73	19
13	ARDWICK	28	8	2	18	47	71	18
14	Rotherham Town	28	6	3	19	44	91	15
15	Northwich Victoria	28	3	3	22	30	98	9

ARDWICK A.F.C. F.A.CUP APPEARANCES

	Player	Pos	1890-1891 Apps	1890-1891 Goals	1891-1892 Apps	1891-1892 Goals	1892-1893 Apps	1892-1893 Goals	1893-1894 Apps	1893-1894 Goals	TOTAL Apps	TOTAL Goals
W.	Douglas	G	1		1		2		1		5	
	Harvie	FB	1								1	
D.	Robson	FB	1		1		2		1		5	
A.	Ferguson	FB			1						1	
J.	McVickers	FB					2		1		3	
J.	Milne	HB/F	1				1				2	
D.	Whittle	HB	1	1	1				1		3	1
	Simon	HB	1								1	
H.	Davidson	HB			1						1	
J.	Pearson	HB			1	1					1	1
H.	Middleton	HB					2		1		3	
D.	Russell	HB					2				2	
W.	Hopkins	HB					1				1	
F.	Dyer	HB							1		1	
E.	Regan	HB							1		1	
W.	McWhinnie	F	1	2	1						2	2
J.	Hodgetts	F	1	2	1						2	2
D.	Weir	F	1	3			1				2	3
	Campbell	F	1	2							1	2
W.	Rushton	F	1	2							1	2
J.	Davies	F			1		2				3	
R.	Milarvie	F			1		2		1		4	
H.	Morris	F			1		2		1		4	
J.	Angus	F					1				1	
W.	Bowman	F					2	1			2	1
F.	Steele	F							1		1	

LANCASHIRE COMBINATION 1893-94

		P	W	D	L	F	A	Pts
1	Blackburn Rovers Res.	16	13	2	1	62	13	28
2	Bolton Wanderers Res.	16	11	2	3	72	26	24
3	Darwen Res.	14	8	1	5	47	22	17
4	Tranmere Rovers	16	6	2	8	29	53	14
5	Lostock Hall	14	6	1	7	49	43	13
6	Newton Heath Res.	16	5	2	9	37	36	12
7	Turton	16	5	2	9	28	43	12
8	Preston North End Res.	16	4	1	11	24	63	9
9	ARDWICK RES	16	3	3	10	18	69	9

Royton expelled for not fulfilling fixture. Darwen Res. v Lostock Hall matches not played.

LANCASHIRE SENIOR CUP 1893-94

20-Jan	H	Rossendale	L 2-4	Douglas	Dyer	Caine	Bowman	Whittle	Regan
1894	R.1		1000	Bennett 1	Pickford1	Steele	Milne	Milarvie	

MANCHESTER SENIOR CUP 1893-94

3-Feb	H	Bury	L 3-6	Stones	Steele	Dyer	Bowman	Whittle	Regan
1894	R1		6000	Bennett	Pickford1	Milne	Milarvie	Hargreaves2	

FRIENDLY MATCHES 1893-94

04-Sep	H	Bolton	L 0-5	Douglas	Dyer	Robson	Middleton	Bowman	Hopkins
1893		Wanderers	2000	Yates	Jones	Morris	Carson	Robinson	
12-Sep	A	Darwen	L 0-7	Douglas	Steele		Bowman		
			1000			Milne	Carson		
18-Sep	A	Stoke	L 0-4	Douglas			Middleton		
			1000	Yates	Saddington		Carson	Robinson	
25-Sep	H	Darwen	L 2-5	Stones	Steele	Robson			
			1000	Yates 1		Lambie	O'Brien 1		
16-Oct	H	Everton	L 2-3	Douglas	McVickers	Robson	Middleton	Stewart	Dyer
			2000	Yates 1	Morris 1	Bowman	Bennett	Milarvie	
4-Nov	H	Fairfield	D 1-1	Douglas	McVickers	Robson	Middleton	Whittle	Whitehead
				Yates 1	Morris	Egan	Carson	Milarvie	
6-Nov	H	Stoke	W 6-3	Douglas	McVickers	Robson	Middleton	Bowman	Saddington
			1000	Morris	Bennett	Steele 2	Davies 1	Milarvie 3	
25.Nov	H	Derby	Abandon	Stones	McVickers	Robson	Middleton	Whittle 1	Regan
		County	65mins.	Yates	Morris	Egan	Davies	Milarvie	
23-Dec	H	Liverpool	L 2-6	Stones	McVickers	Robson	Middleton	Whittle 1	Regan
			3000	Bennett 1	Pickford	Willey	Egan	Milarvie	
25-Dec	A	Newton	L 1-2	Steele	McVickers	Robson	Middleton	Whittle	Regan
		Heath	6000	Bennett 1	Pickford	Dyer	Egan	Milarvie	
01-Jan	H	Wolverhampton	L 1-2	Douglas	McVickers	Robson	Middleton	Whittle	Regan
1894		Wanderers	1000	Bennett	Pickford 1	Dyer	Egan	Saddington	
02-Jan	H	West	W 1-0	Douglas	McVickers	Robson			Regan
		Manchester	1500		Pickford	Dyer		Robertson1	
17-Feb	H	Stockport	W 3-0	Stones	Steele	Dyer	Bowman	Whittle	Regan
		County	1000	Bennett 1	Milne 1	Robertson1	Milarvie	Saddington	
23-Mar	H	West	D 2-2	Stones	Steele	Dyer	Bowman	Whittle	Regan
		Manchester	3000	Hargreaves	Milne 2	Milarvie	Harrison	Saddington	
09-Apr	H	Newton	L 1-2	Steele	McDowell	Dyer	Stenson	Bowman 1	Baker
		Heath	1000	Milne	Pickford	Milarvie	Hargreaves	Hughes	
18-Apr	H	Sheffield	L 0-2						
		United	1000						
28-Apr	A	Stockport	D 0-0	Steele					
		County		Milne	Spittle	Milarvie		Hughes	

CHAPTER 18

MANCHESTER CITY FOOTBALLCLUB
THE BIRTH OF THE BLUES
1894

APRIL 1894

At the beginning of April 1894 it was reported that a few of the ticket-holders and others had made up their mind to start up a new organisation to be called "The Manchester City Football Club Company Limited". At that stage Manchester City had been refused affiliation by the Football Association. However, on Wednesday 4th April 1894 Manchester City had applied for affiliation to the Lancashire Football Association. It was reported that the Lancashire F.A. would grant their request upon production of an agreement showing the new Club had a ground to play on. The ground the promoters had in mind was the Ardwick Enclosure and they claimed that the Landlords, The Manchester Sheffield & Lincolnshire Railway Company, would sign the necessary document within a few days.

The promoters of the City Club held a public meeting on Thursday 5th April 1894 in furtherance of their objectives.

On 15th April 1894, it was reported that the opposition to The Manchester City Football Club had been abandoned and it was now clear for the new Club to get a fair start. The promoters of the new organisation held a public meeting and judging from the crowded attendance and the enthusiasm of those present, Manchester City Football Club should obtain plenty of support.

On 16th April 1894 Manchester City Football Club Company Limited came into being when the club was incorporated under the Companies Acts.

On 23rd April 1894, The Athletic News reported that Manchester City F.C. is now an established organisation, and the prospectus of the new company will be found in our advertising columns. The meeting which was held last week was of such an enthusiastic character that the promoters felt justified in proceeding with the formation of the company. On Friday, 20th April 1894, the Club was successful with their application to the Lancashire F.A. for affiliation (which came into effect on 1st May 1894). The Ardwick Ground was secured, Chesters Brewery Company having let it, together with the whole of the stands, at a reasonable rental. The capital of the Club would be £2,000 in £1 shares, payable by instalments of 2s.6d per share.

It was intended to secure the services of Mr J. Parlby, late secretary of the Ardwick Club, and in doing so the new company would be making a good choice. The Subscription List opened on Saturday 21st April 1894 and would close on 2nd May 1894.

The prospectus showed that John E. Chapman would be Chairman and S. Barnett Holden would be Vice-Chairman. There would be 9 other Directors as shown in the prospectus. A copy of the agreement for the land and stands at

Ardwick with Chesters Brewery Company Limited and also the Club's Memorandum & Articles of Association were available for inspection at the Club's Solicitors.

**Certificate of Incorporation of
Manchester City Football Club CompanyLimited
on 16th April 1894**

The subscriber shares were taken by the Directors and their names and occupations were:

John Edward Chapman (Publican);
Samuel Barnett Holden (Schoolmaster);
Robert Hayes (Telegraphist);
Frederick William Skinner (Manufacturer);
John Robert Prowse (Assistant Schoolmaster);
Alfred Jones (Brewer);
Edwin Hodson (Salesman);
Charles McLaughlin (Agent);
William Heywood (Schoolmaster);
Alexander Strachan (Sign Writer and Decorator) and
Robert Heath (Wholesale Druggist).

> The SUBSCRIPTION LIST OPENED on SATURDAY, April 21; and CLOSES on MAY 2.
>
> # MANCHESTER CITY FOOTBALL CLUB COMPANY, LIMITED.
>
> CAPITAL............ £2,000 in 2,000 shares of £1 each, payable
> 2s. 6d. on Application,
> 2s. 6d. on Allotment,
> 2s. 6d. one month after Allotment,
> 2s. 6d. two months after Allotment,
> 2s. 6d. three months after Allotment,
> 2s. 6d. four months after Allotment.
> Leaving 5s. to be called up later as required.
>
> DIRECTORS.
> John E. Chapman (chairman), Shakespeare Hotel, Stockport-road, Manchester.
> S. Barnett Holden (vice-chairman), 27, Park-avenue, Longsight, Manchester.
>
> W. Heywood,   J. R. Prowse,   G. M'Laughlin,
> R. Heath,   R. Hayes,   F. W. Skinner,
> A. Jones,   E. Hodson   A. Strachan
>
> BANKERS:
> The Union Bank of Manchester Limited (Ardwick branch).
> SOLICITOR: Frank Milne, 5, Norfolk-street, Manchester.
> HON. SECRETARY (pro tem.): R. Hayes.
> OFFICE (pro tem.): 15, Parker-street, Ardwick, Manchester.
>
> The wide and populous district of Manchester, comprising Ardwick, Longsight, Chorlton-on-Medlock, and West Gorton, has now no football team which can be placed amongst those of the first rank in the country.
>
> In promoting the "Manchester City F.C." the Directors' chief object is to enable those most interested in the success of this popular sport to have a direct interest and control in the undertaking.
>
> The club has been affiliated to the Lancashire and Manchester Football Associations already, and it is intended to apply for inclusion into the Football League for next season. An agreement has been entered into between the company and Chesters' Brewery Company, Limited, for the land and stands at Ardwick, which has been used as a football ground since 1887 by the Ardwick F.C., and such agreement with the articles and memorandum of association can be seen at the offices of the solicitor to the company. The articles of association provide that half of the number of directors shall retire annually, but be eligible for re-election. Shareholders will have the privilege of obtaining season tickets for stands at a reduction of 2s. 6d. on the prices fixed.
>
> Worked on sound business principles, there is every prospect that the Manchester City Football Club will be successful, and the directors hope to secure the services of Mr. J. Parlby, late secretary of the Ardwick Football Club, as secretary to the company.
>
> Applications for shares, accompanied with a remittance of 2s. 6d. per share, must be forwarded to the company's bankers. If the whole amount applied for by any applicant is not allotted, the surplus of the amount paid on deposit will be appropriated towards the sum due on allotment, and where no allotment is made the deposit will be returned in full.
>
> Prospectuses and forms of application may be obtained at the Offices of the Company, their Bankers or Solicitor; the "Sporting Chronicle" Office, the "Athletic News" Office, or from any of the directors.

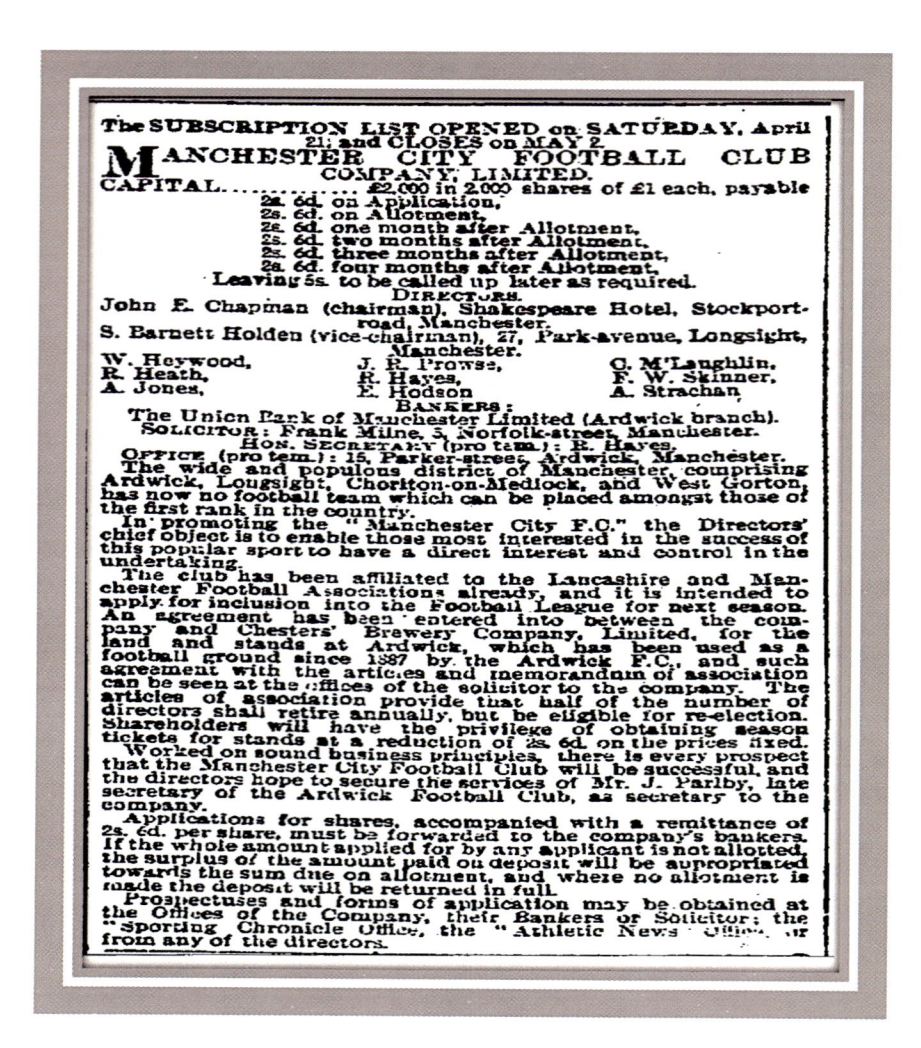

Manchester City Prospectus

John E. Chapman   Chairman

On 30th April 1894, it was reported that the shares had been fairly well taken up and there was every probability of the new Club commencing at once. The affiliation with The Lancashire Football Association was to come into force on Tuesday, 1st May 1894, and it was the intention of the Directors of the Club to apply for admission to the Second Division of the Football League.

On Thursday night, 3rd May 1894, the City Directors held a meeting and proceeded to allocate the shares. There had been so many applications it was decided to keep the list open until Friday, 11th May 1894, when a General Meeting would be held. A Players Sub-Committee had been formed and everything possible would be done to secure a good team. The new Club had nothing whatever to pay for stands or other erections, which were let with the Ground at Ardwick, and a big attempt would be made to gain admission to the Second Division of the Football League for which an application had been submitted.

The Football League Meeting took place on Monday, 21st May 1894, when there were 9 applications for membership to the Second Division. It was mentioned that the Clubs going out were Ardwick (defunct), Northwich Victoria (who found the game too expensive) and Rotherham Town, whilst another vacancy was caused by the retirement of Bootle at the beginning of the 1893–94 Season. The Clubs elected were Manchester City (20 votes), Leicester Fosse (20 voted) Bury (17 votes) and Burton Wanderers (17 votes). The election of League Officials at this meeting did not produce many changes and Joshua Palby (Manchester City) was elected as a Second Division representative to The Football League Management Committee.

The Athletic News commented that it was a surprise that the voting for Manchester City was almost unanimous, which showed a lot of confidence in the organising powers of Mr Parlby to get 20 votes for a Club which had only just been born.

On 28th May 1894, it was reported that Manchester City Football Club was now in full working order, but it was absolutely necessary that considerably more shares should be taken up. Now that the Club had been elected to the League and its future practically assured, there ought to be little difficulty in disposing of at least 1,000 shares for the terms were very easy. If the Ardwick people wanted a Club they would have to provide the cash. The Directors had done all they could up to now and are waiting for the Manchester football enthusiasts to do the rest.

On 4th June 1894, The Athletic News reported that City were engaging players as fast as they could and that they had signed: **Milarvie**, **Bowman** and **Dyer** (all of Ardwick); **Calvey** of Blackburn Rovers; **Smith** and **Wallace** of Blackpool and **Jones** of Everton. Calvey was described as a "fine young fellow" who had played for Blackburn in about half their league matches and all through the Cup ties in the previous season. He had weight and youth on his side and should make a big impression. R.Jones was the centre half of the Everton Combination team but he had often played in League matches. He was described as a finished player, placing the ball with great judgment and a very hard worker. H.Smith, a right full back of Blackpool came with a big reputation which was well earned.

Joshua Parlby and his colleagues were doing their utmost to secure a strong team but it was mentioned that there efforts would be all the more successful if the general public hurried along with their applications for shares for the terms on which the shares could be obtained should suit everybody.

Joshua Parlby Secretary

On 11th June 1894 The Athletic News reported that Joshua Parlby had not been long in getting a team together bearing in mind that the Club had only been in existence for six weeks and the players engaged were as follows:

Goalkeeper	Charles Williams (Royal Arsenal)
Right back	H.E.Smith (Blackpool)
Left back	Frank Dyer (Ardwick)
Right half	Joseph Nash (Nelson)
Centre half	Robert Jones (Everton)
Left half	Walter Bowman (Ardwick)
Outside right	Alexander Wallace (Blackpool)
Inside right	Patrick Finnerhan (Northwich)
Centre forward	Mitchell Calvey (Blackburn Rovers)
Inside left	James Sharples (Rossendale)
Outside left	Robert Milarvie (Ardwick)

The team would cost £21.15s.0d. per week in wages in the winter and £1.10s.0d. per week in wages in the summer.

On 16th August 1894, The Athletic News reported that Manchester City Football Club Company Limited would be holding its first meeting of shareholders during the following week when a full statement as to the players engaged and other matters connected with the new Club would be made. The Ground would be made to look as bright as possible in the Ardwick district and the playing portion had been carefully attended to during the summer months. The pitch had been extended on the Hyde Road End so as to avoid the miniature railway which came across a portion of the turf on the stand side. The new team had a hard match to start the season having to play away at Bury.

On Saturday 25th August 1894, the Manchester City team appeared in full in a trial match before 8,000 spectators and the new "eleven" gave every satisfaction. The City players were a big lot of young fellows and their worthy secretary had every confidence in their ability to hold their own.

The Athletic News commented on Manchester City on 27th August 1894:

"Manchester City have given a lesson to many people on the way to make a Football Club. Some six months ago Ardwick were just about on their last legs and it was decided to form a company to work another Club on the same ground. This was done, they were elected to the Second Division of the League and only a week ago they were exempted for the Lancashire Cup. This shows that the management of the Club is very strong and they deserve to get success.

With all this work to do the team has not been neglected and one that will make a name has been procured. On Saturday afternoon, the first trial game was played and there would be fully 8,000 people present to see the preliminary canter which was very enjoyable as well as promising.

The Ground has been thoroughly overhauled and several raised banks of cinders have been made so there should be good accommodation for fully 15,000 people to see the game.

The players themselves looked in fair condition but their new trainer, James Broad of Stalybridge will have a big job to keep them going as they have a tendency to be on the big side."

The following is a list from which the first team will be selected:

Goalkeepers:	**Charles Williams (Arsenal)**
	Byrne (Leek)
Full backs:	**Archibald Ferguson (formerly Ardwick and Preston)**
	H.E.Smith (Blackpool)
	Frank Dyer (Ardwick)
Half backs:	**George Mann (Blackburn Rovers)**
	Robert Samuel Jones (Everton)
	Joseph Nash (Nelson and Burnley)
	Alexander Rowan (Sheffield Wednesday)
	Walter Bowman (Ardwck).
Forwards:	**Patrick Finnerhan (Northwich Victoria)**
	Mitchell Calvey (Blackburn Rovers)
	James Sharples (Rossendale)
	Thomas Little (Derby County)
	Alexander Wallace (Blackpool)
	Robert Milarvie (Ardwick)

In the trial game on Saturday, there was hardly a man who did not show up well; both goalkeepers did smart work; in fact the defence all round was good. The halves were fair whilst Finnerhen and Sharples were the pick of the front rank with one or two very lively youngsters amongst the reserve lot.

The City colours were Cambridge blue shirts with white knickers.

Robert Jones was appointed City captain.

MANCHESTER CITY 1894-95

On the front row the first three players from left to right are W.Meredith, P.Finnerhan and A.Rowan. On the middle row the three players in the centre from left to right are believed to be W.Bowman, R.Jones (captain) and J.McBride. On the back row from left to right, the first person is James Broad (trainer), the second person is C.Williams (goalkeeper), the fifth person is Joshua Parlby (Secretary), the sixth person is D.Robson and the seventh person is John Chapman (Chairman)

The first match played by City was at Bury.

1st September 1894 **FOOTBALL LEAGUE** SECOND DIVISION
Bury   4   v   Manchester City   2

8,000
Manchester City: Williams; Smith and Dyer; Mann Jones and Nash; Wallace Finnerhan Calvey 1 Sharples and Little 1

Bury kicked off in fine weather. A free kick to Bury was safely cleared by SMITH. This was followed by City pressing around the Bury goal. LITTLE was too clever for Gillespie, and whipping in a beautiful low shot LITTLE scored the first goal of the season for City when the game was only 3 minutes old. Soon afterwards LITTLE experienced hard lines with a shot which went a trifle wide. Bury relieved their goal and took play to the City end, when Miller spoiled an opening by shooting over. City were playing very fast and so far had the best of the game. CALVEY put in a low shot but Lowe saved. Bury, by good play, attacked but DYER got the better of Wyllie before he could shoot, the corner following being cleared. Wyllie then centred but WILLIAMS saved grandly from Plant. Bury were at this point having all the game and City were evidently distressed by the fast play. Bury gained a free kick followed by a corner which Ostler headed in but WILLIAMS saved repeatedly. Miller missed a very easy chance. A nice run by the Bury forwards resulted in another corner and WILLIAMS had to save again. Bury were continuously pressing but were very unlucky. Once WILLIAMS was down and the ball was lying within a yard of the line, but no Bury player could put it through. With 40 minutes play gone Barber equalised and a minute later Ostler scored a beautiful goal. City recovered and CALVEY equalised with a grand shot. At half time the score was two goals each.

In the second half, Bury had a shade the best of the play and WILLIAMS showed some fine form in goal. The Bury defence was not so good. LITTLE particularly being too clever for Gillespie and Lowe had to save some fine attempts. Towards the end of the game, after Barbour had several shots, Miller scored the third goal for Bury. Two minutes from the end Barbour had an open goal and beat WILLIAMS easily for Bury's fourth goal. The result was Bury four goals Manchester City two.

The Athletic News commented that City had a rattling good combination and played a thoroughly good game. City hardly deserved to lose, and on Saturdays form, will want some shaking off. There is not a weak spot in the team, although they did not wear quite so well towards the finish. Little played a splendid game forward, whilst Jones deserved mention in a capital trio of halves. Both Smith and Dyer showed really good defensive power and Williams was in huge form in goal.

Manchester City had been successfully formed as a limited company with an adequate financial base and went on to finish in ninth place in the Second Division of the Football League.

The First Fourteen Years

Two members of St. Mark's Church, **Walter Chew** and **Lawrence Furniss**, played very significant roles in the growth of the Club during the first fourteen years.

A tribute has already paid to the part played by **Walter Chew**. As well as playing for the team and captaining the club for a short period he was secretary from 1885 to 1889. He was a very capable administrator and without his skill and determination during the period from 1880 to 1890 the club would have foundered. He was only twenty six when he retired from the Ardwick Committee in 1890. He did not return to the management of the club but remained a supporter and devoted his time to the Manchester and District Football Association.

Lawrence Furniss joined Gorton in 1884 and captained the team. A serious knee injury in 1886 curtailed his football career. He was on the Gorton Managing Committee with **Walter Chew** when the Hyde Road Ground was secured and the club became Ardwick. He succeeded **Walter Chew** as secretary in 1889 and remained secretary from1889 to1893. In the 1890 closed season, he and John Allison went to Scotland to sign several experienced Scottish players and they also signed several good players from Lancashire clubs, including David Weir who was an England international. Ardwick then had a very good team. **Lawrence Furniss** was Secretary when Ardwick joined the Football Alliance in 1891 and the Football League in 1892. He was later to become a Director and Chairman of Manchester City. He was appointed President after his period as a Chairman and held that position when he died in 1941. When City moved from Hyde Road to Maine Road in 1923, Gary James mentions that there were many who wanted to name the new stadium after **Lawrence Furniss** but he declined that honour.

Walter Chew and **Lawrence Furniss** are now largely forgotten but they should be remembered for the significant contributions which they made to the club and they represent the link and continuity from the formation as St. Mark's to the formation of Manchester City Football Club.

Sportingold Limited

Leading auctioneers of Sporting Memorabilia especially football
But all other sports covered.

Auctions held every two months with Large number of football lots including Programmes, Caps, Medals, Shirts, Menus, Badges, Itineraries, Books, Photographs, Cigarette cards etc.

Valuations undertaken and auction entries welcome, Football, Cricket, Boxing, Tennis, Golf, Rugby Union, Rugby League, Speedway etc.

Contact Chris Williams, 01494 565921
Or 07785 290358
Email: info@sportingold.co.uk
Web: www.sportingold.co.uk

Sportingold Limited